"Kregel's Background and Application Commen[ ]
that title suggests. It offers a succinct, persuasive,
on one or more biblical books, while focusing [ ]
on Old Testament backgrounds and contemporary significance. The high-
quality standard set by the series' initial volumes is preserved in Gary Burge's
newest contribution. Fully aware of the most cutting-edge scholarship, this
commentary wears its learning very lightly. Burge's explanations of Israel
and the church (Galatians), and of household codes (Ephesians) are not to
be missed."

—Craig L. Blomberg,
Distinguished Professor Emeritus of New Testament,
Denver Seminary

"Reading the New Testament 'through Old Testament eyes' is not only
a requirement of historical exegesis but also a theological and pastoral
imperative: the very identity and mission of the church is conditioned
by whether and how Israel's Scriptures become 'our story.' Gary Burge's
*Galatians and Ephesians Through Old Testament Eyes* makes an important
contribution to this essential hermeneutical task. Burge's thorough—
though not overbearing—analysis of Paul's Old Testament intertexts
invites readers to track the theological substructure of Paul's argument,
and thereby to find themselves in God's story of cosmic redemption. Highly
recommended."

—Max Botner,
Associate Professor of Biblical Studies,
Jessup University (Rocklin)

"You cannot read long in Paul's letters before you encounter quotations
from, allusions to, or echoes of Old Testament texts or ideas. Veteran biblical
interpreter Gary Burge attends to these features in two of the apostle's most
powerful letters, Galatians and Ephesians; and he assists those of us less in
tune to hear—and indeed feel—their intense biblical resonances. Unlike
some work in intertextuality, Burge does not rush immediately to the New
Testament readings; he lingers first to listen to the Old Testament on its
own terms."

—David B. Capes,
Director of Academic Programming,
Lanier Theological Library and Learning Center, Houston

"Gary Burge brings his expertise as a seasoned NT scholar to bear on this helpful commentary. Refusing to treat Galatians and Ephesians as isolated Christian texts, the volume skillfully bridges any seeming cultural and theological gaps to Old Testament and Second Temple backgrounds, illuminating the rich range of ancient Jewish metaphors and echoes in these important Pauline letters. In doing so, Burge weaves a tapestry of connections between Galatians and Ephesians to the voice of the Hebrew Scriptures, displaying a unified theological framework in divine, biblical revelation. The commentary is also full of helpful insights concerning relevant Greco-Roman influences within both epistles. This volume will quickly become my go-to commentary to inform my lectures, sermons, and other projects that delve into the language, culture, religious history, and beauty of Galatians and Ephesians. A stellar contribution to Kregel's Through Old Testament Eyes series!"

—Cory M. Marsh,
Professor of New Testament, Southern California Seminary,
Scholar in Residence, Revolve Bible Church

"Those who often measure the quality of a volume by its size will be pleasantly surprised by both the academic rigor and pastoral relevance of this concise commentary. Building on a careful examination of the structure of Galatians and Ephesians—as well as a close interaction of the Greek text—Burge is able to highlight the significance of Old Testament quotations, allusions, echoes, concepts, and institutions within these Pauline epistles. Moreover, in performing such intertextual explorations, Burge opens windows for modern readers to appreciate the power of these biblical texts in contemporary intercultural and intergenerational contexts, especially within a polarized society that desperately craves to hear the gospel afresh."

—David W. Pao,
Academic Dean and Professor of New Testament,
Trinity Evangelical Divinity School

"For two relatively short letters, Galatians and Ephesians can be overwhelming—uncommon words, major theological concepts, reflections of very different social experiences, and biblical echoes bombard the reader in verse after verse. Gary Burge's commentary expertly guides readers through the complexity. The mix of attention to the words Paul uses, the letters' historical and social contexts, and their intricate relationship with the rest of the Bible provide a rich resource. Even more, Burge's own pastoral sensitivity helps readers hear the living voice of these first-century letters to connect their challenge with our world."

—Caryn A. Reeder,
Westmont College

"*Galatians and Ephesians Through Old Testament Eyes* is a fine commentary for the lay reader. It works to defeat biblical illiteracy in the church, and its emphasis on Old Testament backgrounds enlightens the reader to the apostle Paul's own canon. Professor Burge's commentary, intended for 'preachers, teachers, and other readers,' is based on the Greek text and gives good attention to the meaning of words as well as introduces readers to critical issues. Burge is fair to both the Reformed and Wesleyan traditions. A highpoint of his commentary is his vision of 'Paul delighting in the picture of a Roman slave-woman preaching in one of Paul's churches as Jews, free citizens, and men sat attentively.' Burge concludes that Paul wants to overturn 'the old order of the Roman household.' Christians can trust that this commentary on Galatians and Ephesians is well-balanced, sound, easy to read, and yet encouraging the reader to imitate Paul's vision for today."

—Aída Besançon Spencer,
Senior Professor of New Testament,
Gordon-Conwell Theological Seminary

"Burge is a seasoned scholar and an able guide through these two significant letters from Paul. He deftly handles cultural context and Old Testament background, opening our eyes to much that we may miss on our own. The result is a fresh encounter with the text, and motivation and preparation for the preacher and teacher who wants to communicate this word in our day."

—Craig Swanson,
Pastor, First Evangelical Covenant Church,
Grand Rapids, Michigan

# Through Old Testament Eyes

New Testament Commentaries
Series Editors: Andrew T. Le Peau and Seth M. Ehorn

A BACKGROUND AND APPLICATION COMMENTARY

# GALATIANS AND EPHESIANS

## THROUGH OLD TESTAMENT EYES

## Gary M. Burge

ANDREW T. LE PEAU AND SETH M. EHORN
SERIES EDITORS

KREGEL
ACADEMIC

*Galatians and Ephesians Through Old Testament Eyes: A Background and Application Commentary*
© 2025 by Gary M. Burge

Published by Kregel Academic, an imprint of Kregel Publications, 2450 Oak Industrial Dr. NE, Grand Rapids, MI 49505-6020.

**Library of Congress Cataloging-in-Publication Data**

Names: Burge, Gary M., 1952– author.
Title: Galatians and Ephesians through Old Testament eyes : a background and application commentary / Gary M. Burge.
Description: First edition. | Grand Rapids, MI : Kregel Academic, [2025] | Series: Through Old Testament eyes | Includes bibliographical references and index.
Identifiers: LCCN 2024040458 (print) | LCCN 2024040459 (ebook)
Subjects: LCSH: Bible. Galatians—Commentaries. | Bible. Galatians—Relation to the Old Testament. | Bible. Ephesians—Commentaries. | Bible. Ephesians—Relation to the Old Testament.
Classification: LCC BS2685.53 .B88 2025 (print) | LCC BS2685.53 (ebook) | DDC 227/.407—dc23/eng/20240928
LC record available at https://lccn.loc.gov/2024040458
LC ebook record available at https://lccn.loc.gov/2024040459

ISBN 978-0-8254-4518-7

Printed in the United States of America

25 26 27 28 29 / 5 4 3 2 1

*To Greta, Sig, and Atlas*

*In Memoriam*

Kenneth E. Bailey, Ralph P. Martin, I. Howard Marshall,
and James D. G. Dunn—teachers and mentors all

# CONTENTS

# SERIES PREFACE

*The New Testament writers were Old Testament people.* Their minds were populated with Old Testament stories and concepts. Their imaginative world was furnished with Old Testament images, motifs, metaphors, symbols, and literary patterns. When Jesus came and turned much of their conventional wisdom on its head, they largely had Old Testament tools to understand what was going on in order to explain Jesus to others and to themselves. So that's what they used.

For many Christians the Old Testament has, unfortunately, become a closed book. It seems long, mysterious, and boring with a confusing history full of many strange, unpronounceable names. And then there are those sometimes bizarre prophecies populated with strange creatures. Yet my consistent experience in teaching the New Testament is that when I turn the attention of students to relevant Old Testament passages, the proverbial light bulbs go on. The room is filled with "aha"s. Formerly obscure New Testament passages suddenly make new sense in light of the Old. Indeed the whole of each book of the New Testament takes on fuller, richer dimensions not seen before.

The purpose of the Through Old Testament Eyes commentaries is to give preachers, teachers, and other readers this same experience. This series opens the New Testament in greater depth to anyone who wants to see fresh ways that Scripture interconnects with Scripture.

Scholars have long known that the Old Testament influenced the New Testament (an idea known as intertextuality). In fact, more than a millennia and a half ago Augustine famously proposed that we understand the relationship of the two testaments in this way: "The new is in the old concealed; the old is in the new revealed." Yet no commentary series is as devoted as this one is to seeing the richness of Old Testament allusions, references, echoes, and background to illuminate both puzzling passages and explain others in fresh ways.

Practices like baptism, meals, fishing, and fasting; concepts like rescue, faith, sin, and glory; and terms like *wilderness*, *Sabbath*, and *Lord* are just a few of the dozens of words in each New Testament book and letter with deep Old Testament resonances. Sometimes a narrative arc or an argument is also shaped by the Old Testament. An appreciation of this background enriches our understanding and helps us appropriately apply each passage.

In these commentaries you will find four repeating features which will enrich your encounter with the Scripture.

## Running Commentary

Verse-by-verse or paragraph-by-paragraph commentary will include Old Testament background as well as other key information to give readers an understanding of the text as a whole and to answer questions as they naturally arise.

## Through Old Testament Eyes

Periodic summaries offer overviews of chapters or sections. These occasional pauses give the opportunity to step back from the detail to see the bigger picture of how Old Testament themes and motifs are being used by the New Testament authors.

## What the Structure Means

New Testament authors often get their points across through the way they structure their material. The very organization of their writing conveys significant meaning in and of itself. How the events and teachings are linked makes a difference that, while not explicit, is an important part of the message. Again it is important to not take verses out of context as if they were timeless truths standing apart from their original settings, which affect how we understand them.

The authors of the New Testament also deliberately use, for example, repetition, contrast, hyperbole, metaphor, story, and other techniques so they can have the maximum impact on their readers. "What the Structure Means" will highlight these every so often and help us keep track of the overall flow of each book and letter so that the Old Testament background can be seen in its proper context.

## Going Deeper

New Testament writers did not want to merely convey information. They wrote with the needs of the early church in mind. What should their attitude be toward family members who weren't Christians? How should they respond to challenges from Jewish or Roman authorities?

What about internal disputes within the church? These and many other issues were on their minds, and the New Testament addresses them and many more.

Through Old Testament Eyes commentaries will not only leave readers with an enriched understanding of the text but with enriched lives. In "Going Deeper" the authors will unpack the practical implications of each book and letter for Christians and churches, especially drawing from the Old Testament dimensions uncovered in the text.

As much as this series champions the importance of understanding the New Testament's use of the Old, two key points need to be mentioned. First, the Old Testament is not merely a tool for understanding the New. The Old Testament is important and valuable in its own right. It was the Bible of Jesus and the first Christians. They guided their lives by it. The Old Testament needs to be and deserves to be understood on its own terms, apart from the lens it provides for seeing the New Testament clearly. All the commentary authors in this series begin just here as they approach the text. In fact, our hope is that these commentaries will be a window into the Old Testament that will motivate many readers to look more deeply into what some have called the First Testament.

Second, the Old Testament is not the only interpretive lens we need to understand the New. Roman and Greek culture and history, for example, had a very significant influence on the New Testament era. So did the Second Temple period (from the start of rebuilding the temple about 537 BC to the destruction of the temple by Rome in AD 70). Where essential, these commentaries will reference such background material. But the emphasis will be on providing in-depth Old Testament background that readers too often overlook.

While these commentaries are grounded in solid scholarship, they are not intended primarily for an academic audience. For this reason many topics, approaches, and debates found in technical commentaries are absent. This series is for those who want to teach or preach, as well as any serious reader committed to understanding Scripture.

The past is always present. The question is: Are we aware of how it affects us or not? The Old Testament was present with the New Testament writers. They knew that and treasured it. We can too.

—Andrew T. Le Peau and Seth M. Ehorn
Series Editors

# INTRODUCTION

*Interpreting something from another culture* is difficult. Interpreting something from another culture that is two thousand years old can seem almost impossible. And yet we often think that if we examine an ancient book or plaster fresco or pottery artifact long enough, its meaning will simply emerge effortlessly. It won't.

## A Mosaic in Galilee

There is a fourth-century synagogue that was discovered in S. Galilee (Israel) about a hundred years ago. The Beit Alpha synagogue can be found near two Israeli villages (*kibbutzim*) on the side of Mount Gilboa (it is actually in Kibbutz Hefzi-Bah). Sixteen hundred years ago, this ancient Jewish synagogue (and its small Jewish community) lived in a Roman town that sat on the crossroads of two major roads in southern Galilee. Over the next centuries the area sustained a small Jewish community that built its own public synagogue in the AD 300s, and in the 500s, they refurbished it around a beautiful and costly mosaic floor.

However, in AD 749 a massive earthquake destroyed the stone buildings at the site, the area was abandoned, and it wasn't until the 1870s that the ruins of the ancient Roman town were discovered by archaeologists. Jewish immigrants in the 1920s built a settlement here, and in 1928, during their excavations, they found the ancient mosaic floor of the synagogue. They were thrilled. It was the first ancient synagogue discovered by some of the earliest Jewish settlers in modern-day Israel. They protected it, and today, it is a national historic site.

Today you can visit the remains of this fascinating synagogue. You'll see the floor where Jewish worshippers stood more than fifteen hundred years ago. You'll see in the mosaic the names of the ancient artists who crafted it (Marianos and his son Hanina) and learn that they designed other mosaics for Byzantine Christian buildings elsewhere in the region (they were "artists for hire"). They worked up the road in the Christian city of Scythopolis (ancient Beit She'an) as well.

And then if you look carefully and read the display signs at the synagogue, you'll see something that should give you pause. The south end of the floor shows a variety of Jewish symbols (an ark, candelabra, shofar, palms, ritual shovel, etc.). You feel reassured that you can recognize Jewish historic symbols! The north end mosaic tells the story of the near-sacrifice of Isaac (complete with knife, altar, fire, and ram-in-thicket). You feel good again: you know the story and could find it promptly in Genesis. Yes. This is an ancient *Jewish* mosaic. Your interpretative confidence swells.

**Figure G-0.1. The Mosaic Floor of Beit Alpha**

But then in the central, massive installation between the north and south ends, another mosaic sets your head spinning. The center of the floor has a circular mosaic and there are twelve images or characters carefully arrayed around the circle's perimeter. Within minutes you'll figure it out: this is a zodiac wheel complete with the symbols you know today. Taurus, Aries, Capricorn. This is an ancient pagan symbol going back to the Babylonians that was wildly popular among the Greeks and Romans. But there is more. At the mosaic's center—well, the center of the whole synagogue—in the middle of the zodiac wheel, is the Roman sun god Helios accompanied by his four-horse chariot (a *quadriga*) that he rode across the sky.

Immediately new questions come rushing at us. *Why is this here? Why here in a house of Jewish worship, for heaven's sake? Isn't this a brash compromise of the purity of faith?*

When we stand before this mosaic, we are *interpreters*. When we make sense of the mosaic, we are trying to understand its meaning and the beliefs of the people who financed it. And it is puzzling. How could Jews who held to belief in the one God of Israel import images like this into their sanctuary? (Imagine an artist suggesting such a floor in a reconstruction of a Baptist church today.) Of course, a scholar on hand might tell you that other zodiac synagogues have been found in the area from the same period (at Tiberius, Sepphoris). But it will take great skill to speculate about the meaning of this floor.

Were they Greek-speaking Jews (Hellenistic Jews) who held their religious scruples lightly? Did they see the floor as having no religious significance? Did they combine pagan and Jewish symbolism intentionally and, if so, why? Were they like some of us, using zodiac astrology symbols to predict their fortunes and futures as entertainment? But wait. This is sacred space. Why profane sacred space? Or didn't they think they were profaning it?

But here we stand in front of the ancient mosaic. We see the colored stones, we can read the symbols (or can we?), and we see that this has sprung from a foreign culture, a culture that is utterly distant in time from our own. It would be presumptuous for us to say we "understand" this floor, much less its owners. "But they were Jews," we say—thinking about Jewish friends we have in our neighborhood back home. But wait. They were Jews living in a world far distant from anything we can imagine. We may understand bits of this mosaic; but we actually understand less than we think. And it takes great humility for a tourist (much less the tour guide) to walk away from Beit Alpha simply admitting we don't know what it all means, despite the confident pronouncements of the beautiful Israeli National Park Service sign right in front of us.

## A Letter from Paul

This same interpretative challenge confronts us when we hold an ancient book. Perhaps a letter like Galatians or Ephesians is an example. It comes to us with a language that is foreign (Greek). It comes from a cultural and historical context that is two thousand years old, where reflexes were utterly different from our own. And it once lived in a setting of controversy and debate that we have difficulty reconstructing. We can hear one side of Paul's argument (his letter), but we do not possess the other side's views. We are forced to reconstruct the original questions through Paul's answers.

This may sound despairing, but all is not lost. If an average tourist stepped into the Beit Alpha synagogue unaccompanied and there were no Israeli Park Service signs, they would be lost. But with the help of a skilled interpreter who knows the synagogue's history, mosaic art from that century, Jewish tensions with Roman religion, and the design of other Jewish synagogues in the period, we could make good headway in developing some theories. One danger in this synagogue is that we tend to "see what we already know"; that is, we may have in our minds what synagogues look like (or what churches look like) or what zodiacs mean, and we begin to impose on the synagogue meanings that are not there.

We wrestle with these challenges in art museums all the time. I was recently on a tour at the wonderful Detroit Museum of Art, and the docent leading us stopped our group at Caravaggio's famous painting (from 1598) depicting Martha and Mary from the Gospels. The only problem was that the guide did not know the biblical stories about these two women. She admitted it but instead found modern meanings of beauty and piety in the paintings. It was tragic. As an interpreter, she had failed to guide us into the wider biblical context that Caravaggio knew so well. We could have discussed the sixteenth-century world of Caravaggio or even the first-century world of the gospel story. But our guide could do neither. We were all foreigners to what was before us.

**Figure G-0.2. Caravaggio's *Mary and Martha***

When we open a letter from Paul, we must remind ourselves that we are foreigners too. The aim of books like the one you are holding is to give us insights and background that help us interpret accurately what is being said in this ancient letter because if we do not possess these insights, we risk representing Paul in ways that even Paul would not recognize. Therefore, we need a guide or a well-equipped docent to lead us through these ancient words so that we can understand them rightly. We need tips about Paul's Greek phrases, his literary references, his use of the Old Testament, and his ideas as they are embedded in their own historical context.

Here is a small example. Notice Paul's tendency to refer to himself and other Christians as "servants" of Christ. Paul uses the Greek word for this many times (exactly thirty). Romans 1:1 is typical, "Paul, a *servant* of Jesus Christ, called to be an apostle" (emphasis added). But the problem is that Paul did not speak English. The term he used was *doulos*, which in Greek means "slave." And this term carries a load of meaning that might seem unexpected.

The word *servant* softens Paul's meaning because, the truth is, everyone wants to be a servant of Christ, serving him daily. But Paul's idea here is different and certainly more dramatic. What did *doulos* mean in Paul's language and culture? Was it provocative? Was it shocking? Or was it commonplace? Would a successful, well-educated Roman citizen *ever* call himself a *doulos* in the first century? And why are we translating it "servant" at all? Are we softening Paul's voice? Sometimes the meaning—the deeper meaning—is located between the lines and words, and this is where an excellent guide serves us.

# GALATIANS

# INTRODUCTION TO GALATIANS

Paul's letter to the Galatians gives us a glimpse into the earliest days of the apostle's theological career. Unlike the calmly reasoned style of many of his other letters, here Paul uses forceful polemic as if something essential, something vital to the message of the gospel, was in jeopardy. We will learn that he doesn't even open the letter with the standard phrases of courtesy that he'll use in other letters. He's very agitated, but this agitation is only evident when we know how formal letter-writing worked in the ancient world.

He is no doubt at the beginning of his ministry, and we know that Paul has learned about opponents who have denied what he teaches. He is astonished that the Christians of this region have succumbed to false teaching, and he is eager to straighten them out. "I am astonished," he writes, "that you are so quickly deserting the one who called you to live in the grace of Christ and are turning to a different gospel . . ." (Gal 1:6).

In each of Paul's letters, it is vital to understand context or setting. Every letter springs from particular circumstances in Paul's life and arguments found in, say, Galatians are going to be entirely different from concerns expressed in Thessalonians. Galatians is a dramatic case study of this. Just knowing what is happening before and after this letter was penned will determine a great deal about how we interpret it.

Several important questions have shadowed this letter (each championed by lists of scholars), and we will begin by clarifying where this letter stands in Paul's life and thinking. Where has Paul been? What has happened to inspire the conflicts in the letter? Who were his opponents? What did they teach? Why did Paul view their teaching so critically? And when was this letter penned in relation to other major events in the history of the early church?

## Where Was Galatia?

From the intimacy and argument of the letter, Paul has already visited Galatia. The book of Acts refers to Paul visiting Galatia on his second (Ac 16:6) and third (Ac 18:23) tours. The problem is that much of what Paul argues here regarding the Jewish law and Gentile compliance had been resolved at a theological council in Jerusalem (Ac 15) attended by James and the apostolic leaders. And this gathering had taken place before Paul's second tour (see Figure G-0.3).

**Figure G-0.3. Paul's First Tours**

| Paul's First Tour<br>Acts 13–14 | Jerusalem Council<br>Acts 15 | Paul's Second Tour<br>Acts 16–18 |
| --- | --- | --- |

The problem is this: Why does Paul have to argue a theological point following the very council that had clarified that point? If Paul's visit to Galatia was after the Jerusalem Council and that council had decided in favor of Gentile freedom, was the council a failure? Did some reject it? The problem to be solved may be expressed thus: What is the relation between the Jerusalem Council of Acts 15 and the letter of Galatians? And we need to begin by locating Galatia.

Galatia was located in the region geographers call Anatolia (or Asia Minor)—modern-day Turkey. The small, historic ethnic region of Galatia was in North Central Anatolia, where Celts and Gauls had migrated some three hundred years before Christ (Strabo, *Geography* 12.5.1; 567). The Romans recognized it as its own kingdom for many years before Paul began his ministry. A quick look at a map[1] indicates that the cities of Pisidian Antioch, Lystra, and Derbe—the cities of Paul's first tour—were not in this region and instead belonged to the southern area populated by people called Phrygians (see Figure G-0.4). Most early Christian (Patristic) commentators assume this northern location for Galatia because this is how they understood the geography of their own time. And for them, Paul never entered this region until his second tour.

This position, however, was challenged in the nineteenth century by a Scottish New Testament scholar (and archaeologist) named William Ramsay (1851–1939). As an intrepid Victorian traveler using wagons and horses (and who enjoyed tea set out on elegant china by his wife every afternoon in the field), Ramsay journeyed throughout Asia Minor studying what remained of the cities and locations mentioned in the New Testament. And he happened on a remarkable theory that has since been largely substantiated.

Ramsay hypothesized that when Paul refers to the geographic regions of his travels, he did not mean "ethnic" regions, but he was using "imperial" or

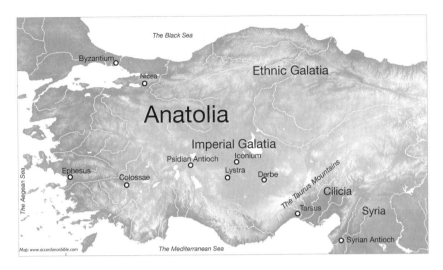

**Figure G-0.4. Map of Anatolia (Ethnic and Imperial Galatia)**

governmental regional designations (1 Co 16:5, 15, 19). It so happened that in 25 BC, Rome had reorganized central Asia Minor and created an imperial region called The Province of Galatia that swept south to the Taurus Mountains and included cities like Pisidian Antioch. And if this was true, when Paul visited this city on his first missionary journey, he was visiting the Roman Imperial Province of Galatia. About two hundred years later (second century AD), Rome again reorganized central Asia Minor, shrinking Galatia back to its northern ethnic parameters.

For many scholars, this question is settled. In the New Testament, Galatia refers to an imperial Roman province that reached south beyond Psidian Antioch. Moreover, Paul prefers going to those areas that are developed with large population centers, where his efforts at evangelism would be rewarded. The southern regions not only had these cities, but they also had roads that facilitated Paul's travel. Ethnic Galatia (the north) was sparsely populated and its road system undeveloped. The crux, however, is here: *Paul visited Galatia on his first missionary tour (Ac 13–14) as well as on his second missionary tour (Ac 16)* (see Figure G-0.5). The remaining question: When did he write his letter?

**Figure G-0.5. Paul and Imperial Galatia**

| Paul's First Tour Imperial Galatia Acts 13–14 | Jerusalem Council The Gentile Decree Acts 15 | Paul's Second Tour Imperial Galatia Acts 16–18 |
|---|---|---|

# The Timing of Paul's Letter

The timing of Paul's letter is a matter of some debate because we need to decide where it falls in relation to the Jerusalem Council of Acts 15 with its formal decree granting freedom to Gentiles. If the letter was before the council, it can be dated to AD 49 and its arguments anticipate the council. If it is after the council, it belongs to the early 50s and shows that the council did not convince every member. Three positions are common.

(1) The so-called North Galatian Theory has been the majority view of the church for centuries. Some contemporary scholars who still defend this position argue that Paul is addressing the churches of this northern ethnic region and that he only visited here on the second tour, hence, after the Jerusalem Council. By this reasoning, Paul's letter refers to the Jerusalem Council of Acts 15 in Galatians 2:1–10. In these verses Paul says he visited Jerusalem with an entourage of colleagues (including Barnabas, Ac 15:2), whom he met with the apostolic leadership. He describes his theological opponents and names James, Peter, and John as "pillars of the church" who affirmed his work (Gal 2:9–10). To sum: this view believes that Galatians *followed* the Jerusalem Council. (Some severe critics in this position believe that Paul does not refer to any decree in Galatians because the events of Acts 15 never occurred.)

(2) Other scholars are drawn to the South Galatian Theory, arguing that Paul's formative visit to Galatia occurred *before* the council on the first tour and that this letter anticipated the arguments of the council. Most scholars concede today that Paul was in Galatia on the first tour, but it remains to be seen if Paul wrote the letter *before* the council. By this view, Paul's description of the visit to Jerusalem in Galatians 2:1–10 refers to the so-called Famine Visit of Acts 11:27–30. And indeed, there are many parallels. These scholars also claim that if the decree of Acts 15 had occurred, then Paul should have mentioned it in his letter. But in Galatians he does not. Plus, they wonder why, after the council, James (who publicly gave way at the council) is still sending out emissaries who contradict Paul (Gal 2:12). This position has much to commend it and will be the view I use as we examine the letter.

(3) Today a mediating position affirms that Paul is referring to [southern] Imperial Galatia in all his travels and that Paul likely *never* entered northern ethnic Galatia. Thus, Paul went to Galatia on *both* tours (his first and his second). However, Paul's description in Galatians 2:1–10 does point to the Jerusalem Council of Acts 15. We cannot know why Paul fails to mention the previous decree from Acts 15, but we have a parallel in 1 Corinthians.

This letter followed the Jerusalem Council as well and here Paul discusses food sacrificed to idols and sexual morality—two issues also settled by the decree. If Paul had the decree, why doesn't he mention it in 1 Corinthians (a letter written after the council)? On this view, Paul had already delivered the Gentile decree to Galatia during his second tour, and it had been rejected by his opponents. But above all, a close comparison between Galatians 2:1–10 and Acts 15 demonstrates a surprising number of parallels in all the major issues: the issues (circumcision and Gentiles), the outcome (Gentile freedom), and the agreement of James and Peter.

**Figure G-0.6. When Was Galatians Written?**

| Paul's First Tour Acts 13–14 | *Position 2 Paul writes Galatians?* | Jerusalem Council Acts 15 | Paul's Second Tour Acts 16–18 | *Positions 1 & 3 Paul writes Galatians?* |
|---|---|---|---|---|

The key here is to see that Galatians is shaped by ideas being debated in the earliest days of the church. And the Jerusalem Council in Acts 15 presents us with the critical issues—the first theological issues—that the early church had to contend with. Some believe it is vital to see the letter as preceding the council. Still others argue that it followed the council and that Paul is forced to revisit the issues of that gathering because the decree of Gentile freedom had been ignored or rejected (see Figure G-0.6).

## The Spiritual Climate

We need to think of the cities of Asia Minor as filled with people with a wide array of religious interests. A city like Pisidian Antioch was a highland trading crossroads where travelers from the "far east" (Syria, Mesopotamia, Persia) might have mingled with Greeks, Romans, and the local Phrygians who were known for their ecstatic worship of the goddess Cybele. Temples from older Greek gods still existed alongside Roman shrines whose gods in some cases simply occupied the older temples. And in this mix, we would find communities of Jews who struggled with the age-old problem of faithfulness to their religion while mingling with the newer Hellenistic cultures around them. Some Jews certainly were won over to this pagan world and compromised much; others held firm to their faith and, as a defensive posture, may have exhibited a rigidity that isolated them.

Paul is writing to Gentiles in the region of Galatia (Gal 4:8–9). In fact, when Paul and Barnabas passed through the Galatian city of Lystra (Ac 13–14), the crowd was so impressed with them that they gave the two men the ultimate speaker's compliment, "The gods have come down to us in human form" (Ac 14:11). They called Paul Hermes (because he spoke so much) and Barnabas they called Zeus (the chief god of the Greek pantheon). Even the priest at Zeus's temple in Lystra tried to sacrifice to them (Ac 14:13). Still others referred to Paul as "an angel of God" (Gal 4:14). To say the least, Paul and Barnabas were distressed. But these Hellenistic religious instincts showed up in other ways. Many there were interested in superstitious beliefs that left them in bondage and fear, and they no doubt paid homage to "spirits" and imagined spiritual forces (Gal 4:8–11).

**Figure G-0.7. The Goddess Cybele**

After Paul and Barnabas had completed their work during their first tour in Galatia (Pisidian Antioch, Lystra, Iconium, Derbe), they departed for Judea and left behind fledgling Christian communities that were fragile but understood the fundamentals of the gospel. These were some of the world's earliest Christian churches. They had no written Christian scriptures but only knew what Paul taught— which likely left them vulnerable—and while Paul was away something happened. It appears that a delegation of teachers from Jerusalem arrived in Galatia in Paul's absence and met with these young churches. And this is when the trouble began. They contradicted Paul's teaching and taught the Galatians that, in some manner, Christians had to take on the markers of Judaism if they were to be fully attached to Christ. Suddenly topics like circumcision and Sabbath observance were a part of the Galatian vocabulary. We refer to this delegation as Judaizers in that they were imposing Jewish law on the Gentiles.

## The Crisis in Galatia

How do we know this? Paul must have learned about this crisis while he was in Syrian Antioch around the time of the Jerusalem Council (see "The Timing of Paul's Letters" for more about locating the letter). He penned Galatians as a furious complaint against these teachers, and using the words from this letter, we can reconstruct what is going on. He is unafraid to call them out personally ("some people are throwing you into confusion," Gal 1:7) and says they should be condemned for what they have done (1:9; 5:10). He even names the culprits as "certain men came from James" (2:12), which tells us that this delegation had originated in Jerusalem, more importantly, from the Christian church there led by James the brother of Jesus (Gal 1:19). In a bit of grim irony, he even says these promoters of circumcision should mutilate themselves (5:12). These are harsh words. Paul feels so strongly about this that he postpones his Second Tour (if we follow the South Galatian theory). And with this view we suspect that the Galatian crisis likely ignited the debates leading up to the Jerusalem Council (Ac 15). It is no surprise that at that council, Paul was intent on having a clarifying conversation with James.

The problem is that these teachers from James have made firm inroads in Galatia. Paul writes, "I am astonished that you are so quickly deserting the one who called you to live in the grace of Christ and are turning to a different gospel" (Gal 1:6). He also says, "You foolish Galatians! Who has bewitched you? Before your very eyes Jesus Christ was clearly portrayed as crucified" (3:1). He is almost in despair as he thinks how these new Christians have suddenly begun to carry the burden of the law and have lost the joy and freedom he had preached to them. "I fear for you, that somehow I have wasted my efforts on you" (4:11). They had returned to slavery (4:9) but now of a type they had never known before: it was slavery to Jewish laws and obligations that had no business in their lives.

The letter to the Galatians is Paul's attempt to confront what these teachers have said and remedy the situation.

## What the Structure Means: On Writing a Letter

The Roman world was similar to our own when it came to composing professional letters. There were rules, and well-educated people followed them. Formal letters followed a model we can easily see in the tiny Third Letter of John. Gracious opening lines identify the writer and his recipient (3 Jn 1:1). This is followed by a prayer of blessings for the reader (1:2–4), the body of the letter (1:5–10), a delicately written ethical exhortation (1:11–12), and a polite close, often with a blessing of "peace" (1:13–15).

Now look at the first lines of John's third letter. Note the elegant details of this opening:

The elder, To my dear friend Gaius, whom I love in the truth.

Dear friend, I pray that you may enjoy good health and that all may go well with you, even as your soul is getting along well. It gave me great joy when some believers came and testified about your faithfulness to

> the truth, telling how you continue to walk in it. I have no greater joy than to hear that my children are walking in the truth. (3 Jn 1:1–4)

Now look at Galatians and note how many courteous elements are missing.

> Paul, an apostle—sent not from men nor by a man, but by Jesus Christ and God the Father, who raised him from the dead—and all the brothers and sisters with me.
>
> To the churches in Galatia: Grace and peace to you from God our Father and the Lord Jesus Christ, who gave himself for our sins to rescue us from the present evil age, according to the will of our God and Father, to whom be glory for ever and ever. Amen.
>
> I am astonished that you are so quickly deserting the one who called you to live in the grace of Christ and are turning to a different gospel… (Gal 1:1–6)

Galatians is a "rebuke letter," penned for someone you might know quite well but who has disappointed you profoundly. In an Egyptian papyrus letter remnant from the third century (P. Oxy. 1.123.5–9), we can hear this tone easily in the words of a father rebuking an errant son, "I am very much surprised, my son, that until today I have not received any letter from you, telling me about your welfare." This is Paul's tone as well. He launches forcefully, abruptly, into his concerns, almost as if he can't help himself. This letter is a rebuke, and because of this, scholars commonly study the letter to see persuasive (or rhetorical) speech patterns known in the ancient world.

The opening lines of Galatians demonstrate Paul's rhetorical style well. Note there is no word of thanks for the Galatians—not even kind wishes for their welfare. Paul can give praise to God for our deliverance from this evil age, but there is no praise to God for the Galatian church (cf. the praise in Col 1:3 or 1 Th 1:2). And why is this? Because they have "so quickly" (Gal 1:6) abandoned the gospel itself. It was not long ago that Paul had been there, and now, before the gospel itself had barely taken root, they had let the core of its message disintegrate.

We should note that scholars often question the authorship of many of Paul's letters. However, seven of Paul's thirteen letters are rarely questioned: Galatians, 1 and 2 Corinthians, Romans, Philippians, 1 Thessalonians, and Philemon.[2] Therefore, scholars are virtually unanimous that Paul is the author of Galatians. The date of Galatians depends entirely on where we locate it in connection with Paul's three missionary journeys. Those who believe the letter precedes the Jerusalem Council date the letter at AD 48 or 49. Those who think it follows the council date it at AD 50–52. The date of the letter is important not simply to establish a chronology of Paul's life but to establish the arguments surrounding the controversy at the Jerusalem Council of Acts 15.

## The Form of the Letter

For a letter that is essentially a rebuke, some have argued that it was hastily written with little order or form. This view is less popular today. Most students of Galatians think that we can find a broad outline (see Figure G-0.8) that helps us follow Paul's thoughts.

**Figure G-0.8. The Form of Galatians**

### Paul's Personal Narratives (1:1–2:21)

*Following an abrupt greeting, Paul outlines the history of his own experiences from his conversion to his meetings with the leaders of Jerusalem.*

**Greeting 1:1–5**
**Paul Rebukes the Galatians 1:6–11**
**Paul's Own Story 1:12–2:21**
   *Paul's Conversion and Call 1:12–17*
   *Paul's Encounters with the Jerusalem Leaders 1:18–2:10*
      *Paul reviews his travels 1:18–24*
      *Paul confronts the Jerusalem leaders: A case study 2:1–10*
   *Paul Confronts Peter in Antioch: A Case Study 2:11–21*

### Paul's Theological Argument (3:1–4:31)

*Paul now provides a theological basis for his argument in defense of Gentile freedom in Christ. He draws from historic Jewish narratives (Abraham, Sarah, Isaac, etc.) to show that the principle of grace is a constant theme in the Old Testament.*

**The Example of Abraham 3:1–14**
**The Nature of Law and Promise 3:15–29**
**Becoming a Child and Heir of God 4:1–11**
**A Personal Appeal from the Heart 4:12–20**
**The Analogy of Abraham and Sarah 4:21–31**

### Paul's Ethical Argument (5:1–6:10)

*Paul commonly follows his theological teachings with a brief exhortation about the personal and moral implications that ought to follow these truths. In this case, Paul shows that genuinely experiencing the grace of God should result in a change in how we live.*

**Freedom, Circumcision, and Law 5:1–12**
**Life in the Spirit 5:13–6:10**

### Paul's Closing Remarks (6:11–18)

*Paul now summarizes the nature of his debate with these opponents, reinforcing the teaching he has delivered in chapters 3–4. He ends with a short benediction.*

## What the Structure Means: How to Launch an Argument

Looking at the overall structure of Galatians we can see that it is organized around three basic steps (followed by a few closing remarks). Unlike many other biblical writings that sustain a theme and develop it carefully, Paul is here trying to put out a fire. To extinguish it, Paul makes three moves.

First, Paul describes what has happened (Paul's Personal Narratives, 1:1–2:21). We will learn that after Paul established churches in Galatia, a team of Christians from Jerusalem had arrived there correcting Paul's teaching and imposing Jewish ritual customs on the Galatians. Worse still, they undercut Paul's authority and suggested that the Galatians should listen to the "headquarters" in Jerusalem and their leaders. Paul rebukes the Galatians for their error, establishes the genuineness of his own conversion and commission, and tells a couple of stories about his journeys to Jerusalem, where these renowned leaders had accepted his teaching and given him "the right hand of fellowship" (2:9).

Second, Paul explains why the imposition of Jewish customs on Gentiles was not only unnecessary but inappropriate theologically (Paul's Theological Argument, 3:1–5:1). At stake is our understanding of the grace of God and how this grace is grounded in the Old Testament. In other words, Paul is teaching nothing novel here but shows how the principle of covenant grace springs from Abraham and includes an invitation and blessing to the nations (3:8). Thus Gentiles can become children of Abraham, and so they too belong to the covenant established with Abraham. Paul is making a fundamental theological argument: membership in the lineage of Abraham is not by blood (or ethnicity) but by faith (3:7). This dramatic inclusion of Gentiles who do not have to adopt Jewish ways was as revolutionary as it was controversial.

Finally, Paul argues that not only is his position theologically correct, but it is superior in promoting the righteousness expected by God (Paul's Ethical Argument, 5:2–6:10). One argument for the ongoing use of the law is that obedience to the law might promote righteousness. Paul upends this view as well. He argues that the missing element of righteousness is the Spirit, which promotes righteousness in a manner the law could not. And ultimately this is what Paul's gospel seeks: the transformation of the person. When it comes to circumcision, Paul urges the Gentile Galatians: do not do it. It is unnecessary and not beneficial. Galatians 6:15 sums up Paul's view concisely, "Neither circumcision nor uncircumcision means anything; what counts is the new creation." Some scholars wonder if Paul may have believed that Gentile adult circumcision was impossible anyway since the law required it to happen "on the eighth day" (see *Jubilees* 15:14; Ge 17:14 LXX; possibly Ro 2:27), and an adult seeking it beyond this terminus would be disobeying the law.

Within this broad outline of Paul's remarks, scholars often point out that we have here in Galatians the rudimentary makings of Paul's earliest theology—which is fleshed out more fully in Romans. Indeed, Galatians and Romans share a great deal in common, perhaps as a rough draft could be compared to the polished essay. After we read the polemical review of Paul's own history with Jerusalem here, the theological core of the letter launches the two fundamental questions that drove his thought. (1) What is the basis of our righteousness with God? What is the role of the law (represented in circumcision), and how do we understand grace? (2) What motive or inspiration will produce the transformation inherent in that righteousness? Does law produce change? Or does grace? Do we make these efforts or does God accomplish this through the work of his Spirit?

These two categories, sometimes labeled justification and sanctification, have become two of the essential ideas that form the basis of Christian thinking. Consider these two passages, which are memorable to us but were revolutionary when Paul first wrote them. We can almost hear him arguing these twin points in his debates in Anatolia's synagogues.

> [We] know that a person is not justified by the works of the law, but by faith in Jesus Christ. So we, too, have put our faith in Christ Jesus that we may be justified by faith in Christ and not by the works of the law, because by the works of the law no one will be justified. (Gal 2:16)

> For through the Spirit we eagerly await by faith the righteousness for which we hope. For in Christ Jesus neither circumcision nor uncircumcision has any value. The only thing that counts is faith expressing itself through love. . . . So I say, walk by the Spirit. (Gal 5:5–6, 16)

In verses like these Paul makes clear that the project of the gospel stands on two ideas: a justification anchored to the grace of God and a transformation anchored to the Spirit of God. As we will see, these were not novelties to Paul. But they were based on teachings in the Old Testament, Abraham's life in particular, and this teaching needed to be recovered.

## Paul's Primary Message

The fundamental concern on Paul's mind is the ongoing role of the Jewish law in the purposes of God. Paul says Gentiles are not obligated to fulfill the law as represented in the requirement of circumcision. But entailments certainly follow. Circumcision was just the beginning, and we can expect that other strictures, such as dietary law and Sabbath observance, were sure to follow. But this leads Paul to think more expansively about the law and its ongoing place even in Judaism. For Paul, Christ was the great disrupter of all things in heaven and on earth—in the pagan world and within Judaism. But to endorse a Christ-formed view of the law, to promote a rearrangement of the duties of the law, this certainly would bring controversy. Paul is not necessarily arguing with those who believe that circumcision (or the law) is a prerequisite for salvation. He is arguing against those who would make circumcision a necessary entailment that marks true believers from those who fail to understand God's will. For Paul's opponents, then, uncircumcised Gentiles live on the margin of God's grace until they choose to be obedient to the law.

From beginning to end, Paul is not simply defending a minor theological point of view in this letter. He believes that an epic shift has occurred in history. Paul has deftly asserted the secure place of Gentile Christians in the family of God and defined for the first time the relationship of the law to the gospel. Certainly, his reframing of the "children of Abraham" was a disconcerting idea to many within the Jewish-Christian world. And non-messianic Jews no doubt wondered about this Gentile-Christian identity. Did they still have a place in Paul's theology? Paul doesn't answer this last question here, but he will feel the weight of it later, and we will find his answer at the middle of his letter to the Romans (Ro 9–11).

In a word, Christ has brought to reality what Abraham's children were meant to be. This is why it is fair to say that Paul did not deny his Judaism, but rather, that he believed he was drawn deeper, through his faith in Christ, into what it means to belong to Israel. God is now making children out of many nations (Ro 4:17; Gal 4:7). This is his first benediction for his churches, and its theological weight is enormous: "Peace and mercy to all who follow this rule—to the Israel of God" (6:16). What rule? The Abrahamic-Messianic rule of grace and faith. What community? The church, now boldly given the Old Testament's most honorific title.

## Galatians and the Old Testament

Throughout his letters, Paul writes like a person who has a deep and intimate knowledge of the Old Testament (which he is reading in Greek). And in many cases when he knows that his audience has these same commitments, he can echo themes from the Old Testament that to us may seem subtle. But every culture does this. When a body of knowledge or a set of images is shared fully between a writer and the audience, allusions suffice. Thus in 4:21–31 Paul can say "it is written" that Abraham had two sons and then he can launch into a discussion of interpreting the lives of Hagar, Ishmael, and Isaac. He assumes his readers know where "it is written" and that they know these stories from Genesis.

But there is more. Each of us are shaped by concepts—and not just stories we can recall. When I refer to "love," things move immediately into my mind that will come from my own cultural or theological context. When I say "law," the same thing happens. This means we need to be alert to terms Paul uses that are really shaped by a framework that is foreign to us. The word *grace*, for instance, has a long history *as a concept* in the Old Testament. And when Paul writes, he likely has this in mind, assuming that we as readers share this same framework.

In Galatians' six chapters, Paul explicitly cites the Old Testament ten times. But these are concentrated in the theological core of the letter in chapters 3–4. In the opening two chapters, the explicit use of the Old Testament is rare (but see 2:16) because here Paul is defending his apostleship and telling stories about his interactions with Jerusalem's leaders. Paul's debate in Galatia centered on correctly interpreting the law *in light of the arrival of the messiah.* And in these debates the Hebrew scriptures were essential. But we have to realize—and here we will point this out regularly—Paul is building a Christian theology in its earliest stages, weaving Old Testament ideas that were simply reflexive or natural to him. He does not need to cite the Old Testament every time he is thinking about the Old Testament. He can reach for the life of Abraham in Galatians 3 and easily presuppose that the great themes from Abraham's life were common knowledge. Or better still, his opponents in Galatia may be using the Abraham story and thus it is already part of an open debate.

One last note. We will refer frequently to the "Septuagint" (often given the abbreviation LXX). This is the Greek translation of the Hebrew Old Testament that was begun about two hundred years before Paul. It circulated widely among Jews who spoke Greek, and we know that it was the text that Paul cited when writing his Greek letters. This is important because, in some cases, the key to understanding a word from Paul is found by tracking that Greek word's use in the Septuagint. Of course, the Old Testament lies behind the Septuagint, but it is written in Hebrew—which Paul also could read—and so both the Hebrew Bible and the Septuagint will come into play.[3]

# GALATIANS 1

*The most famous remark on Galatians 1:1–5* comes from the renowned British commentator who wrote in 1865: J. B. Lightfoot of Cambridge University. "The two threads which run through this epistle—the defense of the Apostle's own authority, and the maintenance of the doctrine of grace—are knotted together in the opening salutation."[1] Paul begins by asserting his own apostolic identity and anchors it to the Lord who commissioned him in his resurrection.

We have already seen how Paul's opening lines bristle with impatience. The main features of a Roman letter appear (author, recipient, salutation). But generally Roman letters began with gracious words of introduction naming the author and blessing the recipient followed by a prayer of thanksgiving. A quick glance at Philippians 1:1–4 illustrates this form easily.

> Paul and Timothy, servants of Christ Jesus, To all God's holy people in Christ Jesus at Philippi, together with the overseers and deacons: Grace and peace to you from God our Father and the Lord Jesus Christ. I thank my God every time I remember you. In all my prayers for all of you, I always pray with joy . . .

But here in Galatians Paul is eager to defend himself and assert his authority. The controversies that are spinning in Galatia have been inspired by his critics, who have undercut his identity as a valid messenger from God. Therefore, Paul is eager to establish his calling as unrelated to human self-appointment. He is passionate and even his grammar provides impulsively written phrases that almost run together.

**1:1** *Paul, an apostle.* Paul lived in a multilingual world. He could work as easily in Aramaic-Hebrew contexts as he could in Roman Greek-speaking contexts. When he was in the former, he likely used the name Saul (Ac 7:58; 9:4), but he also was called "Paul," particularly when he was traveling in Hellenistic circles. He possessed Roman citizenship, and in this case, it was common for Jews to also use a Latin name: *Paulus* (Gk, *Paulos*). In the book of Acts, Luke employs Paul's Roman name for the first time when he leaves Syrian Antioch and arrives at Greek-speaking Cyprus (Ac 13:9).

In most of his letters, Paul introduces himself with some combination of the terms *apostle* or *slave/servant* (Gk, *doulos*). Thus we see in Romans 1:1, "Paul, a servant of Christ Jesus, called to be an apostle. . . ." In Galatians, he is aware of his preferred identity as a *doulos* of Christ (1:10), but he does not lead with this idea here. Paul is an apostle first and foremost, and this is what he wants the Galatians to hear.

## Galatians 1:1 Through Old Testament Eyes: Messengers

This idea of authorized messengers was quite old even by Paul's day. Transactions over a distance required authorized agents, particularly when they required negotiation or explanations. In the Old Testament world, the Hebrew term *shaliach* was one who bore the authority of the one who sent them. (In John's gospel, Jesus is viewed as God's "agent" because he has been "sent" with a message; John 4:34; 5:37; 6:38.) In Jewish writings in Paul's day, Moses was viewed as the *shaliach* (the sent one) of God (see Ex 3:13–15). Thus, when Moses spoke, he bore God's words to his people.

An apostle was an emissary, agent, or representative authorized by another person to bring a message, a gift, or money to another. His authority was entirely based on who had sent him. And Paul wants no debate here: *he is an emissary from God,* "sent neither by human commission nor from human authorities but through Jesus Christ and God the Father" (Gal 1:1 NRSVue). Therefore, if Paul makes a claim that he is an apostle, he must identify his sender. And in this case, he must make it crystal clear that the basis of his ministry, the authority of his teaching, did not have a human beginning. He had been sent by Jesus and God the Father.

Paul is not making a claim here that he is among the original twelve apostles. These Twelve were also "apostles," since Jesus had commissioned them. The term *apostle* was used widely and flexibly. When Paul was in prison in Rome, Epaphroditus was sent by the Philippians to Paul as their messenger

(Gk, *apostolos,* Php 2:25). Still others represented Christ and so, like Barnabas, they could be called apostles (Ac 14:4, 14). In Galatians 1:19, Paul implies that James (the Lord's brother) had this title even though he was not one of the Twelve, and in 1 Thessalonians 1:1 and 2:6, Silas is included as an apostle. In 1 Corinthians 15:7–9, Paul compares his experience of the resurrected Jesus with that of the Twelve. In 1 Corinthians 9:1–2, he defends his apostleship based on his meeting (and commissioning) by Jesus himself. Messengers must have a clear channel of authority passing from their sender into their work. And in cases where this authority-from-Christ is questionable, Paul can refer to false apostles (2 Co 11:5; cf. Rev 2:2). This is likely what Paul's accusers were calling him: a false apostle, not commissioned by God but owning a presumptuous and arrogant self-given authority.

## Galatians 1 Through Old Testament Eyes: Moses, Paul, and Authority

In the Old Testament, a comparison with Moses' authority in Exodus 19 is apt. Following Israel's departure from Egypt and three-month journey to Mount Sinai, the Israelites must discern the source of Moses' authority. Was he a charismatic deliverer who had cleverly defeated the Egyptians? Was he a self-appointed prophet speaking his own words? When they arrive at the mountain, the story makes Moses' authority unassailable. "This is what you are to say," the Lord tells Moses (Ex 19:3). And then Moses is given a divine message that he then relays to Israel's elders. "So Moses went back and summoned the elders of the people and set before them all the words the LORD had commanded him to speak. The people all responded together, 'We will do everything the LORD has said.' So Moses brought their answer back to the LORD" (Ex 19:7–8).

The obedience of the elders is predicated on their confident knowledge that they were not hearing Moses' words, but rather God's words. And when Moses speaks to Israel broadly, he is overshadowed by a dark thundering storm cloud that underscores God's authority now born by Moses. "The LORD said to Moses, 'I am going to come to you in a dense cloud, so that the people will hear me speaking with you and will always put their trust in you.' Then Moses told the LORD what the people had said" (Ex 19:9).

As God was Moses' sender, so Jesus was Paul's sender. Paul will return to the defense of this authority shortly (Gal 1:11–12, 15–17), but above all, he must make the claim at the outset that the resurrected Jesus had "called him"—commissioned him—to do the work that he was doing (Gal 1:15).

This calling also is linked to the desire of God *the Father*. The notion of a god as father was well-known in virtually every Mediterranean culture. And of course, it features in many Old Testament passages as the ultimate description of God's authority over his creation (Dt 32:6; Isa 63:16; Jer 31:9). Therefore, Paul is appealing to the highest source of authority imaginable. As God raised Jesus from the dead, validating his identity as the messiah, so too Christ in his resurrection had commissioned and validated Paul in what he now does.

**1:2** *And all the brothers and sisters with me.* The NIV here takes the appropriate liberty of translating "brothers" as "brothers and sisters." The Greek term *adelphos* (brother) has a generic force here since undoubtedly Paul's communities represented both men and women. The use of "brother" (translated variously) for religious gatherings was common throughout the ancient world and well-known in the Hebrew Old Testament (Ex 2:11; Dt 3:18–20; Ne 5:1; Isa 66:20).

Paul commonly refers to those who are sending greetings with him as he writes (see most of his letters). But in this case, he is reinforcing something important. Paul is not alone in what he has to say to them. He is accompanied by others—not one or two names, but many others who acknowledge his authority and the substance of his message. In the polemics of his self-defense, this will become a vital item.

*To the churches in Galatia.* The term "churches" (Gk, *ekklēsia*) was a common term for any gathering or assembly of people (civic or religious) in the Greek or Roman worlds. In the Septuagint, which was popular at this time, this word was used by Hellenistic Jews to describe God's people, sometimes translated "assembly" (Dt 23:1–2; Jdg 20:2; 1 Ch 28:8). As the early Christian communities grew, this term became their first choice for their formal gatherings (being used 114 times in the New Testament).

We have already seen (in the Introduction) that the location of Galatia has witnessed considerable study, but today many scholars believe that Paul is referring to imperial or Roman provincial titles when citing regions. Imperial Galatia was an important Roman province in the center of Anatolia, reaching south to the Taurus mountains. The regional culture in the southern area was called Phrygia, so when Paul travels here, Luke often says they were in "Galatia and Phrygia" (Ac 16:6; 18:23); that is, they were in the Roman government "state" of Galatia but in the Phrygian territory (like saying you are in Bavaria, Germany). Note that Paul is writing to *the churches* of this area. This would include those communities established during his first missionary tour and revisited on the second tour: Derbe, Lystra, Iconium, and especially the major city of Pisidian Antioch.

But note as well that Paul does not attribute this church as belonging to "God." Paul always commends his churches when he writes. Typically he writes as he does to the Thessalonians, acknowledging the sort of gathering that was here. "Paul, Silas and Timothy, To the church of the Thessalonians in God the Father and the Lord Jesus Christ" (1 Th 1:1; see 2 Th 1:1). He addresses the Corinthians as "those sanctified in Christ Jesus and called to be his holy people" (1 Co 1:2). In Galatians 1:22, he can say that the Judean churches are gatherings "in Christ." But the Galatian churches receive no such honoring description. This is an alarming omission in Galatians, and it signals Paul's view of their well-being.

**1:3** *Grace and peace to you from God our Father and the Lord Jesus Christ.* Every culture has etiquette rules for greetings. Jews would commonly say "peace" (Heb, *shalom*, Jdg 19:20 ESV; 1 Sa 25:5–6 ESV) while Greeks would greet each other with *Chairein!* which meant "grace" (Gk, *charis*, Jas 1:1). (See "Galatians Through Old Testament Eyes: Shalom" below and "Galatians 3:2–6 Through Old Testament Eyes: Grace and Benefaction.") Paul is likely adapting the well-known Greek greeting for his own Christian use.

The early Christians combined peace with grace into their own formulaic greeting, "Grace and peace to you," which is used widely in the New Testament (Eph 1:2; Php 1:2; Tit 1:4; 2 Pe 1:2, etc.). In the Old Testament, *charis* is similar to the Heb *hen* and *hesed*, in which mercy and charity are important cultural values (Ge 19:19; 47:29; 1 Sa 20:8; 2 Sa 16:17). The Old Testament use of *hesed* likely gets at this directly: this is God's loving-kindness (Ex 20:6; Isa 54:8; 63:7; Jer 9:24; 31:3). While gods of the ancient world could be routinely described with terms like *power* and *glory*, Israel is unusual in attaching this notion to Yahweh, pointing to his kindness and loyalty.

The power of this greeting was not lost on Paul, given the present circumstances in Galatia. "Grace" will not be simply a casual greeting but will become the touchstone of this letter. Paul is reminding the Galatians of this grace that has its origins in both the Father and the Son. And it is this idea of grace as the foundation of the gospel that Paul needs to explain.

## Galatians 1:3 Through Old Testament Eyes: Shalom

In the Old Testament, the notion of *shalom* (peace) was not only used commonly as a greeting but could bear a dense set of theological or social ideas. If we translate it as "peace," we run the risk of limiting its many meanings. It doesn't mean the cessation of conflict as much as the well-being of one's personal life, especially of material life (fortunes, health, etc.). For a country, it referred to prosperity and stability. When Isaiah predicted doom for Jerusalem, Hezekiah dismissed it thinking that his reign would be prosperous (or enjoy *shalom*, 2 Ki 20:19).

Theologically *shalom* is used frequently in reference to God. This is the fullest gift that he gives to people. So when Gideon built an altar to God in the book of Judges, he named it "God is *shalom*" (Jdg 6:24), signaling simply that God is one who blesses with flourishing and goodness, with *shalom*. Thus, God creates *shalom* in the heavens (Job 25:2 NLT), and he promises to provide it to his world (Ps 35:27 NLT). When we pray for the *shalom* of Jerusalem (Ps 122:6), we are not simply asking that God would save it from conflict but that he would gift it with a status that supplies well-being and flourishing.

Thus, it is no surprise that *shalom* became a greeting in the Old Testament, ancient Judaism, and even today. It is a comprehensive offering of goodness and prosperity for another person. That Paul uses the term *peace* (Gk, *eirēnē*) is an echo of his Jewish background, his Jewish roots. (See sidebar, "Galatians 6:16: Shalom—Reprise.")

**1:4–5** *Who gave himself for our sins.* At the heart of Paul's gospel is the idea, the fundamental idea, that Jesus' death was a sacrifice for our sin (Gal 2:20; 1 Co 15:3). Sacrifice of an animal in worship was a common practice in the Old Testament (e.g., Ex 29:10–14, 33–37; Lev 4–5; Nu 8:8). During festivals numerous animals were killed at the temple altar. During the seven-day Passover, for instance, fourteen bulls, seven rams, forty-nine lambs, and seven goats were sacrificed. During Tabernacles, a whopping 199 animals were sacrificed over eight days (see Nu 28–29). And this does not count the daily morning and evening sacrifices nor the personal guilt and sin sacrifices (see Lev 1–7). Leviticus 1:4 describes these sacrifices as "atoning" (Heb, *kipper*), which can refer to wiping away, covering, or ransoming someone who is in jeopardy (Lev 17:11); this could refer to the status of the nation or a person. In no case was child sacrifice (or human sacrifice) permitted, although it was known in Canaanite culture (Lev 18:21; 20:1–5; 2 Ch 28:3; 33:6; Eze 16:21; 20:31).

But how Jesus, a person, might be a sacrifice for sin wasn't so clear at the very beginning of Christian history. That a person would die for another has a generic dramatic quality, and Roman literature used this motif as commonly as modern literature and film will use it. Religious uses of sacrifice were everywhere in this world. It is hard to imagine any religious cult in Paul's world that did not incorporate some form of ritual sacrifice. But note what Paul is doing: he is assigning Jesus a role in *religious sacrificial service* (see also Gal 2:20). This is startling and no doubt what set early Christian teaching apart from the very onset.

Paul is alluding to matters that the Galatians need to know in order to better assess their own spiritual condition. The chief idea at the center of the gospel is the generosity of God—and this notion is deeply rooted in the Old Testament. Paul's language here ("for our sins," 1:4) likely echoes Isaiah 53:6 and the language of altar sacrifice in Israel (Mic 6:7; Eze 40:39). In Isaiah, it is the servant of Yahweh who gives himself for the sins of the nation (Isa 52:13–53:12) and who inaugurates an end to the curses that stemmed from Israel's violation of the covenant. This offering, according to Isaiah, brings a second exodus to a new inheritance (Isa 54:3) and even brings a new beginning to creation.[2] This framework of redemption to new-creation in Isaiah is no doubt what Paul has in mind when he imagines the redemptive and restorative work of Christ as an altar sacrifice for our sins.

This generosity is seen when God supplies a sacrifice (a ram) for Abraham before he offers up his son Isaac on an altar (Ge 22:13). This is where God brings his people out of Egypt despite their full embrace of Egyptian religious habits. This is where God brings his people back from exile despite their violations of the covenant. These are acts of generosity, and they form the basis of Israel's covenant with God. In fact, the entire sacrificial system employed at the Old Testament temple was built on this one idea: that the sacrifice of an innocent victim (a lamb, a bull) supplied by God's agents (priests, Levites) could cover the sins of Israel. This too was an act of generosity. Therefore, Paul is reminding the Galatians that whatever they think about Jesus, knowing him as a sacrificial victim unlocks their understanding of the generosity of God. And this one idea will be a gateway to reclaiming their understanding of God's grace.

*To rescue us from the present evil age.* However, Jesus' death on the cross did not simply satisfy the just requirements of a righteous God. Jesus' death set right a world where many believed evil forces held reign. The idea of evil's dominion over this world is common in the Gospels, where Jesus must defeat Satan in order to exhibit the emerging new dominion of God and his kingdom. Jesus is plundering Satan's house (Mk 3:24–29). So elsewhere Paul will say, "Do not conform to the pattern of this world" (Ro 12:2; see Eph 2:2). This pattern is an environment of decay and evil, which Christ came to defeat. Therefore, this is why the Galatians need to see that any who serve the old ways of this world have not been fully emancipated as Christ intended. And above all, the law (which served temporarily within the order of this world) is a part of this passing era: it served as a custodian, a caretaker until the time of the Spirit would emerge (Gal 3:23–35). Paul will say, "Now that this faith has come, we are no longer under a guardian" (v. 24).

These two ideas—the generosity/grace of God and the freedom we have from the law—will become essential ideas to show the Galatians where they have gone wrong. The Galatian world was well-acquainted with gods who demanded much of their followers. They were easily susceptible to religions that would require sacrifice-in-fear lest an angry deity bring some punishment to them.

Clint Arnold describes the nature of the religious world that the Galatians would have known. Living in fear of offending a god, the Anatolian faithful often believed if they violated or offended a god, they would be struck with a malady, and to appease the god, a stone monument (a stele) would be erected with an inscription confessing the offense and exalting the god. Arnold writes about religious steles in the vicinity of Galatia:

> All of the inscriptions represent the deities as austere, powerful gods who take offence at the transgressions of their worshippers. It does not matter if the sins are witting or unwitting; they still solicit the harsh response of the deity. The nature of the sins varies from cultic offences (e.g., violating purity laws, neglecting religious obligations, failing to take part in ritual mystery initiation, failure to fulfill a vow, etc.) to social misdeeds (e.g. stealing, lying, cheating, and even the use of witchcraft to bring harm to someone). The gods are quick to smite the offender with any of a range of maladies, including rendering people mute or blind, putting the offender in a death-like condition, instilling madness, and even striking men and women with serious problems in their genitals. In some cases, the offender or a family member is struck dead by the god.[3]

This is the Galatian world with which Paul must contend. The gospel brought freedom from the threat of deities that would harm if they were not placated. This is the religion of "the present evil age" (1:4) that Paul believes the Galatians have returned to. And it is completely opposed to the God of grace and generosity that he brought to them.

But there is more. If the Galatians were ready-made for a religious framework lacking generosity, a world of expectation (law) and anxiety, they would be susceptible to messengers from Jerusalem or any place who might come to them and argue that Paul's gospel was inadequate. "Paul's gospel was too generous," they could tell the Galatians—and soon, the Galatians changed their minds.

*Our God and Father, to whom be glory.* "Glory" (Gk, *doxa*) was a common term (along with "holy") used as an Old Testament attribute of God (Ex 15:11;

16:7; Ps 4:2; 19:1; Isa 6:3; Eze 1:28). In the Old Testament context, it refers to weight (Heb, *kabod*), as in his significance or honor or "weight" in the world. In Greek it can also mean honor, which is likely Paul's intention here. Paul is providing honor, praise, and acclaim to the one God who can bring about rescue from this world of fear.

*Amen* was a well-known Hebrew affirmation that what has just been said is true (Dt 27:15–26). It often closed prayers (Ps 41:13; 72:19; 89:52).

**1:6–7** *I am astonished.* Paul's astonishment is therefore understandable. Perhaps it was the speed with which the Galatians had abandoned the good news ("quickly deserting," v. 6). It recalls the speed with which the Israelites, having seen the power and grace of God defeat Pharaoh, quickly abandon their historic belief in him and resort to pagan worship practice (Ex 32:8; Dt 9:16). This reversion to Egyptian religion was as tragic as it was catastrophic for Israel. In Paul's context, his shock was parallel. He may be thinking of the short duration of time since he had been with them, mentoring them in the gospel. Either way Paul is amazed that these Galatians, once enlightened with the gospel of grace, would return to the bondage that was unnecessary.

*Turning to a different gospel.* This may be the first time (assuming that Galatians is the first written document of Christian theology) that someone employed the word "gospel" to summarize the essence of the Christian faith. Gospel simply means "good news" (Gk, *euaggelion*). It is a good announcement from any source (the government or God) saying that something terrific has happened or is about it happen. In this case, Paul makes it clear that this news is anchored in what God has done when he called us by the grace of Christ. Notice again Paul is reinforcing his main theme (1:3). The essence of this good news is grace. And this is what the Galatians have lost: a fundamental plank in the teaching that Paul had given them.

## Galatians 1:6–12 Through Old Testament Eyes: The Gospel

The verb *euangelizomai* ("to announce good news") is found multiple times in the LXX regarding messages of immense importance. Messengers bring the good news of military triumph (1 Sa 31:9 ESV, NASB, NRSVue; Na 1:15), and the Lord announces his own victory over his enemies (Ps 68:11 NASB, NET, NLT). Good news can also regard the birth of a son (Jer 20:15) or the anointing of a new king (1 Ki 1:42–43).

Most significant for the New Testament are likely Isaiah 40:1–2, 9; 52:1–2, 7; and 61:1–4 concerning the return of Israel from exile, its freedom from captivity, the restoration of the nation, and the commencement of God's reign.[4]

To announce his ministry and the fulfillment of all these promises from God, Jesus quotes Isaiah 61 in Luke 4:18–19:

> The Spirit of the Lord is on me,
>     because he has anointed me
>     to proclaim good news to the poor.
> He has sent me to proclaim freedom for the prisoners
>     and recovery of sight for the blind,
> to set the oppressed free,
>     to proclaim the year of the Lord's favor.

Paul would know of how Jesus and the early church understood and applied these later chapters of Isaiah. Indeed, he referenced Isaiah 52:7 (see also Na 1:15) when he noted, "And how can anyone preach unless they are sent? As it is written: 'How beautiful are the feet of those who bring good news!'" (Ro 10:15).

Freedom from slavery, restoration, the defeat of God's enemies, and the establishment of his kingdom would all be background of the good news, the gospel, Paul had in mind.

The more difficult question is the nature of this "different gospel" the Galatians have embraced (1:6). Paul is clear that in his mind it is "no gospel at all"—and that it is a perversion of the gospel he represents (1:7). And here for the first time we learn that it has promoters in Galatia. "Some people are throwing you into confusion" (v. 7). Many translations describe this as "troubling you"—the Greek word here (tarassō) refers to something that is disturbed, such as water that makes waves (Jn 5:7) or even upsetting political protest or agitation (Ac 17:8). This is the effect that these teachers are having on Paul's converts, which explains Paul's personal frustration and reactivity.

Who are these people? And what is their agenda? Throughout the letter Paul will allude to these opponents (see 3:1), but he will also indicate that he is no stranger to struggle when it comes to defending the gospel against opponents. In chapter 2, Paul will describe debates he had in both Jerusalem (2:1) and Syrian Antioch (2:11). The gospel of Christ is so remarkable that it will stir contentious reactions.

It is doubtful that these teachers are contesting fundamental ideas such as Jesus' death and resurrection. Rather, they are teaching something that no longer brings "good news" to these Galatian Gentiles. The teaching in some manner jeopardizes the idea that Jesus' death ushered in a grace that satisfied God's every requirement.

Paul's gospel therefore has competition. But his opponents are not simply Jews who reject Jesus and promote the law. Nor are they pagan Galatians who want to blend the gospel with local temple religion. This false teaching in Galatia is a perversion because it has led the Galatians to abandon the gospel (Gk, *metastrephō*), which means to turn one thing into something else. It is to flip something desired (fresh water) into something undesirable (salt water). It could be feasting turned to mourning (Am 8:10) or daylight into darkness (Joel 2:31). Moses changed Egypt's rivers into blood (Ps 78:44). Evidently these are Christian leaders who have inverted the gospel into something it was never meant to be.

The Old Testament illustrates richly the capacity of God's own people to collapse spiritually and promote wrong ideas from within their own ranks. From the dissent in the wilderness wanderings to the false prophets of the monarchy period, Israel was capable of hearing the good news of its rescue and denying it fully. It is Eve having a discussion with the serpent. It is Ahab twisting God's word for himself. In the Old Testament tradition, such behavior calls for nothing less than a harsh rebuke. Isaiah exhibits this tone:

> Woe to the sinful nation,
>> a people whose guilt is great,
> a brood of evildoers,
>> children given to corruption!
> They have forsaken the LORD;
>> they have spurned the Holy One of Israel
>> and turned their backs on him. (Isa 1:4)

Paul's outrage is no different. This is not an alternative interpretation of the gospel; this is a perversion of the gospel.

**1:8-9** *Under God's curse.* Notice how unsparing Paul is toward these teachers. For the apostle, the gospel is a pristine revelation given by God and the legitimacy of every other teaching must be tested by it. It would make no difference if the messenger of an alternative *gospel* were from heaven (1:8) or from this world (1:9)—it makes no difference. They deserve to be placed under a curse.

Today we find this sort of curse language (Gk, *anathema*) odd, but it was common in the Jewish and Hellenistic world surrounding Paul. The word is used in the LXX with some frequency to describe objects or people that deserve destruction (Lev 27:28–29; Dt 7:26; 13:15–17; Jos 6:17–18). "To hell with them" might reflect Paul's tone only if we remember that he means it theologically. They deserve God's judgment.

**1:10** *Am I now trying to win the approval of human beings?* These opponents know what Paul teaches, and they want to amend it. They are Christian missionaries who are willing to contradict Paul. And the fact that Paul is willing to stand his ground at the cost of popularity or reputation signals his passion for this truth and his willingness to pay any price to protect it. He knows that standing up at this moment is costly. In 4:16, he acknowledges that this sort of stand may create enemies, and so it will. But the opposite of this conviction is flattery, speaking in order to win favors or benefits. Later Paul will claim that this is precisely what these teachers are doing (2:11–16). But for him the riskiness and danger of holding firm with an unpopular position lends legitimacy to his truth. He essentially asks, "Why would someone do this were it not for the truth of the matter?" Paul has just invoked a divine curse on his opponents, certainly angering most of them! This behavior would make him an extremist or someone with an intemperate attitude. Divisive perhaps. But for Paul, pleasing Christ is everything (and otherwise, "I would not be a servant of Christ," 1:10).

*A servant of Christ.* The actual term here is "slave of Christ," and this provides a window into how Paul thinks about his relationship with God. Paul commonly refers to himself as a slave (Ro 1:1; Eph 3:7; Col 1:25), which would be immediately shocking to his readers. In a world of strict social hierarchies, Paul has just placed himself at the bottom of any social ladder. But more, Paul is echoing a common Jewish idea represented throughout the Old Testament where people devoted to God were authorized bearers of God's message (Jos 24:29; 2 Ki 9:7; 24:2; Ne 10:29).

It would be easy for us to misunderstand the depth of Paul's meaning here in his Jewish context. We live in a world of voluntary associations that we choose, sustain, or quit with some frequency. In the Old Testament, tribal life within the theological framework of Israel meant that God's relationship with his people was that of a monarch and his subjects, a shepherd who *owns* his flock. He controlled his people's future and could make demands on their present. Thus Abraham (Ge 26:24), Moses (Nu 12:8; Jos 1:2, 7; 2 Ki 21:8), Caleb (Nu 14:24), David (2 Sa 7:5, 8; 1 Ki 14:8; 2 Ki 19:34), Job (2:3; 42:8), Isaiah (20:3), and Israel the nation (Isa 41:8) are called God's servants. They obey his word and regard themselves as having limited freedom.

Paul has embraced this same identity. *He belongs to Jesus Christ.* This is not a casual identity he's picked up. This is an identity that controls him.

Moreover, being a slave demoted your identity, but it could empower your presence because you stood and spoke on behalf of the one who owns you. Just as Moses did not speak for himself in his utterances but spoke on behalf of God, so here Paul is making the same claim. This explains why in the next section Paul describes the origin of this gospel he so keenly wants to protect.

**1:11-12** *The gospel I preached . . . I received it by revelation from Jesus Christ.* These paragraphs are marked by Paul's own sense of urgency about these matters. "I want you to know" is Paul's attempt to reinforce his argument. ("Brothers and sisters," NIV, correctly represents the Greek *anthropoi*, which is inclusive and refers to people generally; 1:11.) Here Paul is appealing to prophetic authority, which means that his teaching is not "from below"; that is, his words are from God ("from above"), and they cannot be described as a human construct—which is precisely what he wants to say about his opponents.

## Galatians 1:11–12 Through Old Testament Eyes: Revelation and the Hebrew Bible

The Old Testament provides a wider, deeper context for Paul's assertion. So much of the ancient world either found their gods to be distant and unmoved by human affairs or present in temple and ceremony. Access to divine power to resolve human problems could come by magic, sacrifice, or ritual. The Old Testament is decidedly different. Here God conveys his will *through spoken word* and expects to be heard and understood. Thus God speaks and creation takes form (Ge 1:3, 6, 9, 11, 14, 20, 24, 26). God speaks and written words appear on stone tablets (Ex 31:18). God speaks and prophets arise (Jer 1:2; Hos 1:1; Mic 1:1; etc.). This provides the Old Testament with a distinctive notion of revelation—God as initiator and his people as recipients—that sets its theological worldview apart. The loss of this sole idea would impoverish the world and leave it in silence. But in a Hebrew setting where this notion is active and alive, where revelation is assumed, the contest centers on which words are indeed divine words and which people can rightly convey them.

An authoritative teacher such as Paul would rarely find his authority in his own brilliance or creativity. Generally, he would claim that it was derivative, stemming from a superior or a mentor, a rabbi perhaps that had formed his thinking. Paul could appeal to this derivative authority when he refers to the teacher Gamaliel of Jerusalem (Ac 22:3). But in the case of Galatians, Paul is saying something else. He was not taught these things by another person in the ordinary way of things (1:12). This is a teaching that has come directly from the resurrected Christ. This is an extraordinary claim, and it echoes what we heard in 1:1. Paul is not a commonplace bearer of theological education. He is a courier of something given to him from heaven.

**1:13–14** *My previous way of life in Judaism.* It is vital that we do not misunderstand Paul here. Paul never thought of himself as once a Jew and now a Christian. His previous way of life (Gk, *anastrophē*) points to the way he viewed matters *within* Judaism. He was a Jew who persecuted the church and tried to destroy it (Ac 8:3). But, as a follower of Jesus, he would never have said he had been converted *out of Judaism*. He was a Jew who had embraced the Jewish messiah (see Gal 2:15).

*Extremely zealous for the traditions of my fathers.* The story that Paul bears (the gospel) is therefore so potent that it not only surprised him, but it utterly changed him. And this is where the apostle wants to lead us. In telling this story he is not only making a claim to the legitimacy of his own credentials in Judaism, thereby avoiding the criticism that he is an outlier or an eccentric Jewish teacher, but he also needs to write convincingly about the strength of his own conversion. In the Old Testament, this is no different than Moses' voice in relation to Israel's struggle with Pharaoh. After meeting God on the mountain, Moses does not return to Egypt and his people with a plan for escape or a convincing argument for Pharaoh. He is a courier, a messenger, bearing another's voice. "This is what the LORD, the God of Israel, says: 'Let my people go'" (Ex 5:1). It was Moses' encounter at Mount Horeb (Ex 3:1) that authorized his call.

Paul is moving within these narrative circles. He is the recipient of revelation, and in this sense, he has virtually taken on the capacity of a prophet. Compare what he says about himself in Galatians 1:15–16 with Jeremiah's or Isaiah's self-understanding (Jer 1:5; Isa 49:1). In 1 Corinthians 14:37, we can hear Paul debating with Christian prophets whom he needs to challenge. Then he reveals his own self-understanding, "If anyone thinks they are a prophet or otherwise gifted by the Spirit, let them acknowledge that what I am writing to you is the Lord's command." His ability to challenge a prophet is that he too, like any prophet, is a courier of the Lord's command.

Of course, some might ask: Is Paul's revelatory encounter a fantasy or is it believable? Is he conveying things that now break his relationship with Judaism? Is he still a Jew after all these years? Paul must now provide his own compelling narrative.

Paul begins with his life in Jerusalem. For a full glimpse of Paul's personal history, we can look at his short autobiographical outline in Philippians 3:4–11, and for his conversion story, we can look at the three descriptions in the book of Acts (9, 22, and 26). Paul grew up in Tarsus within a conservative family (his father was a Pharisee) who promoted Jewish tradition passionately. This explains his family's unusual decision to send their son to Jerusalem where Paul studied under the famous Pharisee Gamaliel I (Ac 5:34). Here Paul says he was trained in "the law of our ancestors" (Ac 22:3), and eventually it appears he worked closely with the Sanhedrin, the religious court of Israel.

## Galatians 1:14 Through Old Testament Eyes: The Spear of Phinehas

Here in 1:14 and in Acts 22:3, as well as Philippians 3:6, Paul uses the word "zeal" (Gk, *zēloō*) to describe his disposition. He was "zealous for the traditions of his fathers" (Gal 1:14). This could be a casual reference to his skill in study (he outdistanced all of his peers). But this term carried significant freight in Paul's world as well as the Old Testament. This word indicates an extreme and sometimes intolerant outlook on those who were less committed to obedience to the law. Its legacy and meaning were fixed in the Old Testament story of the priest Phinehas in Numbers 25:1–9 (Ps 106:30). Outraged by the unrighteousness he witnessed in the tabernacle during the wilderness wanderings, he took up a spear and killed an Israelite and his Midianite wife and was commended for it. The "zeal of Phinehas" became a catchphrase and even inspired an entire violent movement to fight against the Roman occupation of Judea. This identity was so widespread that even one of Jesus' own apostles was Simon "the Zealot"—giving us some idea of his personal politics.

Therefore, when Paul says he is "zealous" for the law, he is linking himself to a potent Jewish tradition, one that has explosive tendencies. It is no surprise that Paul is first introduced in Acts at the stoning of Stephen (Ac 7:58). He is there as a legal witness, no doubt in his mind, representing the Sanhedrin. And he continues this effort by pursuing Christians whom he sees as errant Jews. This is behavior typical of those who prided themselves with zeal and was reflected by passionate Jewish forces from the Maccabees of the second century BC to Judaism's war with Rome in AD 66.

**1:15–17** *God . . . set me apart from my mother's womb and called me by his grace.* The idea that God had set Paul apart before birth anchors him squarely in the prophetic tradition of Jeremiah and Isaiah (Jer 1:5; Isa 49:1). This leads to the suggestion that Paul viewed himself as a prophet with a Jeremiah-like calling. Even Paul's language in 1:15 echoes that in Isaiah 49:1 (LXX). But this plan was crystallized when Paul was interrupted on his way to Damascus. In his conversion accounts in Acts, Paul points to the critical moment when the voice of Jesus intersects his plans (Ac 9:5; 22:7; 26:14). We might imagine that the strength of that voice had to match the strength of Paul's misdirected zeal.

Paul alludes to this pre-conversion story to underscore the transformation—the dramatic encounter—that occurred on the road to Damascus (Ac 9). We cannot underestimate the significance of this for Paul. Given his theological convictions, Paul's encounter with the resurrected Jesus upended his beliefs. And it made clear that his pursuit of the church was in fact a persecution of Jesus who was God's messenger. In each of his conversion accounts, Paul's pre-conversion efforts on behalf of the Sanhedrin are described as hostility to Jesus (Ac 9:4; 22:7; 26:14). In Paul's mind, he deserved judgment not because he was mistaken about the messiah but because the God of Abraham whom he worshipped had *sent his Son* to him and Paul had rejected him. Embedded in this idea is an affirmation not only of Jesus' mission (to reveal God) but his identity (as the Son of God). This is why the crisis on the Damascus Road was so profound. Paul had offended the God of Israel.

But within this encounter, Paul says he was received by Jesus with grace. Grace had replaced judgment. This was not simply a revelation of what was true for Paul; Jesus commissions him to do what he is doing: bringing the astounding reality of this grace to the Gentiles (Ac 22:21). Here then we find the bedrock of Paul's own theological outlook. When his religious preparation and practice placed him in opposition to God, he experienced the unexpected. His earnest religious effort had steered him wrong. His new life would be grounded in this experience, this gracious encounter with Jesus who not only accepted him but gave him a new purpose ("so that I might preach," 1:16).

*So that I might preach him among the Gentiles.* A Gentile (Gk, *ethnos*, "nation") is anyone who is not a Jew. This notion of separation from non-Jews is rooted in the Old Testament. On the one hand, the people of God are to distance themselves from the influence of pagan nations and their evil and idolatrous ways (Lev 18:3, 30; Dt 6:14–15; Jer 7:5–7; 35:15). On the other hand, foreigners who live in their midst are to be treated fairly (Ex 22:21; 23:9; Lev 25:35), and ultimately they can be welcomed into God's family (Ge 12:1–3; Ps 86:9; Isa 9:1–2; 42:1–8; 49:5–6; 55:5). Israelites are even to bring God's message to them (as Jonah was called to do). This is the background to the conflict between Paul and the Judaizers. As we will see in the course of this letter, Paul believes that this Old Testament separation is emphatically resolved in Jesus Christ, who removes this requirement of tribal separation and brings all nations together in him.

*I did not go up to Jerusalem.* David established Jerusalem as the capital of his kingdom about a thousand years before Christ (2 Sa 5:6–10), and it has remained the most important city in Israel to this day. Following the death and resurrection of Jesus and the events of Pentecost, the city became the center of early Christian activity and a hub for many leaders of the fledgling church. For Paul, going to Jerusalem would be an obvious move if he intended to be taught by or receive a mandate from those in authority. He deliberately points out that he didn't do this because that was not the source of his message or calling.

*But I went into Arabia.* Paul's immediate response was to travel *to Arabia.* This is less a matter of geography than an affirmation of the origin of his conversion, and it reinforces the notion that Paul had a prophetic call, not unlike Moses, who also met God on Sinai in Arabia. Recall that there were those who were challenging his apostleship, and this provides the backdrop of this letter. Here Paul is saying that his commission has been purely from heaven and not in consultation with other authorities, even those in Jerusalem. His gospel was God's gospel alone (see 1:1).

## Galatians 1:17 Through Old Testament Eyes: God in the Desert

Arabia was the desert region east of Judea (modern Jordan) and to the south (near northern Saudi Arabia), referred to multiple times in the Old Testament (see 1 Ki 10:15; Jer 25:24). Many Arab tribes lived in these regions and prominent among them were the Nabateans, whose capital city was the famous Petra. Jews had frequent contact with them, and even in Damascus there was a "Nabatean Quarter" where some resided. However, Paul's choice to enter the desert wilderness represented an Old Testament reflex.

Throughout the Hebrew scriptures, Israel had always had their most profound experiences with God in the desert. Abraham led a desert caravan when he came to Canaan at God's direction. Moses fled to the desert of Sinai where God commissioned him (Ex 2–3). Israel itself spent forty years there (Ex 16:35; Nu 14:33). Esau, Jacob (Ge 27:42–45; 28:10–22), David (1 Sa 23:14; 26:2–4), and a host of Israelites (1 Ki 19) found that the nearby eastern deserts were a place of both refuge and revelation. As Deuteronomy says, this is where God shows his ability to feed and clothe us. And it is where God learns (as we do) what is truly in our hearts (Dt 8:1–4).

This motif is clear in the life of John the Baptist, who is not only shaped in the desert but who calls Israel to enter the desert (Mk 1:4–8). Jesus likewise spent forty days in the deserts east of Jerusalem (Mk 1:12–13). Paul's Arabian journey echoes this tradition. He has entered the wilderness in response to a life-altering revelation.

What was Paul doing in Arabia? His career, preceded by years of preparation and culminating in his work in Jerusalem's Sanhedrin, was over. Some scholars believe that Paul began his preaching ministry immediately since there were many Jews in Nabatea. Perhaps this included Syria or even Damascus where, according to one Jewish historian (Josephus, *Wars*, during the Roman siege, 2.561) there were over ten thousand Jews. At least we know that Paul made enough of a stir in Damascus that at the end of this period, Jewish leaders there set a plot on his life (Ac 9:23–25). Still others believe that his destination was Mount Sinai (mirroring Elijah, 1 Ki 19:8–18). But perhaps something more modest is in order. Perhaps Paul was being mentored by Ananias of Damascus and the Christian community in Syria and Arabia. Or maybe Paul now had to regain his footing and digest what had just happened. This was a time of personal self-exploration and reckoning.

**1:18–24** *After three years, I went up to Jerusalem.* Paul spent three years in this region, likely moving in and out of Damascus (in the Old Testament and first-century literature, Damascus is either included in or adjacent to Arabia). And when he did preach in Damascus (Ac 9:22, 27), the Jewish community there threatened to kill him. This hostility would become common in his subsequent missionary tours. Eventually Paul made his way to Jerusalem, and we can imagine that his reentry was not simply awkward but dangerous. His high-profile conversion was known well in the city, and plans were set for his murder there as well (Ac 9:29).

In Jerusalem, Paul visited Cephas (the Aramaic form for *Peter*) for fifteen days and also saw James (or Jacob), Jesus' brother. There is general agreement that Peter was known as a leader of the early church across the Mediterranean while James was likely leading the Jerusalem church (Ac 12:17). But this small note is significant in Paul's argument in Galatians. We will learn that a delegation *from Jerusalem* (Judaizers) is the source of Paul's troubles in Galatia (Gal 2:12), and they are likely contending that Paul does not represent the teaching of the church. Here Paul shows his acquaintance with them—including James—and implies that they heard his story (despite the fears of other Jerusalem Christians, Ac 9:26) and likely discussed his revelation, his mission, and his understanding of the gospel.

*Other apostles.* See comment at 1:1.

*Syria and Cilicia.* Luke adds helpful details here that Paul avoids. Paul's arrival in Jerusalem and his public speaking sparked intense persecution. Not only was he threatened but the church itself was in danger (Ac 9:28–31). So Paul was escorted to Caesarea Maritima, Judea's Mediterranean port, and from there traveled to his home region around Tarsus. Cilicia was a region that in this period was a district of the province of Syria. But Paul singles it out because his own city of Tarsus was there (Ac 9:11).

Syria, on the other hand, was an enormous province with millions of residents and a sizable population of Jews. Its chief city was Antioch (on the Orontes River), which was deemed one of the largest cities in the empire. Paul will say in Galatians 2:1 that after fourteen years he returned to Jerusalem, and if we figure that he began his count from his conversion, we must imagine that Paul was in northwestern Syria for ten years.

These are Paul's "silent years," but this is so only because we have no records of what he did. Paul's family was in Tarsus, and we can speculate what it meant for him to return. But we can also speculate that Paul preached widely in Syria itself. The churches in Judea (outside of Jerusalem) did not know him (1:22), but his reputation had spread quickly (1:23). They said the one who had once been a threat now had become an ally. And because of this God was praised fully.

But it is in Syria that Paul strengthened his public credentials and gained experience in debate that centered on Jesus, his messiahship, and his identity as the Son of God. Eventually Christian leaders in Syria will recruit him, and he will join their work formally in Syrian Antioch.

In this opening chapter Paul has established the authenticity of his own profound conversion, his identity as an apostle, his familiarity with the Jerusalem leadership, his willingness to sacrifice his career for the sake of Jesus, and his zeal to proclaim the gospel in communities throughout Syria. In the debates to follow, his opponents will attempt to discredit him. But this brief biographical narrative will serve as a feature of his defense. He wants them to recall and recommit to the gospel he preached in Galatia—but this has to begin with them relearning the authority of his own life and commission.

## Going Deeper:
## Paul and His Encounter with Grace (Gal 1:11–24)

Paul's story is one of grace (1:15). And in this first chapter the key element is his report of his own encounter with the grace of Jesus. When he expected judgment, he met the generosity and patience of Jesus. And within this he was given the most unlikely of commissions: to go to the Gentiles (1:16). Paul hopes these words resonate with the Galatians. Their lives began with the grace of Jesus (1:6), and their struggle was embracing that this generous grace could likewise belong to the Gentiles living among them. This argument will lie at the heart of the balance of Paul's letter.

How Paul's life is anchored to his encounter with Jesus on the road to Damascus raises some important questions for each of us. *What makes us adhere to our Christian convictions?* Is it our inheritance from our family or community? Is it the pressure of social conformity? Is it respect for tradition? Or the logic of the Christian position? Throughout Paul's life, it is this one encounter that upended everything and became the source of his spiritual and theological certainty.

My mom was born in the Swedish community of Chicago in 1928 and died in 2022. Only recently did I learn this story: One year, when she was about ten, it became clear that her grandmother, whom she deeply loved, was dying. She stood at the foot of her grandmother's bed for countless hours taking in all that she could before her grandmother departed this world. And then one evening, it happened. She stood at the foot of the bed with her back to the rest of the room when suddenly the room was filled with blinding bright light. "My time is coming, and they are here for me," her grandmother said. My mom was confused and swept the room looking for the source of the light and could only see images, faint images behind her. And then it was over. Her grandmother was filled with peace and days later died. When my mom told me this story in about 2000, I asked her what it had meant to her life. "It was the foundation of my certainty. I had seen heaven come down for her." My mom continued to live a vibrant Christian life and, to the very day of her passing, had no fear. One encounter blessed all ninety-four of her years with confidence.

# GALATIANS 2

**2:1** *After fourteen years, I went up again to Jerusalem.* Two questions follow this section of Paul's letter (2:1–10). First, when do we begin counting these fourteen years? Some scholars believe this should be counted from Paul's recent visit to Jerusalem for fifteen days (1:18; Ac 9:26). This has merit since he refers to Jerusalem here ("up *again* to Jerusalem"; 2:1, emphasis added) as if this is a return visit. Still others think that Paul is counting from his conversion, which is the starting point of the autobiographical narrative beginning in 1:13. The problem has to do with the chronology of Paul's life. If we count from Paul's fifteen-day Jerusalem visit, it has been seventeen years since his conversion (three years were in Arabia). If Paul counts from his conversion, then it has been fourteen years since he met Christ. Respected scholars take both points of view (see Figure G-2.1).

**Figure G-2.1. Paul's Early Timeline**

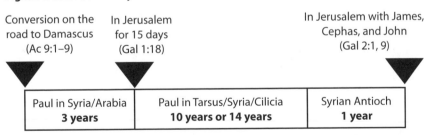

| Conversion on the road to Damascus (Ac 9:1–9) | In Jerusalem for 15 days (Gal 1:18) | | In Jerusalem with James, Cephas, and John (Gal 2:1, 9) |
|---|---|---|---|
| Paul in Syria/Arabia **3 years** | Paul in Tarsus/Syria/Cilicia **10 years or 14 years** | Syrian Antioch **1 year** | |

Either way, from this verse we can reconstruct something important about Paul's own early life. Following his conversion, Paul was in Arabia for three years and then in Syria-Cilicia for ten (or fourteen) years *before* he engaged in his well-known public ministries. Of course, we have no record of his activities in these places. But he was an active Christian either preaching widely or being mentored by Christian leaders. But by the time he enters into a formal ministry that will spring from Syrian Antioch, *he is a mature Christian* with many years of exposure to the fundamentals of the faith.

The second question in this verse has to do with the brief Jerusalem visit itself after his three years in Arabia. Following Paul's conversion and sojourn in Arabia, we know about the fifteen-day visit (Ac 9:26). We also know that later he visited Jerusalem from Antioch with famine relief money (Ac 11:27–30). Then we know that he and a delegation came from Antioch to Jerusalem in Acts 15 to resolve a theological dispute concerning the Gentiles and the first missionary tour (the so-called Jerusalem Council). This is linked to the north and south Galatian theories (see Introduction). The majority of scholars connect Acts 15 with Galatians 2:1–10, but a growing number (myself included) now think that the Famine Visit of Acts 11 may be better a fit with Galatians 2:1–10. This means that the Famine Visit followed the one year Paul spent in Syrian Antioch. Here Paul says he went up to Jerusalem, thanks to a revelation (Gal 2:2), and this is what happened in Acts 11:27. But also, Barnabas was with Paul (Gal 2:1; Ac 11:30). It is also striking that if this Famine Visit is the Jerusalem Council, then Paul should refer to the decree of James in Galatians (Ac 15:13–21), but he does not. This would have strengthened his argument.

*Barnabas . . . Titus.* Barnabas accompanied Paul on his first tour that included Galatia (Ac 13:1) because they had a long history together. It was Barnabas who first trusted Paul's conversion story and brought him into the leadership circle in Jerusalem (Ac 9:27). During Paul's silent years in Syria/Cilicia, Barnabas had become the leader of the church in Syrian Antioch (Ac 11:22), and when he needed help, he traveled to Tarsus to find Paul and brought him into the Antioch ministry. It was in this context that Paul traveled south to Jerusalem with Barnabas with famine relief money.

Titus is not known from the book of Acts, but from Paul's letters we know that he became one of Paul's most trusted colleagues. His first appearance is here on this Jerusalem visit, but he probably accompanied Paul on some of his journeys and became prominent in Paul's ministry at Corinth (2 Co 7:6, 13–15; 8:6, 16). We have one short letter written by Paul to Titus, and here we learn that he had become the leader of the church in Crete (Tit 1:5).

**2:2** *In response to a revelation.* Paul may have come to Jerusalem because of a prophetic decree. This is the picture we have in Acts 11:28 when the prophet Agabus described the coming famine. But this is not Paul's point. Paul is clarifying that he did not come to Jerusalem as if required by the church there. Exactly how this revelation came to him (a dream? a prophecy? a vision?) is uncertain, but its importance is unmistakable. "The point is that he went at heaven's behest, not at Jerusalem's, nor even Antioch's . . . He was not answering a summons or going 'cap-in-hand.'"[1]

Paul also frequently uses language about revelation to refer to the revelation of the gospel itself (Ro 16:25; Eph 3:3) that he had received directly from Jesus, and this too is likely a part of his meaning. God was sending him to the city bearing a message. Galatians itself is evidence that there was some stir about what Paul was teaching. The greater controversy had not broken out yet, but here Paul intuits that his own understanding of the gospel must be cleared up. As the following verses will show, he was right. The upcoming conversations will address not merely the famine and how Antioch can help but also the substance of Paul's message.

Paul says he met with "those esteemed as leaders" (Gk, *dokeō*, "recognized"—an honorific title) who were no doubt Peter, James, and John (Gal 2:9). His revelation from Jesus included the full acceptance of Gentiles as recipients of salvation *that did not require their incorporation into Judaism* through obedience to ceremonial law. As a trained Jewish scholar, Paul knew how controversial this was. To say that the Jewish messiah had arrived in Jesus was one thing; to say that the messianic kingdom was a diverse gathering of Jews and Gentiles was something else again. Paul reached out to the leaders of the wider church to confirm this teaching because just possibly his complaint was with the church in Jerusalem—as will become clear.

*I wanted to be sure I was not running and had not been running my race in vain.* Athletic references in the Old Testament are few, and that of running a race may be limited to Psalm 19:5. Paul likely draws this idea primarily from Hellenistic culture, viewing the pursuit of the Christian life as an athletic contest and commonly employing images from the arena. Thus he is concerned about races that are "in vain" or fail (Gal 4:11; 1 Co 15:2; 2 Co 6:1; Php 2:16, etc.).

The end of 2:2 is easily misunderstood. Paul does not doubt his own convictions here ("running my race in vain"), but he wants to discover if the apostolic leadership disagreed with him; if so, then his own ministry would be subverted. All of his efforts might then be *in vain*. In 2:5 the unflinching convictions of Paul are clear ("we did not give in to them for a moment"). He does not doubt himself, but as we will see, he doubts the consistency of some of these leaders.

**2:3** Co*mpelled to be circumcised.* Here we see the crisis unfold in all its shock. Titus is a Roman name (it was the first name of the emperor Vespasian, AD 79–81: Titus Flavius Sabinus Vespasianus), and clearly Paul's companion was a Gentile and thus not circumcised. Paul refers to him as a "Greek" (2:3), but this was a convention that simply reflected the pervasive spread of Greek culture in the Mediterranean since Alexander the Great. From a Jewish viewpoint, "Greek" is almost anyone who belonged to the Greco-Roman world and who is not a Jew. So Paul can describe his ministry to "Jews and Greeks" (Ro 1:16 ESV; 1 Co 1:22; Col 3:11 ESV) when Paul clearly worked among Romans. But to say that one of his companions *in faith* was a Greek would immediately alert every Jewish Christian present: What happened in regard to Titus-the-Greek in this story would set the course for any Gentile elsewhere in the church.

## Galatians 2:1–10 Through Old Testament Eyes: Circumcision

Circumcision was an Old Testament marker of identity among the Israelite people. It was established in Genesis 17:10–14 when God inaugurated a covenant with Abraham and his descendants. It was a procedure completed on the eighth day of a male child's life and required the surgical removal of a sheath of skin (or foreskin or prepuce) from the child's penis. In the New Testament era, it had become enormously important and along with Sabbath observation, dietary law, the temple, and the Torah, circumcision was a signal marker of Jewish identity.

Knowledge of this was widespread so that Roman writers commonly pointed to circumcision as characteristic of Jews. Thus, the Roman historian Tacitus can say of Jews, "They adopted circumcision to distinguish themselves from other peoples by this difference" (*Histories* 5.5.2). Josephus wrote that the function of circumcision was so that Abraham's "children should be kept from mixing with others" (*Antiquities* 1.192). During the Jewish Maccabean revolt in the second century BC, some tried to surgically remove the evidence of circumcision in order to fit into the Greek world of public baths and athletics. They are severely criticized as "abandoning the covenant" and giving themselves to Gentile culture in the practice of evil (1 Maccabees 1:15). Jewish families who refused to circumcise their sons are listed with those who defiled the temple, built pagan altars, and sacrificed swine in worship (1 Maccabees 1:40). And when Jewish areas were "redeemed" from Gentile influence, the Maccabean leaders forced circumcision on every Jewish male (1 Maccabees 2:46).

This ritual therefore became a symbol of the wide divide in the Jewish worldview between Jews and the rest of the world. Gentiles were called "the uncircumcised"; Jews were called "the circumcised" (see Ro 4:9–12). But the practice was repugnant to Romans, who viewed it as a peculiar mutilation of the body even though it was widespread in the eastern Mediterranean.[2]

But here in Jerusalem, someone (James perhaps) led a delegation of Judaizers who were arguing that Titus (and by extension all Gentile Christians) had to be circumcised (cf. Ac 15:1). How did they detect this? Paul's association with Gentiles was likely well-known. In tribal societies, signals of cultural identity could be seen from someone's speech to their hair and clothes. But we need to see the question about circumcision as all-encompassing. By asking about circumcision, they were actually inquiring whether Titus *kept the law*. Or perhaps: *Was Titus a God-fearer (a near-convert to Judaism) or a full Jewish convert?* In a word, Paul's Antioch delegation learned that some in Jerusalem required that Gentiles convert to Judaism (Gal 2:14) before they could enter the church. They were required to bear the principal marker of Judaism.

And this is what Paul rejected. His language evokes a rhetorical struggle: they were urging or compelling (Gk, *anagkazō*) Titus to be circumcised. This term is often juxtaposed to freedom in Roman writing and could be linked to conquest or enslavement. For Paul, this imposition was a form of slavery for a Gentile. But rhetorically Paul will pick up the term in 2:14 to accuse Peter of exactly what is going on. Peter is *forcing* Gentile Christians to conform to Jewish traditions. The term appears again in 6:12—once again, circumcision is a marker of bondage for a Gentile.

**2:4** *Some false believers had infiltrated our ranks.* Paul's grammar here runs away with him, something every translator tries to clean up. Galatians 2:4 begins a thought ("because of false brothers secretly brought in" ESV) but never concludes it (2:5 begins another sentence). This is not uncharacteristic for Paul, whose anger and sense of urgency in this make his writing collapse. The problem is that *false brothers* have been *brought in* secretly to this debate. This language is important. These opponents are false siblings (Gk, *pseudadelphoi*), unlike the Galatians who are true "brothers" (1:11; 3:15). They have not simply infiltrated this debate; they have been brought in, smuggled in, inserted with sleight of hand—like spies. Have sympathetic members of the Galatian church invited in these Judaizers from Jerusalem? We do not know. But Paul labels them spies, a term with widespread military usage, from the Greek Trojan horse account to Israel's reconnaissance of the Holy Land under Joshua (Jos 2:1–3). And their effort would result in the loss of freedom (recall the language of compulsion in Gal 2:3).

**2:5** *The truth of the gospel.* See "Galatians 1:6–12 Through Old Testament Eyes: The Gospel." Paul was unflinching in his resistance. It was not simply about the ritual procedure itself; it was about the theological grounding of the gospel and what submission to that procedure implied. He would not acquiesce or retreat ("we did not yield to submission for even an hour!" 2:5 literal traslation).

This rare term (Gk, *eiko*) suggests drawing back or retiring or submitting. Paul would not. And the reason for this is that it would result in the corruption of the gospel *in principle*. If grace were truly anchored to the generosity of God (and not performative markers of ritual), then these requirements were false. Note that the language here is plural ("we did not . . ." 2:5). This resistance is not peculiar to Paul, but he is speaking for his delegation, including Titus and Barnabas—and perhaps the church in Syrian Antioch as well.

This is Paul's first use of the term *truth* (Gk, *aletheia*, 2:5, 14; 5:7). It had a long currency in Greek writing to mark what is real and reliable from what is not, and—in the Old Testament—the LXX uses it to translate words that refer to the reliability, constancy, or solidity of God, even his faithfulness. It is an essential characteristic of God (Ps 51:6 ESV) and is the opposite of deceit (Pr 11:1; Mal 2:6). This is the basis of trusting God, represented well in 2 Samuel 7:28, "For you are God, O Sovereign LORD. Your words are truth" (NLT). Jews writing with the Old Testament in mind would often employ multiple ideas to get at this concept: faithful and righteous. Therefore, what Paul is defending is not merely a point of view. He believes he is defending the essence of God's character.

**2:6–8** *High esteem.* The level of Paul's frustration now reveals its true pitch. He is keenly aware of those in Jerusalem who were held in "high esteem," and everyone knew "whatever they were"—early and original followers of Jesus (2:6). Paul likely is alluding to the three "pillars" he mentions in 2:9 (James, Peter/Cephas, and John). But he refuses to give them the social ranking others did for two reasons. First, they were not the source of his understanding of the gospel in the beginning (1:18) and second, his faith came about through divine revelation (1:15–16). This gospel that he understood had never been enlarged or deepened by these leaders. Their one contribution came in validating Paul's own commission (2:7).

Here we see one of the earliest fault lines beginning to surface in the early church. Leaders in Jerusalem recognized that Paul held a unique commission to go to the Gentiles ("the uncircumcised") just as Peter was commissioned to go to the Jews ("the circumcised," 2:7). But were these two fledgling messianic movements—one anchored in Syrian Antioch, another in Jerusalem—going separate ways? Did the Jerusalem leadership accept Paul with a wink, figuring that he preached a deficient gospel and that the purest form of faith was found in the circle of Jesus' earliest followers (the Twelve)?

Paul's defense is firm: he "had been entrusted" (Gk, *pisteuo* as passive, Gal 2:7) with this gospel; but who had invested such trust in him? God himself. Note how everything turns on the conviction springing from Paul's own experience with God. The same Lord who made Peter an authorized messenger ("apostle," 2:8) of the gospel is the same Lord who likewise made Paul such a messenger. Therefore, those who opposed Paul's work are in fact opposing the one who commissioned Paul. This use of direct comparison was a common rhetorical strategy in antiquity to elevate someone or something being questioned. In Acts, Luke uses this regularly to favorably compare Paul with Peter and so elevate Paul's status.[3]

*Apostle.* See comment on 1:1.

**2:9-10** *Esteemed as pillars.* The crux of this debate for Paul is in locating the views of those who were widely recognized as major leaders. Some view the use of "esteemed" (Gk, *dokeo*) as ironic or sarcastic, and it could be translated "reckoned" or "seemed to be" pillars.[4] "Thought to be pillars" gives this nuance well. The NIV removes all hint of this. These three men in Jerusalem were Jacob ("James"), Cephas ("Peter"), and John (the son of Zebedee, Mk 1:19–20)—the brother of James who had been martyred (Ac 12:2). Peter and John always figure prominently in the gospels together and, with James of Zebedee, are a close circle around Jesus. However, with James' death, the brother of Jesus, also called James, joined the other two. This second James is the author of the New Testament letter.

Paul shows that rather than subvert Paul, they in fact gave him full and complete acceptance. "The right hand of fellowship" (Gal 2:9) was a common expression (never "the left hand") to express friendship personally, or more formally it meant approval and endorsement or perhaps the sealing of a relationship—even covenant-keeping. This preference for the symbolic right hand was common in the Old Testament where promise-keeping was involved. It was also used metaphorically for God, as in Isaiah 41:13: "For I am the Lord your God who takes hold of your right hand and says to you, Do not fear; I will help you." Similarly, see Psalm 144:7–8, 11 (emphasis added):

> Reach down your hand from on high;
> deliver me and rescue me
> from the mighty waters,
>     from the hands of foreigners
> whose mouths are full of lies,
>     whose *right hands* are deceitful. . . .
> Deliver me;
>     rescue me from the hands of foreigners
> whose mouths are full of lies,
>     whose *right hands* are deceitful.

Paul's use of "pillar" (Gal 2:9) in reference to these central leaders was likewise common. God said he was making Jeremiah an "iron pillar" (Jer 1:18), and the leaders of Egypt were called pillars (Isa 19:10 ESV). A pillar would be easily recognized in any public architecture of the time. Its wide currency could be used metaphorically for a person of stature in a community, not unlike our use today. But it may have been a more honoring gesture. Were these three being compared to the Old Testament patriarchs as foundational characters? The term was clearly used by later rabbis for this purpose.[5] Paul frequently used Old Testament temple images for the church (2 Co 6:16) just as Israel used temple images. Most would know the twin pillars in front of Solomon's temple (1 Ki 7:15–22) and see it in the imagery for its own national life (Ps 114:2). Pillars even figure in the eschatological picture in the Apocalypse (Rev 3:12). Keener thinks this temple application is plausible, particularly when we see how Peter's own name (Cephas = "rock," Mt 16:18) is used to signal the building of Christ's church.[6]

*The grace given to me.* Therefore, Paul has honored the status of these leaders and recorded their act of generosity and confirmation. Paul includes these approving words because he knows well that at least one of the three had betrayed these assurances. The leadership recognized that Paul bore an authentic and compelling message and commission from God. Describing his spiritual experience as "grace given" was common to Paul (Ro 12:3; 15:15; 1 Co 3:10), and he hoped that this would describe believers as well (Ro 12:6; Eph 4:7). But grace given in the context of commission begins to evoke the root meaning of grace (Gk, *charis*), which means "gift." It could also be a gifting from God (Gk, *charisma*) or a gift generously or graciously given.

*The Gentiles, and . . . the poor.* The drama and authenticity of Paul's gift is signaled by what God had called him to do. We are mistaken if we underestimate the scandal of this calling. Jewish boundary-making kept Gentiles strictly apart, and this view was embraced by the early Jewish Christians. (See comment on "So that I might preach him among the Gentiles" at 1:15–17 and "Galatians 2:11–18 Through Old Testament Eyes: Meals, Gentiles, and Separation.") Peter's entry into Caesarea in Acts 10 illustrates this when he must return to Jerusalem to make an accounting of himself (Ac 11:1–18). If God was not the author of this grace extended to Gentiles (evidenced in the Spirit), then who was? Peter—the man who witnessed this dramatic turn of events with Cornelius—was now in Jerusalem during Paul's visit, and Paul would have rightly expected him to support the generous acceptance of Gentiles.

Ongoing care for the poor made sense during this Famine Visit. Judea had had a series of droughts, and without its own river system, the Judean countryside was vulnerable. Antioch, on the other hand, had a major river (the Orontes) which gave it agricultural stability and rapid urban growth. Syrian Antioch was one of the largest cities in the Roman Empire. The reminder to Paul and Barnabas to care for the poor (Gal 2:10) acknowledges the need that they have come to address. Jerusalem's early church was poor: it was sharing its possessions (Ac 2:44–45), it was experiencing rapid growth, and it was being persecuted by its city.

Care for the poor was a major Old Testament ethic that was a duty to all Israel (Dt 24:10–22; Ps 14:6; Isa 3:14–15; Am 8:4–6). The giving of regular offerings for the poor likewise expressed a personal duty and, in the prophets, was a hallmark of righteousness. Therefore, the leaders are asking for nothing novel here but instead a reminder with a unique application. The church now may be the recipient of this covenant duty.

Therefore, on this visit recounted by Paul, the apostle understood that important progress had been made. The leaders had conceded to Paul's refusal to circumcise Titus, and they affirmed Paul's unique calling to go to the Gentiles. And in response, the leaders were knitting these Gentile communities back to Jerusalem with expectations that were shared within Israel's covenant communities. Paul left this meeting no doubt satisfied. His message and commission had been affirmed, and he agreed to the moral obligation to bring Antioch's wealth to needier believers in the south. Throughout his career Paul remained faithful to this agreement. During his third and final missionary tour, he aimed to bless the church of Judea by collecting offerings from all of his Gentile congregations—and have their delegations deliver this aid to Jerusalem.

## What the Structure Means:
## Paul's First Case Study (Gal 2:1–10)

This is now an important turning point. Paul is keen to defend his own authority and the authenticity of his message (see Figure G-0.8 under "The Form of the Letter" in the Introduction). Paul's first visit to Jerusalem as a follower of Jesus was after his conversion (Ac 9). This second visit is described here in Galatians 2:1–10 during his Famine Visit (Ac 11).

I argued that this second visit outlined in Acts 11 is being retold here in Galatians 2 (see comment on 2:1). But what Paul has done is important. This second visit supplies him with his first case study on the centrality of grace, particularly for Gentiles. While in Jerusalem, the "pillars" of the church had received him warmly, accepted his commission to the Gentiles, and backed down when some urged that the Gentile Titus should be circumcised (2:9–10). For Paul, this should be a precedent. Peter, James, and John were each at this gathering, and they endorsed Paul and his understanding of the gospel. Paul is now ready to supply a second case study (2:11–21).

**2:11** *When Cephas came to Antioch.* It is difficult to establish when this second conflict happened. All we know is that at some point, Cephas (Peter) was in the church of Syrian Antioch,[7] no doubt after the Famine Visit just described in 2:6–10.[8] So far Paul is narrating his story chronologically and there is little reason to think he does otherwise here. Paul's opposition to Peter here stands in stark contrast with the "right hand of fellowship" mentioned earlier in 2:9.[9] This means that 2:11 is really a continuation of the story just told. The Greek has an important contrasting conjunction here (Gk, *de*) that could be overlooked. Literally it is, "But when Cephas came . . ." or perhaps, "However, when Cephas came . . ." This strengthens the contrast with the amicable gathering in Paul's first story.

Since Paul does not provide a setting for the story (cf. 2:1–10), this event must have been recent and fairly well-known. While Peter was in Syrian Antioch, he was comfortable mixing with Gentiles. This would make sense given Peter's own experiences in Caesarea in Acts 10 and the recent agreement in Jerusalem. But when the Judaizers from Jerusalem arrived, Peter drew back from the Gentiles and separated himself.

*I opposed him to his face.* This phrase does not infer hostility but is a common expression of a personal encounter (Ac 25:16 ESV, NASB). However, Paul apparently did this before an audience (Gal 2:14), which would make this a dramatic and potentially shaming encounter.

**2:12** *Men came from James.* The conventional understanding is that James (in Greek here, *Jacob*) had sent these men. But this is not precisely what the text says. Saying you came from someone does not imply commissioning by them (see Paul's language in 2 Co 1:16; 11:9; 1 Th 3:6), which could easily have been said. Paul does not say James sent them.[10] These men have come from the Jerusalem church generally where James is in leadership and may well have been self-commissioned. Nor do we know why they came and so should not suggest wrongful intentions on their part. Peter may have known them (though he does not name them) or knew what they represented: the commitment within the Jewish mission to sustain Jewish custom. Now Peter (clearly allied with the Jerusalem leaders) finds himself in a *foreign mission* exercising the freedom demanded by Paul, Barnabas, and Titus. His reflex may have been innocent—to eat with these new guests—but the story suggests that he was not drawn to them as much as he wanted to avoid the Gentiles ("he drew back," Gal 2:12 ESV). At stake in his mind was his reputation. If the Jewish Christians were practicing separation (from Gentiles)—something the Antioch Christians rejected—then Peter may have felt that his reputation with James and John was at risk.

*The circumcision group.* Here we have our first evidence that there was indeed a partisan movement afoot in the church. This circumcision group (literally, "those from the circumcision," compare Ac 11:2) which Peter fears likely represents Jewish Christians who openly expected Gentile separation and circumcision for Gentile believers. These are the people Peter was called to lead in Galatians 2:7 ("the circumcised"). The language of sharing meals is code in this culture for acceptance and fellowship.

*He began to draw back and separate himself.* Remarkably, Peter sensed the jeopardy of this moment and decided to break fellowship with the Gentiles who were in the Antioch church. This is all the more remarkable because, in Paul's mind, Peter had been with Gentiles formerly—and perhaps the story of Peter's important conversion of Cornelius (Ac 10) had become well-known. In Acts 11, Peter had even defended his decision to eat with Gentiles despite public criticisms from this circumcision group (11:1–4). But here Peter's fear gets the better of him, and in an attempt to pacify his critics (and his critics in Jerusalem), he separated himself.

## Galatians 2:11–18 Through Old Testament Eyes: Meals, Gentiles, and Separation

The expectations for purity, particularly in the Second Temple period, were stringent. One could not enter the Temple in a ritually unclean state. However, we also know that being in a state of impurity was almost unavoidable. This included common things like diet and clothing and concerns about sources of impurity (corpses, bodily fluids, skin diseases, etc.). People moved from a state of clean to unclean regularly, and the only remedy was washing in ritual baths.

Gentiles were also considered unclean, and therefore devout Jews would keep a distance from them. We see this described in Ephesians 2:11–18 where Paul says the "dividing wall" between Jews and Gentiles can be removed in Christ (2:14).

It was inevitable that Jewish-Gentile contact was a regular feature of life in the Diaspora. But for strict Jewish teachers, separation was a mandate. In Leviticus 20:26, Israel is called to be separate or set apart from other nations, and this stems from ideas in the Old Testament about mixing (Lev 20:24–26; Ezr 10:11). But the key Old Testament passage is Deuteronomy 7:3–4, "Do not intermarry with them [Gentiles]. Do not give your daughters to their sons or take their daughters for your sons, for they will turn your children away from following me to serve other gods, and the LORD's anger will burn against you and will quickly destroy you."

This was strongly reinforced in the post-exilic period when calls for purity were a response to the perception that the exile was caused by faithlessness to the covenant. Nehemiah warns Israel not to intermarry with non-Jews (Ne 13:3, 23–27). Ezra 9 is a lengthy soliloquy against intermarriage with Gentiles, describing their culture as unclean and filled with pollutions (9:11). Malachi shares these same concerns. His charge is that Israel must not "profane the covenant" (2:10). Malachi viewed Israel's interest in other gods as infidelity, marrying foreign gods (2:11), and therefore Israel must be separate and righteous.

In the later intertestamental period, the Book of Jubilees writes, "Separate yourself from the Gentiles and do not eat with them." Josephus explains Jewish life to his Roman readers and notes how such separation was required by the law (*Ag. Apian*, 2.257). This separation may be the origin of the Pharisees (which Paul belonged to) who took Gentile separation seriously, particularly when sharing meals.

## Going Deeper: Conflict and Doctrine (Gal 2)

Galatians 2 is a story about doctrine and conflict. Paul is persuaded that his understanding of grace and the law is correct, and here we see that not only in this letter but in his record of his behavior in Antioch, he is willing to engage in conflict in order to persuade his opponents. Perhaps for some, *conflict* is too strong. But the picture is clear: Paul is willing to argue until he wins the day.

Are there times when conflict and argument do more harm than good? And in those times, should we step back in humility and consider how concessions are needed? At other times, our commitment to a theological view is essential and worth struggling for (consider the Reformation). When do we know when to concede and when to fight? Perhaps our difficulty today is that too many of us choose to argue, and so we have created a culture that is deeply divisive and polarized. And the unity of the church has suffered. Sometimes we need to take a stand; but how often do we confess that our arguments have been unfounded and should be reconsidered?

In many churches, questions surrounding gender and gender identity have brought enormous division. Should women be trusted with the same leadership and preaching authority as men? Should the church welcome LGBT believers as they would anyone else? In each case, even if we hold firm convictions, we need to speak into these issues with love, charity—and humility. And we need to decide clearly which issues are central and which are peripheral. Most of us agree that charity is needed in minor disputes, but perhaps this is true in major ones as well.

I recall attending a theological conference and listening to a young scholar argue that women's authority over men in church violated biblical teaching and that any who believed in female leadership did not hold to inerrancy. Afterward I asked this eager zealot how I stood with God since I endorsed women's ordination. His answer was quick, "It is a salvation issue, and you have placed yourself in spiritual jeopardy." I kept wondering if this sort of high-conflict response was helpful to anyone (despite it being in error) and if it contributed to the well-being of the church.

**2:13** *Hypocrisy.* Paul notes that the community of Jews in Antioch had broadly accepted Gentile converts. And this included Peter. But he adds that even Barnabas, the man who had brought Paul into ministry in Antioch (Ac 11:25), likewise joined his critics. Recalling Paul's long history with Barnabas, this development must have been stunning, and given that Paul repeats it here, it must have remained in Paul's thinking for some time.

**2:14** *Not acting in line with the truth of the gospel.* See comments on "Turning to a different gospel" at 1:6–7.

The depth of Paul's outrage now surfaces in these deeply polemical sentences. Note that Paul does not say that Peter conceded. Paul certainly would have mentioned this in order to list it as another victory for his view. Not only did Peter refuse to side with Paul, but the Antioch Jewish Christians refused as well.[11] For Paul, it was a double betrayal, and no doubt, as he considered his mission, at this point he would have to think that work among the Gentiles would have to proceed outside the orbit of Antioch. As Acts shows, Paul's missionary work from here began to move further west and likely was centered in Corinth or Ephesus (and possibly Rome, Ro 15:24).[12] Were Barnabas and Paul reconciled? Acts 18:22 may imply this.

*You live like a Gentile.* Paul's accusation is likely an echo of what the followers of James had been saying about Peter, "You are a Jew,—but here you are acting like a Gentile" (author's translation)—that is, joining with Gentiles in table fellowship as if separation did not matter. For Paul this behavior is a dangerous denial of the gospel, and it showed the sort of pressure the Jewish community in Jerusalem or Antioch could place on the James delegation. Paul is critical that now the converted Gentiles must take on Jewish culture (Gk, *ioudaizein,* "to Judaize"). This is an important term, and we must not read too much into it. The argument at this point may not have been that Gentiles had to be circumcised to be saved but that Gentiles must take on the markers of Jewish culture in order to belong to the church. At this early stage, the ethnicity (the language, diet, ritual habits) of Judaism was being imposed on Gentiles. And for the Jewish Christians, their worry may have been about purity. Were these new Gentile Christians going to observe the purity requirements every Jew knew so intimately?

**2:15–16** *We who are Jews by birth . . . know. . . .* This is now Paul's epistolary turning point. He moves from describing a troubling event, a case study in wrongheaded theology, to the basis of his theological position. In addition to addressing the problem of the Antioch conflict, Paul is also suggesting that the same conflict has arisen in Galatia, and by extension, the Antioch story can serve Galatia as a case study. For many interpreters, in these next few verses Paul is establishing the theological position for which he will argue in chapters 3 and 4. And these chapters no doubt summarize the core of Paul's theological thinking, which he represented in each of his presentations of the gospel where Jews were present.

## What the Structure Means:
## Galatians 3–4 and Romans 3–4

When we read Galatians 2, it is difficult to know where Paul's story about Antioch ends and where his polemic about grace begins. A new section begins at 3:1 but here in 2:15–21 Paul rushes forth, and his words almost spill over each other. Here we are listening to Paul's earliest formulation of his view of grace. For him it is a passionate, burning idea, something he certainly felt was at the core of his own life. In chapters 3 and 4, Paul lays out the groundwork of why his views are sound and anchored in the Old Testament.

These chapters are almost a rough draft of what we can read in Romans 3–4. Both sections of Paul's writings echo similar themes, but in Romans the text is tightly organized and more confident. These verses from Galatians come with the heat of polemic; Romans exhibits the calm rhetoric of theological argumentation.

*Sinful Gentiles.* Paul was sympathetic toward the Gentiles, and so he is not lodging a harsh criticism of them. This is simply a practical description of those who lived outside the revealed law. In the Old Testament, this strict separation of the world into two camps was common. "Blessed is the one who does not walk in step with the wicked or stand in the way that sinners take or sit in the company of mockers" (Ps 1:1; also 58:10; Pr 12:12). "Sinner" was so common that Jews employed it to describe those whom they disagreed with or who rejected their positions (1 Maccabees 1:34). It is used against Jesus as one who eats with "sinners" (Mt 11:19; Lk 5:30).

*Justified by faith in Christ.* See "Going Deeper: Being in Christ According to Paul (Gal 5:6)."

This word group (Gk, *dikaioō,* "to make righteous," "to justify," "to acquit") is one of the most important Pauline words we have (twenty-seven of thirty-five New Testament uses belong to Paul), and it appears frequently in both Galatians (eight times) and Romans (fifteen times). It can also be translated "made righteous" (since righteousness, *dikaios,* stems from the same root). Essentially this is a term from the Greek courtroom. It is a verdict of innocence or righteousness, as is clear in Matthew 27:19 when Pilate's wife calls Jesus "innocent" (*dikaios*) while she simply means he is not guilty (see Lk 23:47; Php 4:8). The standard of this righteousness could either be the public law (in Greek usage) or God's law (in Jewish usage). The person in question has been set right in relation to some standard. For a theologian such as Paul, the standard is always God's righteousness.

*Not by the works of the law.* We want to keep in mind that Paul is arguing from ideas that Jewish Christians—his opponents in this setting—would already agree to. His objection is going to be against works that have become tokens that divide Jews from Gentiles and thus destroy fellowship.

## Galatians 2:16 Through Old Testament Eyes: Paul's Use of Psalm 143:2

When Paul writes that "by the works of the law no one will be justified," he is echoing an important text from Psalm 143:2 (LXX 142:2), "for no one living is righteous before you." This is also used in Romans 3:20 ("Therefore no one will be declared righteous in God's sight by the works of the law") and no doubt became important to Paul. But this was nothing new to Jews in Paul's day. Some Jews would reject the notion that one could claim a rightful standing before God by virtue of righteous works (Isa 59:2–19). Covenant promise was the only basis of positive standing before God.

Paul does change the word "no living person" to "all flesh" (*Gk, sarx*) as it is in the Septuagint, and this gives a more dramatic presentation to his idea, pointing perhaps to our human frailty. But he also adds "by the works of the law" to his allusion to the Psalm. This is the crux of his argument. Activity which is outlined in the law cannot be the basis of our security before God—and this is precisely what the debate in Galatians was all about. Circumcision was required in the law, but it is less consequential than one might think. For Paul, the covenant grace of God found in Jesus Christ is the only basis of divine security.

Many Protestants have concluded that Paul's objection is against works that lead to salvation *gained by pursuing righteous works*—the "works of the law." Paul points out that this is not the issue since there is agreement already *among Jews* that such salvation cannot be achieved by effort but instead is a result of God's covenant and grace. Recently scholars have argued persuasively that what Paul has in mind is not salvation-by-works but instead markers of Jewish covenant purity, responses, as it were, to God's covenant love. These "works" then are covenant obligations and signals of Jewish piety. In Qumran, for instance, applicants for membership were vigorously tested for such "works" to see if their devotion was sufficient (1QS 5.21–26). In Paul's setting, the most obvious two issues had been circumcision and food laws, both of which had become nonnegotiable markers of those who obeyed God. What had once been routine Jewish practices of Jewish identity had now become tests that every Gentile had to pass.

*Faith in Christ Jesus.* The problem here is not law versus grace. Jews understood grace. The problem is that Paul's opponents (the delegation from James, Jewish Christians from Jerusalem) had made peripheral markers central and so judged the Gentiles by those markers. Instead Paul reminds them that our righteousness is anchored to "faith in Christ Jesus" (Gk, *dia pistesōs Iesou Christou*). There is a long technical debate about how we understand these terms.[13] Literally the text says we are justified "through faith"; nonetheless, "Jesus Christ" is in the Greek genitive and can be read two different ways. The first option is "the faith belonging to Christ," meaning something that Jesus has done such as his faithfulness in going to the cross. Otherwise it could be an objective genitive, meaning that Christ is the object of our activity (or faith). Interpreters accept both readings, but the objective reading for the genitive (that Christ is the object of our faith), suggested throughout the letter, seems most compelling.

This objective understanding is confirmed when we see Paul clarify it in the second half of the verse. We put our faith into Christ Jesus (this time, *eis Christon Iesoun*). Therefore, Paul is forcing his opponents to think Christianly, to recall the foundation of how justification is established: it is grounded in our utter devotion to Jesus and nothing else. Hence those who would require circumcision or disqualify believers based on diet are simply mistaken.

## Going Deeper: Add-ons to Faith (Gal 2:15–16)

We can sympathize with what these Jewish Christians were thinking. For them (as for us), the foundation of salvation was utterly in Christ. However, they also believed that righteousness based on grace had real and important entailments. And the absence of these entailments put in question whether this saving faith was indeed true and active in a person's life.

Paul has to say twice in Galatians 2:16 that our identity as believers is anchored purely in Christ Jesus and nothing else. We too believe this in theory. But it doesn't take long before a fellow believer speaks with conviction about the necessary outgrowths of faith that we should see working in a person's life. And when these are absent, such people are judged.

In Paul's context, he sees this happening to his Gentile brothers and sisters. He recognizes what is at stake is the loss of a fundamental idea: that grace alone brings us into God's kingdom and sustains us there. Nothing else.

Today it is not uncommon to find Christians dividing over identity markers that were unknown just a generation ago. If I promote social justice or the study of race theory in America, or even question if the United States is a divinely anointed nation, I will quickly find critics who might agree that we are one in Christ but that my mistaken political or economic beliefs are wrongheaded and not biblical. One pastor stood firm against leaders in his church who demanded to erect a huge American flag in the sanctuary during the past election! His loyalty to his country and God were loudly questioned. I have published two books critical of Christian Zionism and have had to learn to live with critics who say that only one view of Israel is permissible to God.[14] One writer assured me that I was "going to hell" simply for this theological-political view. We have become prone to attaching political or religious markers to the church no different than these Jewish Christians. Paul would apply many of these words in Galatians to us today.

**2:17** *We Jews find ourselves also among the sinners.* This is the first hint of a pastoral and theological accusation that Paul must address fully in Galatians 5. The charge is that those such as Paul, who promote grace entirely found in Christ, might also be promoting sinfulness *because* they feel set free to do as they wish. And this would include the table fellowship in Antioch. If it is sinful for a Jew-in-Christ to mix with a Gentile-in-Christ, then Paul asks rhetorically, "Doesn't that mean that Christ promotes sin," or literally, he asks, "Is Christ a servant of sin?" Paul rejects this forcefully. To label Gentiles as sinners (and thus excluded) while Jews are righteous (and protecting boundaries) is wrongheaded, as Paul has shown in 2:15 (citing Ps 143:2). Everyone, all "flesh," shares the same sinful position. Paul's use of the word *servant* ("servant of sin") held an original meaning of someone who serves at table. And for some commentators, this would have had meaning for this Antioch fellowship.[15] Paul might have challenged these people with the image of Jesus as *servant* (Gk, *diakonos*), serving a table of Jews and Gentiles, something the Jews were claiming was sinful. Jesus then becomes the host of sinful behavior, something they hopefully would find absurd.

**2:18** *If I rebuild what I destroyed.* What does Paul think he has destroyed in 2:18? Now Paul pursues the opposite scenario from the one he's arguing against in 2:11–14. Recall that Paul was critical of Peter for enforcing religious separation (with Gentiles). He believed that in Christ this wall of division (see Eph 2:11–22) had been destroyed, that Jewish and Gentile believers in Christ might be one. But imagine, Paul says, if he changed his mind and reinstituted (rebuilt) religious separation in Antioch. What would this mean? It would mean that Paul's earlier attempt to destroy it had been a sinful deed. But perhaps more significant for Paul would be his awareness that rebuilding religious separation would deny the very essence of the gospel he had embraced. This would indeed be a catastrophe.

**2:19-20** *I have been crucified.* Paul now gives the rationale for why in 2:18 it is impossible for him to revert to the position held by Peter. This is one of the most famous verses Paul ever penned. It encapsulates the very essence of the gospel, possibly articulated here for the first time in writing by the apostle.

The issue for Paul is not that he has taken up a new theological position, or that he has gained some new insight from the scriptures or discovered new compassion for Gentiles. It is about death. His death—and Christ's death. Something seismic has shifted in how Paul thinks about everything. The key to his meaning is in 2:20: "I have been crucified with Christ and I no longer live, but Christ lives in me."

For Paul the idea of conversion was not simply an acknowledgment of Jesus as the messiah. It involved dying *as Jesus died* (Ro 6:4–6; Php 3:10).[16] At least in part this refers to his utter identification with Jesus crucified, Jesus as outcast (so in Gal 3:13, Jesus became a curse). If this was his new identity, then those who were deemed outcasts (Gentiles) were certainly among those with whom he could live. This is what Paul means in Philippians 3:10 when he writes that he is "becoming like him (Christ) in his death." Paul had taken on a new standing in the world, and this standing has affected his relationship to the law (Gal 2:19). The law for him was "no longer the ultimate norm in ethics."[17] But it would be wrong to think that Paul was rejecting the law (Torah) as he embraced Christ. Note that he does not say that he died with respect to the Torah as if the law did not matter. He rather died *through the law* (Gk, *dia nomou*), which he will take up more later (3:11–14, 19–25). Christ was born under the law to redeem those under the law (4:4–5) so that a new work would commence within the lives of those in a Torah-driven life.

This dying, however, also included a new life (2:19b). "I died . . . so that I might live for God." Paul understands that something in him has been left behind and something new has been taken up. In 5:24 he says this death separated him from an old self (his flesh) with its sinful passions and desires. But it also opened him to a new life filled with the Spirit (5:25) through which he can please God because God's own Spirit is directing his paths. Therefore, Paul views himself as a person who can look back on his former life and now look at his present life and measure a critical difference. He now lives with Christ living in him (2:20), which means he no longer views himself as a person pursuing Torah performance as a means of pleasing God; he views himself living a transformational life created by Christ's saving work on the cross but also by Christ's gift of life (shaped by the Spirit). This idea of Christ indwelling the believer was common to Paul (Ro 8:10; 2 Co 13:5; Eph 3:17; Col 1:27). It is achieved by the Spirit indwelling the believer (Ro 5:5; 8:9, 11, 15–16).

*The life I now live.* Therefore, Paul's bodily life has undergone a reorientation not just in his thinking but in his experience. Notice how he continues to use the first person in these verses ("If I rebuild," "I died," "I no longer live"; 2:18–20) because he is giving witness to his own experience, which links with the testimony he began at the start of the chapter. This continues to be a part of Paul's story. "I live by faith in the Son of God" could easily be translated "I live in trust" since the word itself bears both meanings (Gk, *pistis*, "faith"/"trust," 2:20b). This life of trust is Paul's response of gratitude for what God has given him: Christ has loved him and given himself for him.

Therefore, returning to the present crisis, Paul is saying that now he sees things differently. He has been awakened by an existential encounter that bears transformational spiritual realities. And he cannot think about Gentiles the same way any longer. *Gentiles who are similarly attached to Christ, similarly indwelt by his Spirit, should likewise enjoy full public endorsement by the church.* To use Torah-driven markers for who is in and who is out would be to regress to Paul's old self.

Scholars frequently try to find the center of Paul's thought by promoting either justification or participation (sometimes known as mysticism). But these verses show the needlessness of this choice. For Paul, conversion involves both features: a sacrificial death dealing with sin and a Spirit-led transformation. One without the other misrepresents Paul's understanding of the work of Christ.

## Going Deeper: Paul and the Gift (Gal 2:19-21)

Some readers will recognize that this is the title of an important technical theological work written by New Testament professor John Barclay from the University of Durham, England. Barclay is challenging us to rethink Paul's perception of what he discovered in Christ. It was a gift—which came from God and therefore was transformative. The implications of this for Paul were compelling and profound. Gifts were not simply received and taken; they were gestures of relationship and obligation. This is why Paul can talk about the generosity of God in grace while at the same time talking about our obligations to obey. Both were included in the ancient concept of "gift." Barclay explains this in detail and shows how we have no cultural parallel to it in the modern western world. [18]

We have a glimpse of this in the Old Testament story of Abraham. [19] Barclay points out how God offers the patriarch a stupendous gift of land and descendants. But how do we understand this gift? Is it based on Abraham's righteousness (Ge 17:1)? Or his obedience (Ge 22:15–18)? Deuteronomy clarifies that this gift originated in God's "love" (7:8) even though these recipients of divine favor had a long history of disloyalty and sin. The "gift" and its acceptance are predicated on a binding relationship *that comes with expectations*. God is both loving and generous but also a God who can be jealous and angry; he has steadfast love to a thousand generations and repays those who ignore him (Dt 7:9–10). We here have two halves of God's character (loving care; firm anger), which have troubled many theologians. But, Barclay shows, this is resolved when we see how gifts functioned in the ancient world. Divine benefaction led to relationship and ideally it transformed the recipient of the gift. This is how God's mercy and grace is balanced by his justice and expectations.

In Galatians 2:19–21 we read what may be the first time that Paul explains what happened to him in his conversion. Of course, it included the identity of Israel's messiah and with this came reflection about his life and work, including his death on the cross. But the full embrace of this gift meant something transformational: *Paul was crucified; Christ lives in him; he lives trusting/believing in the Son of God. And he will live a life mirroring that of Christ.*

This is important because for Paul, Christian faith was not merely a theological idea or an ethical position (though he teaches in these arenas regularly). Christian faith began with experience. It was personal. He met Christ, and Christ began to dwell in him through the Spirit.

Which makes us wonder if Paul would always recognize our preaching today. Particularly in conservative circles, sound teaching and moral instruction often make up much of what we present to audiences. Oddly we fail to talk as often about the indwelling Christ, the Holy Spirit, or the full transformation of our lives, as Paul does here. For Paul, transformation lives on the other side of a relationship, a relationship found in the graciousness of God. It is not a transformation that can be found in the law or demanded. It is born when we see what remarkable gifts we possess and who has given them.

**2:21** *I do not set aside the grace of God.* In this verse, "set aside" could better be translated "reject" or "nullify" (Gk, *atheteō*). Paul's closing statement summarizing his story now explains why he cannot reject everything that he has just described. He cannot reject the generosity or the gift that God has given to him. In this context, to refuse a gift would be to insult or shame the giver. Paul will not do that.

But it would also be foolish. Paul knows that righteousness could not be achieved by living out the precepts of the law. This was the view that held wide agreement among Jews in this period.[20] Keener says it well: "The problem then is not with the law *per se*, as if it is unrighteous in itself; rather the problem is with trying to be justified by the law. The problem with law is not that it is wrong to observe it, but that it is wrong to believe that doing so makes one right with God."[21]

This now is the end of Paul's own witness to his early experiences with how grace should be applied in the burgeoning multicultural setting of the church where religious markers were being tested and the Jewish centrality of Torah would come to terms with the gift of Christ. In what follows, Paul will continue his argument for grace, but he will do so by referencing the Galatians' experience and the scriptures themselves.

# GALATIANS 3

**3:1** *Who has bewitched you?* Paul is now developing an argument that began in the early verses of chapter 1. The first basis of his argument against Torah performance was the agreement in Jerusalem (2:1–10) when Titus was not circumcised. This was an agreement to which James, Peter, and John concurred. But a test case for this agreement followed when Peter came to Antioch (2:11), and in this awkward moment, Paul held firm.

The second and third bases for Paul's argument now appear in chapter three. First Paul will argue from the Galatians' own experience (3:1–5) and then move to an interpretation of the Old Testament and the story of Abraham (3:6–14). Together these three arguments are Paul's attempt to make his case for the new reality that now exists in Christ and how this new reality has social implications for how Christians live in the world.

Paul turns to the Galatians directly in 3:1 with a tone we have not heard since 1:6. Paul is here likely referring to the provincial area of imperial Galatia in southern Asia Minor (see comment on 1:2). He commonly referred to Christians with reference to their city (2 Co 6:11; Php 4:15), but here we have a province. We can only speculate where this church was.

Paul is utterly dumbfounded that the Galatians could make a mistake on this scale. Paul rhetorically asks who "bewitched" them (3:1). This translation misrepresents what Paul implies. The root word (Gk, *baskainō*) means "to cast a spell" or "to show an evil eye"—meaning a glance of envy or a curse given by the eye. (*Baskania* means "slander" or "envy.") The early church fathers suggested that the Galatians' piety was met with envy by their opponents, and this brought a demon on the church.[1] Paul is thus suggesting that while the fault of the Galatians is severe, still, the blame also rests with those teachers who have distorted their vision. The casting of spells associated with witchcraft was condemned in the Old Testament (Dt 18:10–11; Isa 47:9; Mic 5:12).

Note the irony in 3:1b. If a curse was given through the eye, the true vision Paul wants them to hold is a vision ("before your very eyes") of Christ crucified. This "portrayal" (Gk, *prographō*) is a formal rhetorical term describing the dramatic telling of a picture that moves the audience emotionally. Paul had presented them with a picture of Christ on the cross (earlier in his first visit?), and this vivid image should hold them fast against any who would distract them.

## Galatians 3:2–6 Through Old Testament Eyes: Grace and Benefaction

We hear regularly in Galatians about the grace of God and the gift of the Spirit. But we need a contextual understanding of grace to understand them rightly. We live in a transactional society (based on modern economic realities) in which we think of transactions as one-way rather than in terms of "relationships of reciprocity."[2] Consequently interpreters of Paul think about grace as the transfer of something that is then possessed by the recipient without expectations.

Something freely given meant that a gift was given without coercion (not that it was given without entailments). So while a gift is given at no cost, it is not received "without cost." The acceptance of a gift (or benefit, hence benefaction) meant that obligations followed this acceptance. And to fail to respond would ruin the relationship—the very thing the act of grace was meant to create. This reciprocity is presupposed throughout all of Paul's discussions about gift and response, grace and discipleship, and theology and ethics.[3]

This reciprocity can be illustrated easily from Roman and Greek writers, but the idea that grace creates relationship and expectation spans centuries of time, including the Old Testament. Givers of grace could be known as patrons, and gratitude was the expected response.

This idea underpins the basic framework of the entire Old Testament. God approaches Abraham with generous gifts and then expects relationship tied to a covenant. The word for this reciprocal loyalty was *faith* or *trust*, which is precisely what Abraham demonstrates. The deepest human flaw is to be unaffected by this generosity, to be an ingrate. This position, to neglect the giver and claim the gift, would have been shocking to Paul and all of his contemporaries.[4]

**3:2-3** *Did you receive the Spirit?* In the Old Testament, the Spirit was generally given to individuals who were appointed by God for special responsibilities. The Lord filled Bezalel with the Spirit and chose him to "make artistic designs" for the tabernacle (Ex 31:1–5; 35:30–33). The Lord told Moses that he would give some of the Spirit that was on him to seventy other leaders of Israel (Nu 11:16–30). The judges of Israel also received the Spirit for their roles (Jdg 3:9–11; 6:33–35; 13:24–25; etc.). The Spirit came upon kings (1 Sa 10:6–10; 16:13) and prophets (2 Ch 15:1–8; 20:14–17; Mic 3:8; etc.).

That pattern changed, however, at Pentecost when the Spirit came not just on leaders and not just on men but on all who were in Christ (Ac 2:4, 16–18, 38; 8:14–17; 10:44–48). Indeed, this development was prophesied long before (Isa 44:3–5; Joel 2:28–29).

In chapter 3 Paul now turns to the Galatians' own experience. They know that they received the Spirit, and this solidifies their identity alongside Abraham (3:14). This means that their spiritual identity is unquestionable. But he asks if this gift came through Torah-obedience or through belief in Christ crucified. Was it a gift born from efforts to live out the law more fully or was it an encounter much as Paul himself has described earlier? This is rhetorical because they (and Paul) know the answer. Christ is a gift, the Spirit is a gift, and therefore, it cannot be supplemented with rites of religious practice. We begin all things in emptiness and what we have is given by grace. Therefore, the implication is that any who would reduce this gift or require a supplement to it has regressed terribly to a spirituality that originates in *the flesh* (Gal 3:3).

This contrast between the Spirit and the flesh is intentional here (see further 5:16–23). But there might be a secondary meaning here. Circumcision is indeed about "the flesh," and Paul uses it literally and metaphorically in Galatians 6:12. Therefore his critique is poignant: the Galatians have a spiritual life that began as a gift, and now they literally and figuratively have been told to return "to the flesh." They are thinking that these ritual acts may perfect them (*epileteō*, see *telos*; NIV "trying to finish").

## Galatians 3:2–5 Through Old Testament Eyes: The Holy Spirit

When Paul refers to the indwelling of the Spirit, he is not describing something foreign to a Jewish reader. The notion of God dwelling amid his people was well-known in the Old Testament (Ex 25:8; 29:45–46; Lev 26:11; Nu 35:34). The Spirit was particularly a promise held for Israel in its restoration (Isa 32:15; 42:1; 44:3; 59:21; 61:1; Eze 36:27).

In the Second Temple period, the Spirit was viewed as either linked to an office (priest, prophet) or viewed as present among those with great piety or religious Torah-obedience.[5] Here Paul describes the Spirit as a gift, which he assumes *any* in the Galatian church could receive. Given that Gentiles were viewed as sinners, this makes the gift all the more remarkable.

**3:4–5** *So much in vain?* Paul is driving his point home. Have the Galatians experienced the graciousness of God with no result (Gk, *eikē*, "in vain," "pointlessly," or "for no reason"; cf. Gal 4:11; Ro 13:4 ESV; 1 Co 15:2).[6] This would suggest that the Galatians' discipleship had failed; that they had relapsed to a place of immaturity. It is not as if they did not believe in Christ—Paul's opponents believed in Christ—but Paul recognizes that there is something more that they have missed. They recognized Jesus as messiah but did not realize the entailments of life in Christ and the gift of the Spirit. In this sense, they were limited.

But Paul repeats the question more forcefully (3:5). Are the Spirit and the miracles the Galatians have witnessed the result of Torah observance or through the gospel Paul had preached to them?

This opens an entirely new window into what was normal experience for Christian identity in these early years. Paul can appeal to the Spirit because this was the signal of conversion and discipleship (Ro 8:15; 1 Co 2:12; 2 Co 11:4; Gal 3:14). This is the very least that a text like Romans 8:9 can mean: "You, however, are not in the realm of the flesh but are in the realm of the Spirit, if indeed the Spirit of God lives in you. And if anyone does not have the Spirit of Christ, they do not belong to Christ." It is reminiscent of the conversion of Cornelius in Acts 10 where the Spirit's entry into the story confirms this Gentile's salvation. The Galatians were experiencing the Spirit; they were experiencing miracles. But they did not connect this experience with the theological insight needed here. Therefore, Paul is suggesting that the problem in Galatia is a deficient discipleship, void of the thoughtful understanding required in this situation and hence lacked insight into the deeper dimensions of what Christ has offered them.

## Going Deeper: Paul and the Spirit (Gal 3:1–6)

These verses tell us that, in Paul's mind, Christian conversion is not simply a theological or moral set of commitments. It is the Son of God indwelling his followers—facilitated by the presence of the Holy Spirit. Here Paul points to an experience he doesn't think needs to be debated since it is self-evident. Galatian discipleship already included the Spirit and miracles.

The question that a modern church may ask is simply this: How do we see evidence of the Spirit at work today? If we do not see miracles or transformed lives, if we have few signs of the Spirit but instead simply a thorough knowledge of what we believe, are we much different than the Galatians Paul is trying to correct?

**3:6–7** *So also.* These verses represent a continuation of 3:1–5 and the opening word (Gk, *kathōs*) and could be translated, "in the same manner." What the Galatians had experienced Paul will now show from the life of this most illustrious patriarch. Throughout the section to follow (3:6–14) we find Paul employing the Old Testament extensively (six citations in nine verses). The only comparably dense set of Old Testament citations is found in Romans 3 or Romans 9–11.

*Abraham "believed God."* Paul first told the Galatians that confirmation of their identity as belonging to God should be found in the Spirit—and this gift is not achieved by Torah observance (3:1–5). But this pattern of gracious gift and whole-hearted response is modeled by none other than Abraham himself, the patriarch of Israel's faith and nationhood. We might say that Paul's aim in the remaining chapters of Galatians is to affirm to these Gentiles that they are indeed Abraham's children (3:7, 9, 29; 4:22, 28, 31). Thus in 3:29, "If you belong to Christ, then you are Abraham's seed, and heirs according to the promise." If they are Abraham's children, then they have little to worry about from those who would suggest their faith is inadequate.

Abraham's faith as noted in Genesis 15:6 is cited three times in the New Testament (Ro 4:3, 20–24; Gal 3:6; Jas 2:23). This is no doubt Paul's foundational argument and is assumed in this chapter and the next. The point at the present time is not that the Galatians should imitate Abraham and believe as he believed (as if their imitation was deficient). These Galatians already have faith! The point is that since they have already been joined to Abraham *by faith*, the Galatians are now his heirs and join in the Abrahamic blessings. Abraham's faith represents a response of trust (Gk, *pistis* as "trust"), which he demonstrated by his obedience to the covenant requirement of circumcision (Ge 17) and his near sacrifice of Isaac (Ge 22).

But what did it look like for Abraham's faith to result in righteousness? Paul may well be defeating a commonly held view in which the faith of Abraham was important because it exhibited true obedience (and hence, fidelity to laws such as circumcision). Here the debate was: did Abraham obtain righteousness because of his faith or because of his faithfulness? Because of his trust in God or because of his obedience to God?

Paul moves decidedly in the former direction. Rather than see faith as linked to covenant obedience, Paul knows that Abraham's justifying faith (when he believed God's promise in Ge 12:1–3 and went to the land God promised, seen in Ge 12:4–7) preceded the covenant he received from God (Ge 15:18). In addition, this justifying faith was received without circumcision (Ge 17:9–14), which means that *Abraham was a Gentile exactly as the Galatians were.* And as a Gentile this great patriarch obtained righteousness without circumcision. This then opens the way for new prospects for Gentiles. It was faith that enjoyed God's notice—not Torah-obedience.

*Children of Abraham.*[7] This is where Paul has been headed throughout. Access to Abraham's heritage is not, then, by ethnicity nor by Torah-obedient ritual. It is by faith. At this point we have to pause and take in what Paul has just written. This is a world where theologically anchored ethnic privilege was commonplace, where ritual participation reassured those who were "in" these places of privilege but excluded those outside those places. Paul has thrown open the doors. If faith is the key to Abraham's heritage, Gentiles have full access. To use Paul's metaphor from Romans, Gentiles are grafted into the ancient tree of Israel with Abraham at its root (Ro 11:17).

**3:8–9** *Scripture . . . announced the gospel in advance.* See comments on "Turning to a different gospel" at 1:6–7 and "Galatians 1:6–12 Through Old Testament Eyes: The Gospel."

## Galatians 3:8–9 Through Old Testament Eyes: Paul's Use of the Old Testament

In these verses we gain a window into how Paul views the Old Testament and how he is willing to apply it to his own context. He claims to find in the story of Abraham the essence of the gospel he has been carrying to the Gentiles. He writes, "God . . . announced the gospel in advance to Abraham" when he promised blessing to the Gentiles (3:8).

Although 3:8b is a hybrid citation of Genesis 12:3 and Genesis 18:18, it is an accurate rendering of Genesis's intent (see also Ge 22:17–18; 26:4; 28:14). Paul has now shown how the inclusion of the Gentiles is linked to Abraham. And this linkage is something foretold and anticipated. For Paul, this is the gospel hidden away in the ancient words of Genesis 12:3: "All peoples on earth will be blessed through you." This is the third of three promises Abraham received (first, many descendants; second, land) but it was the most neglected. For Paul, land and descendants (what we might call today an ethnic nationalism) mattered little: it was the redemption of the world that mattered, and here in Abraham, Paul found the mandate. All nations would join in the blessing of Abraham just as historic Israel had. In Romans 4:13, Paul even took this to its fullest application: the promise of blessed inheritance was for the world (not for the land of Canaan).

The term "blessed" is ambiguous in English and even in Greek (*eulogeō*), but it is a Jewish concept. In Greek it simply means to speak well of someone. But the Jewish idea here is to bestow grace and honor and prosperity to someone (Ge 28:3; Nu 6:24–26; Dt 28:3–6; Ps 28:9; 128:5). No one disputed that Abraham was the source of blessing. The only question was the means by which this prospering and honoring might come about.

## Galatians 3 Through Old Testament Eyes: Abraham

It would be hard to underestimate the importance of Abraham in the Old Testament or in Second Temple Judaism. Paul refers to Abraham sixteen times, and these are concentrated in Galatians and Romans. Romans 4 is no doubt his most important treatment.

The Old Testament narrative from Genesis 11:27–25:11 makes Abraham the first of the patriarchs, and although Israel will take its name from Jacob, still, Abraham's place only grew within the Jewish tradition (see its New Testament summary in Ac 7:2–8). Abraham was known as a friend of God (2 Ch 20:7) and no doubt was viewed as the father of the nation. His name, Abram, means "exalted father" (Ge 17:5), and his original home was in Ur of the Chaldees (in southern Mesopotamia), where he lived with his father Terah's clan. His wife, Sarai, and his brothers, Nahor and Haran, also become important to his story.

After a move north to Harran and after his father's death there (Ge 11:26–32), Abram migrated west, at seventy-five years old, with Haran's son, Lot (hence Abram's nephew), followed the fertile crescent along the Euphrates, and made his way to Canaan. This was in response to God's prompting and promise (Ge 12:1–3) that in Canaan he would find a land that would be his, and here he would find blessing and grow a nation. We should not imagine this as a small, solitary migration. Abram was traveling with many from his father's tribe.

Abram arrived in Canaan and settled in Hebron. Here God's promises were reconfirmed through a covenant (Ge 15:1–21) binding God to his gift—and to this overture Abram responded in faith: "Abram believed the

LORD, and he credited it to him as righteousness" (15:6). This response of faith and righteousness is noted throughout the New Testament (Ro 4:3, 20–24; Gal 3:6; Jas 2:23) as a template for faith as a response to God's grace. Thirteen years later, God visited Abram and Sarai again, confirming his promises and changing their names: Abram would now be Abraham ("the father of many nations," Ge 17:5) and Sarai would become Sarah.

Due to their childlessness, Sarai offered her slave, Hagar, as a concubine (which was in accord with custom), and Hagar gave birth to Ishmael. However, the promise of Sarah's own pregnancy was fulfilled despite her old age (Ge 18:1–15; 21:1–7), which brought her Isaac. The drama of his fulfillment is underscored in the story when Abraham's faith was tested when he was told to sacrifice Isaac (Ge 22:1–14). Abraham and Sarah lived to an advanced age (175 and 127 years respectively). Abraham buried Sarah in Hebron at the cave of Machpelah (near the oaks of Mamre), and eventually Abraham was buried there too.[8]

Chief among the legacies of Abraham were the three promises given to him in Genesis: land, progeny, and blessing to the nations (Ge 12:1–3). The land and lineage promises rose to prominence, assuring Israel a national destiny (Dt 1:8; 6:10; Isa 63:15–64:11, etc.) as interest in the nation and its divine privileges were remembered and cherished. However, the third promise—that Abraham's legacy would be a blessing not simply for Israel but for *all nations*—was neglected. This is the genius of Paul's theology: he locates in Christ the source of this blessing that will extend to all nations—namely, the Gentiles.

Second Temple Judaism developed Abraham's profile dramatically and made him legendary as a man who modeled belief and obedience, as well as perfect fidelity to the law (before the law was given). His righteousness was renowned and contributed to Israel's share in the kingdom of God that was to come. As such he was the ideal ancestor of Israel, and every Jew celebrated the esteemed title of children of Abraham (Mt 3:9; Lk 3:8). This attribution to Abraham was so popular that John the Baptist challenged it as a false security: "And do not think you can say to yourselves, 'We have Abraham as our father.' I tell you that out of these stones God can raise up children for Abraham" (Mt 3:9; see also Jn 8).

Therefore, when Paul employs Abraham as a model for how we understand the inner workings of faith and grace, it is no small matter that he uses Abraham. Paul could hardly employ a stronger argument for his audience. If this was true for Israel's greatest patriarch, then Paul's argument should be true for everyone.

**3:10** *Works of the law.* Few sections of Paul's writing have received the degree of debate as Galatians 3:10. The issue is: What does Paul mean when he refers to works of the law? Is this a universal pronouncement that a person cannot gain saving righteousness through personal efforts to please God (this is a traditional Protestant view)? Or is this a continuation of Paul's argument from chapter 2, indicating that those who pursue Torah-obedience and prohibit Gentiles from joining with Abraham are in jeopardy (this is what is called the New Perspective on Paul)? Is this an explicit contrast between "faith and works" or a subsidiary argument for what has transpired in Galatia?

## Galatians 3:10–14 Through Old Testament Eyes: Faith and the Covenant

In these verses we see how completely Paul was convinced that any relationship with God begins with faith and ends with faith (Ro 1:17). The basis of the covenant was faith (never the law), and any who would argue differently did not see the grace of God rightly nor could they see that same grace at work in Christ.

This idea that faith and grace are foundational ideas in the Old Testament is often missed by readers of the New Testament. God's approach to Abraham (when he had no merit, no knowledge of the law) is based entirely in grace. Paul will employ one simple example. In Genesis 15, when God establishes a covenant with Abraham, the patriarch is not circumcised (which occurs later in Ge 17). In Romans 4:10, Paul emphasizes this as a key that unlocks our understanding of God and all people. It is not the merit achieved through righteous achievements that secures our place with God; it is his surprising grace that finds us when we have little claim to it.

If Abraham is the foundational figure for Israel in the Old Testament, the Exodus is the foundational event in its establishment. Even Israel's departure from Egypt—the critical salvific story in the entire Old Testament—is based on grace. When Israel had nothing to offer of merit in Egypt, still, God showed his loving-kindness. "Give thanks to the LORD, for he is good. His love endures forever. . . . [He] swept Pharaoh and his army into the Red Sea. His love endures forever" (Ps 136:1, 15). God saved his people from slavery in Egypt (Ex 12–14) and generously gave them food and water in the desert (Ex 16–17) *before* he gave the Ten Commandments (Ex 19–20). This faithfulness and kindness stands in stark contrast to the story of Israel's remarkable complaints in the wilderness, climaxed perhaps by their desire to return to Egypt. Still, God is faithful to their restoration as his people.

All of this underscores the same idea: *grace precedes law* in the Old Testament. The loving faithfulness of God and his generosity to his people provide the basis of their confidence in life. Despite many examples of Israel's failures from the period of the Judges right through to the exile, God's faithfulness to his people remains because it is not anchored in performance but in his loving-kindness (Heb, *hesed*).

*As it is written: "Cursed is everyone who does not continue to do everything written in the Book of the Law."* See comments on 5:3. For the average Jew, life under the law was a blessing. But most recognized that keeping the law perfectly was impossible. Thankfully, sacrifice and ritual purification made restoration possible. For them, to read these words now from Deuteronomy (27:26) and have them applied by Paul in this context must have been shocking. The problem lies in the original intention of the passage in Deuteronomy. Rather than cursing those who are under the law, the curse rests upon *those who disobey the law*. But now Paul is applying this curse to his opponents who are *promoting the law*. Paul has reversed the aim of the warning. Keener remarks, "Whereas Jewish people understood from scripture that they were blessed and those who walked in the ways of the Gentiles were cursed, Paul argues from scripture that some Gentiles were blessed (Gal 3:8; Gen 12:3) and that those under the law (or under the law in the wrong way) are cursed (Gal 3:10, citing Deut 27:26)."[9]

The larger context of Deuteronomy 27–30 suggests what the later Old Testament prophets make clear. Israel will inevitably break the law (Dt 28:58–68; 30:1–3). This larger narrative says Israel will be scattered because of these curses (28:63–65, 68) and predicts their return to the Lord (30:1–10). It had become broadly accepted that the law itself could not be a refuge from judgment. The prophets insisted on Israel's failures under the law. Jeremiah 11:3 echoes Deuteronomy 27:26 just as Ezekiel 20:11 uses Leviticus 18:5 (a similar warning to obedience). The same insistence is clear in Second Temple Jewish writing.[10] Paul's word to those promoting the law, therefore, is that their position *without the messiah* was a place of jeopardy and judgment. Only in Christ could a true refuge be found.

**3:11** *No one who relies on the law is justified before God.* In their worldview, the lawless (Gentiles) lived under a curse while those embracing the law (Jews) lived with God's blessing. Paul has completely reversed this equation. New Testament scholars have come to wide agreement that stereotyping Judaism as a faith driven by works-salvation is incorrect. (Jews understood the grace of God fully through election and covenant.)[11] However, in a faith that was so fully conscious of law and the importance of responding to God's love by obedience, a life of Torah-obedience could have shaped many views regarding their own righteousness.[12] In the present context, Paul's argument (3:11) is that, *unlike Abraham*, anyone who seeks righteousness without faith is under a curse. He would likely go further saying that any who seek righteousness without *faith in Jesus* were likewise in jeopardy. To miss the grace of God and a response of faith is to fail to understand God rightly—and this could happen to anyone.

*Because "the righteous will live by faith."* Paul now cites Habakkuk (2:4 ESV, NASB; cf. Ro 1:17) to confirm this understanding. A life that does not spring from faith is misdirected. Faith and trust is how people are to understand their relation to God. But now in Galatia this misdirected outlook is being applied to Gentiles for whom faith has been and should always be the center of their life with God (see the sidebar).

The NIV use of "rely" in 3:10 may lead to confusion. The Greek text literally says, "those who are on the basis of law" or more idiomatically, "those who commit themselves to the law" or "base their salvation on the law."[13] Paul is not thinking about Jews who are merit-seeking or bent on works-righteousness. Paul is describing someone whose life is defined by religious practices that set them apart rather than living within the gift of God's grace. McKnight says it well: "Paul is setting alternative approaches to God: either through faith or through obeying the law."[14] And the latter is a failed path.

## Galatians 3:11–12 Through Old Testament Eyes: Habakkuk 2:4 and Leviticus 18:5

Paul's use of these two Old Testament citations in 3:11–12 is some of the most contested in all of his writings. Paul contrasts Habakkuk 2:4 (Gal 3:11) and Leviticus 18:5 (Gal 3:12) in a manner few Jews of his day would recognize.

Habakkuk was an Old Testament prophet who likely appeared during the close of the seventh-century BC (though this is debated).[15] During a time when a Chaldean army from near Babylon was sweeping the world with breathtaking violence (Hab 1:1–11), the prophet acclaims

God's sovereignty over history and interprets this conquest as judgment on unrighteousness (1:12b). The question for Habakkuk is simply: How should he (or Israel) stand in history and observe such evil? Israel could protest or resist—or one could rely on God's faithful purposes. "See, the enemy is puffed up; his desires are not upright—but the righteous person will live by his faithfulness" (Hab 2:4). In other words, the righteous person is set apart by his demeanor toward God; he trusts in God's provision. He is not proud. This, of course, is quite different than Paul's meaning in Galatians 3:11.

Paul's citation of Habakkuk 2:4 has presented various questions. Perhaps Paul is taking one view of the Habakkuk text. Does "by faith" attach to the verb (the righteous will live *by faith*), which implies an obedience characteristic of faithful living that would more naturally fit the original context of Habakkuk? Or does *by faith* attach to the noun (the one who *by faith* is righteous), which is the usual Protestant reading underscoring Paul's emphasis on justification by faith? This is compounded by the fact that the Hebrew text of Habakkuk 2:4 seems to support the former reading. Thus Jews (and Paul's opponents) might see Habakkuk 2:4 as supporting Torah-obedience. Paul then has upended the meaning of the verse.

On the other hand, Habbakuk may be pointing back to and interpreting Genesis 15:6 and exhorting Israel that a life rightly lived is a life in imitation of Abraham who trusted God's goodness and thereby lived a life of comprehensive faithfulness. The dichotomy we see here may be entirely artificial. For Paul, faith and faithfulness worked hand in hand.

Nevertheless, Paul is trying to make a contrast between faith and law, between those whose lives are centered on the gift and those whose lives are centered on obedience. This explains his abrupt phrase in Galatians 3:12a "The law is not based on faith" (lit. *The law is not by faith*). Paul is out to correct a mistaken notion of the law's relationship to righteousness.

Paul uses Leviticus 18:5 in two texts: Romans 10:5 and Galatians 3:12. In the first, he sets up contrasts with Deuteronomy 30:12–13; in the second, he employs Habakkuk 2:4. Text contrasts such as these were common in Jewish exegesis.[16] The challenge is finding the connection Paul is making between 3:11 and 3:12 (with Lev 18:5 and Hab 2:4) and understanding his logic.

Both Old Testament citations refer to *living* and here Paul has set up a contrast or antithesis. Life can be pursued either by faith or by works. However, the law does not promote faith but instead promotes effort—and this is the dichotomy that Paul wants us to see. Barclay remarks, "The compressed argument in 3:11–12, contrasting Hab 2:4 with Lev 18:5, reinforces the incapacity of the Torah. Because no one is found 'righteous' in the sight of God within the terms of the Torah, righteousness is promised (in Habakkuk) on the basis of faith; and the Torah concerns not faith but the practice of its own commands."[17] Leviticus 18:5 then is a summary of what is required by the law: a thoroughgoing effort. But this effort cannot be a replacement for a faith righteousness modeled on Abraham.[18]

**3:12** *The law is not based on faith.* Paul is working out contrasts between law and faith, and parsing this contrast is delicate since we must not misrepresent Paul's high respect for the law. Keep in mind that Paul is engaged in a debate in these sentences, and here he is anticipating an argument from the opposing side. Therefore, he must establish that Abraham's faith was not righteous *because* it demonstrated obedience (circumcision) but was righteous because it was quite simply trust in God's promise. (See "Galatians 3:11–12 Through Old Testament Eyes: Habakkuk 2:4 and Leviticus 18:5.") He finds the principle of faith in Genesis 15:6 (Gal 3:6), and as he knows, the law was given centuries later. His citation of Leviticus 18:5 (also Ro 10:5) reinforces a view of the law that his opponents may well have defended; that is, if their identity with God was grounded in the law, they were obligated to live entirely by the law as they worked out their lives in this work, within a covenant life. And from this perspective the enforcement of circumcision would make sense. This would build immediate boundaries between Jew and Gentile, marking out Jewish life as somehow exclusive, entitled, and elect. And by this logic, if Israel is separate from the nations (the Gentiles), then the problem in Galatia becomes inevitable.

This failure to see covenant and faith rightly thus puts adherents to the law in jeopardy. They cannot be righteous (3:11) and are even under a curse (3:10) if they misuse the law in this manner. Here, however, we have to stress again that Paul is not being critical of the law. He is critical of its misuse and of misunderstanding it. The law cannot be the basis of the covenant or a relationship with God. On the other hand, it can orchestrate life in this world for those who live within the covenant.

**3:13** *Christ redeemed us from the curse of the law.* Paul here returns to 3:10 where he talked about the curse that rests on those who misapply the law. Since the law is not an avenue for righteousness, God has provided an escape from this curse through Christ. "Redemption" refers to gaining freedom for someone who is in captivity (slavery, war, etc.) and buying their release. This is the work of Christ. On the cross (3:13b) he enacted in a representative fashion what could have been the fate of all humanity. The NIV has "hung on a pole" (Gk, *xulon*, meaning "wood," hence a tree, beam, or pole), but this really refers to the cross (Gk, *stauros*, "cross"). The curse pronounced on any crucified victim comes from Deuteronomy 21:23 (cf. 27:26) and referred to the exposure of a person after capital punishment, but it soon became a metaphor simply for anyone crucified. But this idea of being cursed *by God* meant (according to Deuteronomy) that the person was placed outside the covenant and the land, left to live with Gentiles. This means that the cross removed Jesus to the outside, exiled from the blessings enjoyed by God's people but into the very places where Gentiles dwelt.

**3:14** *The promise of the Spirit.* This is where Paul's argument leads. The redemption of Christ works on behalf of the Gentile because, as a cursed outsider abandoned on the cross, Christ now has joined the Gentile—and in Christ's death and resurrection God has granted his approval of his Son's position. *Therefore, all those who belong to Christ enjoy Christ's approval before God*, thus making them capable of obtaining the blessings of Abraham. Paul says this carefully: "...that the blessing given to Abraham might come to the Gentiles *through Christ Jesus*" (emphasis added). It is not simply that Jesus died for Gentiles too, thus cleansing sin, but that Jesus died *in order* to bring Gentiles into a redemptive status before God and Israel.

Paul's unexpected conclusion (3:14) is found in the Spirit. The Spirit is not mentioned in the original stories about Abraham. Here Paul may be "reading God's initial blessing to Abraham in the light of its later flowering in the prophetic promises that God will pour out his Spirit in the new covenant (e.g., Isa. 32:15; Ezek. 36:27–28; Joel 2:28–29). Perhaps he is particularly reading Abraham's blessing in the light of Isaiah 44:3."[19] The proof that this is the case is found in 3:1–5, where the reception of the Spirit was one of the chief hallmarks of conversion. This was a sign throughout the early church of God's embrace of those who were formerly left on the outside but now had been welcomed in (Samaritans, Ac 8:4–13; Gentiles, Ac 10:44–48).

Paul has now come full circle. What is transpiring in Galatia is the fulfillment of God's great promise, both of the Spirit and of the inclusion and blessing of the Gentiles. Notice how Paul shifts his language to the plural: "He redeemed us"; "so that by faith we might receive" (emphasis added). This is a word spoken to Jews and Gentiles, *both of whom* lived in jeopardy. There is a problem for both and a redemption for both as well. Abraham's covenant gave birth not only to a nation but genuine blessing as well for the Gentile.

**3:15** *Brothers and sisters.* This is a helpful and accurate expansion of the Greek singular (*adelphos*, brother); see comments on 1:2.

*Let me take an example from everyday life.* Paul now brings home his idea by referring to binding covenants. The principle is simple: no one can change the substance of a covenant that has already been ratified—particularly one that has been in place and confirmed for centuries. Most scholars think that Paul has in mind here inheritance covenants, where promises with real benefit are given to people. Such promises would become meaningless if they could be easily erased.

**3:16–17** *The promises were spoken to Abraham.* Paul now provides a case study of covenants in the story of Abraham, likely referring to the promises that God gave Abraham regarding land and descendants (Ge 15 and 17). The law was given 430 years following these covenants with Abraham (Ex 12:40). The Abrahamic pattern of a trusting acceptance of God's gift and the promises that accompanied it was not annulled by the law of Moses. Therefore, the principle of grace/response continues to operate even among those who live on this side of Moses' covenant.

Paul must be careful, however, because in this case study of Abraham the promises are given to Abraham *and his seed* (progeny, descendants, or offspring, Ge 12:7; 13:15; 15:13, 18; 17:7; 24:7). This could be interpreted to mean that the beneficiaries of the promises to Abraham would be those who alone share his physical lineage, namely, those with Jewish ethnicity. And if this were the case, how would Paul's use of the Abraham covenant help place Gentiles within that covenant? Here Paul does something creative in that he gives dramatic interpretation of the promise.

While we may find Paul's logic difficult, it was not uncommon in his day. The term "seed" (Gk, *sperma*) could be either singular or plural, and one's view could be used to argue a point. We have numerous examples of Jewish writers in this period doing this.[20] In Abraham's case, the Old Testament views this progeny as strictly limited to those who descend from Isaac (Ge 17:19–21) and excludes Abraham's seed resulting in Ishmael (Ge 16; 21:8–13).[21] This means the seed of Abraham was limited to Isaac alone.

Following this logic, Paul then argues that the *ultimate seed* of Abraham is the messiah, Christ. Thus, Christ is the true heir of the promises of Abraham's covenant—and those who are attached to Christ thus become heirs along with the patriarch.

On the other hand, it may well be that the Abrahamic promise was collective, referring to many (like our English "offspring"), and this could be argued within the promise itself that this seed will be enormous like the dust of the earth, the stars in the sky, and sand at the sea. But Paul wants to abandon this view, perhaps because he looked at Jewish history and recognized that the promised blessing to the Gentiles had failed to appear. Therefore, the mechanism by which this blessing would come had to be another, namely, the Christ.

**3:18** *If the inheritance depends on the law.* See comments on inheritance at Eph 1:13–14 and 5:5.

Paul now says there is a choice to be made. His own view is that the catalyst for messianic blessing has always been the grace of God, demonstrated through the life of Abraham. This is the origin of Israel's "inheritance"—a critical word for Jews (see "Galatians 3:18 Through Old Testament Eyes: The Inheritance of Abraham").

Paul underscores that God "gave" these promises. This then is the basis of inheritance: it is God's generosity, not a legal claim. Paul then takes up a position in opposition to a prevalent view of his day. Inheritance is not to be seen as a legal claim against the giver; inheritance is determined by the good will of the giver who is making promises. To leverage law over God in order to claim your promises would the height of error.

## Galatians 3:18 Through Old Testament Eyes: The Inheritance of Abraham

Few ideas were as important as inheritance within the Old Testament and the writings of the Second Temple rabbis. An inheritance was secured through a will, which listed specific promises. But among the promises it received, Israel highly valued the gift of nationhood (a "great nation") and land (Ge 15:7–8; Nu 33:54; 34:2; Dt 25:19; 26:1). Paul uses the term *inheritance* because it draws us back to Genesis (and Deuteronomy) and touches on a fundamental value in his audience. These were the national promises that inevitably excluded Gentiles. These promises even went further and, in Paul's day, were interpreted as a promise to inherit the *entire world* (see Ro 4:13)![22]

Paul recognizes all of this. That is why in this section of Galatians he pointedly remarks that such inheritance is not a possession to be held as if it were a privilege. Instead, all promises come as gift, and those gifts require responses that either disqualify or affirm the recipient. When divine gift devolves to privilege and entitlement, and (as a result) the relationship with God is compromised, prophetic criticism comes next. This is precisely the role of the Old Testament prophets in their assessment of Israel's life. Just because the nation was ethnically tied to

Abraham did not exempt them from judgment (Eze 7:2–6; Hos 5:1–7; Am 8:1–2; etc.). And this isn't far from what Paul is saying in Galatians 3.

**3:19** *Why, then, was the law given at all?* Paul must now explain the value and function of the law if it is not here to make a legal claim against God's covenant. If the promises of God have been made available apart from the law, the law had little use (apparently) in the program of God. To be sure, Paul's answer here is critical since if he shows disregard for the law—in a Jewish religious world that loves the law—he would be discredited utterly.

The traditional interpretation is to see Paul's view of the law negatively. That is, the law was given *because of* the errors regarding Jewish behavior. But others wish to see something different and more positive here. Paul says the law was given "because of transgressions,"[23] and here it could either be that the law was God's instrument to reveal the true sinfulness of his people or that the law was given as a remedy to that sinfulness (hence its sacrificial system). Either way, the law was a temporary expedient unmasking the true state of affairs in Israel until the coming of the seed (Christ) that was promised. In this sense, the law was preparatory until Christ, a custodian perhaps, showing sin clearly and thus making Christ's gift that much clearer. In Romans 3:20, Paul contends that "through the law we become conscious of our sin." Similarly, he argues in Romans 7:7, "I would not have known what sin was had it not been for the law." Romans 5:20 says the giving of the law was the means by which sin would increase.

Paul has thus made two affirmations: (1) the law was given to reveal sin; and (2) the law had a temporary role until the coming of Christ, where the complete solution to sin could be found. Finally, Paul adds one more idea (3:19c). It was common in Paul's world to say that the law was not given directly by God to Moses but instead was given through intermediaries, likely angels (Ac 7:38; Heb 2:2; Jubilees 1:27; 2:1; Josephus, *Antiq.* 15.5.3). The Old Testament gives no evidence of this (see Ex 3:2), but conjecture about it was widespread and accepted. This meant that God had given the law to a mediator who then passed it to Moses who was a secondary mediator. Moses then distributed the law to all Israel. If this were true, Paul is hinting that, while the law came through a mediator, the promised gift given to Abraham came directly from God. The promise is thus elevated in importance while the law is subordinate.

**3:20** *A mediator, however, implies more than one party; but God is one.* The exact meaning of 3:20 has eluded interpreters for as long as there has been interpretation.[24] Literally the verse says, "The mediator is not [just] one; but God is one."[25] The NIV expands its meaning: "A mediator, however, implies more than one party," which, of course, is an interpretation and which seems the right one. Paul's less-than-successful sentence here (hence the wide confusion) likely says the God who spoke to Abraham is one (which is a central credo in Judaism, Dt 6:4–5; Ro 3:30), but in the case of the law, there was more than one mediator. This reinforces the comparison Paul has been making throughout this section between law and promise.[26]

**3:21** *Is the law, therefore, opposed to the promises of God?* Paul is still concerned to show that as a teacher, he respects and values the law. He believes that the law has played an important role for God's people, guiding them in righteousness and setting the stage for Christ. Therefore, Paul's promotion of the promises and gift of God (modeled through Abraham) is "absolutely not" opposed to the law. Instead, they have worked in concert.

*If a law had been given that could impart life. . . .* The problem Paul has to face is the clear Old Testament teaching that the Torah (or law) gives life (Lev 18:5; Dt 6:24–25; Pr 3:1–2). On the one hand, Paul may be thinking that the Torah supplied Israel with a *way of life,* but this is different than the power of God to *make alive.* This can only be done by God's initiative. However, Paul's argument goes further. He has argued that the problem is that the law itself is tethered to sin. It triggers sin and reveals it. His language is even dramatic: the law is imprisoned (Gk, *sugkleiō*) by sin (Ro 11:32).

Relying on the works of the law is futile (Gal 3:10) and cannot be an avenue to righteousness. A sixth-century African priest (Fulgentius of Ruspe) once said it well: "Law without grace, then, can expose disease but cannot heal."[27] The only full and successful resolution of sin is in the grace of God discovered in Christ.

**3:22** *Scripture has locked up everything under the control of sin.* Paul now sums up his argument to this point. "Scripture" is likely referring to the great expanse of the Scripture's teachings that view history as fixed in a state of sin. Note that Paul does not say "everyone," but rather says "everything" (Gk, *ta panta*). This means that the problem is not simply in Israel. Jews and Gentiles—the entire world—lives with this burden of brokenness and sin. As Paul does in Romans 1–3, he here is hinting at a wide scope for the problem of creation's predicament. The law, given as a gesture of grace, was a guide that charted a path through this turmoil.

*So that what was promised . . . might be given to those who believe.* In the desperation of their dilemma, those both under the law (Jews) and those outside the law (Gentiles) might find Christ, God's echoing gesture of Abrahamic grace. The gateway to this relief, to this escape from the world's crisis, is simply faith-as-trust in the one who can bring righteousness where there is none.

**3:23** *Held in custody.* It would be easy to see the "custody" referred to as something negative. But here Paul introduces a new term (Gk, *phoureō*) to describe our condition. This word can also mean "to guard or watch over" (2 Co 11:32). The idea, then, is more protective than punitive, which parallels what Paul says in Galatians 3:24 about the law as a guardian. "Locked up" in 3:23b, then, refers to how the law *restrains* (not imprisons) us. The world is locked in sin (3:22), and now the law has constrained Israel. In an age where sin is rampant, Paul may have in mind a course of life given to Israel in Torah that protects as a parent creates inflexible rules for the child who lives in a world of danger.

**3:24** *The law was our guardian.* The law was more precisely a mentor or tutor (Gk, *paidagōgos*, often in English, *pedagogue*), which describes a guide, guardian, or mentor of youth (the NRSVue "disciplinarian" misses the nuance), and in this sense the law was both protective and strict. The roles of such guardians in Roman culture were carefully defined and inflexible *because* they were protecting the immature from the world. They were often slaves who were deeply trusted, who walked young men to school each day, protecting them from either molesters or immorality. They took on this assignment when the boy was only a child and ended the duty when he passed through puberty.

**3:25** *Now that this faith has come.* Paul has the temporary role of the pedagogue in mind when he sees the law as a temporary expedient. As a boy was released from his pedagogue at puberty, so too Christ has introduced a new era of freedom and maturity. By embracing Christ by faith and receiving the Spirit, Israel has the opportunity to move into maturity, enjoying a righteousness independent of the law.

## Going Deeper: The Law as Our Custodian (Gal 3:25)

In many respects, law has a protective function in our immaturity. This can be seen today from practical family examples to larger issues of civil law and even the Ten Commandments. I remember memorizing these commands when I was in catechism many years ago and thinking that if I just master these, I'll be fine with God.

But what is tragic is when we meet adult Christians who continue to live "under the law"; that is, they look at the Bible as the rulebook and try to determine what is permitted and what is prohibited. They have never matured. Paul envisions a Christian maturity in which the Spirit's guidance and wisdom take control. Instead of not stealing because of the eighth commandment, we do not steal because (hopefully) we understand God's deeper desire for my conduct and the harm we can do to others. By God's Spirit we can internalize God's character into our own character such that our actions more automatically conform to his will. After we have regularly and consciously practiced the habits of not stealing, of praying, or of showing compassion, we live according to God's desires without having to make a deliberate decision each time. This is part of the "process of being conformed in the image of Christ for the sake of others."[28]

This is not an entirely new concept in the New Testament. The Old Testament prophets were thinking similarly. When Jeremiah talks about a renewed heart (31:31–34; 32:39) or a heart to truly know God's will (24:7), or when Ezekiel talks about a new Spirit that will enter Israel (36:26–27), they are imagining a new way for God's people to relate to him. The New Testament (and here, Paul) is making the claim that this imagined time has now arrived in Christ.

**3:26–27** *Children of God.* Paul has concluded his explanation of the place of the law (3:15–25) and now returns to his main subject, providing perhaps a summary conclusion. Recall that the problem in Galatia was the critique of Gentile Christians because they were not living out the Jewish laws as dictated by a delegation of Judaizers from Jerusalem. Paul now returns to Gentile life in Christ and says what must have sounded remarkable: *"In Christ Jesus you are all children of God."* Notice how Paul changes from "we" to "you." He is addressing the Galatian Gentiles again.

The intent of the NIV is to be inclusive (all persons are "children" of God), but the Greek actually refers to "sons" of God (Gk, *huioi*; also 3:7). We understand this title comes from a patriarchal culture, but it bears nuances that can be missed. Sonship implied privilege, inheritance, and status, and Paul will focus on inheritance in 3:29. Divine sonship was the most elevated status in the Old Testament for Israel (Ex 4:22–23; Jer 31:9; Hos 11:1), and in the Second Temple period the righteous of Israel bore this title (Sirach 4:10; 2 Maccabees 7:34).[29] Paul is applying to Gentiles the most sought-after title of Israel.

Paul had already indicated that the Galatians were "sons" of Abraham (3:7) or, as Paul will write in Romans 4:11, "He [Abraham] is the father of all who believe." In Galatians 3:26, in the Greek text, Paul even advances "all of you" to the beginning of his sentence: *"All of you are sons of God"* (emphasis added). Gentiles have now joined Jews as "sons" of Abraham and "sons" of God in a community of belief in Christ and can share the same identity. This is a dramatic shift for any Jewish teacher to promote. Dunn says, "As 'faith' has replaced the law as the distinctive mark of the 'sons of God,' so 'Christ Jesus' has replaced ethnic Israel as the social context of this sonship."[30]

*All of you who were baptized into Christ have clothed yourselves with Christ.* In 3:26 Paul described faith as the gateway into life in Christ. Now he refers to baptism, and together these two reflect how the early church viewed initiation into the Christian community. No doubt water baptism is in mind, as it was practiced by John the Baptist and Jesus' followers (Ac 2:38; 1 Co 1:13–17). The early church frequently referred to baptism in the Spirit (Mk 1:8; Jn 1:33; Ac 1:5) as well.

Paul describes these Gentiles as further *clothed with Christ.* This idea of taking on a new identity as donning new clothes appears in the Old Testament (Isa 52:1; 61:10; Zec 3:3–4).[31] Together these metaphorical images supply us with a comprehensive picture of what it means to belong to Christ: full identity and transformation.

**3:28** *You are all one in Christ.* See "Going Deeper: Being in Christ According to Paul (Gal 5:6)."

This is one of the most celebrated verses penned by Paul in Galatians. It is often repeated and applied in countless contexts in the church. And yet here Paul is making it his concluding statement for this part of Galatians. This proclamation of inclusion and unity appears also in 1 Corinthians 12:13 and Colossians 3:11, but, unlike these passages, Paul here includes women and men in the list of possible divisions in the church. Some have pointed to sayings circulating in Greek and Jewish contexts where men thanked God that they were neither women, slaves, nor barbarians. But the provenance of these prayers is dubious, and we wonder how widespread they were.[32]

As Paul elaborates on the unity of the church and his desire to break down walls that divide, he offers three pairs of contrasts that cover the flashpoints of life together in the church. It is wrong to do as some would and say this verse simply presents all categories of persons as capable of gaining salvation. There is more here because Paul knows that a wider disruption of social life has occurred in Galatia, and he aims to repair it. Paul envisions a community where the hierarchies and divisions of the world weaken as we mature in Christ and eventually fade away. Therefore, there are deep social and justice implications that can be rightly drawn from 3:28.

The number three is often used in the Old Testament to signal completeness (Ge 40:10–22; Nu 22:28; 1 Sa 3:8; 1 Ki 18:34; Jnh 1:17). Paul's list of three pairs thus suggests completeness without being exhaustive. He could well have added, "Neither young nor old, neither rich nor poor, neither well nor sick," and more. Christ removes all barriers between those who are in him.

## Galatians 3:28 Through Old Testament Eyes:
## Genesis 17:9–14

Scholars have debated the origin of these three pairs in Galatians 3:28 (Jew/Gentile; free/slave; male/female). Some believe that Paul has in mind Genesis 1:27, where a variety of verbal parallels link the references to male and female.[33] Genesis 17:9–14 is a more likely background, where we read the specific requirements for circumcision. In Genesis 17, Israel is to distinguish between all three pairs: Israelites who are circumcised (Gentiles are not); free Israelites and their household slaves who are circumcised (but their free laborers are not); and men who are circumcised (while the women are not). This then creates an ideal: to be Jewish, free, and male.[34]

This restricting triple-criteria may have been upended in Christian baptism where these categories simply did not matter, or, better, they could not be used to exclude. Men, women, slaves, free, Jews—and here in this setting, Gentiles too—were fully included. "Christian baptism ignores the distinctions required by the covenant of circumcision and provides a basis for unity in the Christian community."[35]

*Neither Jew nor Gentile.* Paul's use of Greek and Gentile is almost interchangeable in verses such as this (see also Ro 1:16; 3:29), and here he underscores a contrast between Jews and Greeks (*hellēn*, see comments on Gal 2:3) It shows us how the Jews viewed the world: the circumcised and the uncircumcised, those who belong to Israel and those who do not.[36] But this was a worldview that stemmed from the law, which required strict boundaries between Jew and Gentile, and following Paul's thinking in the previous paragraphs, this outlook now must disappear in Christ. The Galatian Gentiles thus provide a model for how ethnic/cultural/racial divisions are affected by our new identity in Christ. This does not mean that cultural identity is lost but that our cultural place, especially among those in power, is no longer privileged.

*Neither slave nor free.* While Paul's reference to gender resonates with the modern reader, this pair of terms would have sounded absurd to a Roman reader. Paul's Roman world was a slave culture where slaves were visible every day and where many citizens owned slaves. This world was filled with social hierarchies, and slaves lived at the very bottom. But here Paul suggests that a believing community will not find slavery tolerable with a life in Christ. We can see this at work when Paul writes a letter to Philemon on behalf of a runaway slave, Onesimus, urging the slaveowner to focus not on their relative hierarchy but on their mutual standing as brothers in Christ (Phm 1:16). The early Christians further modeled this value by describing themselves as *slaves of Christ* (Ro 1:1; Gal 1:10).

*Nor is there male and female.* Joel's prophecy (2:28–29) says there will come a time when the Spirit will no longer be reserved just for men who had special responsibilities (see comments on Gal 3:2–3). He says the Spirit will fall on both males and females, and even on slaves of both sexes ("Even on the male and female slaves, in those days I will pour out my spirit," NRSVue). Paul's second and third divisions fall in line with both of these, especially since, as we've seen, he also emphases the Spirit in this chapter (Gal 3:2–5, 14). Yet Paul knows this is a divisive feature of social life. Paul does not use the usual terms for men and women but cites the exact language of Genesis 1:27 (*male and female*). This is no doubt evocative of the portrait of the garden before the fall, when male and female lived in perfect harmony and without sin. But even in Paul's own experience, he saw that women were moving into the ranks of the church in large numbers.

Women, for instance, were in organized ministries: Priscilla (Ac 18:2; Ro 16:3), Eudoia and Syntyche (Php 4:2–3), Junia (Ro 16:7), and Phoebe (Ro 16:1). The church had women who served as deacons (Ro 16:1–2; 1 Ti 3:10–11), prophets (Ac 21:9; 1 Co 11:5), and formal caregivers (1 Ti 5:3–16). We fail to notice that when Paul adds greetings to the end of his letters many of these names are female. Paul writes acknowledging fifty-four men and thirteen women in his letters. Twenty percent of these people are women. And some of them he describes as "co-workers" (Gk, *sunergoi*), the same term used for men (Ro 16:9, 21). We could easily translate *sunergoi* as "colleague" and thus easily translate Romans 16:3 as "Greet Prisca[37] and Aquila, my colleagues in Christ."

## Going Deeper: Jew nor Gentile, Slave nor Free, Male nor Female (Gal 3:26–28)

Paul's list of divisions in Galatians 3:28 covers some of the most prominent tensions that have troubled human society throughout countless generations. Racial/ethnic/tribal divisions, social status divisions, and gender divisions are like a plague in the world. The reflex to look at another race and express judgment, superiority, and exclusion is common in every country and within every people group, fueling reactive immigration policies and practices around the world. We also have our own version of social hierarchies, and while slavery is outlawed, still, we view the homeless and the poor with similar disregard. In many countries, society has improved in its equalizing of male and female opportunity, but still, we have far to go, and every woman knows it.

As Paul writes here, he is thinking particularly about life in the church. The church should be an enclave of welcome and equality unknown elsewhere in the world. At least in the church, we should have in Christ the ability to overcome racial strife, to welcome the stranger and the poor, and to accept women so that they enjoy privileges of leadership and respect equal to that of any man.

It is impossible to appreciate just how radical Paul's thinking is in Galatians unless we are able to reconstruct some of the social realities of his Roman world. The idea that Jews and Gentiles would break down social barriers would surprise both groups. Greeks and Jews would happily separate from the other. The picture of slaves and citizens worshipping side by side would also surprise. And to be sure, the notion that women would be freed from the limits set down by society and be viewed in every way as men's equals would no doubt shock.

This is a radical rearrangement of life and Paul understands this. I can imagine Paul delighting in the picture of a Roman slave woman preaching in one of Paul's churches as Jews, free citizens, and men sat attentively. This was Paul's vision for his churches, and it certainly would be his vision for our churches as well.

Many churches disagree on gender roles for men and women. But Paul's passionate argument here is that the church must upend entrenched social traditions that have no place in the kingdom of Christ. If we feel strongly about slavery, we should feel just as passionate about women in the church. We can imagine some ancient churches excluding slaves due to their social status. Paul would object. We can also imagine a modern church marginalizing women due to their gender. Paul would also object.

Perhaps the most heartbreaking experience I have had teaching in a seminary is talking with women who grew up with a list of things they could not do in church. *They had internalized these.* These are gifted women called into leadership. And so we might ask a fundamental question: What are we doing to promote equal participation of women and men within our churches?

**3:29** *You are Abraham's seed.* Paul uses the language of belonging to describe our identity with Christ: "If you belong to Christ." This is parallel to Paul's usual language of being "in Christ," employed frequently in about seventy verses throughout his letters (see Ro 8:1, 9). In Romans 7:14–25, Paul uses this ownership metaphor for slavery, ownership, and discipleship. The metaphor shows immovable ownership that another cannot remove.

Paul has already discussed how the seed (or descendants) of Abraham are identified through Christ (Gal 3:6–9, 16–19) and implied that those who then belong to Christ likewise are linked to Abraham (3:9). Now he makes the link explicit. *Those who belong to Christ are Abraham's seed.* He will say this with equal force in Romans 4:11–12. It is hard to imagine the power of these words. Claiming descent from Abraham was a Jewish prerogative. But Paul has been arguing that neither bloodline nor works of the law are what locate the true spiritual family of Abraham in this new messianic era. It is faith (Gal 3:9; Ro 4:16). Christ has upended—or better, returned—Israel to the expectation of faith that was known in the beginning with Abraham in Genesis.

*Heirs according to the promise.* Paul's use of sonship language inevitably leads to matters of inheritance. While inheritance was typically passed from father to son (Nu 27:1–11; Dt 21:15–17), many Old Testament passages concerning inheritance refer to the land that is promised to the people as a whole (Dt 12:9–10; 31:7; Ps 105:9–11).[38] (See also comments on inheritance at Eph 1:13–14 and 5:5.)

When Paul uses this language, he again is stepping into the sacred realm of Jewish privilege. Membership in Abraham's family means sharing the inheritance that springs from him. And this is based on the promises God had made to Abraham. Paul will develop this idea of inheritance further in chapter 4. But here he wants it clear that any who would disqualify the Galatian Gentiles if they do not follow the law are completely mistaken. These people are sons (children) of Abraham, the seed of Abraham, and heirs of Abraham—given their faith in Christ, their reception of the Spirit, and their baptism.

## Going Deeper: The Promised Inheritance (Gal 3:29)

Paul says in 3:14 that the promise awaiting messianic believers is the Spirit. And this may be what he refers to in 3:29. Paul also may be thinking of the messiah Jesus as the promise since he is now the fulfillment of the promised seed of Abraham (3:16). In chapter 4, Paul links God's promise to the inheritance of Isaac and the promise of citizenship in the Jerusalem that is "above"—namely, a Jerusalem in heaven (4:26).

In this verse, however, Paul describes the promise in connection to Abraham and inheritance. What were these promised inheritances? In the Old Testament, Abraham is promised two gifts within his covenant with God: a land and a nation. And these became the premier gifts of national identity throughout Old Testament history.

If Paul is echoing these promises, he is subverting two serious features of Israel's identity and suggesting that Gentiles will share in them. If so, this is how Abraham will be a father to "many nations"—which includes the Gentiles (Ge 17:4). This is how Abraham will be a blessing to "the nations" (Ge 22:18). This is how Paul can reinterpret the land promise of the Old Testament and say that it refers to *the entire world* (Ro 4:13).

Why is this important? The promise of land and nation based on ethnicity (ethnic nationalism) is used throughout the world today to justify exclusion, and frequently, violence. Thus, some will say that Hungary is for ethnic Hungarians and all others should depart; Germany is for ethnic Germans; Serbia is for Serbs. This is a part of the American story as well. We can ask if this is equally true in modern Israel where ethnic nationalism is woven intentionally into the nation's identity. Legislation called the Nation-State law ratified in 2018 (and upheld by the Supreme Court in 2021) declared that Israel exists for Jews and only Jewish self-determination would prevail. What might Paul think about marginalizing 21 percent of Israel's population who are not Jewish?

In Galatians he insists that Christians (despite their ethnicity) are heirs to Abraham's promises.

# GALATIANS 4

**4:1–2** *The heir is subject to guardians.* This paragraph flows neatly from 3:29 where Paul has mentioned how the Galatians are both children of Abraham *and heirs.* Now Paul wants to expand on inheritance and weave it into his understanding of the law. A child (though an heir) cannot inherit until the time set by his father, and this makes him little different than a slave who cannot inherit. Therefore, this young heir is subject to guardians. The term here is different than 3:24. Paul says we were subject to administrators (Gk, *epitropoi*) and trustees (Gk, *oikonomos*). These are almost synonyms referring to guardians of an estate, perhaps estate managers. Thus, this person protects the inheritance until an appropriate time. (See "Galatians 3:18 Through Old Testament Eyes: The Inheritance of Abraham" and comments on inheritance at Eph 1:13–14 and 5:5.)

**4:3** *We were underage.* Paul is targeting this interim period, when someone owns the promise of an inheritance but does not have access to it. In this interim we are enslaved while living under the law (Eph 1:18). This is a theme that appears in the gospels. There are those who live in a household, following all of the rules (Lk 15:25–29; 17:7–10), and yet view their life as slavery (Lk 15:29) and find no joy in their father or master.

*The elemental spiritual forces.* The spiritual world of Old Testament writers was populated with various beings, angelic and demonic. Job 1–2 refers to two royal counsels held in God's presence that are attended by "the sons of God," Satan and angels. We find a similar scene in 1 Kings 22:19–23. Those who make sacrifices to demons are condemned, equating these activities with idol worship (Lev 17:7; Dt 32:17; Ps 106:36–37). Zechariah 13:2 also equates idols and unclean spirits, suggesting that these spirits are causing prophets to speak falsely. This sort of world view carried over into the New Testament, especially as seen in Jesus' confrontations with demons and Satan.

Paul could have in mind these cosmic forces that manipulated the world. Or he could also be thinking about the commonplace influences of sin and base human nature. Commentators are divided. But at least, Paul has in mind that in this era *before Christ*, we did not have the power or capability to manage as we do now. Worse yet, he will describe the law as one of those forces under which his fellow Jews have been living (Gal 4:8–10). The point is that, before Christ, humanity (and Judaism) had far less agency than it imagined.

**4:4–5** *God sent his Son.* The "set time" Paul anticipates here echoes the son's awaited time of inheritance, when maturity has finally arrived (4:1–2). This time is marked by the arrival of God's Son. It is noteworthy that "son" is being used throughout this passage because of Abraham and inheritance. The symmetry of 4:6 is overt: Jesus is the truest son of Abraham, and he is God's Son, but now believers can claim sonship for themselves. *The Galatians are sons like Jesus and so stand in the same place of inheritance.*

*Born of a woman.* The phrase does not imply anything more than Jesus' full humanity (Job 14:1; 15:14; Lk 7:28). The following phrase, "born under the law," refers to his life within the Jewish world of law-keeping. Jews in this era expected the messiah to obey the law expertly. But like a Trojan Horse, since Jesus belonged to the law, he was capable as a representative within the law to defeat the subjection the law gave.

*To redeem those under the law.* Redemption (Gk, *exagorazō*) refers to purchasing someone's freedom, hence, to buy off or ransom (Gk, *agorazō*, "to purchase"). The image of redemption is used prominently regarding how the Lord brought Israel out of Egyptian slavery (Ex 6:6; Dt 7:8; 9:26; 13:5; 15:15; 24:18; 2 Sa 7:23; Ne 1:8–10; Ps 74:2; 77:15). God continued to be their source of hope for redemption (Ps 19:14) from death (Ps 49:15; 103:4; Hos 13:14), from enemies (Ps 106:10; 107:2), from oppression (Ps 119:134), and from sin itself (Ps 130:7–8). Here in Galatians 4:5, the subject of the ransom is likely Jews who live under the law.

*Adoption to sonship.* While there is no formal adoption law in the Old Testament, God is often referred to as the father of his people (Dt 32:6; Ps 68:5; 89:26; 103:13; Isa 63:16; 64:8; Mal 2:10). If not exactly having adoption in view, this nonetheless suggests that God in some sense incorporates his people into his family. We also find a stronger image in God adopting the king of Israel as his son (2 Sa 7:14; Ps 2:6–7). Might Paul be implying that all of us in Christ share in his royal status?

In its immediate context, the adoption Paul speaks of might refer to Gentiles since they are not natural sons. But it might encompass Jewish liberation as well as Gentile adoption, both gained through the work of

Christ. Indeed, redemption and sonship (Gal 4:5) are linked when, in the context of God liberating Israel from Egypt, he calls Israel his "firstborn son" (Ex 4:23).

Paul may also have in mind the idea that Jesus is the only true seed or son of Abraham (Gal 3:16), which makes *everyone* who comes to faith in Christ have the capacity to become a true son (Jews and Gentiles). By Roman law, the adoptee had the same legal status as a natural heir. Either way, believers, including Gentiles, are now adoptive sons and this means possessing the privilege of inheritance. Thus in 4:7, "since you are his 'son,' God has made also an heir" (author's translation). By giving us "adoption," Paul underscores that this is a gift, initiated by God's own decision and not a privilege earned. See the close parallel in language in Romans 8:15–17.

**4:6–7** *God sent the Spirit of his Son.* The Spirit is the first gift of inheritance received by all those who are heirs. Note, however, how Paul describes this as "the Spirit *of his Son*" (emphasis added), meaning that the Spirit borne by believers is Jesus' Spirit (Php 1:19). And since Christ is the seed of Abraham and the Son of God, the gift now alive in the Galatians (Christ's Spirit) draws them uniquely into a divine life not known before. Not only do we share sonship with Christ, but we also are co-heirs with him (Ro 8:17), meaning we are fully sharing in aspects of the Son's divine life.

This is a major theological move by Paul. He has now connected the historical Jesus (born of a woman) to the eschatological gift that comes alone from God. Jesus is the axis point around whom all events turn. He completes the historic connection to Abraham and completes the experiential connection to God.

This is why in Galatians Paul points to the Spirit as the most important marker to signify that Gentiles are fully a part of Abraham's (and God's) family (Gal 3:2–5, 14). Circumcision (demanded by Paul's opponents) was not the true marker: only the Spirit signified complete identity with Christ. Paul returns to the second person ("you are his sons," 4:6) to reinforce this for his Gentile readers.

## Galatians 4:1–7 Through Old Testament Eyes: God as Father

The Hebrew word "father" (*ab* or *av*) is used frequently in the Old Testament due to its patriarchal culture. The household is led by the father, tribal leadership uses the term, and God is described as father. Names often use this as a prefix or suffix as a confession of faith: Joab (Yahweh [*Yo* or *Jo*] is Father [*ab*]) or Abijah (Father [*ab*] is Yahweh [Jah = *Yah*]).

The metaphorical idea of God as father was widespread and developed numerous features (Dt 1:31; 32:6; Isa 1:2; 63:16; 64:8; Mal 2:10). Israel was God's son (Hos 11:1) and the king was God's son (Ps 2:7). This evoked ideas of God's trustworthiness and loving authority (Ps 103:13; Pr 3:12). As a child with a father, he shelters and protects (Ps 89:26). But fatherhood also implies obedience (Isa 64:8; Jer 18:6–7), and so severity could be expected.

In the Second Temple period, "Father in heaven" was a common phrase in Jewish prayers. "Father and Lord" and "Father and Master" were also common (see Mal 1:6). Jesus' use of "father" in the gospels stands out, particularly in John (115x). The early church remembered how Jesus prayed in his native Aramaic, and *Abba* entered the vocabulary of the earliest Christians. That Paul in Galatia can tell these Greek-speaking Gentiles to use a term that was foreign to them would be odd if the word was not already in use during worship.

*Abba Father.* This is a rarely used term in the New Testament. It is Aramaic for "father" and may be an echo of the Aramaic ministry of Jesus that now survived in the Greek-speaking churches of Paul. Jesus uses it in Mark 14:36, but elsewhere it only occurs in Romans 8:15. This is the language of a child and evokes intimacy and trust by a child who is crying out (Gk, *krazō*; also, Ro 8:15). Again, Paul is reinforcing how Gentiles have a remarkable place as heir and son who can experience a profoundly intimate relationship with God. Galatians 4:7 sums this up carefully: We have been redeemed from slavery; we are God's sons; and since we are sons, we are heirs. And the Spirit has sealed this truth for us. Christ is in us, and this makes an unbreakable bond.

**4:8–11** *Now that you know God.* The alternative life lived *after Christ—* which these Galatians have experienced—is a life governed by knowing the truth and being known by God. The knowledge of God was a widely promoted value in Paul's world, and it is central to the Old Testament understanding of fidelity to the covenant (Jer 31:34; Hos 2:20 ESV, NASB), while "the nations" were known for their absence of this knowledge (Ps 79:6 ESV, NASB; Jer 10:25 ESV, NASB). But Paul corrects himself, saying that even if these Gentiles are oblivious sometimes to the truth, still, *they are known by God.* This too is a major Old Testament idea (Ge 18:19 ASV; Ps 1:6 ESV, NASB), and it points to God's initiative and grace, his effort to love even the mistaken.

*Turning back.* It is clear from 4:11 that the Galatians had already begun to adopt Jewish religious customs as demanded by these delegates from Jerusalem. Paul finds this baffling. Once someone has experienced freedom, why would they return to slavery? Recall that this is a slave culture and so the Galatians would know it well. In Paul's mind, the Gentile life lived *before Christ* was a slavery not to the law but to those "who by nature are not gods" (or literally to "gods which by nature are not," 4:8). Paul refers to these forces as "weak and miserable" (4:9) because devotion to them led to superstition, fear, and impoverishment. This reflex to return to Roman religion must have been common in Paul's Gentile churches (1 Co 8:4-6), but he sees it as a devastating compromise of their faith.

In addition, they are observing sacred days, months, seasons, and years (Gal 4:10). Every culture in this world held religious calendars. The division of the year into months and weeks following lunar cycles was likewise everywhere. Days could be lucky or dangerous or powerful. But almost always these festivals were linked to the Roman or Greek gods and their sacrifices. Judaism also organized the year around festivals (Passover) and sacred days (Day of Atonement). Sabbath no doubt was the most important, and in the Jewish mind, it was the chief demarcation between Gentile and Jewish life.[1] Therefore, when someone argues that Gentile converts must adhere to the works of the law, recognizing the religious calendar was a part of the expectation. Paul says the Galatians are already observing these—and it may be a mix of all the above.

## What the Structure Means: Pathos (Gal 4:11–20)

Keener explains at length that Paul's approach at this point in the letter is rhetorically called "pathos."[2] This was one of Aristotle's three approaches to argumentation: pathos/emotion, logos/logic, and ethos/character. Employing emotion was a carefully negotiated device in antiquity. In a world of constant oral presentations, audiences were alert to how the speaker could move them to action. In 4:11–20, note the many ways that Paul is employing pathos or emotion in his attempt to win over the Galatians: "I fear . . . I have wasted my efforts," "I plead with you," "It was because of an illness," "you would have torn out your eyes," "I am perplexed." In previous verses, note how Paul is making a logical theological argument (*logos*). In chapter one, Paul establishes his own authority (or *ethos*) as someone to be heard (*ethos*).

This demonstrates that Paul was a skilled rhetorician. He understood public communication and was successful with his audiences.

**4:12-14** *I plead with you.* Paul now makes his appeal to the Galatians personal and evocative. If they are choosing to return to works of the law, they need to remember that Paul himself is not living under the law *so that* he could reach the Gentiles like those in Galatia. In other words, they are moving into space that Paul had already abandoned. He recalls being with them in Galatia, where they together shared a trusting and respectful relationship ("You did me no wrong," 4:12). On occasion Paul has had to defend himself from charges of wrongdoing (2 Co 7:2; 1 Th 2:3–12), but Galatia had no such history.

*An illness.* Ancient audiences did not always respond to infirmity with compassion. In the popular culture of the day, an illness or disability could be a sign of sin or a curse from a god. Compare with this the expectation among Greeks and Romans (in statuary) that pious or ideal persons displayed bodily perfection. Paul clearly was infirm in Galatia (cf. 2 Co 12:7), but he notes that they did not detest him or reject him. The last term (Gk, *ekptuō*) originally meant "to spit" ("you did not spit at me"), and some wonder if Paul was judged as having "the evil eye" (or was tormented by demons). Spitting was a protection against it—but the word also became a metaphor for rejection. But the Galatians did none of this. They received him as if he were an angel or even Christ himself (see Abraham's meeting with angels in Ge 18; cf. Ge 33:10; 1 Sa 29:9; Zec 12:8).

**4:15** *Your blessing.* Paul continues to evoke empathy, asking them if they are willing to offer a blessing on Paul and his views in the current controversy. He remarks that while he was with them, their love for him was so great that they would have "torn out" their eyes and given them to him. This exaggeration may support a theory that Paul's ailment had to do with his vision. Perhaps he was in pain or could not see well. In 6:11 Paul signs this letter himself and almost apologizes for his large and awkward writing, which may be another sign of an eye problem. On the other hand, tearing out one's eyes was also a popular idiom for generous and sacrificial love because the eyes were so precious. Records show Roman politicians making speeches saying that "they sacrificed their eyes" to serve and defend the people.[3] This is akin to the modern saying: "I'd give my right arm for you."

## Going Deeper:
## Paul and the Pastor's Heart (Gal 4:12–16)

I have read Paul many times. And in my own mind I have built up this image of him as the supremely intellectual debater moving from synagogue to amphitheater persuading audiences about the truth of the gospel. But a close reading of these verses shows something different. Paul is not using *pathos* simply for effect (see "What the Structure Means: Pathos [Gal

4:11–20]"). He is genuinely bewildered and perplexed, he is confused—he refers to these people as brothers (and sisters) and dear children. In other words, as a strong leader, Paul is unafraid to show his heart.

I am convinced that much of modern preaching centers on *ethos* and *logos*: stature and reason. *Pathos* is probably used much less than the other two.

Perhaps we might call it charismatic presence and the clever or winsome spoken word. In modern language, *pathos* might describe transparency or the willingness of the pastor to show emotion. The Greeks knew well that the slight movement from *logos* to *pathos* suddenly displays our own feelings and honesty and it links us to a person's heart immediately. This is what Paul is doing here, not for the sake of manipulation, but because of his deeply felt commitment to the Galatians.

I once heard a brilliant sermon about our mortality. The pastor explained the reality of decline and death from 2 Corinthians 5:1–5. It was sober and well-reasoned. Then the curtains opened. The staff had imported the gear for an entire hospital room. The pastor sat on the edge of the bed and described those from the church who had died in such a place. And then he moved to his own death—and how the heartbeat monitor might be the last thing he'd hear. He was moved, and we could see the sobering emotion welling up. At once this sermon—which had appealed to our minds and was now moving to *pathos*—came home powerfully and touched our whole beings.

**4:16** *Your enemy.* Possibly the Jerusalem delegation had described Paul as an opponent or an enemy, at least someone not to be trusted. And so he asks here if the Galatians were also choosing this designation now to name their relationship. This is *pathos* in full form (see above "Going Deeper: Paul and the Pastor's Heart") where he pushes his readers to see an extreme form of their position. Paul had only told them the truth (of the gospel? of Christ?), and his simple assumption was that they would receive it with joy. Is Paul piling on guilt here? Indeed.

**4:17–18** *That you may have zeal.* Zeal can regard any determined, energetic action (2 Sa 21:2; Ne 3:20). In particular it can relate to one's passion for God and his ways (2 Ki 10:16) or for how God carries out his own designs (Isa 9:7; 37:32; 42:13; Eze 5:13; 36:5). In the honor-shame culture of the Ancient Near

East, it is not surprising that zeal is associated with honor, whether one's own (Nu 25:11) or God's, especially when he is rejected (Nu 25:13; 1 Ki 19:10, 14; Ps 69:9; 119:139; Eze 39:25).

The zeal of "those people" (Gal 4:17) mentioned by Paul, however, is wholly misplaced. They think they are defending God's honor, but they are quite wrong. Paul uses "zeal" twice in this verse (see also 1:14). To be zealous over another could mean being envious of them—or passionate about their welfare. In this case, however, their zeal is up to "no good" (4:17). Their aim is to break the bond between Paul and the church and then make these Galatians as "zealous" as they are. The NIV "alienate you from us" (4:17) really derives from the word for shutting someone out (Gk, *ekkleiō*), and this may be a clue to what is happening. The Greek text does not have "from us" and instead implies a threat. Paul's opponents want to convert them to make them zealous or they would be excluded from the body of Christ if they do not follow the law.

*It is fine to be zealous.* Zeal was an important word in Jewish discussion about faith. Paul realizes, however, that zeal can move in two directions. It can be excessive and lead to judgment and rigidity (1 Co 3:4), or it can inspire spiritual passion (1 Co 12:31). In writing to the Galatians, he can describe himself as being zealous for them. In the present case, the purposes of this zeal are not helpful but he knows he walks a fine line. He wants the Galatians to be passionate but to be so about the right things.

**4:19** *The pains of childbirth.* Here Paul frames discipleship and growth in terms of labor pains and childbirth and begins with an emotionally endearing title, "My dear children" (Gk, *tekna mou*). *Tekna* refers to small children who are still being formed in maturity. It was Paul's custom to think about his disciples using the metaphor of a parent with a child (1 Co 4:14; 2 Co 12:14; Php 2:22). His deep desire is that they would not simply see their faith as a long walk of obedience but instead as a long walk of formation. The gospel is about having "Christ in you, the hope of glory" (Col 1:27). Here we get a glimpse of Paul's understanding of what it means to enter the faith. Baptism and the gift of the Spirit do not automatically seal a disciple's identity. It is the beginning of a process of transformation that is only possible through baptism and the Spirit. Only one thing matters, Paul will write in Galatians 6:15, and that is a new creation.

**4:20** *I am perplexed.* Everyone knows that in-person communication is more persuasive and satisfying. Our use of digital communication, such as Zoom, leaves us feeling that something has been missed. Worse, the tone of our despair (or anger or affection) can be misunderstood if the right words are not chosen. Paul is aware of this in his letters. He often expressed his desire to be present in his churches (Ro 1:11; 2 Ti 1:4) and would say things such as how he was present with them in his heart (1 Co 5:3; Col 2:5). The Galatians may even feel that Paul's absence made him less persuasive because clearly the Judaizers had direct proximity to them. They could persuade by spoken word and presence while Paul could only write from afar.

A good speaker will name these problems out loud and defuse their power. Paul does wish he could be there in Galatia. If he were with them, they would hear his authentic voice (Gk, *phōnē*; NIV: "tone") and then understand his heart-broken perplexity.[4]

**4:21-23** *Abraham had two sons.* This is Paul's final argument against those who wish to bring the Gentile Galatians under the law. Throughout he has said the defining principle in our relationship with God is faith in the gift of God. He illustrated this from the Galatians' own experience (3:1-4) and from Abraham's experience (3:6-9). He now wants to reinforce his view by returning to Abraham, the great patriarch. Here he works not with Abraham's faith but with the covenant that stems from him. Paul finds in Sarah and Hagar an allegory that he wants to employ for his case. He takes three steps: (1) the question and the challenge presented by the story, 4:21-23; (2) the interpretation of the story, 4:24-27; and (3) the application of the story's principles, 4:28-31.

*Are you not aware of what the law says?* Paul wants to draw his readers back to the Old Testament (4:21), but his motive may be that the Judaizers in Galatia may have already done this. They may be using the Abraham/Sarah/Isaac story to show that the Galatians should imitate Isaac, who was circumcised (Ge 21:4). Paul, however, believes there is a deeper meaning in the Genesis story.

Paul provides a brief review (Gal 4:22-23; see also "Galatians 3 Through Old Testament Eyes: Abraham"). Abraham's disappointment at seventy-five years of age is palpable in the Old Testament. This disappointment lived alongside God's promise to provide him a son and hence was the foundation for the nation that was to come. Everything was in jeopardy without a son.

His wife, Sarah, then offered her Egyptian slave, Hagar, to Abraham to serve as a concubine, taking Sarah's place. This may seem odd to us, but in antiquity, it was not uncommon for a man to secure a male heir like this (Ge 30:3, 9). Hagar's child would be considered Abraham's son without qualifications. But eventually, God's promise was fulfilled when Sarah was beyond childbearing years and became pregnant. The result: Sarah's son was Isaac; Hagar's son was Ishmael. Both were viewed as Abraham's sons (Ge 16:15; 22:2), although the story repeatedly refers to Isaac as Abraham's "only son"

(Ge 22:2, 12, 16). Both boys were circumcised. Paul then notes that Ishmael was born "according to the flesh" (Gal 4:23), which likely means "by natural means" (though for Paul, "flesh" can take on other meanings), and Isaac was born by divine promise.

These details about Sarah and Hagar are vital because Paul is about to work with them in unexpected ways. Note that ethnicity and circumcision did not create the covenant link to Abraham. Both sons had this. Instead, Paul will show that it is only the promise of God (received by faith) that connects anyone to the patriarch.

**4:24-26** *The women represent two covenants.* Paul's interpretation of the Sarah-Hagar story would be surprising to any Jew (and to the Judaizers). But he explains that this is an allegory[5] (NIV, "taken figuratively"), and its deeper importance lay just beneath the surface.

Paul creates an alignment of covenants, people, and activity that disrupts the usual interpretation. Both sons represent covenants. Paul links Ishmael to Mount Sinai and slavery; he links Isaac to Mount Zion and freedom (see Figure G-4.1). Both mountains were well-known. Mount Sinai is in the distant southern desert in Arabia, where Moses received the law. Mount Zion is the hilltop where Jerusalem is located. Paul's interest is tracking what happened at Sinai.

Hagar (as a slave) represents Sinai, and she aligns[6] with the earthly city of Jerusalem, *which is a city in slavery.* This might literally be taken as true since Rome conquered the city in 63 BC and kept it captive.

But Paul sees more here. Jerusalem and her children are enslaved to the law. What does Paul have in mind? They are not likely the residents of the city itself nor the Jerusalem church. He is targeting those Jewish Christians *from Jerusalem* who are troubling Galatia, imposing the law on them.

**Figure G-4.1. Paul's Allegory of Abraham's Two Sons (Gal 4:21–31)**

| Law/Flesh | Faith/Promise |
|---|---|
| Hagar (the slave) | Sarah (the free woman) |
| Born according to the flesh | Born according to God's promise |
| Ishmael: No claim to inheritance | Isaac: May claim the inheritance |
| Children are to be slaves | Children are to be free |
| Covenant from Mount Sinai | Covenant from Abraham |
| Earthly Jerusalem | Heavenly Jerusalem |
| Now in slavery | Now in freedom as children of promise |
| **Paul's Opponents (Judaizers)** | **Paul's Followers in Galatia** |

Note carefully what Paul has done. He has linked the outlook of the Judaizers with Hagar, a slave woman, instead of linking them with Abraham and Sarah, who represent the traditional path of Israel's redemption. In other words, Hagar gained Ishmael for Abraham through *works*, while Sarah gained Isaac for Abraham through *faith*. The position of the Judaizers is therefore the same as Hagar, while Paul (as well as the Galatians) possess the privileged link to Sarah. Note also that Ishmael was circumcised in Genesis 17, just like Isaac (v. 23–27). In Paul's argument, then, he demonstrates further that *even circumcision* cannot gain automatic covenant blessing. It is hard to overstate the shock of this argument.

*The Jerusalem that is above.* Of course, the one covenant that matters belongs to Abraham. Here Paul is thinking about the story of Sarah and Isaac—the story of faith and promise—and where this alignment leads. It does not lead to the earthly Jerusalem but to a heavenly Jerusalem, a city of freedom.

Judaism had long taught that the earthly Jerusalem was a weak model of what God desired. On Sinai, Moses was shown the pattern (from heaven) for how to build the tabernacle (Ex 25:9, 40), and this led to widespread expectation that God was holding another Jerusalem in abeyance for his people. This is attested by numerous sources written in the Second Temple period.[7] For Paul, this Jerusalem will be a city filled with Christ's followers, a city shared by all races without regard for ethnic privileges.

*She is our mother.* Thinking of Jerusalem as a mother figure bearing the children of Israel was not unusual in the Old Testament (Isa 50:1; 51:17–18; Jer 50:12; Hos 4:5). But to follow Paul's allegorical alignment, the heavenly Jerusalem connects back to Sarah, the mother of Isaac, the mother of all who live with faith.

## Going Deeper:
## Christian Allegiance to Jerusalem (Gal 4:26)

David deSilva, a senior New Testament scholar at Ashland Seminary, makes the following observation on Galatians 4:26:

> Paul might find himself perplexed at the interest of twenty-first century Christians (especially the more evangelical Christians) in ... [and] their investment in the promotion of the interests of earthly Jerusalem and the modern State of Israel. Galatians is decidedly not a Zionist text. The "present Jerusalem" is not the focal point of the promise; the God of Jew and Gentile is interested in peace and justice for all people, not the one-sided privileging of any people at the expense of another. In light of Paul's redefinition of who

constitute Abraham's seed, Christians might consider whether their first allegiance ought to be not the State of Israel . . . but to Israeli and Palestinian *Christians*, with their agenda to actively promote the mutual good of these brothers and sisters in Christ.[8]

**4:27** *Be glad, barren woman.* Paul sums up his argument (as he often does) citing from the Old Testament. This is a citation from Isaiah 54:1 in the Greek Old Testament, the Septuagint. Isaiah 54 is a passage of comfort for the exiles of Judea who have lost hope. It promises that God would return to his people, take them up in their loss (barrenness), and once again be Israel's husband. "For a brief moment I abandoned you, but with deep compassion I will bring you back" (54:7). Isaiah promises many children in this redemptive future and the building of a temple beyond anyone's imagining. "I will rebuild you [Jerusalem] with stones of turquoise, your foundations with lapis lazuli. I will make your battlements of rubies, your gates of sparkling jewels and all your walls of precious stones" (54:11–12). This imagined temple could hardly be the stone temple of Paul's day; it must correspond to something grander, something never seen.

This is the *heavenly* Jerusalem in Galatians 4:26 (see Rev 21:10–21) and no doubt Paul imagines the promise here as fulfilled in Christ. Now with the expansion of believers in every tribe, the promise to Sarah and Abraham to bless many nations is realized. Sarah's offspring through Christ will now bless the nations of the world (Ro 4:13).

**4:28–31** *Children of promise.* This is now Paul's pastoral application, which makes clear that these issues belong to the Galatians he is writing to. As he summarizes in 4:31, the Gentile Galatians belong to the "free woman" (Sarah) and not to "the slave woman" (Hagar). They are free with respect to works of the law, while we can assume Paul believes that the Judaizers belong to Hagar and are in slavery to the law.

*Persecuted the son.* Paul now returns to the Genesis story to mine one more feature in it. Genesis describes a rivalry between Sarah and Hagar that resulted in Hagar's removal from Abraham's family (Ge 21:8–21).

Throughout Israel's history, conflict had been sporadic with those tribes who lived in the eastern deserts of Syria and Arabia (Ps 83:5–6), described ostensibly as descendants of Ishmael. Judaism explained this ancient conflict through the Isaac/Ishmael story. Sarah's negative reaction to Ishmael may have come from the episode found in Genesis 21:9. Here the two boys are playing (Ishmael is fourteen years older), but the verb in the Greek Old Testament (*paizō*) can mean both "play" or something worse: to mock, to make fun of, to scorn, or to play with cruelly. Was the older Ishmael mocking Isaac? "Mocking" is the term used in Genesis 21:9 in the NIV. There is a long Jewish tradition viewing the scene in this way, and the Septuagint regularly uses *paizō* negatively (Jer 15:17; Pr 26:19).[9] This is why Sarah reacts as she does (Ge 21:10); the older boy is mocking the younger. The descendants of Hagar and the descendants of Sarah thus have a history of conflict. Since Paul has aligned the Judaizers with Hagar, he is pressing the allegory further: the present conflict in Galatia has a precedent in the behavior of Sarah and Hagar and their immediate descendants.

In Genesis, Sarah presents Abraham with these concerns about Hagar. Sarah urges her husband, "Get rid of that slave woman and her son, for that woman's son [Ishmael] will never share in the inheritance with my son Isaac" (Ge 21:10). Paul cites this text in Galatians 4:30 (see Ro 9:7; Heb 11:18) almost precisely but gives it a surprising application. Sarah's worry was that Ishmael might make a claim on Isaac's inheritance. In the Galatian context (4:31), because these Galatians belong to Sarah (and the Judaizers belong to Hagar), Paul employs the story to suggest that just as Abraham and Sarah sent away Hagar and Ishmael, so too should the Judaizers be told to depart Galatia.

What is at stake here? Two items are central: protection from persecution (prefigured in the Isaac/Ishmael story) and protection of inheritance. Paul wants the Galatians to realize that they are the true heirs of Abraham and Sarah, and the pressure they feel is unnecessary though inevitable. The key word here is *freedom*: Sarah is the "free woman" (4:31; also 4:22–23, 26, 30), and those like Isaac are also to live in freedom. This theme of freedom will now bridge to chapter 5, where Paul will pick it up and explain how freedom can be used and misused.

# GALATIANS 5

**5:1** *It is for freedom that Christ has set us free.* Paul now summarizes what he has been saying for two chapters. The consequence of embracing faith in the promises of God leads to freedom, while the return to Jewish legal obedience leads to slavery. Freedom has been Paul's theme since 2:4, and here he wants his readers to know what is at stake. The loss of freedom has costs, and if the Galatians make the wrong choice here, the outcomes will be dire. Freedom appears in Paul (2 Co 3:17) as one of the key benefits of living in faith, which is why someone who preaches another gospel (Gal 1:7) is deserving the harshest language.

## Going Deeper: Freedom (Gal 5)

Freedom is the central theme of Galatians. And it was no doubt an organizing idea around which Paul reflected theologically on the work of Christ. For Paul, we are free from the curse of the law (3:10–14; 5:1, 13) because this freedom was won by Christ on the cross, where we are also freed from sin and its compulsions. But we are also set free to live empowered by the Spirit that generates a life not remotely matched by the law. All of this together means that we are free to become someone we have never been before—released from condemnation and legal expectation, guided by God himself through his Spirit.

This transformation is the genesis of Paul's understanding of how we might live with one another differently. With lives directed by love, we create communities that bypass the social, racial, and gender boundaries Paul describes in 3:28. This is what makes Paul so different from his context: he finds the resurrection/transformation of the human heart not through disciplined obedience but through a divine work of God. He will still write about concrete expectations for how we should live, but he will never employ these as rules that undercut the grace he knows in Christ.

Oddly, though, we sometimes confuse what Paul is describing with modern political ideas. I recall during a contentious period in the COVID-19 pandemic of 2020 when a church member wanted to debate freedom. He said, "Freedom in Christ means I don't have to wear a mask." Here we have a complete confusion about Paul's understanding of freedom. "Actually," I mentioned, "Paul said that we are being offered slavery in Christ, and in that slavery, we would find freedom from sin."

Paul's frequent exhortation to Christians was to *stand firm* (Gk, *stēkō*), a command that makes us imagine a military formation. Stand fast in the Spirit (Php 1:27), in your faith (1 Co 16:13), in the Lord (Php 4:1; 1 Th 3:8), or even in the traditions (2 Th 2:15). Standing fast implies resistance to an oncoming force (Rev 2:2, 19), and here Paul refers to a yoke of slavery. A yoke (Gk, *zugos*) is a wooden guide harness for an ox (crossing the shoulders of the ox), but due to its long shape, the term also can refer to a scale. Its metaphorical use is widespread and not entirely negative. A disciple can be yoked to a master (Mt 11:29), and in Judaism, a yoke describes devotion to Torah (*m. Abot* 3.5). But Paul's reference to slavery gives a darker view where the metaphor can refer to slavery from war (Lev 26:13; Isa 14:25). A yoke meant subservience and, in the present instance, subordination to the law from which Paul wants to protect Gentiles (Ac 15:10).

## What the Structure Means:
## Freedom from and Freedom for (Gal 5:1–12)

Scholars try to reconstruct the most accurate way to organize Paul's thoughts. When we remember that chapter divisions and verse numbering did not exist in Paul's day, we are not bound by the divisions in our modern Bibles. Galatians 5:1–12 is a good example. Its organizing themes are freedom and the law, but this is not primarily linked to 5:13, where freedom is abused, but to 4:21–31, where we learn about Sarah and Hagar, freedom and slavery. These twelve verses are the great passionate climax of Paul's argument about the law and freedom. But note that in 5:1 we are *free from* something—namely, the law. But in 5:13 we are *free for* something—namely, a life infused with God's Spirit leading to love.

When we allow Paul's argument to guide our understanding of the key sense-units, then the coherence of Paul's thought becomes clearer.

**5:2-3** *Mark my words! . . . Christ will be of no value to you.* Now we see with clarity what the delegates from Jerusalem are aiming at: *they want the Galatian men to be circumcised.* This deed would then become a token that those who let themselves be circumcised would then agree to obedience to the whole law. Paul's Greek underscores this: he says the Galatians would be "submitting themselves" to circumcision (Gk middle or reflexive voice).[1] He later will say that circumcision is of no value (5:6; Ro 2:25–29), so it is not the act itself that is on his mind. It is the decision itself, the choice to voluntarily restructure their relationship with God.

For Jews in this period, circumcision was the ultimate marker for the Gentile who wanted to join the synagogue. Jews were even called "the circumcised," as if this marker was the prominent identifier. And it kept many Gentiles back. So Paul is firm (Gal 5:2 NIV, "Mark my words," in Gk, "Look!" *ide!*)—this is a major tragic step. But it is also a turning point which explains Paul's sharp rhetoric. "Christ will be of no value to you at all" (5:2). Paul draws a bright line between these choices: to live by the promise of grace in Christ or to submit to the rules of Jewish law. Circumcision in effect subverts the gift of grace offered by Christ, dissolving it and its benefits entirely. And the result is simple: anyone stepping through the door of circumcision will then be obligated to obey the entire law because this would be a reformulation of their spiritual life. At a fork in the road, they have chosen a path and thus turned their back on Christ.

The challenge that Paul sees here is not that those who choose the law will then need to keep it perfectly. No Jew believed this. The problem is that the gift offered by Christ is incompatible with any other decision, any other means to find God—which includes employing the law of Moses. This choice will then make Christ obsolete because his system of righteousness built on grace is our only means of freedom and hope.[2]

**5:4** *Alienated from Christ.* This verse mirrors what has already been said. "Justified by the law" is here reflecting the decision to be circumcised. Alienation from Christ is reflecting Christ having no value to you. These sentences underscore that Paul is talking about theological systems and how one must choose a path that leads to righteousness.

*Fallen away from grace.* This phrase has led to numerous debates. Does this mean that the Galatians, once saved, now could make a choice that removed them from salvation? The severity of the decision before the Galatians is now placed in the starkest terms. Paul sees this choice to find safety in the law as a choice that disconnects us from the realm of Christ's grace. This is like a flower falling from the stem that gave it life or a ship failing to hold course as it navigates the shoals.[3] This is a decision that removes us from the domain of grace completely.[4]

**5:5** *Through the Spirit we eagerly await.* Both Paul and the Judaizers agree that the aim of our life is finding a righteousness that is acceptable to God. And this righteousness would be finally revealed in the final judgment. Here Paul draws a strong contrast in Greek: *but we* await . . . and the "we" is emphatic.[5] The flip side of the Galatian choice to return to the law is now found in the Christian life that is led by the Spirit. Note how here and throughout Galatians Paul includes the Spirit as the necessary power that completes our Christian identity (Gal 3:2, 5; 4:6). We are joined to Christ and receive the benefits of his righteousness, but we also receive the Spirit that sustains us until we see the glory God has promised us in the resurrection (Ro 5:1–5; 2 Co 5:5; Eph 1:13–14). The Spirit sustains us as God's strengthening when our faith—which we hold in God's grace—weakens. Hope refers to confident expectation (not disguised uncertainty) and investment in what is assured.

**5:6** *Neither circumcision nor uncircumcision.* Paul continues to make his case for a life "in Christ" (see comment at Gal 3:29) that is led by the Spirit. This is about a new status found in Christ that makes ritual gestures unnecessary. Paul was indifferent to circumcision in the sense that he did not oppose Jewish families using this rite for their sons (Ac 21:21), but he opposed its requirement for Gentiles as a spiritual prerequisite.

## Going Deeper:
## Being in Christ According to Paul (Gal 5:6)

One of the striking phrases we see in Galatians are the words "in Christ" (see 2:4, 16; 3:14, 26, 28; 5:6). The phrase *en Christō* occurs twenty-five times in Paul's letters, and about eighty-three times he writes *in Christ Jesus* (*en Christō Iēsou*), but the meaning is the same. Paul also uses "in the Lord" forty-seven times. This is something that belongs distinctively to Paul since it occurs elsewhere only in 1 Peter (1 Pe 3:16; 5:10, 14).

There are two general ways that Paul employs this. First, it can be objective, where Paul describes an event that belongs to Christ's work. Romans 3:24 is typical: "all are justified freely by his grace through the redemption that came by [Gk, *en*, "in"] Christ Jesus." Second, Paul may have a subjective meaning in mind where he refers to believers having an identity that is lived mystically in the life of Christ. Thus Romans 8:1 says, "Therefore, there is now no condemnation for those who are in Christ Jesus." This phrase is used so frequently that Dunn can say, "Paul's perception of his whole life as a Christian, its source, its identity, and its responsibilities, could be summed up in these phrases."[6]

It is a mistake if we think of these words as synonymous with "being a Christian" or "belonging to the church." For Paul, it is far more. This is not simply a new label we wear to signify our belonging (although this is a part of it); this draws in something more: a lived lordship under Christ and some sense of a transforming personal experience empowered by the Spirit that substantially changes who we are. This refers to an indwelling in which our lives are swept up into the life of God. In Jesus' farewell discourse in John, we hear something similar: *Those who love Jesus and keep his word will be loved by the Father, and both Christ and the Father will make their home with them* (see Jn 14:23).

Therefore, being in Christ includes a mystical sense of living with the divine presence of Christ, and this shared experience is what made for mutually recognizable identities within the church.

*Circumcision.* See comments on 2:3 and "Galatians 2:1–10 Through Old Testament Eyes: Circumcision."

The believer who is directly connected to God through Christ and thus enjoying the benefits of this intimacy ("children of God," 3:26; "heirs," 3:29; "*Abba*," 4:6) hardly needs to supplement this status. But Paul here is striking at the deepest division he knows: The Jew/Gentile or circumcised/uncircumcised division. As in Galatians 3:28, these evaporate, and the marker of Jewish privilege now is no longer effective (Ro 2:25–29).

*Faith expressing itself through love.* The faith that is characteristic of Jesus' followers now finds a supplement: it is a faith made effective and energized in love.[7] The principle of love is what Jesus' life featured (Gal 2:20) and now is reflected in his followers. Paul says this expressly in Romans 5:5: "God's love has been poured out into our hearts through the Holy Spirit, who has been given to us" (see also Ro 8:35–39). Note that in 5:2–6 we see the "Christian triad" of virtues—faith, hope, and love, the "quintessence of the God-given life in Christ."[8]

Paul's term for love here is *agapē*. This was a relatively unused word in secular Greek and occurred rarely in the Greek Old Testament. But the New

Testament Christians adopted it as their own unique vocabulary for what they had seen in Christ (72x in Paul; 116x in the New Testament; the verb *agapaō* occurs 143x in the New Testament). Here was a term that expressed the sacrificial generosity of God and, along with "grace," could become the profile of God's gift to us in Christ (2 Co 13:14; 1 Ti 1:14).

## Galatians 5:6 Through Old Testament Eyes: Love as Agape

We know that the term *agapē* was appropriated and celebrated in the writing of the early Christians. References to it abound in the New Testament, and certainly it would have made many native Greek readers curious about why it suddenly came into primary use.

Greek was known for its careful nuances of meaning, particularly in the classical era. This was true for words for love. *Phileō* was generally used to express affection, and forms of the word were used for friends or a kiss. Here there was mutual attraction. *Stergō* likewise referred to affection, but it generally appears for parents and children or the love of a people for their king. The verb *eraō* described a romantic love between a man and a woman and often carried sensual nuances. Derivatives such as *eros* (erotic) belong here. But *agapaō* is odd. It had little use in classical Greek literature and generally appears in the Hellenistic era.

The Old Testament does, however, offer related ideas. When God acts generously on behalf of either humanity (in creation) or Israel, this activity is an expression of his *character*: that of goodness, righteousness, and love. Deuteronomy talks about God electing Israel as an example of this loving commitment, and this becomes the basis for the great call to Israel that the nation should love and obey him (Dt 6:5).

The Old Testament prophets take this further. Hosea, particularly, does something risky, given the world of fertility cults: the God of Israel is depicted as a spurned lover/husband who nevertheless loves Israel (Hos 2:19–23). "And I will take you for my wife forever; I will take you for my wife in righteousness and in justice, in steadfast love and in mercy" (2:19 NRSVue). The later prophets do the same. Jeremiah can refer to God's everlasting love (31:3).

We think that the wide use of *agapē* among Christians came from the Greek Old Testament where the *agapē* word group occurs over three hundred times. The verb *agapaō* (or the noun, *agapē*) was regularly used to translate a Hebrew verb for love (*ahav*). But in many of these texts, we cannot distinguish successfully between its use and, say, *eraō*. Agape seems almost synonymous with other Greek words for love, and so clear lines of meaning are blurred. We can see this increasing use of *agapē* in other writings of Intertestamental Judaism (the Apocrypha, Qumran). The love of God—and the reciprocal love of his people to him and to their neighbors—defines the essential expression of a faithful life in this period. But this love is less emotional than it is acted out. For example, God's Torah is a gift of love, but demonstrating reciprocal love is shown through obedience (Dt 11:1; 19:9).[9] Thus, how you behave is elevated above how you feel.

By picking up this one word and making it the mainstay of God's expression for his world, the New Testament—and particularly Paul—is doing something stunning. In the New Testament, *agapē* is the central concept to depict God's relationship to his creation and our relationship to him and each other (the *agapē* word group occurs about 320x). Thus, it is not surprising to see Deuteronomy 6:5 and Leviticus 19:18 working together (Mk 12:28–34). Because God loves us, we ought to love one another—a command that is repeated in the New Testament (Ro 13:9; Gal 5:14; Jas 2:8, etc.). But Jesus even goes further, something unknown in this era. He calls us to love our enemies as well (Mt 5:43–48).

The use of *agapē* may have originated as an expression of self-giving love, where its object has no inherent attractiveness (cf. *eros*). But this is uncertain. Nevertheless, if we were to examine the New Testament standing within a Roman religious context, the repeated use of "love" would absolutely stand out. The New Testament had elevated love to be a premier feature of religious and moral life, and it quickly became known as a distinguishing mark of followers of Jesus.

**5:7-10** *You were running a good race.* Paul now turns to an athletic metaphor from the racetrack: "You were running well; who cut you off?" (au. trans.). (Regarding running, see also comments on 2:2.) The picture is of a runner whose pace has been broken by an unjust competitor (the NIV translation "cut in on you" is not referring to circumcision but see 5:12). This is his plea, now revisited from 4:12 and 5:1. The form of this distraction is these false teachers, the Judaizers, who keep them from the truth, and their tactic is persuasion (5:8), compelling them to run in a different direction. If they have followed Paul's argument thus far, they should recognize that this teaching is not from God.

*A little yeast.* Paul is likely using a well-known proverb (also in 1 Co 5:6) that speaks to how one bad influence can yield widespread destructive results. Yeast is an edible fungus that grows throughout the world, and when an active source is placed in the dough, it will permeate the dough and make it rise. Here Paul imagines that the Galatian church is the dough—and these teachers are the yeast whose influence must be stopped before the entire batch is ruined.

### Galatians 5:9 Through Old Testament Eyes: Yeast

Yeast (or leaven) was common throughout the ancient world. Its first use extends back to about 4000 BC, and it was well-known for making bread, beer, and mead. As any baker knows, it takes little to ferment a surprisingly large amount of dough. In the Old Testament, it appears prominently in the Passover story, when all yeast had to be removed from the Israelite homes before the feast so that only "unleavened" bread was eaten (Ex 12:14–20). The reason for this instruction was that families needed to be ready to leave Egypt on a moment's notice, and leavened bread took time to rise. They might not be able to delay their departure for that (Ex 12:11, 33–34, 39).

Yeast also became a metaphor (Mt 13:33), often negative, for influences or corruptions that can spread like yeast "invades" the dough. Thus, in 1 Corinthians 5:7–9 Paul tells the Corinthians to sweep out the old leaven (yeast) of evil.

*Take no other view.* Paul continues to plead with the Galatians to stay the course and ignore those who distract (also 1:7). The root idea of this verb (Gk, *tarassō*) is to stir something up (Jn 5:4) or to cause commotion, fear, or crisis. It is a strong word for the emotional experience in Galatia. Moreover, he is persuaded that these teachers will come under judgment (Gal 5:10) for what they are doing.

**5:11–12** *The offense of the cross.* It is impossible to determine from the context what accusations may have come against Paul in 5:11. It is also impossible to imagine from his writings that he promoted circumcision. Scholars offer many hypotheses, but two stand out: (a) Perhaps some knew from his pre-conversion activity that he was a zealot for Jewish practice, and his opponents see his preaching then as disqualifying his critical views now or (b) more likely Paul is being criticized because in certain Jewish-Christian contexts, he was relaxed about circumcision, though in 1 Corinthians 7:18 he did not call for the removal of circumcision. In Acts 21:17–26, we hear a rumor that Paul forbids Jews to circumcise their sons. To prove his fidelity to the law, James asks Paul to take new Jewish converts to Christ to the temple to adhere to traditions (vows, purification). In addition, Paul had Timothy circumcised (Ac 16:3) in Lystra, not far from Galatia. Perhaps this story is circulating. Clearly Paul is willing to adapt to the cultural expectations of any setting he is in (1 Co 9:20), and in Jewish settings he could view circumcision as a cultural or traditional affair. But even in 1 Corinthians 7:19 he affirms, as he does in Galatians and Romans, that circumcision counts for little.

## Going Deeper: Cruciformity (Gal 5:11)

The *idea* of the cross is something unique to Christianity. Paul found it difficult to explain since crucifixion was so abhorrent to the Roman way of thinking. We have very few accounts of crucifixion in the Roman world because no one wanted to describe it. Paul knew this. In 1 Corinthians 1:18, he admits what the Corinthians already knew: the cross was idiocy or folly or stupidity (Gk, *mōria*) to those who were the thought-leaders of Paul's day. In contrast to the wisdom of his world, Paul says he preached the crucifixion of Jesus (1 Co 1:23), which any Greek would find unsophisticated and an example of an impoverished religion.

But Paul found this offense not only in the content of the gospel but in the content of his life. He openly spoke about how the cross was a self-defining marker for how he lived. He can say that he has been crucified with Christ (Gal 2:20) and his life bears the marks of loss (Gal 6:17).

Christians recently have embraced the term "cruciformity" to express this life of voluntary loss. In 2021 Michael Gorman's celebrated book, *Cruciformity: Paul's Narrative Spirituality of the Cross*, changed our conversation and introduced new vocabulary. He calls it a "spirituality of the cross" that embraces "loss and descent" as features of how Paul sees spiritual maturity.

This decision *for cruciformity* has come clearest to me through the students I have known. When I meet them years later, I see what decisions they have made. One brilliant student I remember was premed in our college, and after medical school, he joined a large practice in Minnesota. He was quickly very successful. I was speaking at a conference in Minnesota fifteen years after he began working. And one afternoon, there he was—greeting me, introducing me to his wife and young children, and asking if we could meet up late that night.

When we did, within minutes, I knew he was depressed. He didn't like anything about his life. But it came down to this: His partners in the practice wanted to raise their rates and begin taking care of fewer and fewer poor people. Their goal was to meet a higher target income for each physician. He already felt he was paid generously, but his wife wasn't on his side: she wanted "a house on the lake," a euphemism everyone in the Midwest understands.

I asked him why he entered medicine in the first place. He referred to his internship in downtown Chicago, where he volunteered serving in clinics that cared for the poor. He felt so alive then. This was why he was a doctor: to heal the needy in the name of Christ. "But what would it cost you to return to your original vision?" I asked.

"Financially?" he asked.

"In every way," I answered.

He said it was like choosing a cross, and it might kill him.

The conversation reminded me of Matthew 16:25 where Jesus says, "For whoever wants to save their life will lose it, but whoever loses their life for me will find it."

*Why am I still being persecuted?* Paul's persecution by these Judaizers persisted *because* he continued to preach a gospel of faith and promise and criticized religious legal practices on theological grounds. To do otherwise was to empty the cross of its dramatic power. The scandal of the cross was not simply a cultural embarrassment (1 Co 1:23), it also scandalized the instincts of a religious perspective promoting religious merit or performance. The Greek, *skandalon*, refers to something that trips you up or make you stumble (Ro 11:9). And this is precisely what the cross is doing to teachers from Jerusalem.

*Those agitators.* This new term for Paul's opponents has a legacy of referring to militants or those leading uprisings (Ac 21:38). But his next words are even more forceful. He wishes that those who promote circumcision would go further—and make themselves eunuchs. He uses the middle voice ("and make eunuchs of themselves").[10] In the Old Testament, eunuchs were prohibited from the assembly of God's people (Lev 21:17–20; Dt 23:1) and widely despised. Paul then is making an ironic point: those who would "cut off" Gentiles now should "let slip the knife" and so cut themselves off.

In Galatia we know of the cult of Cybele, where self-castration was practiced. Rabbis were so opposed to it that they deemed it worthy of exclusion from the covenant community. Likewise both Greeks and Romans wrote against it in the strongest language. Paul's words are as surprising as they are severe and indicate the depth of his anger about what he sees in Galatia.

**5:13–15** *Called to be free.* Paul has now completed the major force of his argument against the law and circumcision. But he is aware that if he sets aside the law as a guide for righteous living and promotes the Spirit's guidance, his critics may well say that the absence of law will promote lawlessness. Paul is keenly aware of this charge, and here he discusses it directly. Galatians 5:13–15 also provides an introduction to 5:16–26. The harsh lines drawn in the preceding chapters run the risk of dividing the body in Galatia. And so the exhortation to employ freedom judiciously is not simply a call to personal righteousness (though this is important) but a call to live together in unity. Given the sharp boundaries drawn between Jew and Gentile—and now between Gentile Christians and Jewish Christians—Paul sees the call to unity as primary.

*Do not use your freedom to indulge the flesh.* Paul uses the term *flesh* in two ways. On the one hand, it is a common description of our bodily life. Thus in 1:16 he writes about the time after his conversion, "I did not confer with flesh and blood" (lit.). This use does not mean that our bodies (our flesh) is intrinsically evil.

On the other hand, he also uses "flesh" to refer to our human condition of sin. "After beginning by means of the Spirit, are you now trying to finish by means of the flesh?" (3:3; Ro 7:5, 18). In later verses (Gal 5:16–17), he will show that what is on his mind is a state of being intrinsic to human life—namely, sin (again, not that our bodies themselves are evil).[11] Sin is not just something we are inclined to indulge; it is central to who we are (Ro 7:14–20). And it is only the Spirit that can put this typical life in reverse. In Galatia, the church risks a regression and descent into this degradation (sin). The return to the common life of the world, void of the Spirit's leading, results in disagreements and even violent conflicts (Gal 5:15). The reverse posture is one where freedom leads to love, humility, and service (5:14).

*Love your neighbor.* Earlier Paul cited Deuteronomy 27:26 (Gal 3:10) with its dire description of human inability. Now Paul cites Leviticus 19:18 as the essence of what it means to fulfill the law: love now empowered by the gospel will satisfy what the law desired. While in Galatians 3:10 Paul was critical of any who participated fully in the works of the law, now 5:14 explains why for Paul the law still holds prominence. It is fulfilled in the gospel, which completes what the law sought. For Paul, embracing the gospel, receiving the Spirit, and living a life transformed by love is the truest fulfillment of the Torah. Therefore, if the Jewish-Christian missionaries wish to employ the law, then they too must acknowledge that love is at the heart of what the law promotes.

## Galatians 5:14 Through Old Testament Eyes: Leviticus 19:18

Leviticus 19 belongs to the Holiness Code of Israel (Lev 17–26), which is preceded by rules for sacrifice (Lev 1–7), for priestly ordination (Lev 8–10), for purity (Lev 11–15), and the Day of Atonement (Lev 16). The Holiness Code is a lengthy section that governs the conduct (or ethics) of Israel as it crafts a covenant community in harmony with God's law. Rules for sex (Lev 18) and conduct during festivals (Lev 23) are covered.

Chapter 19 is a collection of personal rules that often mirrors the Ten Commandments (Ex 20:2–6; Dt 5:6–10) and creatively applies them to practical settings. Within its list, verses 11–18 govern personal conduct and call for justice and charity in social contexts. Here the code refers to lying, deception, theft—even exploitation of non-Israelites.

But at the root of these commands, Leviticus 19:17–18 lays out a rule for charity and love that is set apart from attitudes of revenge, enmity, and grudges (19:18) and offers the central rule that undergirds them all: *You shall love your neighbor as yourself.* The basis for this appears at the end of the chapter (19:33–37). Because Israel had seen mistreatment in Egypt (19:34), it should understand what it means to suffer from discrimination and loss. Therefore, this love described in 19:18 must include the "stranger" (RSV) or "alien" (NRSVue) or "foreigner" (NIV). Those living outside Israel's covenant deserved the same treatment as those living within. To underscore the seriousness of this, most of these commands end with a strong, final pronouncement, "I am the LORD your God," which, like Leviticus 19:34, recalls the God "who brought you out of" Egypt (Ex 6:7; 20:2). This is who God is and this is what he wants.

In the New Testament, Leviticus 19:18 is the most cited text from the first five books of the Old Testament (the Pentateuch or Torah): "Love your neighbor as yourself." In Leviticus this is the summary statement outlining how Israel must integrate a moral life within its ritual ceremonies. This love command is used by Paul here in Galatians 5:14 but also in Romans 13:9, where Paul lists some of the Ten Commandments and sums them up: "whatever other command there may be, [they] are summed up in this one command: 'Love your neighbor as yourself.'" James calls this "the royal law" (2:8).

Many scholars believe that this regular use of Leviticus 19:18 was central to Jesus and soon became a repeated phrase among his followers. When asked about the primary commandments by a lawyer, Jesus said, "'Love the Lord your God with all your heart and with all your soul and with all your mind.' This is the first and greatest commandment. And the second is like it: 'Love your neighbor as yourself.' All the Law and the Prophets hang on these two commandments" (Mt 22:37–40; also Mk 12:28–31; Lk 10:27). Love is also a central theme in the gospel and letters of John (Jn 15:12; 1 Jn 3:11). It was not uncommon in Judaism to inquire about the essence of the law. For many, Leviticus 19:18 summed up the whole law.[12]

## Going Deeper: Love Your Neighbor (Gal 5:14)

The beautiful and hard command of Leviticus 19:18 no doubt became a profound memory of Jesus' ministry and something that was repeated by the teachers of the early church. But it is a difficult command.

Andrew DeCort is a former student of mine who, after earning a PhD in ethics from the University of Chicago, began his career in Ethiopia. He worked there for years in reconciliation efforts. This led to invitations to speak throughout the world. But as he called for reconciliation based on Leviticus 19:18, factions in Ethiopia threatened to kill him and ultimately forced him to leave, interrupting his career there. Today he has online classes and a remarkable newsletter that talks about neighbor-love in countless world settings. You can sign up for it at andrew-decort.com. (You can also find out about the neighbor-love global movement at www. nlglobal.org.)

Ethiopians aren't the only ones who find this call to love others a challenge. When I take students to Israel, I always want them to meet with local living communities—Jews and Arabs—to hear them out and put a face on the struggles there. A few years ago I had thirty students at a large Jewish settlement south of Bethlehem where the rabbi of the synagogue hosted us warmly. He spoke for a half hour and then asked for questions. That is when it happened. One of my students cited Leviticus 19:18 and asked, "Is the Palestinian your neighbor?" It was one of those moments where I (as the professor) stopped breathing. The room went silent.

But the rabbi's answer was remarkable, and I will never forget it. "The Palestinian is not my neighbor. Leviticus 19:18 only tells me to love Jewish neighbors." The students were stunned and went silent, and I could tell that they, like Paul, wanted to universalize this commandment to include all neighbors.

This is the difficulty, however: We might be quick to criticize the rabbi for narrowing the scope of love rather than expanding it. But isn't it true that we would all prefer to narrow the love we offer to those who share our ethnicity or nationality? Wouldn't we rather socialize with only those those who share our particular theological beliefs, political preferences, or cultural values and practices? We may not exclude Jews or Palestinians, but we need to ask: Who do we marginalize? Who do we think doesn't deserve our aid? Who are those we think of as enemies? And what excuses do we easily make for not showing the love Jesus called for?

**5:16–18** *Walk by the Spirit.* Freedom in Christ does not mean freedom to do whatever we want (5:17). It does not mean that we can ignore moral obligations or duties to our communities. For Paul there is no such thing as freedom in this sense (see "Going Deeper: Freedom [Gal 5]"). Human life is enslaved by inevitable sin. The gospel does not promise a life emancipated from all constraints; it instead offers to destroy the slavery of sin and replace it with a new master: Christ.

Paul explains this carefully in Romans 6:15–23, where the slave analogy is explicit. The gospel promises that our old slavery to sin will be replaced with a new slavery to righteousness (Ro 6:18). The human condition is so dire that without the intervention of God, we will revert to our sinful state (the flesh). Therefore, freedom "to be my best self" without God does not exist. True freedom comes when our lives are conformed to the design of our creator. It is at this moment that we become all that we were meant to be. And when we do this, we "fulfill" the law of Christ (Gal 6:2).

This sets up for Paul a direct conflict between the Spirit and the flesh (5:17–18). They are at complete odds because the flesh (our innate human nature, not our physical bodies) pursues the interests of sin while the Spirit pursues the things of God (see comment on "indulge the flesh" at 5:13). The struggle of human life and possibility is not a struggle between our wills and the power of sin. This is a struggle that will fail. The struggle is between our innate sin and the power of God's Spirit, which empowers us and enables us to be fully human for the first time. We are creatures dependent on our creator, and sin is ultimately a movement away from that dependence. Our restoration is a return to this dependence. The gospel, in this sense, is a reclamation project. No concept could be further from a modern notion of freedom.

But notice how Paul says in 5:16 that we must not "gratify" the desires of the flesh. This word (Gk, *teleō*) refers to the completion or fulfillment (Gk, *telos*) of something, giving a thing what it really wants. This connects with Paul's use of "walk" at the beginning of 5:16. The result of life in the Spirit is a matter of walking (Ps 1:1—a very Jewish formulation), choosing where your feet take you—and your walking always has a destination (*telos*). For believers, Paul sees real moral agency here. We are not incapacitated *if we are living in Christ*. We participate in the active defeat of sin only with the power of the Spirit. In Romans 6:19, he refers to "offering yourselves" to sin. So now we see that, while through the gospel God reclaims and restores us, we still play a role in sin's defeat.

And the law (Gal 5:18)? As Paul wrote in 3:23–25, the law served as a custodian or guardian, the law provided constraints on our sinful instincts *until* faith was revealed (3:23). Thus Paul imagines a new life, a Spirit-directed life, that is no longer "under the law" (that is, the law of Moses; 5:18) because this new life is far superior.

**5:19–21** *The acts of the flesh.* Paul now invites a comparison. He lists fifteen features of unrestored human life, life lived "in the flesh," that would be recognizable ("obvious," 5:19) to any ancient (Ro 1:18–21) or modern reader. He begins his list with three sexual sins and follows this with two items common to pagan society (idolatry, witchcraft). Then follows eight descriptions of a riven society, broken by anger and conflict. The list ends with two terms (drunkenness, orgies) that might describe the social life accompanying such living.[13] It is the cumulative effect of this list that is important. Such a society indulging in this would be "an unhappy and dangerous place."[14] Together these things represent the "works of the flesh" (5:19 ESV, NET, NRSVue; "acts of the flesh" NIV), and this is probably an echo of "works of the law" (2:16; 3:2, 5, 10). Of course, Jews and Jewish-Christians would have found this list reprehensible as well. But Paul is unrelenting in contrasting what it can mean when someone steps outside the realm of the gospel and into the realm of the flesh (which, without the Spirit, is precisely where those living under the law live).[15] This would be a world of unrestrained sin.

**5:22-23** *The fruit of the Spirit.* Paul next provides another list, this time a virtue list[16] (and one of his most celebrated) describing the outworkings of a life shaped by the Spirit. The metaphor of fruit was widespread in antiquity, both among Jews and Romans, in ethical instruction.

## Galatians 5:22 Through Old Testament Eyes: Fruitfulness

In the Old Testament, abundant fruit attests to God's creativity and lavishness (Ge 1:11–12; 29). In the context of redemption and liberation from slavery, the Promised Land is portrayed as exceedingly fruitful (Ex 3:8; Nu 13:26–27; Dt 8:8; Ne 9:25). While God offered this freely to his people without any preconditions, continued fruitfulness was linked to obedience (Lev 25:18–19; Dt 28:1–11; 30:1–10). Indeed, disobedience leads to judgment (Jer 4:26).

Metaphorical uses of fruitfulness are also abundant. Israel is often compared to a vineyard that God cultivates (Ps 80:8–9; Isa 5:1–7), hoping for fruitfulness (Isa 27:2–3) but sadly at times finding only bad fruit (Isa 5:2–4). In addition, a blessed individual, one who walks in God's ways, is fruitful (Ps 1:1–3; 72:3; 92:12–15; Pr 11:30; Isa 32:17; Jer 17:7–8; 31:27; Hos 2:21–23), whereas the wicked bear bad fruit (Ps 1:4; Jer 2:21; 6:19; Hos 10:13).[17]

Likewise, Paul's use of this image evokes the picture of the natural produce of a vital and healthy tree: love, joy, peace, forbearance, kindness, goodness, faithfulness, gentleness, and self-control. The list provides a portrait of serenity, tolerance, charity, and self-discipline that any ancient or modern reader would admire.

But it also signals the dynamic on Paul's mind. The flesh is not set against *human effort* (it controls human capacity) but is juxtaposed to the Spirit. God's Spirit grounds Paul's hope for a renewed life. The Spirit produces fruit (while the flesh requires work appropriate to its kind). Note that here the term (fruit) is singular. The entire array comes together in a Spirit-directed life (which avoids any talk of specializing in one virtue while leaving others behind).

There are five well-known virtue lists in the New Testament (2 Co 6:6; Gal 5:22–23; 1 Ti 4:12; 6:11; 2 Ti 2:22; 2 Pe 1:5–7). Many of these virtues are repeated, but one is constant throughout: love, which recalls Paul's use of Leviticus 18:19 in Galatians 5:14. This list, as Paul will say in 6:2, comprises the "law of Christ," belonging to those who "belong to Christ Jesus" (5:24;

also 3:29), evoking again the idea that Christian freedom lives under a new headship or mandate (having left the mandate of the flesh behind). Christian freedom *is freedom* because it produces the virtues of Jesus untethered to the demands of sin.

## Going Deeper: The Fruit of the Spirit (Gal 5:22–26)

Paul never imagined Christian discipleship as a set of moral requirements imposed by the Bible or the church. Despite his moral exhortations, this was not the keystone to the arch.

I taught for twenty-five years at one of the leading evangelical colleges in America. I was amazed at how many of these young college students, usually formed in strong churches and believing families, understood what discipleship was: a long-haul effort to discipline themselves so that they would look like Jesus. And for many of them, the failure to do this successfully put their salvation in jeopardy. Some failed, and the failure led to the collapse of their faith.

Paul understands that this sort of effort will fail (Ro 7:15). Christian life begins with Christian birth, and this is discovered within the generous and gracious gifts of God. *By grace we have been saved* (Eph 2:5, 8). But it leads to a new creation (Gal 6:15), a transformation, a resurrection if you will, which means we evolve into something else. However, generating the moral energy to bring about this change does not belong to us. Transformation begins with God, whose Spirit continues our rebirth and sustains our transformation. It is through our participation with the Spirit that we become like Jesus. Thus, if Galatians 5:22–23 becomes a checklist or assignment of Christian virtue, we have already failed.

This is why Paul quite intentionally refers to these transformational features of our discipleship as "fruit." Fruit grows from a healthy tree. A tree never tries to grow fruit; rather, the fruit is simply a by-product of its flourishing life. For us, fruit is a by-product of a Spirit-directed life. But once we mature, once we recognize this growth, we begin to have real agency. Our *new-creation-in-process* life begins to grow stronger, and we experience capacities we never before imagined. We can walk in the Spirit (Ro 8:4); we can yield ourselves to Christ (Ro 6:16); we can "work out" or work through our salvation (Php 2:12) so that we begin producing more and more fruit.

The second error is to itemize this fruit. It becomes a checklist so that we find that, while we might be successful at self-control, we can take a pass on patience. Galatians 5:22–23 is not a scorecard. It is a composite picture of what the Christ-shaped life looks like. Paul instead imagines something truly supernatural. "It is no longer I who live, but it is Christ who lives in me" (Gal 2:20 NRSVue). Or in Colossians he refers to "Christ in you," which is the hope of glory (1:27). This means that all of Jesus will emerge, and a mature discipleship will begin to exhibit the entirety of Jesus' resurrection in us.

**5:24** *Crucified the flesh.* Paul now closes off his argument by echoing 5:16. But here he uses language that was not only peculiar but offensive to any Roman reader. Crucifixion was never used as a metaphor because of its ugliness and shame.[18] But Christians embraced it (due to Jesus' crucifixion) and made it a tool in their moral arguments. Thus Paul can say "I have been crucified" (Gal 2:20) and "the world has been crucified to me" (6:14). It is hard to underestimate the surprise this would evoke in an ancient reader. But this is what Paul promotes. *As Jesus was crucified on the cross, so too should our flesh be crucified if we belong to Christ.* "Crucified" is in the Greek aorist tense, referring to a singular action. This is what happens when a person enters into Christ and is filled by the Spirit. The flesh is crucified once and for all. This is the activity played out in Romans 7. Coming under the ownership of Christ means the death of something left behind.

*Passions and desires.* In Galatians 5:19–20, Paul listed the activities of the flesh. But here we see that what must be crucified is the emotional enticement that precedes these activities. The works of the flesh have power because they play on desires and emotions that falsely offer satisfaction.

**5:25–26** *Keep in step with the Spirit.* These verses are a preface to what is coming in chapter six, since there is a natural division between 5:24 and 5:25. Since Paul has made his case that the Christian life is defined within the context of gift/grace, faith, and the Spirit, he now wants to apply these principles, particularly the principle of love, to life in the church. Living by (keeping in step with) the Spirit echoes "walk by the Spirit" in 5:16 and could be an all-encompassing portrait of what it means to live in Christ. The second verb, "let us keep in step with the Spirit" ("let us walk" RSV; "let us also be guided" NRSVue; "let us keep in step" ESV), is not the same as walking. The verb (Gk, *stoicheō*) refers to being in alignment, walking in formation, marching, or, if used metaphorically, being in agreement. The NIV "keep in step" captures the concept well. The Spirit is not simply something to possess or a marker to show Christian identity. The Spirit is active and moving, someone to follow and imitate. The Spirit is to be shadowed in our own lives.

*Conceited, provoking, and envying.* In Galatia, the fruit of the Spirit should be evidenced in how Christians treat one another. If 5:15 is any indication (biting and devouring), they are not doing well in this. *Conceit* in Greek is a compound adjective ("empty glory" or pursuing vanity), and this has led to the Galatians provoking each other (or to challenge or irritate each other, as in an athletic match or combat) and envying each other. Paul's insights here are apt, particularly in a community that is closely defining what it means to be a true believer. Especially where there is talk about the Spirit, competition and elitism is bound to erupt. This would be true not only of the Judaizers, for whom a more rule-driven view of the faith operated, but also of Paul's followers, who might view themselves as having a unique gifting by the Spirit. Both positions can give birth to division.[19]

# GALATIANS 6

*Paul turns now to practical issues in the church* (begun in 5:25), and this is similar to how he ends many of his letters with advice and exhortations. But this is not to say that ethics and theology are separated in Paul's mind. How we live is connected to what we believe. Thus, Paul's emphasis on the transformational work of the Spirit in Galatians 5 spills naturally into directions for personal conduct. At the center of Paul's thinking is a life that is not known for its adherence to religious markers but for being transformed by the Spirit. Galatians 6:15 might summarize this entire section: "Neither circumcision nor uncircumcision means anything; what counts is the new creation." He assumes that when this new creation emerges in us, the "law of Christ" (6:2) is fulfilled.

## Going Deeper: The Law of Christ (Gal 6:1–2)

We often have difficulty imagining what Christ asks of us. For some, our discipleship is a matter of tradition. We have inherited a way of living—cultural habits—and these define us (and our faith). For others, discipleship is linked to a decision made years ago where we "accepted Christ," and this decision secured our salvation and defines us occasionally well, sometimes poorly.

When Paul writes in Galatians 6:2 about the "law of Christ," he is thinking like a Jew for whom such language is not only comfortable but loved. Paul would never imagine that discipleship is a matter of tradition or a once-for-all decision. Discipleship means coming under the rule (law or *nomos*, can mean "rule") of Jesus. It means a lifelong keeping-in-step with his commands. For Paul, freedom is not about doing as we wish.

Paul never believed in that sort of freedom. When left on our own, we become our worst possible selves.

Paul imagines freedom from something (the flesh, sin) and new subordination to Christ. We are freed from one master (Ro 6:17) but now are owned *as slaves* to another, to whom we are obedient (Ro 6:16). Freedom from the law is never traded for absolute freedom (I do not have the capacity to manage that); but freedom from the law is traded for the headship or mastery of Christ *in whom* I can become what I've always truly wanted to be. Ironically, genuine freedom comes on the other side of a new slavery; freedom comes when I yield myself to the rule of Christ and am then set free to become who I desire to be.

**6:1-2** *Brothers and sisters.* See comments on 1:2.

*If someone is caught in a sin.* It is striking that in a letter exhibiting more combative rhetoric than any of Paul's other letters, these disagreements do not exclude our duty to show compassionate care for one another. When factional conflict has broken out, Paul may be exhorting the entire church, and particularly those whose lives and conduct are marked by the Spirit. The person who is "caught" in any type of trespass (the word in Gk refers to a slip or to stumble or being led astray) is someone who has been surprised by the discovery of their sin (or surprised that they are found out). This is the full force of the Greek term behind "caught" (*prolambanō*) in the verse. It might refer to a sin that someone is unaware of, or it might refer to a sin that is concealed.[1] While the sin is not mentioned, the list given in 5:19–21 might be on his mind.

But while this discovery might be cause for outrage, Paul sees the community's response as a test of spiritual maturity. This is what it means to live the Spirit-transformed life that he has called for. The aim is the sinner's restoration (not judgment), and this is to be done in a "spirit of gentleness" (NRSVue). The term "gentle" here (Gk, *prautēs*) was used for taming something, such as a wild beast. More commonly it denoted a calm and friendly demeanor, someone who is not reactive.

*Burdens.* The term (Gk, *baros*) had a wide use, and it could be any weight someone carried. Its application was flexible: the weight could be finances, health, suffering (Mt 20:12), or the burden of the law (Mt 11:29–30). Paul can even use it to refer to the "weight of glory" promised to believers (2 Co 4:17 ESV, NASB; see also Ro 8:18). Here the idea is a difficulty borne by a fellow believer—a difficulty that calls for help.

*The law of Christ.* Paul thought of himself as living under Christ's law (1 Co 9:21), and this is understandable given his Jewish background and vocabulary. He could compare this to those Jews who lived "under the law" (1 Co 9:20). But what could Paul's use of this unusual term mean? Certainly, he did not see the commands of Christ as the Judaizers saw the law of Moses. "Law" here can also be translated "rule," and this decreases the confusion. Paul lived under the "rule of Christ."

No doubt this thinking harks back to memory within the church of Jesus and how he interpreted the law. But more, how Jesus viewed life *was utterly different*. Thus in Galatians 5:14 ("love your neighbor") Paul has Jesus in mind.[2] In carrying burdens, Paul may well be thinking of the *example of Christ*, which means loving another even if it means loss.[3] In 1 Peter 5:7 (quoting Ps 55:22), we are told to give our burdens to God to bear them for us: this exhortation, then, is a call to reciprocating burden-bearing *as God* has done. The true north of Paul's moral compass, then, is the love command elevated by Jesus and now offered as a means of fulfilling the Old Testament law (Gal 5:14a).

**6:3-5** *They deceive themselves.* The second problem is with someone who is overly confident in their view of themselves (which may have fueled the conflict in Galatia).[4] In contrast with the spirit of gentleness in 6:1-2, this likely refers to spiritual pride, which does not pursue the virtues of 6:1-2. Burton describes this well, "Conceiving ourselves to have no faults, we have no sympathy with those who have faults and refuse to make their shortcoming any concern of ours."[5] The result is self-deception. This verb (Gk, *phrenapataō*) comes from the root for deception (*apataō*), for leading someone astray or to deceive. Its prefix (*phren*) originally meant the abdomen (the seat of emotion, thought, self), and so it intensifies Paul's meaning: this is to lead one's mind astray, to be a victim of self-deception.

The solution is courageous self-examination (6:4; 1 Co 3:13; 1 Pe 1:7). But the effort is not purely "self-awareness." It is testing our work (in Gk, *ergon* "work" is moved to the front of the sentence for emphasis). Paul's interest is not in enlightenment but in scrupulous honesty about our behavior.

*Take pride.* Galatians 6:4 could be translated as "then they can boast." Paul is not giving license to boasting, for he sees this in a negative light (Ro 3:27; 1 Co 1:29; 2 Co 5:12). This verse connects to Galatians 6:3 and the person who deceives himself. Self-examination should lead to humility and an awareness of sin. Once this is done, we might have new *confidence* in our conduct, thanks to our discernment. The problem is the examination of others (6:4b—comparing ourselves to someone else), which leads to criticism and judgment so typical of those who have inflated self-assessments.

*Carry their own load.* The load in 6:5 echoes the burdens of 6:2 with a different nuance. Here Paul uses a different word, meaning "the things we carry" in our ordinary lives. He is underscoring the personal responsibility each has to be aware of our routine conduct. The discerning community, we might say, understands the difference between personal responsibilities each of us must bear and the overwhelming burdens carried by others who need our help.

**6:6** *Share all good things.* This theme of generosity and sharing in another's needs continues in 6:6, while doing good (6:10) will be the conclusion of all that is said in 6:6–9. In this case, Paul exhorts the community to share liberally with those who are instructing them. This opens a number of ideas.

First, at this early stage we see the development of recognized teachers in Galatia as they had at Corinth (1 Co 12:8). And they are to share "all good things" with such teachers, which easily means material support (food, lodging, money). Even though Paul maintained a trade, still, he could expect support from his churches (1 Co 9:11–12; 1 Ti 5:17–18). But note that the leading word here is "share," and not "pay."[6] This is typical for how the early church viewed its life (Ac 2:43–47). The support for these teachers was not a debt but a social obligation springing from the character of their community.

Second, these teachers were likely taught by Paul and endorsed by him, which made them special opponents of the Judaizers from Jerusalem. If targeted, they would require even more support. But this instruction fits under the same umbrella as we saw in 6:2. Here we have a vision of a community that is known for its generosity and mutual support of one another. In such a community, the financial burdens of pastors and teachers would not be overlooked.

**6:7** *Do not be deceived.* In 6:3 Paul already discussed self-deception, and now, in 6:7, he does it with more severity. The verb form itself (Gk, *planasthe*) can either be passive (NIV, "do not be deceived"), or it can be a middle voice (do not deceive yourselves). The latter is best, given what we have in 6:3. Paul's target is those who exploit their newfound freedom in Christ and assume that God will not know the difference between a Spirit-freed life and occasional indulgences of the flesh. He will. Ultimately God sees "in secret" (Mt 6:4–18). In the long term, then, the spiritual choices we make will bear fruit for better or worse, implying that, in the end, God will judge those choices (1 Co 3:13–15).

*A man reaps what he sows.* Paul references an Old Testament motif here that would be familiar to a primarily agrarian society.

> As I have observed, those who plow evil
> > and those who sow trouble reap it. (Job 4:8)
> A wicked person earns deceptive wages,
> > but the one who sows righteousness reaps a sure reward. (Pr 11:18)
> Whoever sows injustice reaps calamity,
> > and the rod they wield in fury will be broken. (Pr 22:8)

> Sow righteousness for yourselves,
> > reap the fruit of unfailing love. . . .
> But you have planted wickedness,
> > you have reaped evil. (Hos 10:12–13)

Our actions have consequences; therefore, we need to consider them seriously. Evil deeds tend to result in wicked outcomes. From good works come blessing. As is the case with proverbs, these are wise sayings, not hard-and-fast rules (see Ps 126:4–6; Mic 6:14–15). Except for the ultimate judgment that God brings, it is a general principle in this life of how the world works.

**6:8–9** *Sows to please their flesh.* Paul continues the image of reaping and sowing. The temptation is for believers, even those who have long lived within Christ's grace, to regress and indulge "the flesh" (those impulses to sin that are native to who we are). This is a further probing of self-deception (6:3, 7), and, simply put, it describes Christians who disregard the importance of their own sin. This leads to decay (NIV, "destruction"). The word *decay* (Gk, *phthora*) in secular Greek had numerous meanings and can also be used for death or even shipwreck (1 Co 3:17; Rev 8:9). This behavior destroys and corrupts (shipwrecks!) the community Paul is trying to save in Galatia. The mutual generosity and kindness, the burden-sharing and self-restraint, now could be lost by those who are no longer keeping in step with the Spirit (Gal 5:16).

*We will reap a harvest.* Paul now focuses the agricultural metaphor (6:7–8) on the harvest itself (6:9; 2 Co 9:6–10). After planting and tending, the outcome of these labors takes time. Despite our fatigue or impatience, there will be a harvest. Paul wants the Galatians to take the long view and not succumb to their weariness. This is about investment. We cannot expect that exhibiting the fruit of the Spirit will necessarily have immediate results. But an investment over time, a long faithfulness in the same direction, will change our communities. Galatians 6:8 explores the reverse: an indulgence in the flesh likewise corrupts the future and destroys our communities. An investment in health and goodness will bring life. When Paul refers to the harvest, however, he also has in mind the judgment that will unmask who we truly are and how we have truly contributed.

**6:10** *Let us do good.* What is the present time (Gk, *kairos*; NIV: "opportunity") before us? It is the present, complete with its imperfections and conflicts. It is this time when we demonstrate who we really are. The fruit of the Spirit grows easily in a time of tranquility and prosperity; but the test of virtue is how they operate under duress.

Paul here sees two assignments. First, believers should (literally) "do good things for all people." Because he refers to the church in 6:10b, this first assignment means that the world outside the church also deserves the goodness growing within the church. This undoubtedly contributes to the church's witness in the world. The gospel is not simply to be proclaimed; it is to be exhibited and lived. This recalls the apocryphal saying attributed to St. Francis of Assisi, "Preach the gospel at all times, and if necessary, use words."

Second, Paul underscores the importance of the family (or "household"; Gk, *oikos*) of believers who deserve the same, if not more (NIV, "especially"). Given the social setting of these churches in the Roman Empire, many Christians likely lost some of their networks of support because of their faith. This generous sharing was a feature certainly of the earliest Christians who met in houses (Gk, *oikoi*, as here) and likely formed household gatherings. These were churches (Gk, *ekklēsiai*), but this could also literally mean *gatherings* as in "household gatherings" (Ro 16:5; 1 Co 16:19; Col 4:15; Phm 2). They were the family of God (Eph 2:19; 1 Ti 3:15; Heb 3:5–6). In addition, Paul used the language of brother (and sister) for believers twenty-nine times.

**6:11** *Large letters.* Paul used professional scribes, and in Romans 16:22, we even have one scribe's name (Tertius). This was a convention in antiquity to give a manuscript a professional quality that would evoke the respect desired. Today we understand the value of a well-designed and printed letter. Paul's habit seems to have been ending his letters with his personal handwritten note (1 Co 16:21–24; 2 Th 3:17; Col 4:18; cf. Ro 16:17–20). At the end of 2 Thessalonians (3:17) he writes, "I, Paul, write this greeting in my own hand, which is the distinguishing mark in all my letters." In Galatians, he points to his large letters, which almost sounds like an apology since he did not have professional-quality writing skills. Many speculate that Paul may have had a hand injury, or perhaps he was nearsighted (Gal 4:13–15). Or he may be providing a security here against false letters in circulation attributed to him (2 Th 2:2). Others wonder if he writes these notes to emphasize his closing comments. In Galatians 6:12–16, he returns to themes that he doesn't want them to miss: the flesh, circumcision, the law, and so forth.

**6:12–13** *Those who want to impress people.* Here we must imagine Paul scratching out these words roughly with a quill pen (if he were writing on papyrus or vellum) or an iron stylus (if his tablet had a wax surface) while his professional scribe looks on and winces. He begins with an irony. These Judaizers want to put on a "good face" (NIV, "impress people") by means of "the flesh." This idiom was used by athletes, who are stripped down for sports, who wish to do well.[7] But here the showing in the flesh is circumcision, something that both Greek and Romans despised. Thus, these missionaries want to mark "the flesh" of these Galatians, shaming them in their own local Galatian context.[8] The language evokes insincerity and dishonesty.[9]

But as we have seen, "the flesh" bears a double meaning for Paul, including as a theological term for a sinful impulse opposed to God's Spirit (3:3; 4:23, 29; 5:16–19), an outlook Paul has attached to the Judaizers' efforts. The flesh and circumcision create a clever pairing when we see how it fits Paul's polemic.

*The cross of Christ.* In cities like Jerusalem, Jewish Christians were persecuted by fellow Jews who did not think they were obeying Torah. Worse yet, Jewish Christians were fellowshipping with Gentiles (such as here in Galatia). The cross of Christ was a scandal (see comments on 5:11) because in its preaching, Christians like Paul were announcing a way of salvation apart from adherence to the law of Moses. If these agitators did not require Gentile converts to be circumcised, this was proof that they were not Torah-obedient. This then became the basis of their persecution. However, if they can succeed in imposing Torah-obedience on Gentiles, they can return to Jerusalem boasting of their efforts (6:13b).

*Keep the law.* A further critique of these opponents is that they do not keep the law anyway, which makes their promotion of circumcision hypocrisy. It is difficult to know how these Jewish-Christians are failing in Paul's mind. Were they liberal in other matters (just not circumcision), and so when compared to the Pharisees, not fully obedient? Is Paul making a more sweeping observation that all obedience fails to achieve a saving righteousness (Ro 2:12–29)? In Romans, Paul then can say that any such disobedience can dissolve the merits of circumcision (Ro 2:25; Gal 3:21; 5:4). But Paul may also be thinking along the lines of 5:14—neighbor love—which fulfills the law and so satisfies the "law of Christ" (6:2). By this standard, these opponents have disqualified themselves.

**6:14–15** *May I never boast except in the cross.* If the Jerusalem missionaries are eager to boast in their successful promotion of Torah-obedience (6:13), Paul is eager to boast as well—but not in his achievements or what he has accomplished in Galatia. His confidence is anchored to the cross of Christ (Ro 3:27; 5:11; 1 Co 1:31; 15:31; Php 2:16; 3:3). What the missionaries sought to avoid (the cross, Gal 6:12) Paul now wants to elevate.

We often fail to understand here the importance of what Paul has just said. The word *cross* (Lat, *crux*; Gk, *stauros*) was unmentionable in polite Roman society and can be seen in how the Romans avoided using it (see comments on 5:11).[10] But it was an undeniable and paradoxical fact of Christian preaching. And this perhaps unveils more powerfully how Paul has set himself apart from worlds of Torah-obedience and the Roman Empire that shaped him. He now was committed to a righteousness no longer anchored to the law of Moses nor to the values of Rome. Paul had found in Christ a covenant of grace anticipated by Abraham *that was a fuller expression of the purposes of the Old Testament.* His embrace of the cross signaled that Paul had turned a corner; his unflinching commitment to the cross was no doubt as offensive to Romans as it was disturbing to his former Jewish friends. In Philippians 3:8, he can say that *everything* that once gave his life meaning now may be discarded for the sake of knowing this Christ: "I consider everything a loss because of the surpassing worth of knowing Christ Jesus my Lord, for whose sake I have lost all things. I consider them garbage, that I may gain Christ and be found in him, not having a righteousness of my own that comes from the law, but that which is through faith in Christ—the righteousness that comes from God on the basis of faith" (Php 3:8–9).

*The world has been crucified to me.* In this sense, if the cross has been central to Paul's understanding of Jesus Christ, he understands that taking this position of promoting the cross has meant dramatic loss for him. This means that every belief system and all values promoted by the world around him have been canceled. His life has been utterly disrupted, and there was no going back. Not only does this elevate the fact of Jesus' crucifixion in his preaching, but for Paul, the gospel includes elements of our own crucifixion: "I have been crucified with Christ and I no longer live, but Christ lives in me" (2:20). The experience of baptism/belief/Spirit then becomes a baptism into Christ's death (Ro 6:3), a burial with Christ's burial (Ro 6:4) *so that* we can be raised with Christ and become a new creation (6:4).

## Galatians 6:15 Through Old Testament Eyes: New Creation

When Paul refers to a new creation in 6:15, some wonder if he is borrowing concepts from the Hellenistic world. But this is not the case. The Old Testament prophets also looked at the difficult moral and political climate of their day and anticipated an era (an *eschatological* future) when God's creation would begin anew. This is especially true of the book of Isaiah, which can say, "See, I will create new heavens and a new earth. The former things will not be remembered, nor will they come to mind" (65:17). Or similarly, "'As the new heavens and the new earth that I make will endure before me,' declares the LORD, 'so will your name and descendants endure'" (66:22). While throughout the book of Isaiah we hear that judgment will come both on Israel and on the nations, nonetheless, Isaiah climaxes with the plans of hope that God has for both Israel (Isa 62) and the nations (66:18–21). Given that Isaiah celebrates how those from Israel and those from the nations are both united in worship of God, it's not surprising that Paul uses Isaiah's image of new creation to also celebrate how Jews and Gentiles are one in Christ. Isaiah never saw this promise of new creation realized, but the New Testament is announcing that its fulfillment has begun.

N. T. Wright has been a champion of new creation theology in the New Testament and has highlighted how this call in the New Testament is an express fulfillment of what Isaiah promised. The promise of the gospel is not simply the salvation of believers; it is about God's intervention in his creation to inaugurate a new beginning or the re-creation of the world. In Galatians 6:15, Wright compares Paul's list of circumcision, uncircumcision, and new creation with 1 Corinthians 10:32 where the apostle writes "Jews [circumcision], Greeks [uncircumcision] or the church of God." Thus the church is the inauguration of the new creation that is begun in Christ and will be completed at the end of time.[11] The unity of Jew and Greek into a single body, the church, is that new creation.

*A new creation.* For many, Galatians 6:15 is the anticipated climax of the letter. The verse uses a Greek conjunction (*gar*) to link the thought of verses 14 and 15: ". . . and I to the world; *for* neither circumcision nor uncircumcision. . . ." Because Paul will not stand on ritual (circumcision), he has broken with those who promote it *because* ritual no longer matters to him. For Paul, circumcision *of the flesh* is of little value compared to circumcision "of the heart" (Ro 2:28–29).

Paul sees the work of God in the gospel as the transformation—the resurrection—of humanity, a reclaiming of what God had created so that creation can begin anew. This is the new creation, which has truly eschatological features: What religion might promise for the future can now be realized in Christ. As Adam was the first of God's creatures, so now Christ can be compared with Adam—a second Adam whose life-giving Spirit inaugurates a new reality (1 Co 15:45). Stepping into the death and life of Christ is when we put on a new nature (Col 3:10).

**6:16** *Peace and mercy.* The blessing of peace was commonplace in Israel. It represented the Hebrew *shalom* (Nu 6:24–25; Ps 125:5; 128:6), which was used extensively in the Old Testament. It is no surprise that the term appears in the New Testament ninety-two times among Jewish-Christian writers who knew the convention. The combination with mercy was also common. The famous benediction of Aaron in Numbers 6:24–25 includes the blessing of peace but adds mercy in the Greek Old Testament (which is not in the Heb text).

Paul concludes with a blessing, which was customary for letters in this period. While this might be a simple assignment, Paul has written here one of the most controversial verses of his career.

## Galatians 6:16 Through Old Testament Eyes: Shalom—Reprise

See also the sidebar, "Galatians 1:3 Through Old Testament Eyes: Shalom."

Few Hebrew terms are as recognizable to modern readers as *shalom*. The word comes from the verb "to make something complete or sound" (1 Ki 7:51; Ne 6:15). The root of the verb (*shlm*) was flexible and in conversation inquired about a person's well-being (soundness) and contentment—and thus the sense of peace or tranquility. Its literal use referred to the absence of war or enemies (1 Sa 7:14), but broadly it meant harmony and goodness in life. Thus, in the prophets it can be a measure for the just and moral life of the nation (Isa 2:2–4; Mic 5:4–5).

By the New Testament era, the Hebrew *shalom* was used widely, both in its original Hebrew form among Jews or in Hellenistic churches as the Greek *eirēnē*. It could be a blessing, ("Jesus said to the woman, 'Your faith has saved you; go in peace,'" Lk 7:50) or a greeting ("Again Jesus said, 'Peace be with you,'" Jn 20:21). But it was also a quality of life—as in the Old Testament—that brought flourishing ("The mind governed by the flesh is death, but the mind governed by the Spirit is life and peace," Ro 8:6; see also 5:1). Peace is not simply the cessation of hostility but the active pursuit of goodness from which springs tranquility and flourishing.

Many point to the misuse of shalom in Psalm 122:6 in the modern church, "Pray for the peace of Jerusalem: 'May those who love you be secure.'" It is a modern problem because today it has been given a political application. Even less helpful is the seventeenth-century translation in the KJV, "Pray for the peace of Jerusalem: they shall *prosper* that love thee."

What has happened? This verse has been used as a promise of prosperity for those who support the politics of modern Jerusalem. Christians throughout the world believe that praying for the prosperity of Jerusalem and its *Jewish residents* is a modern spiritual duty. This is then linked to Genesis 12:3 ("I will bless those who bless you, and whoever curses you I will curse"). Then the prosperity gospel is a short step away.

Indeed, we should pray for the peace of Jerusalem—and every other city. Promoting the *shalom* of Jerusalem (and Lagos, Cairo, and Toronto) is to passionately petition God and actively pursue the moral qualities that make for goodness and flourishing.

The problem in 6:16 arises when we ask whom this blessing is for. Clearly it is for "all who follow [walk by] this rule [standard]" (see also Gal 5:25)—namely, those who follow the gospel Paul has been defending. A literal Greek rendering could be: "and to all who walk by this rule, peace be upon them—and (Gk, *kai*) mercy even (Gk, *kai*) on the Israel of God." When Paul refers to Israel, what does he mean? Is he asking peace for the church and mercy on Israel, *even those who reject the gospel*? Is he including the agitators from Jerusalem? Given his strong words about them (1:8–9), this may seem doubtful.

Keener cites no fewer than six interpretations that are possible,[12] but the options may narrow to three: (a) Paul is blessing ethnic or national Israel without regard to Jesus; (b) Paul is blessing Jews who have converted to Jesus, which includes the Judaizers from Jerusalem; or (c) Paul is blessing those "who walk by this rule"—namely, all believers in Christ who follow Paul's teaching about grace. Without doubt the third option enjoys the vast majority of scholarly support.[13] This would be a fitting climax to his letter. This then provides a poetic alignment of two groups: the true followers of Jesus whether (a) Jewish or (b) Gentile.[14]

Throughout Galatians Paul has imagined that Gentiles share in the blessings of Abraham and so, together with messianic Jews, they form a new creation, the church, which now continues the faith community designated as Israel. This then is Paul's most dramatic point as he "redraws the definitions already implicit in his argument."[15] For Paul, the "Israel of God" represents those living within the messianic era, who continue Abraham's faith, who bear the Spirit, and who understand the "rule of Christ." It is Jews and Gentiles living together forming a "new creation" (Gal 6:15), a new person (Eph 2:15), and a shared citizenry (Eph 2:19). Wright summarizes effectively: "The rhetorical weight of placing this solid but world-defining phrase at this point in the letter can hardly be overestimated. Paul knows exactly what he is doing. He is underlining the message of the whole letter; to take the phrase differently would be to undermine that message."[16]

Nevertheless, Paul has not lost hope in non-messianic Israel. He mourns for them in Romans 9, explaining that not all who descend from Israel belong to Israel (9:6), and explains in Romans 11 that they are branches broken off from the great olive tree of Abraham (11:17). He still holds out hope, however, for Israel-after-the flesh (1 Co 10:18), that even though they are "enemies" of the gospel, they are beloved (Ro 11:28) and may be re-grafted to the ancient olive tree if they do not persist in unbelief (Ro 11:23).

**6:17** *The marks of Jesus.* Now for the first time Paul shifts from describing the trouble in Galatia to the difficulties of his own ministry. He has suffered for the gospel. Paul's reference to "the marks" on his body (*stigmata*) has always stirred curiosity. Older commentators have wondered if Paul is referring to the practice of scarring slaves (Paul views himself as a slave of Christ, Gal 1:10) or perhaps tattoo marks worn by followers of pagan gods. Today most think Paul is referring to his hardships, including his stoning at Lystra (Ac 14:19) or his flogging (2 Co 11:25). Such suffering is what it meant to participate in Christ's death—it is bearing in his body "the death of Jesus" (2 Co 4:10). A list of these travails can be found in 2 Corinthians 6:4–6 (troubles, hardships, and distress, beatings, imprisonment, riots; hard work, sleepless nights, and hunger). In 2 Corinthians 6:7–10, he outlines how he has been treated as an imposter, worthy of death and punishment, sorrowful, and poor. Discipleship for Paul was an exercise in bearing the cross and embracing loss. And above all, persecution was the one experience that he knew he shared with Christ.

And so, this is a warning. Paul has had enough. The efforts to contradict his teaching, undermine his authority, and rob believers in Galatia of their freedom must stop.

**6:18** *The grace of our Lord Jesus Christ.* This is Paul's farewell to the Galatians. Similar endings can be found at the close of many of Paul's letters. The usual Greek ending should be "farewell," but here Paul uses his favorite word, "grace," as a characteristic Christian closing. For him this word summarizes the distinctive identity of Jesus' followers, and no doubt, it was picked up and imitated not only in the New Testament but throughout Christian history.

*Be with your spirit.* Generally, Paul uses spirit to refer to God's Spirit; this may be the only time he is actually referring to the human spirit or life lived within each person. This is the only time Paul concludes a letter with an intimate title, "brothers" (NIV, "brothers and sisters," see comment on 1:2). This evokes the sense of intimacy these early Christian communities felt. Their bond was not a narrow nationalism nor ethnicity; it was a common experience of the transforming power of God given in Christ as a gift. Despite all of Paul's harsh words to the Galatians here, still, his affection for them remained, reflected in this final word.

*Amen.* This was a common closing to a benediction as an affirmation of what had just been said. *Amen* is Hebrew (*'āmēn*) and was usually used in groups to express concurrence to what has just been said (1 Ki 1:36; 1 Ch 16:36; Rev 5:14; 543x in the Old Testament).[17] It meant "So be it"—from the Hebrew root for "making something firm." Paul uses it as a conclusion to prayers and doxologies regularly (see Gal 1:5; Ro 15:33).

# EPHESIANS

# INTRODUCTION TO EPHESIANS

*Ephesians has enjoyed the admiration of Christian* readers far beyond what one would expect. For some, Paul has reached the apex of his writing ministry, making Ephesians the crowning achievement of his career. We can barely compare this letter with Galatians. That letter was hotly polemical and represented Paul at a raw early moment, when some of his earliest churches had been sabotaged by emissaries from Jerusalem. In Galatians sentences break apart under the weight of Paul's urgency and frustration. It is a staccato hammering home the centrality of grace and the freedom he discovered in Christ. Galatians was probably written in AD 48 or 49, perhaps a dozen years after Paul's own conversion.

Ephesians comes from an entirely different setting. Years have passed. Paul has traveled extensively throughout the Mediterranean world, planting churches in numerous major cities. He has penned several letters addressing problems and giving directions to fledgling churches that have little if anything to study. Possibly some Jewish Christians possessed some rough collections of Jesus' teachings and were familiar with the Old Testament. But most of the believers were Gentiles (as we have here in Ephesians) whose thinking was steeped in Roman custom and religion.

Paul is a different person when he writes Ephesians. He has by now written various letters, including the magnificent letter to the Romans where we see how his thinking about the faith has matured, expanded, and deepened. He has also experienced sharp opposition from those who opposed his work, particularly in the synagogues. This opposition climaxed with his trip to Judea (Ac 21:17) following his third missionary tour when he was rescued from a mob and arrested (Ac 21:30–33; 23:10). After being transported to Caesarea on Judea's coast, he remained under guard, waiting for an audience with Felix, the Roman governor of the province. Paul remained here for two years (24:27) until another Roman (Festus) assumed the governorship. Because of continuing threats, Paul "appealed to Caesar," taking advantage of his invaluable Roman citizenship (25:11). Essentially, he asked for an imperial (or federal) trial to sort out these provincial charges. Thus, Festus put Paul on a ship and sent him to Rome (27:1–2), where he remained for an uncertain time awaiting his hearing.

This is why Paul refers to himself as a "prisoner for the Lord" (Eph 4:1) and an "ambassador in chains" (6:20). Ephesians (along with three other "prison epistles," Colossians, Philippians, and Philemon) were all written from this imprisonment in Rome.[1]

Paul was under "free custody" in Rome, which meant he could entertain visitors and send out letters. We can imagine, then, Paul welcoming emissaries from a variety of churches bringing him aid. In Philippians we have the name of one such messenger (Epaphroditus) who visited him from Philippi (Php 2:25–30). We also know that Paul used some of these disciples to serve as couriers, carrying letters to many of his churches. Ephesians and Colossians were sent out together and carried by the same courier named Tychicus (Eph 6:21–22; Col 4:7–8).

## To Ephesus? From Paul?

Unlike Galatians, Ephesians lives at the center of an active scholarly controversy. Various questions have followed its interpretation for over one hundred and fifty years.

*To the Ephesians?* The titles we use for the Greek manuscripts of Paul's letters were attached to them sometime in the second or third centuries due chiefly to some reference within the letter to their destination. Philippians 1:1 is an example ("to all God's holy people . . . at Philippi"). Ephesians, however, was different. Ephesians 1:1 says Paul is writing to "God's holy people *in Ephesus*" (emphasis added). However, some important Greek manuscripts do not include the reference to "Ephesus" and leave the letter without a destination.[2] Other important manuscripts keep it. This has led scholars to wonder if Ephesians is not a letter at all as we think of, say, Galatians. Perhaps it was a circular letter designed to go to many locations. It also has an impersonal feel and does not contain references to persons as we have at the end of Paul's other letters (see Ro 16).[3] This is all the more remarkable since Paul spent more time based in Ephesus during his third tour than he spent in any other city.

At best we can say that it was written to Gentile Christians (2:11; 3:1) who are in churches not founded by Paul (3:2–3; see Col 2:1, "for all who have not met me personally"). And in this sense we might think of it as an essay—or a dissertation that is communicating to multiple churches about their need for unity and for public conduct befitting those who belong to Christ.

*From Paul?* While the authorship of Galatians has never been seriously doubted, many today wonder if Paul actually wrote Ephesians despite two verses that refer to him (1:1; 3:1). In fact, the majority view among New Testament scholars is that Paul is not the letter's primary author. The basis for this is not mere skepticism but unmistakable evidence within the letter. It is not that the ideas or the theology in the letter stand apart—they all cohere with Paul's writing elsewhere—but questions about things like vocabulary, style, and the unusual reuse of key words. Certain ideas are missing, while others are framed differently than we expect. This led to the suggestion that a disciple of Paul writing at a later date produced this letter *in Paul's name.*

Critics point to vocabulary. There are forty-two words here that do not appear elsewhere in the New Testament and fifty-two that do not appear in any of Paul's other letters. For instance, Ephesians will refer to "the devil" (*diabolos*), while Paul regularly refers to Satan. Then there are words in Ephesians that seem to be used differently ("mystery," *musterion*; "head," *kephalē*; and "fullness," *plērōma*). The problem with these concerns is that a new context can explain a new vocabulary. Plus, if we look at the rate of variation, 1 Corinthians, 2 Corinthians, and Philippians are no different from Ephesians in the number of unique words used.

Some also point to the style of the letter. Rather than providing rhetorical questions and an abrupt urgency of argument, Ephesians exhibits a fluidity and almost poetic style that we rarely see in Paul. This is true, but the point may be exaggerated. Writings are shaped by the audience and purpose for which they are written. Moreover, we know that Paul used professional scribes (amanuenses) for at least some of his letters (see Ro 16:22), and we must remember that these writers did far more than compose dictation.[4] They *contributed* to the composition in ways that might surprise us today. In an era of high illiteracy, the guild of scribes promised to produce elegant and correct Greek. And as anyone who has been edited before knows, an ambitious editor can change your style, whether it is appreciated or not.

Other more subtle arguments have been suggested against Pauline authorship, but these are examined in more technical introductions. Today's discussion centers on whether the theological perspective in Ephesians matches the emphases elsewhere in Paul. For instance, Ephesians and Colossians both emphasize the cosmic role of Christ, something rare elsewhere in Paul. This represents a singular shift in theology: the church and its spiritual battles as well as its welfare and future are now center in this letter. Scholars have wondered if the letter implies a date long after Paul's death or if it exhibits theological strains that seem peculiar. For instance, in Ephesians 4:11 Paul lists gifted officers in the church—but were these offices in existence in his lifetime? The argument, though, could be circular: *there were no such church offices because Paul did not write Ephesians (or for that matter* 1 Timothy). If we admit his authorship, evidence emerges for that very thing. The truth is that a different time and setting made for new concerns, and these being addressed here would be different from, say, those in 1 Corinthians.

*Ephesians and Colossians.* It is likely that that these two letters left Rome at the same time. But, in addition, they have a literary relationship we see no place else in Paul's writings. The similarities are surprising. About one-third of the vocabulary in Colossians appears in Ephesians, and their endings are almost identical (Eph 6:21–22; Col 4:7–8). There are also numerous verses that are parallel.[5] This has led to the suggestion that perhaps Paul had Colossians before him as he wrote Ephesians or at least drew from the same notes as he composed the two letters. Of course, the critical position has always been that the secondary writing, Ephesians, was written by an imitator, and this can either be benign (it was written by a follower of Paul who is honoring him), or it can be critical (Ephesians then being a forgery).

Once we recognize the widespread use of an amanuensis and a changed context, we understand that these things will shape a letter's vocabulary and message. However, even conservative scholars like Frank Thielman and David deSilva admit that the authorship question is not easily solved. Scholars looking for a distinctive "Pauline signature" may be using criteria that would disqualify some of Paul's "assured" letters. At least it is defensible to say that in Ephesians we either have Paul's own writing or Paul's voice, penned possibly by a disciple, and the setting is later in the mid-first century, when life in the church has changed.[6]

In 1976, the ever-prescient G. B. Caird concluded, "When all is said and done, the problem of Ephesians remains. It is curiously unlike the other Pauline letters. There are difficulties in attributing it to Paul. But these are insignificant in comparison with the difficulties of attributing it to an imitator."[7]

With this in mind, from here we will refer to the author of Ephesians as Paul.

## The Old Testament in Ephesians

The author of Ephesians is clearly a Jew whose Greek has been shaped by Hebrew. We may see examples of Hebrew style in his Greek. These are called Hebraisms, occurring here both in unusual grammatical forms and the way he refers to Gentiles (Eph 2:11–12). But overall "it is sure beyond the slightest degree of doubt that the author of this epistle knows the Old Testament and makes use of it."[8] Here we have allusions to the Old Testament (though an explicit citation formula is only found at 4:8 and 5:14).[9] Thoughtful interpretations of those texts show Paul's theological intentionality and sophistication reminiscent of Rabbinic Judaism but also of his other letters (see 1 Co 10:1–4).[10]

Ephesians has about seventeen references to the Pentateuch (chiefly Exodus and Deuteronomy) and thirty allusions to the prophets (mostly from

Isaiah). In eleven cases we read echoes from the Psalms and ten references to Wisdom writings. However, primary attention is given to the use of Genesis, Psalms, and Isaiah.[11] Generally these Old Testament references come from the Greek Old Testament (the Septuagint or LXX).

These citations and allusions generally serve Ephesians' theme of creation restoration and the inclusion of the Gentiles in a renewed world. The notion here is that God's ambition is the reclamation of his creation and ushering in the harmony, peace, and justice that he had envisioned from the beginning. However, Paul's use of these ideas in the Old Testament is highly nuanced. On occasion he may cite an Old Testament text and alter some words to give it a new application (Eph 4:8; Ps 68:18), or he may cite something that is not in the Old Testament at all (5:14). Instead, we usually find allusions, such as the language of 1:20–23 where Paul is likely drawing from Psalm 110:1 (109:1 LXX) and Psalm 8:6 (8:7 LXX). Here Paul describes the enthronement of Christ, echoing the enthronement language of the Hebrew kings in the hymnic liturgies.

Or we find something like Ephesians 2:13–17 where Paul draws ideas and words from Isaiah's writing about a future era of peace and reconciliation promised to Israel—and now Paul wants to apply this to the messianic age and the church. Lincoln points out that many of the main themes in Ephesians do not appear in the Old Testament—such as the reconciliation of Jews and Gentiles (Eph 2:11–22)—and this explains Paul's limited use of the Old Testament.[12]

We see how Paul employs Psalm 68, describing the glorious movement of Yahweh from Mount Sinai to Mount Zion (Jerusalem) where he is enthroned in his temple. Ephesians 4:8 follows Psalm 68:18 closely, but Paul makes three changes (one very important) so that the citation will fit the Christian setting of Christ's resurrection and enthronement. We will discuss this further in the commentary below.

These many "echoes of scripture" indicate that Paul is a man whose mind has been saturated by the Hebrew scriptures. He can employ the Old Testament with the most subtle of nuances, typical of the synagogue teachers of his day, because he lives a life of debate and interpretation regarding these same scriptures. What is important theologically is how free Paul is to find meanings in these scriptures that were not originally intended in order to apply them in fresh contexts and give them to Jesus where we'd least expect it.

## The World of Ephesus and Its Neighbors

Ephesians and Colossians were penned in Rome and carried by Tychicus to western Anatolia (or the "Roman East") to be received by the Gentile Christians in those regions. These churches were likely established on Paul's third missionary tour (Ac 18:22–20:1) when he remained in the area for two years (Ac 19:10). Even if we are uncertain if our letter belonged to Ephesus, we can be confident that it went to the regions nearby. We therefore benefit from understanding this area and knowing the largest city there. Roman colonial efforts in the region were well-advanced when Paul came to Ephesus. Psidian Antioch in central Anatolia, for example, became a Roman colony in 25 BC. But in the region of Paul's likely interest, Ephesus was enormously influential and certainly shaped by Roman culture.

  *Location.* The city of Ephesus was built on the western edge of Asia Minor (modern Turkey) and, in the Roman Empire, grew to rival the great cities of the empire such as Rome, Alexandria, and Syrian Antioch (see Figure E-0.1). Before the Roman period, it was at various times conquered and held by numerous empires—the Greeks, the Persians, Alexander the Great—because everyone recognized its strategic value as an Aegean port. It even defended its own local autonomy for many periods. But by the first century BC, the city was firmly in Roman hands and became one of the great trading centers of the Mediterranean/Aegean world.

**Figure E-0.1. Map of Western Anatolia (Asia Minor)**
Ephesus was an important port on the western edge of
Asia Minor that came under Roman control in 129 BC.
(See also the map of all of Asia Minor in Figure G-0.4.)

The prosperity of Ephesus stemmed, like most Roman cities, from this location. It was situated on the Cayster River, which provided abundant water, and built on the coast, which provided an enormous port connecting it to the wider Roman Empire.[13] Trade moving east-west from central Anatolia simply traveled down either the Cayster River valley or the wide Meander valley from cities like Laodicea, Hierapolis, or Colossae. Or trade came from further points east, from cities like Psidian Antioch. This meant that Ephesus was a commercial success. It grew to a population of over two hundred thousand people and soon was home to some of the most spectacular Roman architecture in the world. Today remarkable mosaics are being uncovered that testify to the city's wealth.[14] Its theater held twenty-four thousand spectators. A colonnade-lined street led to the magnificent harbor. An enormous market (*agora*), baths, gymnasia, an odeon similar to the one in Corinth (for lectures and music), and an athletic stadium have all been found and excavated. We also now can see astonishing hillside apartments for the wealthy, complete with their wall frescoes. Writers from the period describe a medical school, public festivals, and athletic events drawing in people from distant provinces.[15]

*Religion.* The patron goddess of Ephesus was Artemis, twin sister of Apollo, daughter of Zeus (called *Artemis Ephesia*, who eventually was identified with the Roman Diana; see Figure E-0.2). She was among the Olympian gods who protected girls and women, particularly in childbirth. She was also depicted with a bow and arrow and deer, as a goddess who protected hunters. She was venerated widely throughout the Roman Empire, and numerous Artemis cults flourished.[16]

**Figure E-0.2. The Goddess Artemis**
Artemis has been viewed as a symbol of fertility, but scholars
today debate these peculiar objects on her chest. For years they were
viewed as breasts, but today we think they may be ornaments on a necklace,
painted eggs on a decorated harness (using the Roman egg and dart motif),
or the scrotums of bulls. Either way, they are linked to fertility.

Her largest temple stood in the city of Ephesus from as early as 500 BC and was at the time the largest temple of any sort in the world. It was even built entirely of marble. Despite various natural disasters that ruined it, the temple was rebuilt multiple times and always in marble, testifying to the wealth of the city and the devotion of its population. Roman historians (Pliny) provide its dimensions: 425 x 220 ft (130 x 67m) and supported by 127 columns six feet thick (2m) rising to 60 ft (18m) each. [17] Also thirty-six of them were overlaid with gold. This made the temple four times the size of the Parthenon in Rome. In the Roman period it was deemed one of the great wonders of the world, the ornament of all Asia. Unfortunately, little remains today of the temple except its foundation and some debris. [18]

A series of festivals recognized events around the life of Artemis, and these celebrations offered sacrifices, processions, celebrations, and athletic contests filling the city with patrons. Participation in these events was a sign of loyalty to the city (and later to Rome) as well as a signal of respect for Ephesian values. Visitors would crowd the city each spring to attend these festivals because Ephesus claimed to be Artemis's home. However, Artemis worship, complete with shrines and temples, appeared throughout the Roman Empire, but Ephesus had successfully tied its own fate and prestige to this most popular goddess.

*The Emperor Cult and Mysteries.* The circumstances that led to the writing of Ephesians spring from the cultural values at work in the Roman East. The Artemis cult, centered on her temple, was an enormous driver of the city's wealth and influence: the temple owned enormous lands and water sources and often was a civic benefactor, building roads, fountains, and public buildings. These investments—including the festivals—brought foreign money to the city, benefiting all. To offend or ignore this system meant you didn't understand civic obligation.

Society in this world was deeply religious. And this instinct wove through every feature of life. Those of us in the West often think about our modern lives as divided between the secular or commonplace—and the religious. This division would have felt foreign in antiquity. This was a world where universal vulnerability (health, food, war, spiritual forces) led to a quest for security and protection; this meant appeasing the supernatural forces controlling life. Frequently themes of life, death, and fertility (aided by magic, rituals, and secret liturgies) were enacted, giving comfort to followers for whom power and protection were desired. Many lived in fear, believing that malevolent spiritual powers were everywhere.

Cults flourished throughout the empire, and in some cases, they were devoted to a primary deity (Artemis or Isis perhaps) or countless secondary gods. They were usually secretive and selective, admitting only those who were truly devout. We think of these as "mystery religions," but they lived alongside the more public or imperial religions. Devotion to Dionysus, Attis, Isis, or Mithras are just a few that flourished. It is not surprising that many Christians were influenced by these widespread beliefs, and Paul must speak to them.

Alongside these explicitly religious activities, devotion to the emperor began in the era of Augustus, who had a temple for "the divine Caesar" built in Rome. Cities built temples for the emperor (especially Augustus), and in provinces cities won the coveted title of *protector* of imperial devotion. Such imperial temples sponsored festivals (such as the emperor's birthday), gladiatorial games, and sacrifices. But in every case, devotion to the emperor was a sign of personal and communal devotion to Rome and commitment to the Roman project in the world. At the opening of the New Testament era, Ephesus constructed temples to Artemis, Augustus, Tiberius (son of Augustus), and to the people of Ephesus.[19]

*The apostle Paul.* While Paul was in Judea, a Jew named Apollos came to Ephesus from Alexandria and began teaching (Ac 18:24–28). Since his zeal to teach was greater than his understanding of the faith, Priscilla and Aquila took Apollos aside and mentored him so that he would know things "more adequately" (18:26). Then when Apollos moved on to Corinth, Paul returned to Ephesus on his third tour and spent three months speaking in a synagogue (19:8). Here he learned that many under Apollos's instruction knew little about the Spirit and Christian baptism (19:1–7). Paul baptized twelve of them, and they spoke in tongues and prophesied (19:6). But due to severe conflicts with synagogue leaders, Paul left there and entered the Hall of Tyrannus (19:9) where he taught for two years. We are uncertain about this location. This could have been a guild hall, a lecture hall, or a school. Tyrannus means "tyrant" and could refer to the legacy of a teacher, the landlord, or its patron. It could even have been a nickname now lost to us.[20]

Acts provides a lengthy section on Paul's time in Ephesus (Ac 19:1–41), not only because of the importance of the city but also the nature of Paul's willingness to resist its patron deity. Paul's ministry grew enormously with miracles, healings, and exorcisms, as well as public gatherings to hear Paul preach. But this is when Paul found himself embroiled in a controversy with the silver craftsmen of the city. These were artisans who made silver shrines and replicas of Artemis that were sold to pilgrims and patrons of the temple. One man named Demetrius offers a substantial speech in Acts, saying clearly that Paul's preaching was a direct threat to his business and the reputation of Artemis, "who is worshiped throughout the province of Asia and the world" (19:27). Essentially Paul was threatening the Artemis cult of the city.

Demetrius and his friends inspired a mob who kidnapped Paul's companions, Gaius and Aristarchus, and dragged them into the city's theater. Paul wanted to intervene, but for safety his companions held him back (19:30). A Jew named Alexander then spoke in their defense but was drowned out by the cry of the mob, "Great is Artemis of the Ephesians!" (19:34). An Ephesian civil servant then calmed the crowd and declared that Paul had done nothing against Artemis and that the problem was simply financial—and the city had courts to handle such charges. But, he said, rioting was a serious charge for which the crowd was liable, and with that, the mob dispersed (19:35–40).

After this, Paul left Ephesus and traveled to Macedonia revisiting the churches he had established on his second tour.

## The Message of Ephesians

Ephesians describes a grand vision for the church, its place in the world, its qualities, and its mission to create a society unlike any known in the Roman world. To do this, Paul sweeps up many of the themes that appear elsewhere in his writing, giving Ephesians a summary-feel, which reviews and reinforces his teachings. Stott remarks:

> The whole letter is thus a magnificent combination of Christian doctrine and Christian duty, Christian faith and Christian life, what God has done through Christ and what we must be and do as a result. And its central theme is "God's new society"—what it is, how it came into being through Christ, how its origins and nature were revealed to Paul, how it grows through proclamation, how we are to live lives worthy of it, and how one day it will be consummated when Christ presents his bride the church to himself in splendor, "without stain or wrinkle or any other blemish, but holy and blameless" (5:27).[21]

But certainly, as Paul imagined, sending a circular letter to churches embedded in the culture of the Roman East, replete with religious superstition and imperial demands for devotion, he knew he had to address an array of themes from Roman life that contradicted the gospel. The first of these must be *expected public devotion* to the imperial cult of Augustus and the civic goddess Artemis. It is hard for us to imagine these pressures and how refusal to participate brought enormous exposure. Coins, public statues, reliefs, temples, and even the calendar were all devoted to Augustus. He had reorganized the eastern provinces, ended the disarray of his predecessors, and decreed a new calendar based on his life and achievements.[22] This was thoroughgoing propaganda and sought to make the empire cohesive and provide the average person with a coherent understanding of how the world worked. Augustus was a "savior" and so the gods were working through him. When Paul uses the language of empire and tells his readers that God has given Christ victory over all authorities, the implications for Rome are clear (Eph 1:21–22). Jesus is the Lord of history, which puts him in direct competition with Rome.

Second, because the Roman East was filled with mystery cults and deep beliefs in malevolent spiritual powers, Christian identity had to answer the question of power. Were the forces of the spiritual or magical world more or less powerful than Christ?[23] For this, Paul portrays the Christian life as locked in battle with these powers and the Christian as armed defensively (6:10–20): "For our struggle is not against flesh and blood, but against the rulers, against the authorities, against the powers of this dark world and against the spiritual forces of evil in the heavenly realms" (6:12). He also portrays the Christian life as a divine attachment that rescued them from the realm of darkness and ushered them into the light (5:8). Paul frequently views believers as "in Christ" (1 Cor 1:2; 2 Cor 5:17; Gal 3:26; Col 1:2), meaning they belong to Christ and thus are under his protection.

In addition, Paul is aware of divisions in the Christian communities. As a Jew, he recognized the deep divisions between his community and the Gentiles. These problems had been exacerbated in the mid-first century when Christian identity and Jewish identity were parting ways. However, in Roman eyes, Jews and Christians were easily confused. The church had Jewish roots but held beliefs that led to Christian expulsions from synagogues. While Paul held limited hope for "non-believing Jews," still, he believed that Jews and Gentiles attached to Christ possessed something unexpected. Paul explicitly describes the Jew/Gentile division and shows that in the church, the prospect for dividing walls to come down and building genuine peace is possible (2:14–15). Together we are a part of one another (4:25) and together parts of one body, the body of Christ (5:30). This is an exhortation and encouragement that has universal implications for every era where divisions based on race, nationality, or preference prevail.

Finally, Paul knows that any young Christian community growing in a Roman city will be examined for its loyalty (since religion is wed to imperial allegiance). It will be examined for its "citizenship" to see if its faith, departing as it does from the imperial religions, is a defective and dangerous set of commitments subversive to imperial rule. This community is aware of Paul in prison (4:1) and this word may have spread, further damaging the public reputation of the community. Thus, Paul profiles the ideal ethics of this community so that they would be above reproach (4:1–3; 5:3–20). He reinforces the importance of submission to those gifted by the Spirit (4:11–15) and outlines living honorably in the community. He encourages them to love broadly (neighbors to leaders) and so exhibit the character of Christ (4:15–16): "Follow God's example, therefore, as dearly loved children and walk in the way of love, just as Christ loved us and gave himself up for us as a fragrant offering and sacrifice to God" (5:1–2).

We must recall that Paul has not been to these churches near Ephesus for some time. After his work there, he was imprisoned and carried to Rome. Possibly seven or eight years have passed and as anyone might expect, the church is absorbing Roman values or assimilating back into the culture from which it originated. Some in the church have not heard Paul personally, and so their attachment to him was weak (3:2). Ephesians is Paul's call to these Christians to recenter themselves and return to the teachings Paul had given to them in person.

## The Form of the Letter

Many have struggled to find a useful literary structure in Ephesians. Some believe it has a loose organization and considerable spontaneity in its outline. At least we can see a clear division at 4:1, where Paul seems to shift from broad theological insights to practical calls for Christian living. But even this observation has been challenged: ethics appears in the first half just as theology interweaves the second half. We see a clear formal opening with praise and thanksgiving in 1:1–23. There is also a formal closing in 6:21–24 typical of many of Paul's letters and parallel to the end of Colossians (Col 4:7–8). Beyond these broad parameters, commentary writers generally find their own outline, which often consists of a list of topics. Mine is seen in Figure E-0.3.

**Figure E-0.3. The Form of Ephesians**

### A Formal Greeting (1:1–2)

### The Theological Body of the Letter (1:3–3:21)

**A Benediction (1:3–14)**
**Paul's First Prayer of Intercession (1:15–23)**
**God's Power to Redeem (2:1–10)**
**God's New Humanity (2:11–22)**
**Paul's Role as Steward of God's Grace (3:1–13)**
**Paul's Second Prayer of Intersession (3:14–21)**

### Christian Conduct (4:1–6:9)

**Walking in Unity (4:1–16)**
**Walking in Holiness (4:17–32)**
**Walking in Love (5:1–6)**
**Walking in Light (5:7–14)**
**Walking in Wisdom (5:15–6:9)**

### A Personal Appeal (6:10–20)

### Closing Remarks (6:21–24)

John Stott's enormously helpful, practical commentary provides a simplified outline (see Figure E-0.4) that is as brilliant as it is clarifying.[24]

**Figure E-0.4. Stott's Outline of Ephesians**

### A New Life (1:3–2:10)

**Every spiritual blessing (1:3–14)**
**A prayer for knowledge (1:15–23)**
**Resurrected with Christ (2:1–10)**

### A New Society (2:11–3:21)

**A single new humanity (2:11–22)**
**Paul's unique privilege (3:1–13)**
**Confidence in God's power (3:14–21)**

### New Standards (4:1–5:21)

**Unity and diversity in the church (4:1–16)**
**A new set of clothes (4:17–5:4)**
**More incentives to righteousness (5:5–21)**

### New Relationships (5:21–6:20)

**Husbands and wives (5:21–33)**
**Parents, children, masters, and servants (6:1–9)**
**Rulers and authorities (6:10–20)**

### Conclusion (6:21–24)

# EPHESIANS 1

**1:1–2** *Paul, an apostle.* Paul expresses no need to defend his role as he does in Galatians. (See comments on "Paul, an apostle" at Gal 1:1.) He has by now easily and comfortably appropriated the title "apostle." He is a messenger, a courier, and a bearer of a message from an established authority. Here he says his sender is Christ, who commissioned him on the day of his conversion. His own account of this commission in Acts 26 makes this clear when Paul repeats Jesus' commissioning words:

> Now get up and stand on your feet. I have appeared to you to appoint you as a servant and as a witness of what you have seen and will see of me. I will rescue you from your own people and from the Gentiles. I am sending you to them to open their eyes and turn them from darkness to light, and from the power of Satan to God, so that they may receive forgiveness of sins and a place among those who are sanctified by faith in me. (Ac 26:16–18)

Paul is thus a "servant and a witness" (Ac 26:16), living out his commission to the Gentiles. But note that he understands that, theologically, this commission—and all of Jesus' work—is linked to the will of God. Jesus cannot be understood apart from God, and in Ephesians we will see this theological integration expressly.

*God's holy people.* The Greek term behind "holy" (*hagios*), which has a rich Old Testament background, is often translated "saints" or "holy people." But Paul is not addressing two audiences here (holy people in Ephesus and the faithful in Christ Jesus). These refer to the same community who find their holiness through their faithfulness.

## Ephesians 1:1 Through Old Testament Eyes: Holiness

The Old Testament consistently refers to Israel as holy, chosen from the world as a nation *set apart*. The Greek Old Testament uses the Greek *hagios* to express this. "You will be for me a kingdom of priests and a holy nation" (Ex 19:6 LXX). Since God is *set apart* from creation and thus is *hagios,* so too Israel should be *hagios* (Lev 11:44–45; 19:2). Israel is called to have an identity belonging to God but also is expected to conduct itself in ways that evoke the character of God. Spiritual belonging and personal ethics are thus linked as twin theological affirmations. These ideas are distilled in Romans 6:22, "But now that you have been set free from sin and have become slaves of God, the benefit you reap leads to holiness (*hagios*) and the result is eternal life." We both belong to God and are directed to live godly lives.

Paul understands all of this and applies the Old Testament expectations of Israel to the Gentile church in Ephesians. This alone is remarkable because it is the first hint in Ephesians that Paul views these Gentile Christians as having a place akin to Old Testament Israel. But in this case, it is Christ who has made the church holy (Eph 5:26) and calls the church to lead a life of holiness.

*In Ephesus.* See "To Ephesus? From Paul?" in the Introduction to Ephesians. In some manuscripts the reference to Ephesus is missing. Ephesians may have been a circular letter or essay sent to the churches in western Asia Minor located in Ephesus and cities east (Laodicea, Colossae, Hierapolis). Both Ephesians and Colossians were sent out together using the same courier (Tychicus) and our manuscripts referring to Ephesus may have come from an Ephesian archive. Some wonder if Colossians 4:16 ("see that . . . you in turn read the letter from Laodicea") might be a reference to a copy of our Ephesians coming from Laodicea to Colossae.

*Grace and Peace.* See comments Galatians 1:3 and "Galatians 1:3 Through Old Testament Eyes: Shalom." This is Paul's usual greeting (1 Co 1:3; 2 Co 1:2, etc.), but it stands apart from common greetings at the time, combining grace with the Hebrew *shalom* (here Gk, *eirēnē*). Greek readers might be puzzled but, for the early Christians, it combined two of their most important values. It was a greeting but also a prayer that the grace of God and peace would be with them. Rather than a cliché, it became an important spiritual blessing.

**1:3–14** It was Paul's custom, and that of most writers, to begin with a prayer blessing his readers. Paul does this in 1:3–14 and then begins in earnest with his personal message in 1:15. Many believe that Paul's prayer continues to 2:10 dividing neatly into two halves: praise for what God has done (1:3–14) and an appeal to God for the enlightenment of his people (1:15–2:10). This section of twelve verses is actually one continuous sentence in Greek that the NIV has helpfully divided up into multiple sentences. This makes it complex with numerous clauses and has led some to wonder if we are looking at portions of liturgies that Paul is employing from the worship life of the church.

It may be clarifying to see the prayer in three parts. Paul is outlining the three activities of God, which follow a minor trinitarian theme. Following the initial words of praise, first is the work of the Father, whose plan involved his role in the redemption of the world (1:4–6). Second is the work of the Son, who revealed this plan and accomplished much of it on the cross (1:7–10). Third, we read about the work of the Spirit, who completes this plan and secured us within God's will (1:11–14).

## Ephesians 1:3–14 Through Old Testament Eyes: Blessing

Blessing was a major cultural idea in the Old Testament. It meant the transfer of goodness or well-being to another and was the opposite of cursing, which transferred harm. The Greek Old Testament translated the Hebrew as *eulogeō*, which literally means "speaking a good word" (over another). Thus, a father could bless his children directly (Ge 27:1–4), utter a prayer for blessing (Ge 49:25), act to benefit another (Ge 14:19–20), or conduct a ritual showering blessing on all present (2 Sa 6:18). However, in the Old Testament, blessings were generally good things provided in this world: good weather, rich harvests, many children, and general prosperity.

In the New Testament era, formal blessings were generally reserved for the priests who alone could utter them in the synagogue. Blessings of God were expected to precede every formal prayer, and the famous blessing of Aaron was used liturgically, anchored to Numbers 6:22–26: "The Lord said to Moses, 'Tell Aaron and his sons, This is how you are to bless the Israelites: Say to them, "The Lord bless you and keep you: The Lord make his face to shine on you, and be gracious to you: The Lord turn his face toward you and give you peace."'"

**1:3** *Every spiritual blessing.* The aim of 1:3–14 is to praise God for what he has accomplished. While Old Testament blessings generally affected the mundane things of this world (see "Ephesians 1:3–14 Through Old Testament

Eyes: Blessing"), Paul recognizes that God has accomplished something far greater. Through his plan accomplished through Jesus, he has brought about blessings—rich goodness—that affected the "heavenly realms" (Gk, *epouranios*). This phrase is used five times in Ephesians (1:3; 1:20; 2:6; 3:10; 6:12) to underscore that the work of Christ on our behalf is cosmic and eternal. But these blessings are also *spiritual*, which is not a reference to the Holy Spirit as much as an indication of where this blessing operates. This is a blessing for the unseen dimensions of reality that affect our inner life, which host both forces of darkness and the power of God (3:10; 6:12). Ephesians gives great clarity to this multi-dimensional view of the world. Our commonplace daily existence is affected by powers we cannot always see but must learn to discern. (See comments on "the elemental spiritual forces" at Gal 4:3.)

**1:4–6** *He chose us in him.* It is possible to read more into these verses than is warranted, and Christian scholars have done so for centuries. They have often taught a fatalism or predestinarian view of life that is out of keeping with Paul's intentions. As Marcus Barth concludes, "Ephesians cannot be considered the charter for the eternal predestination of one part of humankind for bliss and the other for hell."[1] For Paul, "election" is something nuanced. Paul begins by saying that God has had a plan from the beginning of creation, which has included the call or choice (Gk, *eklegomai*) of a people to advance his saving program in the world. In the Old Testament this election of Israel was a corporate election, meaning that Israel *as a nation* served the purposes of God (and individuals within Israel were responsible for being obedient to this plan). Israel was not chosen to uniquely receive salvation but to uniquely be the means by which salvation and blessing would come to all nations (Ge 12:1–3; Isa 2:2–3; 25:6–8; Mic 4:1–2). They were chosen as a means, not an end—that is, as a means to show God's justice to the nations and to proclaim his praise (Isa 42:1; 43:20–21). When Israel failed, exile awaited them.

Here Paul says something similar. The church—including those Christ-followers in Ephesus—also figured into God's plan. God has chosen them (this is the right meaning of *eklegomai*) to play a vital role by being set apart to proclaim a message of salvation.[2] "In his sight" (Eph 1:4) is not in the original text but is used to reinforce that we are called "to stand before him" as a subject might stand before a king.[3]

But note it was not a calling to status as if it gave birth to some spiritual exceptionalism. It was an election to holiness and blamelessness. God called his people to be holy as he was holy (Lev 11:44; 20:7). Personal humility should accompany all who recognize that they share in a divine plan that stretches back to creation. Blamelessness in the Old Testament refers to a sacrificial animal at the temple that has no blemishes but is perfect to present to the Lord (Lev 22:21; Nu 19:2). It also expresses a disposition to be obedient to God (Ge 6:9; Job 1:1, 8; 2:3; Ps 15:2; 19:13; etc.).

*Adoption to sonship.* See comments on "adoption to sonship" at Gal 4:4–5. This selection or choice by God calls the church to holiness but also secures us as adopted children ("sons"), all motivated by his love, pleasure, and will. The NIV "predestined" (1:5) represents the Greek *proorizō*, which, as with "chose" (1:4), should not be over-interpreted. *Proorizō* describes a decision made in advance and so echoes the plan of God seen in 1:4. God's plan was not a finely worked out determinism but a decision from the start to bring men and women into his family to participate in this plan. Since Gentiles were not Jews, they are "adopted sons," bringing them in with the full rights of natural children. The NIV keeps the word "sonship" due to its cultural importance: *sonship* communicates inheritance and a place of privilege within a Roman family. In our contemporary culture this includes men *and women*.

*His glorious grace.* In the Old Testament, glory regards God's self-revelation (see comments on 1:17). These activities of God—providing a redemptive plan, calling his people to holiness and sonship—are expressions of his grace. We have been invited in as true agents of God's efforts in the world. It is God's generosity and love for his world that initiates all of these plans. They are freely given *through the One*—that is, through Jesus—who has been the instrument in human history to achieve these good ends.

**1:7–10** *In him we have redemption.* Regarding the Old Testament background, see comments on "to redeem those under the law" at Galatians 4:4–5, where Paul also links the idea of redemption to adoption. This is something that only those who have joined God's plan and who are his children can say: they are redeemed. This is a term (Gk, *apolutrōsis*) used most frequently in the release of slaves or war captives. It suggests setting someone free from captivity *so that* they can live a new life. In this case, our captor is sin (Ro 6:7–8; 7:13), and the payment for our release is Christ's blood on the cross (also Eph 2:14–16; 5:2, 25; Col 1:20). Again, this cross-work of Jesus is an expression of God's grace; that is, God was at work in Christ exhibiting his grace for all to see (2 Co 5:19). Christ's death did not change God's mind; it expressed God's mind.

## Ephesians 1:7 Through Old Testament Eyes:
## The Hebrew Concept of Redemption

The biblical world of the Old Testament made frequent use of the idea that something that is lost, sold, made captive in war, or held against its will—or something held as a result of a covenant—could be released or set free if a payment were made. In non-biblical Greek, *apolutrōsis* (seen here in Eph 1:7) is the abstract noun that described this process of payment-and-release and always required a *ransom* (see Ex 21:8 LXX). The root idea derived from the large word group for releasing something or letting something go (Gk, *luō*). The token given to trigger this release was *lutron* (Gk; see Mk 10:45 where Jesus uses it to express how his giving of his life achieved this ransom). The one who facilitates this release is a *lutrōtēs* or "redeemer," used twice in the Old Testament for God (Ps 19:14 [18:15 LXX]; 78:35 [77:35 LXX]). Thus it is accurate to view Jesus as our redeemer, given his sacrificial cross-work that Paul has in mind.

The Old Testament no doubt served as the background to Paul's thinking here. For example, the Lord claimed ownership of every firstborn—from lambs to sons (Ex 13; 34:20)—and so they had to be redeemed if the Israelite wanted to retain them. This was a reminder of the costliness of Israel's Passover escape from Egypt when the Egyptian firstborn had died (Ex 12:29). To reinforce this memory, a redemption ceremony required Israelites to bring their firstborn sons to the tabernacle for redemption (Nu 18:15–16) and the payment of five shekels served as the "redemption price" (Gk, *lutrōsis* in the LXX). Note that in Luke 2:23 Jesus' parents know this and bring Jesus to the temple for his redemption.

But the redemption concept was widespread. In war, captives could be redeemed. In times of economic loss, daughters sold into slavery could be redeemed (Ex 21:8). Israelites who were impoverished and had sold themselves into slavery could likewise be redeemed (Lev 25:47–49). Even one's land inheritance that had been sold could be redeemed in order to return it to its rightful owner (Lev 25:25–26; 47–55). The idea here is that something can return to its right status despite loss or captivity.

Leviticus 25:23–24 shows how this protects Israel's Promised Land: "The land must not be sold permanently, because the land is mine and you reside in my land as foreigners and strangers. Throughout the land that you hold as a possession, you must provide for the redemption of the land." The foundational idea here is that the holy land never belonged to Israel (ancient cultures always viewed their gods as owning tribal territory). And so if its rightful owner is God, Israel-as-foreign-resident could not do as they wished with the land. This means that it could not be sold at the whim of an Israelite. But if it were sold, then a redemption plan must be in place.

Redemption therefore was tied to restoration, to the idea that something lost or misplaced or sold could be recovered and returned to its intended place. For Paul, this is precisely what Christ has done (see his eight uses of the word, Ro 3:24; 8:23; 1 Co 1:30; Eph 1:7, 14; 4:30; Col 1:14). Jesus' death on the cross was a *lutrōsis*, a redemption payment, freeing and restoring humanity *so that* it could return to that place it was intended to be.

*The mystery of his will.* Wisdom and knowledge are not viewed by Paul as common intellectual ability. Wisdom in the Old Testament belongs properly to God, and it is given to humanity so that they can live successfully. For this reason, it is often compared with power (Jer 10:12) or the law (Pr 28:4; NIV: "instruction") or even the Spirit. It is a revelation, and as such it provides humanity with knowledge, which is a divine gift (as is revelation). To "make something known" (Gk, *gnōrizō*) is mentioned six times in Ephesians (1:9; 3:3, 5, 10; 6:19, 21) and simply "knowing" (Gk, *ginōskō*) three times (3:19; 5:5; 6:22; *gnosis* once, 3:19). This moves the concept of knowledge to the foreground in Paul's thinking.

We have already seen (see the Introduction) that a vast array of Roman cults coexisted in Roman cities like Ephesus or Colossae. These groups were called *mystery religions* because they held secret, arcane rites and knowledge that could not be openly divulged. When Paul refers to wisdom, knowledge, and now mystery (1:9), he is drawing on a vocabulary well-known to these groups.[4] But here he claims that the deep secrets of God have been revealed and can be found in Christ. The divine plan that had been set for creation was now open for all to see. Thus Paul is not saying that the plan of redemption is mysterious; he means that it was a plan that had not been disclosed until now. This is in keeping with the Old Testament, where God is not a keeper of secrets but the revealer of mysteries. He unveils the meaning of dreams (Ge 40; 41:15–16; Da 2:1–18; and especially 2:19–23, 26–28, 45–47), and his purpose is to reveal what is hidden so his people can obey (Dt 29:29; Jer 33:3).

Here once again we hear the same rhythm: God has a plan (Eph 1:4), which he had determined before creation (1:5) and was his purpose in Christ (1:9). In other words, what is unfolding in the present time is something divinely appointed, something the Ephesians need to see and celebrate.

*Fulfillment.* When Paul says the plan (Gk, *oikonomia*) for the fullness of time has reached its fulfillment, he shows that he is drawing from Old Testament and Jewish apocalyptic writings that said similar things. In the Old Testament we read the vision regarding God's divine plans for history that he gives to Daniel: "He changes times and seasons; he deposes kings and raises up others. He gives wisdom to the wise and knowledge to the discerning.

He reveals deep and hidden things; he knows what lies in darkness, and light dwells with him" (Da 2:21–22; see Nebuchadnezzar's response in 4:37). Second Temple Judaism affirmed this same view. Consolation for the years after the exile was found in understanding that God had a grand plan for Israel that could not be seen in the present circumstances (Tobit 14:5; 4 Ezra 4:37).

The world awaited a crisis or conclusion when God would intervene and act. *Oikonomia* refers to a master plan or someone who plans, like a household manager (cf. the word's link to *oikos,* "house") or perhaps an administrative plan. This echoes Paul's previous themes. The great plan of God, now revealed, signals that a pivotal time has emerged. He refers to it as a plan for the "fullness of time" (NRSVue), which means it will be the conclusive and decisive story of humanity. Therefore, what is emerging is *cosmic.* It will affect heaven and earth. It is not just that this fulfilling will "bring unity" (NIV) but that this is the summing up of history. The Greek term here (*anakephalaioō*) means "summing up," as a speaker might do when he or she pulls together the threads of an argument at the end. God's plan is a summative activity that he had prepared for all of creation, including the "heavenly realms" (1:3; 1:10, "heaven").[5]

**1:11–12** *We were also chosen, having been predestined according to the plan of him who works out everything in conformity with the purpose of his will.* Paul now turns from the divine plan for creation (1:10) to its participants, the church, and indicates how they are affected. Paul repeats the three ideas confirming our participation (chosen, predestined, plan) and says again that all of this is unfolding in connection to God's will (1:9, 11). This removes all uncertainty. But the key is that we are God's possession and therefore not participating in some comforting religious activity but are now in league with God's efforts in the world. Paul uses a peculiar word to express this. We are "chosen" (Gk, *klēroō*) which is related to the word for inheritance (*klēronomia,* 1:14). It is not that we possess an inheritance but that *we are an inheritance,* belonging to God who is the heir.[6]

*For the praise of his glory.* This is the great crescendo of God's ancient plan. His purpose for us within creation is that we would be holy and blameless before him (1:4) and that we would live lives that bring praise to his glory (1:12). This is the mandate expressed in the Old Testament for Israel. All of God's activity was so that Israel would recognize his glory and praise his name (Isa 43:7, 21; 48:9–11; Jer 13:11). As Paul connects being chosen with revealing God's glory (Eph 1:4–6, 11–12), so does the Old Testament (Isa 44:23; 60:21; 61:3). Now Paul has given this mandate of Israel to the church. The Ephesians were privileged in one regard. They were among the first generation of believers who could witness the unfolding of God's final plan and understand it

(1:12). They put their hope in Christ because they understood that, in him, history had turned a new corner.

**1:13-14** *When you believed, you were marked in him with a seal, the promised Holy Spirit.* Regarding the Spirit, see comments at Galatians 3:2-3 and "Galatians 3:2-5 Through Old Testament Eyes: The Holy Spirit."

The "promised Holy Spirit" may refer to what the prophets looked forward to (Eze 36:26-27; 37:1-14; Joel 2:28-29) and then what Jesus himself said (Lk 24:49; Jn 14-16; Ac 1:4-5).

Ephesians 1:13-14 requires an exact translation from the Greek to connect the primary subject (you) to its verb.

> *In him [Christ] also you,*
>> having heard the word of truth
>>> (the gospel of your salvation in which you believed)
> *have been sealed by the promised Holy Spirit*
>> (which is[7] a guarantee of our inheritance,
>>> for the redemption of those possessed/preserved [by God]);
>> to the praise of his glory.

At once it becomes clear that the source of praise in this section of the prayer is that God has not only called us into adoption and chosen us within his now-revealed plan, but he has sealed us, marked us, with the Holy Spirit. This promise comes in two forms: (a) the Spirit is a marker and (b) the Spirit is a down payment. The sealing (Gk, *sphragizō*) was a mark of ownership in the ancient world. It could be used on a document or even a jar to guarantee that the contents are safe. But above all it signaled the identity of the owner. Thus Paul understands that the Spirit is God's Spirit, setting apart his people as his (1:14). Second, Paul views the Spirit as a prepayment, earnest money, a guarantee or a deposit whose full sum will be paid in the future (2 Co 1:22). In Genesis it is a pledge—that is, a security deposit that is returned when a debit is paid (Ge 38:17-20). Thus Paul sees our lives as sharing an interim blessing with God as we await the final closing of history where our full redemption will be complete.

*The gospel of your salvation.* See "Galatians 1:6-12 Through Old Testament Eyes: The Gospel."

*Who is a deposit guaranteeing our inheritance.* Passing on an inheritance was a common practice in the ancient world as it is today. Since land was the main source of wealth and security in that time, most of the laws governing inheritance in the Old Testament deal with how real estate was to be passed down a family line (Nu 27:1-11; Dt 21:15-17).

The land of Canaan is also referred to as the inheritance that God promised to his people (Nu 34:2; Dt 4:21; 12:9–10; 31:7; Ps 105:9–11). This is what a good father would give to his children (Pr 13:22) to provide for their future well-being.

As Moses is giving his final instructions to the nation, he asks the people to recall how God gave each of the tribes of Israel portions of land. What did the Lord receive? Not land, but the people themselves are his inheritance (Dt 32:8–9). In Jeremiah 10:16 the prophet flips the image—God is the inheritance of his people.[8] (See also comments on inheritance at Eph 5:5.)

---

## Ephesians 1:14 Through Old Testament Eyes: God's Special Possession

When Paul describes the church as God's own possession, he uses the Greek *peripoiēsis*. This refers to something special that has been acquired. Thus in 1 Peter 2:9 we read a list of descriptors for the church, "But you are a chosen people, a royal priesthood, a holy nation, God's *special possession* (*peripoiēsis*) . . ." For Peter, this provides three titles for God's people in Christ directly from the Old Testament. *Peripoiēsis* is used in the Old Testament in Malachi 3:17 (LXX) in this manner for Israel. Israel is God's special possession.

*Peripoiēsis* can also mean something "preserved" or "kept back" as the preservation of a remnant in a war (2 Ch 14:12 LXX; 1 Th 5:9; Heb 10:39). This is similar to something "held" or possessed. In this case, Ephesians 1:14 would then read, "the redemption of the saved remnant."[9]

This is important because Paul is now using a title for Israel and applying it to the church. This connects with Ephesians 1:18, where God inherits his holy people—which is this special possession. Paul now understands that the community of Christ consists of Gentiles and Jews who believe in Christ, and they now carry privileged identities once only reserved for Israel.[10]

---

**1:15–23** *Giving thanks for you.* Paul has now completed his elegant litany of praise for God, naming the work of the Father through the Son that is now sealed in our lives through the Holy Spirit. We can thus see that chapter 1 is easily divided in two parts: Paul's opening blessing of God (1:1–14) and Paul's prayer for God's people (1:15–23). He blesses God for what he has done through Christ, and he prays for us that we might understand the fullness of what this means.[11] Two themes stand at the heart of Paul's final intercession:

knowledge (1:17–18) and power (1:19–22). These two frequently stand side by side in the New Testament. Not only is correct understanding needed so that we can tell truth from error, but an encounter with God's power is required so that we can be assured not only that the gospel is true but that it directly affects our lives. Knowing and encountering will be the twin virtues of this maturity Paul prays for.

Offering a prayer for one's recipient was typical of letters in this period.[12] We can see this in most of Paul's letters (Ro 1:8–10; 1 Co 1:4–9; Php 1:3–11; Col 1:3–12; 1 Th 1:2–5; 2 Th 1:3; Phm 1:4–6). Its absence in Galatians is noteworthy and no doubt tied to Paul's frustration and exhortation. It is also absent from Ephesians, but for different reasons.

**1:15–16** *Your faith in the Lord Jesus.* Paul is thankful initially because he knows that the gospel he preached in Ephesus has taken root. They have not been disturbed by false teaching (as witnessed in Galatia) nor by eschatological fantasies seen at Thessalonica. Their faith in Jesus and their love for all God's people provides a simple formula for what a growing Christian life can look like.

*Your love for all God's people.* Paul is also grateful that they love all "the saints" (ESV; Gk, *hoi hagioi,* see comments on 1:1). We should see this love as directed not simply to fellow believers in Ephesus but (as Paul says) "to all." Beneath these words we should see Paul's profound commitment to a love that crosses ethnic barriers, particularly Jews and Gentiles. Paul will return to this in 2:11–22 in what is perhaps his most eloquent description of this barrier-crossing love. A unity without a devotion to diversity is a small achievement barely worthy of the greatness of the gospel.

**1:17** *I keep asking the God of our Lord Jesus Christ, the glorious Father.* See "Galatians 4:1–7 Through Old Testament Eyes: God as Father."

Paul here begins his petition directly and is careful to describe whom he is addressing. When he says "the God of our Lord Jesus Christ," he is making a statement similar to the Old Testament references to the God of Abraham, Isaac, and Jacob found when God first appears to Moses (Ex 3:6, 15–16; 4:5), promising to rescue the people from their troubles.[13] God is known through his activity among his people when he brought them out of slavery in Egypt, the primary story of redemption in the Old Testament. By this phrase, then, Paul means that Jesus has been fitted into the history of Israel. God is known through his activity in Jesus.

"Father of glory" (NIV: "the glorious father") is a Hebrew combination reflecting the Old Testament idea that God displays his splendor or brightness (his glory) to us as we encounter him, and this is a feature of his authority and power (Ex 24:17; Isa 4:2; 35:2; 60:2). Perhaps the principal Old Testament passage regarding glory comes when Moses asks God to see his glory (Ex 33:18). God agrees and answers his request in this way.

> Then the LORD came down in the cloud and stood there with him and proclaimed his name, the LORD. And he passed in front of Moses, proclaiming, "The LORD, the LORD, the compassionate and gracious God, slow to anger, abounding in love and faithfulness, maintaining love to thousands, and forgiving wickedness, rebellion and sin. Yet he does not leave the guilty unpunished; he punishes the children and their children for the sin of the parents to the third and fourth generation." (Ex 34:5–7)

Glory is God's radiance shown to the world through visible manifestations of his character—his compassion, love, forgiveness, and justice—visible in Jesus (1 Co 2:8; 2 Co 3:18; 4:4–8) and visible within those who belong to him (Ro 5:2; 8:21; 15:7; Php 3:21; Col 1:27).

*The Spirit of wisdom and revelation.* This is the first subject of Paul's prayer. In the past, interpreters were eager to see this wisdom and revelation as a *human capacity* of self-discovery. But this is doubtless not the case. Throughout the Bible, wisdom is divine wisdom as attested by the book of Proverbs, especially chapters 1–9. The poem of Job 28 considers the ingenuity and energy of people to find what is hidden deep in the earth, yet they fail to find wisdom because they are looking in the wrong places. Only God is the source of wisdom. In Isaiah 11:2 a promise of divine wisdom and understanding is given for the "anointed one" (identified as such in Isa 45:1), and it is echoed in Isaiah 42:1—a text used by Jesus to inaugurate his ministry in Nazareth (Lk 4:18–19).

"Revelation" refers to matters not yet disclosed that only God can reveal (see comments on "the mystery of his will" at 1:7–10). Therefore, this must refer to the Holy Spirit (NIV) who will enable us to comprehend the meaning of what God is doing. Some interpreters believe that since the Spirit is already at work in believers, this cannot be a prayer for another gift of the Spirit. But this too narrowly confines the many ways the Spirit works *and continues to work* in our lives. In this case the aim of the gift is knowing God better. In the Greek, this wisdom and revelation *leads to* knowledge (wisdom and revelation *in him*).

Note that this prayer is not for the accumulation of knowledge as an end in itself. It is certainly not knowledge about the world. The *knowledge of God* would certainly include thinking rightly about him (and here theological orthodoxy can be mentioned). But it is also knowledge *about* God. It is not only cognitive, but experiential. If we are sons (and daughters) (1:5), we have access to a knowledge not available commonly. This means that our understanding of the world *as the world* is not the aim of this gift. It is a supernatural disclosure that only God can deliver.

**1:18-19** *That the eyes of your heart may be enlightened.* Blindness is a frequent image in the Old Testament for disobedience or not being able to see the truth (Isa 42:18-20; 44:9-10; 59:9-10; Zep 1:17). Spiritual darkness is a condition that only God can relieve (Isa 29:18; 35:5; 42:16). One way the eyes can become enlightened is through God's law (Ps 19:8; 119:105). Light is also equated with understanding and wisdom (Da 5:14 ESV).

Paul's request (Eph 1:18) reinforces what we saw in 1:17. However, the participle ("enlightened")[14] links with the foregoing, meaning that the wisdom and knowledge sought can be gained because the inner light of our hearts has *already* been enlightened. That is, enlightenment is not another gift, but it confirms that wisdom and revelation are strictly divine gifts stemming from God's spiritual work. We may then translate this as: "that he may give you the spirit of wisdom and revelation in the knowledge of him, having had the eyes of your heart illumined" (literal translation). Because of what has already taken place, we now can pray for further illumination.

The Greek refers to eyes that are filled with light. And in this case, they are portals directly to the heart so that enlightenment may rest there. In antiquity, the heart was not the seat of emotions but represented the totality of a person: thought, feeling, judgment (they did not know how the brain functioned). It was at the center—it pumped blood, which bore life throughout the body—and so Paul prays that this clarifying light will permeate every aspect of who we are.

*In order that you may know the hope to which he has called you, the riches of his glorious inheritance in his holy people, and his incomparably great power for us who believe.* The wisdom and revelation sought in 1:17–18 has three purposes, each following one another in successive clauses in 1:18–19. First, the *hope* of the gospel may refer to life after death, but Paul does not say this. It is more likely pointing to new prospects that we possess here in this world. The plan of God is now afoot in history (1:3–14) and believers are participants in it. Something has begun in the arrival of Christ, and history itself has been put on notice.

Second, the *glorious inheritance* is God's (note "his") and is located among "God's people" (Gk, *hagios*, "saints," see 1:1).[15] As we saw above ("Who is a deposit guaranteeing our inheritance" at 1:13–14; also see 5:5), his people are called God's inheritance (Dt 32:8–9). When we fully recognize that is how God views us, we are overwhelmed.

The final purpose in Paul's prayer is *power*. Paul prays not only that we will discover new hope and our place in the inheritance within God's plan but that we would see the exceeding greatness of God's power. This again underscores the experiential nature of the gifts Paul prays for us. When Paul introduces the gospel in Romans 1:16, he says he is not ashamed of the gospel, for it is the power of God for salvation. Power (Gk, *dunamis*) was one of the most widely used terms in the Roman world. It could be used in philosophy to describe the forces sustaining creation, or it could be used in popular cults to describe spiritual forces that bless or threaten life. If we were living in the first century, power would be what makes religion effective because it improves our capacity for protection. Popular religion did not turn on reason. It turned on power and what activities could generate it. For Paul to miss this deep desire for power would be to miss one of the yearning desires of anyone alert to the spiritual forces in this world.

## Going Deeper:
## Power and the Global South (Eph 1:18-24)

The western world, built on Enlightenment principles, is less comfortable with power than are most Christians living in the Global South. For these believers, evidence of a successful pastor might be his or her ability to exhibit Christ's power in healing and deliverance. For the West, such evidence might be found in an intelligent, winsome sermon that tells us truths we want to take in.

I was once friends with a West African Anglican bishop who has since died. We were at a university discussing the church and ministry in Africa and the West. He told me that *every priest* in his diocese was ready to exorcise demons, defeat malevolent powers, and pray for healing. I told him I'd like to visit one of his churches to witness this. He thought about it for a moment but then declined. "I understand—but we don't need more Western tourists in our churches. We find that their skepticism dampens the power of the Spirit." I must have been visibly hurt. He continued, "I feel sorry for your church in America. It has been built on the back of the Enlightenment and thinks that 'reason' lives at the heart of the gospel. It does not. Power is at the heart, and we in Africa understand this."

**1:19–20** *That power is the same as the mighty strength he exerted when he raised Christ.* The Old Testament associates God's power with his great act of salvation when he brought Israel out of Egypt (Ex 32:11; Jos 4:23–24). God's power overcame Pharaoh's (1 Sa 10:18; 2 Ki 17:7), and he granted power to Israel (Ps 29:11; 68:35). His power is greater than any who might oppose him (2 Ch 20:6).

Christian theological affirmations must always center themselves in Christology (our understanding of Christ) and Paul models this for us. The proof of successful religion in Paul's world was not reasonable explanations but powerful exhibitions (see above "Going Deeper: Power and the Global South"). This explains the prominence of miracles throughout the Gospels and Acts. And it explains why Paul refers to power as much as he does (forty-nine times). Paul viewed his own successes among Gentiles as a display of signs and wonders, the power of God, exhibited through him (Ro 15:19; Eph 3:7). He says to the Corinthians, "My message and my preaching were not with wise and persuasive words, but with a demonstration of the Spirit's power, so that your faith might not rest on human wisdom, but on God's power ... for the kingdom of God is not a matter of talk but of power" (1 Co 2:4–5; 4:20).

While the cross was a display of God's power (1 Co 1:18), the greatest display of this power was in the resurrection (Ro 1:4; 1 Co 15:43). For him, Christ is "the power of God" (1 Co 1:24). So here in Ephesians 1:19–20, Paul's proof of the power for which he prays is found in the resurrection. This was a display of God's "mighty strength" (1:19).[16] This is why most of the preaching of Paul does not begin with the cross. It begins with the resurrection, which was a confounding and unparalleled event in history. But Paul is aware that even this display of power is compelling only to those "who believe" (1:19). The Greek[17] says it is "for those who believe"; that is, this is power for the advantage or benefit of believers so that they will be empowered similarly.

## Ephesians 1:20 Through Old Testament Eyes: Psalm 110:1 and 8:6

Psalm 110:1 refers to the King of Israel and his elevation to God's right hand: "The LORD says to my lord: 'Sit at my right hand until I make your enemies a footstool for your feet.'" The parallel thought is in Psalm 8:6 ("You made them rulers over the works of your hands; you put everything under their feet"). Psalm 110 seems to describe a future king whom God will call to rest while God himself defeats all of his enemies. Many scholars think that it had a messianic use in Second Temple Judaism, and this is why it appears in the gospels (Mk 12:36) and, in particular, at Jesus' trial when Caiaphas asks if Jesus is the Messiah. Mentioning "sitting at the right hand," as does Psalm 110:1, Jesus responds, "I am. . . . And you will see the Son of Man sitting at the right hand of the Mighty One and coming on the clouds of heaven" (Mk 14:62).

Psalm 110:1 is used in the New Testament (Col 3:1; Heb 1:3–4; Rev 5:1, 7, etc.) to describe the exaltation of Jesus after the resurrection. It must have served as a common reference point to explain the fate and future of Jesus the resurrected Messiah since Jesus had now assumed the role of Israel's king.

Here we learn that Jesus has been exalted to God's right hand (Eph 1:20) and God has placed all things under his feet (1:22). These are allusions to the Greek version of the Psalm (Ps 109:1 LXX).[18]

*Heavenly realms.* But what was the end result of this resurrection? Not simply that Christ returned to life but that he was seated, enthroned, at God's right hand (a place of honor) in the heavenly realms. This is a direct echo of Psalm 110; Jesus has now assumed the divinely appointed position of Israel's king (see "Ephesians 1:20 Through Old Testament Eyes" above). The location of Jesus' placement is in heavenly realms, which means that Jesus is not simply "in heaven," but he now has a role of dominion over those regions where spiritual powers exist—some for good (1:3) and others for evil (6:12).

**1:21-22** *Above all rule and authority, power and dominion.* The ancient world (including Paul) believed that the seen and unseen world were populated not by impersonal forces but by personal beings that could bring blessing or evil.[19] (See comment on "the elemental spiritual forces" at Gal 4:3.) Recall the divine status of the Roman emperors in this period. The NIV makes this sound impersonal, but the Greek text is otherwise: "far above all who rule, all who have authority, all powers, and those who claim lordship" (author's translation; Gk, *kuriotēs*: see *kurios*, "lord").[20] "Every name that is invoked" (1:21) is literally "every name that is named" or "every name that is called upon." Colloquially it means every dignitary who bears a title and who is named and dignified.[21] The idea here is comprehensiveness both in position and in time (in the present and the future). Every realm is subject to Jesus, and we can assume this includes Rome as well as unseen arenas of struggle ("against the rulers, against the authorities, against the powers of this dark world and against the spiritual forces of evil in the heavenly realms," 6:12). That is, Jesus now has power on such a grand scale that there is no location where his power is not dominant.

**1:22-23** *For the church.* The comprehensive rule of Christ is for the benefit of the church. He is the head—a term that can have a wide variety of uses (see comment on 5:23)—whose chief interest is in taking care of the church, his body (2:23, a metaphor Paul will use in each of the next four chapters; also Ro 12:3-8; 1 Co 12:12-26). This metaphor is important to Paul for it illustrates the link between believers and Christ. The body will receive gifts from Christ as in 1 Corinthians, and here Christ becomes the church's patron and protector. All that he has become is for the care, nurture, and preservation of his followers.

*The fullness of him.* This "fullness" (Gk, *plērōma*) is rightly attributed by the NIV to the church (it is ambiguous; see 3:19). Literally: ". . . which is his body, the fullness of him who fills all things in himself." This phrase is as difficult in English as it is in Greek, and the interpretations of it are legion. Christ, who is blessed with all fullness, has now filled the church (with himself). But what fills Christ? Colossians may help where this phrase repeats. It is the fullness of deity, the fullness of God himself, that is in Christ (Col 2:9), and this then is what fills the church. This is likely an analogy from the Old Testament and the temple. In the Old Testament the glory of God "fills" not only the temple (Isa 6:1; Eze 43:5) but the earth (Nu 14:21; Isa 6:3; Ps 72:19; Hab 2:14). The wisdom of God, the love of God, and the Spirit of God likewise fill the world. In Jeremiah 23:23–24, God fills "heaven and earth." In this respect, the church is filled with the glory (or presence) of God, a glory that now has appeared in Christ.

Older interpreters have suggested that the term "fullness" may also come with a hidden meaning. *Plērōma* was used in gnostic religions a century after Paul to describe the "totality of divine attributes, powers and manifestations" held by rulers in the spiritual world.[22] Did it have this nuance in Paul's day? If so, these beings were a part of the realm now conquered and ruled by Christ (Eph 1:20–22). But now Christ holds the very attributes—fullness—possessed by them.

In the end, Paul is blessing God in chapter 1 for his glorious and overwhelming plan for his creation. Motivated by grace and love, God has worked for the redemption of his world and set apart a people who will be his collaborators to advance that effort. Their community—the church—is equipped for this task through the Spirit and through the power unleashed by that Spirit, which can defeat any authorities or powers that may come against it. Christ has risen to defeat these powers and now is enthroned with God as ruler. Indeed (as Ephesians will show) there will be conflict in the heavens and on the earth, but the success of this struggle is already assured because of the cosmic and comprehensive victory that God has accomplished in Christ.

# EPHESIANS 2

**2:1–10** *We are God's handiwork.* Ephesians 2 builds on Paul's prayer to God (1:2–23) that blessed him for his glorious redemptive plan in history. Chapter 2 finds Paul outlining what possibilities emerge once this plan unfolds in a person's life. He begins with a description of our dire human condition (which has many echoes from Ro 1–3) and the *new person* that we become (2:1–10). The second half of the chapter describes the *new society* that emerges when Christ's followers begin to live into the gospel itself (2:11–22).

Ephesians 2:1–10 consists of Paul's grim diagnosis of humanity and our hopeful prospects. It describes sincere pessimism for humanity when left to its own devices (2:1–3) and the optimism we can celebrate when we find grace (2:4–10). It moves from despair to faith: what by nature we are and what by grace we can become. All of this redemptive effort is an expression of God's love for us (2:4). The result is that we are *God's handiwork* and not our own handiwork (2:10); we praise God for lifting us out of the quagmire we find ourselves in.[1] Some have even viewed 2:1–10 as the "most effective summary we have of the Pauline doctrine of salvation by grace through faith."[2] Others have seen in it a distilled presentation of Paul's writing in Romans 1–5.

**2:1–3** *Dead in your transgressions and sins.* We usually think of sin as breaking laws. Likewise the Old Testament speaks of it as disobeying God's commands (Lev 26:43; 2 Ki 10:31; 2 Ch 19:10; Ne 9:29). But sin is not just transactional. It is also relational. The relationship is broken as with rebellion (Ex 23:21; Dt 1:26; Jos 22:16; Ne 9:16; Isa 53:6). Sin seeks to dominate and ensnare (Ge 4:7; Pr 5:22).

Paul lists three realities about our human nature related to sin: we are dead in sin (Eph 2:1), we have succumbed to the ways of this world (2:2–3), and thus we live under the judgment of God (2:3). Each is critical. This is a stunning indictment that is as dramatic as the solution Paul will pronounce in 2:4.

Ephesians 2:1 is difficult to read and translate because the primary clause ("he made us alive") is delayed until 2:5. A comparison of translations will show that some translators move the verb forward from 2:5 to 2:1 and open the verse with something positive ("And you he made alive . . ." RSV). Paul's "impetuosity"[3] leads to difficult syntax, and this translation lends more clarity. This does not mean that Paul writes Greek poorly. This is his dramatic style to suspend his main thought. Death in sin is given a series of descriptions (numerous clauses) which ends with Paul's hopeful resolution in 2:5.[4] Little effort should probably be given to distinguish transgressions and sins since both represent the same concept.[5] But the key idea here is that death is the prospect for those who sever themselves from God. Paul generally uses death in two ways. He can refer to spiritual death as being cut off from God (Ro 6:23; 7:10, 24; 8:10), and he can refer to what some call "sacramental death"—that is, the death of our old self at baptism (Ro 6:2–13). These must be carefully distinguished. Here Paul is reminding the Gentiles of Ephesus that the former is their story: they were spiritually dead in their indulgence to sin.

*In which you used to live when you followed the ways of this world.* The NIV's "you used to live" translates an idiomatic phrase ("you used to walk") that was common in the Old Testament (Ex 18:2; Lev 18:4; Dt 10:12–13). Thus, Paul can refer to "the sins in which you walked (see comments on "live a life" at Eph 4:1 and on "walk by the Spirit" at Gal 5:16–18). This use of "walking" is frequently used in Paul (thirty-one times) to express how we live (ethics) and appears in Jewish writing regularly. Moral ethics—how to live—in Judaism was called *Halakah*, or "how to walk." But this walking among these Ephesians has been in step with the trends (Gk, *aiōna*, "ages") of secular life (Gk, *kosmos*, "the world"), meaning a context without interest in God or even hostile to God. But worse, it is a context dominated by "the ruler of the kingdom [authority/power] of the air." This is a clear reference to Satan (Jn 12:31; 2 Co 4:4) and underscores the seriousness of life in this secular domain. This ruler is a spiritual force (Eph 2:2) that is prompting and urging the sinfulness of those who are living lives of death.[6]

*The cravings of our flesh.* The indulgence of sin (2:1) now finds another expression. Not only did some walk in the ways of the world, but we (Paul here shifts to the first-person plural, including himself)—all of us (Gk, *pantes*)—directed our lives by the passions of the flesh, and we succumbed to the desires and thoughts of the flesh.

This is Paul's first use of "flesh" in this letter (Gk, *sarx*, nine times in Eph), and for him, it is a technical word. It does not refer simply to our material bodies, which are created by God and good. It refers to the fallen inner impulses that dictate our conduct (see comments on Gal 5:16–24) and can be influenced by the ruler of the air whose work is to corrupt this inner self.

When corrupted it becomes "the impulse to self-gratification, self-serving, and self-assertion that is antithetical to 'the mind that was in Christ Jesus' (Php 2:5–11)."[7] Paul therefore sees our problem (unlike many Greeks) not simply in the ruin of ordinary life *due to the corruption of this world* (as if our context were the issue) but instead as a problem stemming from within, impulses from within a person's life itself, and this interior corruption has ruined the world.

*Like the rest, we were by nature deserving of wrath.* Few verses in Paul stir as much controversy as Ephesians 2:3. First, "by nature" has seen enormous over-interpretation among those who want to find this willful sinfulness in the nature of who we are, reaching back to our birth (original sin), the first human (Adam), or even God's will at creation (seen in his decrees). This is a tragic over-interpretation of Paul's intent in Ephesians 2:3. Paul is referring to the universality and comprehensiveness of sin, a depravity that has woven itself into our very personhood. The phrase "by nature" (Gk, *phusei*) points to a condition known since birth. Simply put, sin is natural to us (see Ro 5:12; 2 Esdras [4 Ezra] 7:62–69). Paul does not refer to its origins or causes.[8] It is a dire portrait, but as we see in Ephesians 2:4, it is a tragic state that is not stronger than God's love.

Second, the "wrath" of God is likewise an arresting word now directed toward our condition. But this too requires nuance. This is not like human anger, impulsive, reckless, arbitrary, and unwarranted. Wrath is God's response to evil.

It is as personal as his love and grace. Evil represents all that is hostile to God and inimical to his righteousness. Evil promotes injustice, harm, and sin (Ro 1:18–32). Wrath is "righteous anger," which those who love what is good and true and life-giving will value and respect. The more profoundly one loves the things of God, the more profoundly one takes comfort in his swift judgment of evil.

## Ephesians 2:3 Through Old Testament Eyes: The Wrath of God

Few concepts in the Old Testament are more misunderstood than God's wrath. It is a common theme and no doubt influenced the thinking of Paul not only here but throughout his letters. Paul uses the term (Gk, *orgē*) twenty-one times. In Ephesians he refers to it in 2:3; 4:31; 5:6.

It is a mistake to compare God's wrath to human anger that can be fitful or unpredictable. It is not the emotion we are familiar with. Wrath is a term describing a feature of God's permanent attributes. Wrath is his response to sin and evil, which are inimical to his holy and righteous character. "It is as permanent and as consistent an element of his nature as is his love."[9] This means that God's reaction in wrath is inevitable because it is linked to his thoroughgoing life of righteousness.

We can see this in the Old Testament when God declares the destruction of Sodom and Gomorrah (Dt 29:23) or the demise of Nineveh (Na 1:2–6). Such devastating sin inspires God's wrath. However—and here is a key feature in the Old Testament—God's wrath is also mixed with mercy, showing how his love of goodness lives alongside his repudiation of sin. Hosea 11:8–10 illustrates this well.

> How can I give you up, Ephraim?
>   How can I hand you over, Israel?
> How can I treat you like Admah?
>   How can I make you like Zeboyim?
> My heart is changed within me;
>   all my compassion is aroused.
> I will not carry out my fierce anger,
>   nor will I devastate Ephraim again.
> For I am God, and not a man—
>   the Holy One among you.
>   I will not come against their cities.
> They will follow the LORD;
>   he will roar like a lion.
> When he roars,
>   his children will come trembling from the west.

In Ephesians 2 Paul is describing the extent of humanity's thoroughgoing life of sin, God's inevitable response to it, and his enormous patience. But above all, Paul immediately follows 2:3 with a description of God's rich mercy. In Christ, God has offered a way of escape from the dilemma of humanity's inevitable sin and God's inevitable wrath. Christ is God's gesture of love and mercy, and those who flee to him in faith (2:5) will discover God's grace expressed through the cross.

**2:4–10** *But because of his great love for us.* These verses describe the true reality of who we are before God. If 2:1–3 were the end of the story, we should rightly despair. But it is not. Paul now describes what God has done (2:4–6) and why he did it (2:7–10). In a word, these verses describe life lived under God's grace, a grace defined as God's love and mercy.

These opening words unveil the truest character of God. "But God" is emphatic in Greek (Gk, *ho de theos*) and bridges the grim diagnosis in 2:1–3 with this new hopeful possibility. The Greek *de* is a conjunction that often presents an alternative view of things. "On the other hand" translates this as well. Paul then piles up phrases to show how God is rightly to be viewed, which literally reads: "God who is rich in mercy on account of the great love with which he loved us." This is the prelude to the great affirmation of 2:5, "God . . . made us alive with Christ."

Love and mercy are the two profound character traits of God displayed in the gospel. But they are also revealed in the Old Testament in one of the Bible's pivotal scenes. When Moses meets God on Mount Sinai and asks to see his glory, the Lord reveals his name and his character: he is the Lord (Yahweh) who is merciful and gracious, slow to anger and abounding in steadfast love and faithfulness (Ex 34:5–8). This episode was so foundational that it became a touchstone for the Old Testament understanding of God (Nu 14:18; 2 Ch 30:9; Ne 9:17; Ps 86:15; 103:8; 111:4; 112:4; 116:5; 145:8; Da 9:9; Joel 2:13; Jnh 4:2). (See also comments on Ephesians 1:17.)

**2:4–6** *God . . . made us alive with Christ.* The problem of course is that we were dead thanks to the many ways we sinned (2:1–3). And given God's righteous anger toward sin and evil (2:3), his *expected* disposition should have been condemnation. But we were dead, and dead people can do nothing to remedy their situation. They contribute nothing. And this is the incongruity of the gospel. When least deserving, God gifted us with life due entirely to his generosity (2:5). Hopelessness met love.

The NIV can barely show what the Greek makes clear. We are not simply "made alive" but we are "made alive together" (*suzōpoieō*) with Christ.[10] Our new life is thus linked to Christ's life, our resurrection to his. As Paul writes in Romans 6:5, "For if we have been united with him in a death like his, we will certainly also be united with him in a resurrection like his." Our complete unity with Christ means that we are linked to him on his cross (Ro 6:3, 6; Gal 2:19; Eph 2:1–5), we were buried with him (Ro 6:4; Col 2:12), and we were made alive with him (Ro 6:5; Eph 2:5–6; Col 2:12–13). And Ephesians 2:6 completes the story: we are also seated with him (that is, "enthroned together," again *sun* prefixes the verb) in the heavenly realms (see 1:20). As Christ was crucified, buried, raised, and ascended—so are we!

This is what God has done. He has not simply saved us from our sins, but he has attached us to Christ in such a way that our lives are subsumed in his. His power is now within us, and those forces of darkness that rule these heavenly realms that sabotage and corrupt us no longer can dominate us. Paul here is describing a spiritual exaltation that is a far cry from what most of us think about when we reflect on salvation. Far beyond going to heaven, Paul is describing a substantially different life anchored to spiritual realities and powers that coexist with Christ.

**2:7** *In order that in the coming ages he might show the incomparable riches of his grace.* Paul now describes why God has done this (2:6–10). His aim is revelation, to show each coming generation[11] his deepest character. He will diagnose the world justly, and he will also provide a way of escape. Grace, here described as "the incomparable riches of his grace," is what God desires to show to the world: he is kind and generous. Paul has listed phrases that encapsulate why the good news is good news. God will be encountered as love, mercy, grace, and kindness *despite* what we have done to his creation or ourselves.

## Ephesians 2:8 Through Old Testament Eyes: Saved by Grace (Abraham and Habakkuk)

When Paul offers his opening thesis in Romans, it is vital for him to show that this idea of grace is nothing novel. His citation in Romans 1:17 ("The righteous will live by faith") is taken from Habakkuk 2:4 ("The righteous person will live by his faithfulness"). For many Christians this comes as a surprise. Is the God of the Old Testament really a God of grace?

A fundamental idea in the Old Testament is that grace—the generous initiating love of God—is at the center of any thinking about God and Israel's privileges. With God's covenants came expectations as well but, in some cases, these could cloud the greater notion of God's gift and goodness. Abraham was visited by God in Canaan with little merit that could deliver the dreams he wished for. But "Abram believed the LORD, and he credited it to him [Abraham] as righteousness" (Ge 15:6). After four hundred years in Egypt, Abraham's descendants (now called Israel) demonstrated little righteousness. Nevertheless, God's good and generous character saved them from Pharaoh and led them to his mountain. It is only *after* God has acted to save and binds himself in covenant that he brings the law to his people. Throughout the wilderness wanderings, despite Israel's sin and disbelief, still, the Lord sustained his commitment to Israel as a nation (Dt 6–10).

Thus, in Old Testament theology, grace precedes law and is the foundation on which law is built. Obedience is seen as grateful response, not as an endeavor to find favor. Paul knows this and therefore looks for the one verse that represents it well (Hab 2:4). But he also knows about Genesis

15:6, and this too becomes foundational to his argument (Ro 4:3; see comments at Gal 3:6; cf. Jas 2:23; see also "Galatians 3:10–14 Through Old Testament Eyes: Faith and the Covenant").

When Paul writes Ephesians 2:8 ("For it is by grace you have been saved, through faith—and this is not from yourselves, it is the gift of God") he is writing not merely as a Christian but as a Jew. He is presupposing this enormous Jewish theological framework and taking God's grace to a new level *exactly* as prophets like Isaiah predicted. God was eager to extend his grace and love to the Gentiles. But this would occur only through the cross, which would end all personal religious merit.

Paul sees God's work in Jesus Christ as one more example—no doubt the supreme example—of God's gracious activity. The gospel exemplifies the loving-kindness (Heb, *hesed*) that echoes through so many Old Testament stories. Paul would never have said he changed religions when he accepted Christ. The gospel was the messianic fulfillment, continuation, and application of themes he had known all his life. In Christ, the deepest secrets, the fundamental ideas of the entire Bible, were being revealed.

**2:8–9** *It is by grace you have been saved.* These verses are some of the most frequently memorized in the New Testament. And it is for good reason, since they encapsulate the essence of the gospel itself. Three central terms for Paul appear here: grace, salvation, and faith. All of this is a gift because we were utterly unable to rescue ourselves from our own inevitable death. Faith is our simple trust (Gk, *pistis*, meaning "trust") in him to rescue us. But note carefully how Paul constructs this: *We are not saved by faith* as if our faithful effort, the strength of our belief, or the orthodoxy of our commitments have saving power.[12] We cannot rely on works or conduct, which we use to earn God's approval. *We are saved by grace.* Caird writes, "Anyone who tries to live by such religious book-keeping finds he is never out of debt."[13] This is why there cannot be boasting (2:9). Paul uses variations of the term "boasting" fifty-six times in his letters, showing that for him this is a primary concern. It is self-congratulatory self-promotion and for Paul, empty confidence.

Some interpreters point out that Paul's language here is unusual. "Have been saved" is in the perfect tense, indicating something that transpired in the past but now has significance in the present.[14] This has led to some using this verse to say that we were saved at Christ's death ("When were you saved? At the cross!").[15] Paul is simply reminding the Ephesians that in their embrace of Christ (past) they were saved, and this reality is now with them (present).

**2:10** *We are God's handiwork.* Paul's entire discussion has been leading to this point. "We" (that is, the believers in Ephesus) are "what God has made"; we are his masterwork, his work of art.[16] But the key term here is "his" (the pronoun is advanced to the head of the sentence, ESV; NIV: "God's") because salvation is a gift from God and a gracious and generous effort accomplished by him alone. We are no longer "ours." If salvation is a liberation or a redemption (Eph 1:7, 14), then we belong to the one that has rescued us.

For Paul the ultimate promise of the gospel is never in the reorganization of human effort or the education or improvement of society. It is necessary to restart creation, to make something new from the old, to be re-created. In 2 Corinthians 5:17 Paul writes, "Therefore, if anyone is in Christ, the new creation has come: The old has gone, the new is here" (also Gal 6:15; see "Galatians 6:15 Through Old Testament Eyes: New Creation"). The project of the gospel, therefore, is not about repair. It is about rebuilding. This theme of new creation is vital to Paul, and it leads to one purpose: righteousness (Ro 1:17). The result of this gift is transformation expressing itself in good works. If the world cannot see God's grace (Eph 2:7), they will see the good works exhibited by his followers.

*Created in Christ Jesus to do good works, which God prepared in advance for us to do.* We have now come full circle. This is the completion of the plan that God laid out for his creation (1:11). God understood he needed to redeem and recover his creation, and now, Paul reminds us, we who belong to Christ are a part of this. The term "prepared in advance" (Gk, *proetoimazō*) means to arrange something ahead of time. This does not need to be overly complicated. Paul does not indicate when this plan was made. We know simply that God has a plan for the renewal of his world, he made this plan beforehand (it is not spontaneous), and now we learn that we are assuming the role he planned for us within it. (Regarding "the gift of God," Eph 2:8, and the paired expectation that we "do good works," Eph 2:10, see "Galatians 3:2–6 Through Old Testament Eyes: Grace and Benefaction.")

**2:11–22** *One new humanity out of the two.* The twin themes of Ephesians 2 are alienation from God (2:1–10) and alienation from one another (2:11–22). The first half of the chapter probes the desperate condition of Gentiles whose choices have estranged them from God and led to death: "You were dead in your transgressions and sins . . ." (2:1). The second half probes something equally tragic. The sin described at the beginning of the chapter carved deep divisions in human society. Paul knew this firsthand. As a Jew (a conservative Pharisee) he had been raised with a profound dislike for Gentiles. And no doubt Gentiles returned the favor. If Ephesians 2:1–10 describes a "new person" that can emerge from the gospel, Ephesians 2:11–22 describes a new humanity that comes with it. In Romans 5:1; Paul wrote that the result of our salvation is "peace with God." Now he is able to say that peace is the new attribute of those communities that were deeply estranged (2:14).

**2:11** *You who are Gentiles by birth.* Paul begins by describing the situation that these Gentiles had found themselves in. The word "Gentile"[17] simply means nation (Gk, *ethnos*), and it was a Jewish idiom to refer to any people who did not belong to the *Jewish* nation. But they were also called the uncircumcised (*akrobustia*, Jdg 14:3; 15:18; 1 Sa 14:6; 17:26, 36; 2 Sa 1:20; 1 Ch 10:4; Ro 3:30; 4:9; Gal 2:7; Eph 2:11). This work is the medical term for foreskin, the sleeve of skin found naturally on the end of the penis that is removed by circumcision (see "Galatians 2:1–10 Through Old Testament Eyes: Circumcision"). Jews, on the other hand, referred to themselves as "the circumcision" (Gk, *peritomē*), which literally means "to cut around something." It gained special application in the circumcision ritual (to "cut around" the penis to remove the foreskin). Both Gentile and Jewish status is found *in the flesh* (Gk, *en sarxi*; NIV: "Gentiles by birth," and Jews "in the body"). Both phrases use *sarx* and the symmetry is intentional. These are real differences, but they belong to an order of things that now must disappear. They are not simply physical; they are markers of categories that are as superficial as they are outdated.[18]

**2:12** *You were separate from Christ.* Paul now supplies a short catalog (2:12) of losses that belonged to Gentiles who lived without Christ. They quite simply did not belong to God's people. They were not citizens of Israel; they were "foreigners to the covenants, . . . without hope and without God." The notion of citizenship (Gk, *politeia; polis* means "city") was not because Rome had given Israel national status but because they possessed a covenant "of the promise" (2:21) with God in the Old Testament, establishing their national place. Paul (or Luke) uses the term in Acts 22:28 to claim his Roman citizenship for his defense. So here, inasmuch as the Gentiles do not belong to these covenants, Gentiles cannot belong to Israel. This led to harsh discrimination against Gentiles in Jewish circles, which Paul knew well. But as we saw in Galatians (see comments on Gal 3:8–9), the covenant of Abraham (on which these hopes were built) also included blessing for *all nations*—a teaching conveniently ignored by many Jewish teachers. In Ephesians 2:19 Paul will repeat these words so it is clear: this citizenship, long denied, now belongs to Gentiles.

**2:13** *You who once were far away have been brought near.* The phrase "but now" (Gk, *de nun*; sometimes translated simply "now") is frequent in Paul (sixteen times) who uses it to show a major shift in circumstances (Ro 15:23, 25; 2 Co 8:10–11) or thought (Ro 7:15–17). It is tempting to translate it in caps, BUT

NOW, to underscore its prominence in this sentence. The extremely hopeless circumstance of the Gentiles is about to be reversed. The language of "far and near" comes from Isaiah 57:19: "'Peace, peace, to those far and near,' says the LORD. 'And I will heal them.'" He will repeat the phrase in Ephesians 2:17. (See "Ephesians 2:13 Through Old Testament Eyes: Paul's Use of Isaiah 57:19.")

This new community has been possible only because Gentiles, who had no part in it formerly, now are "in Christ"; and as Christ is central to this new creation, so Gentiles will be included. But it is also, secondly, that the blood of the cross has achieved this Gentile possibility. While the law and sin posed insuperable obstacles for Gentiles, the cross now has accomplished what nothing else could. Paul will explain this further in 2:14–18.

## Ephesians 2:13 Through Old Testament Eyes: Paul's Use of Isaiah 57:19

Paul's use of *far* and *near* in Ephesians 2:13 is from the Greek translation of Isaiah 57:19 ("'Peace, peace, to those far and near,' says the LORD. 'And I will heal them.'"). In its original context, this was a word of comfort for Israel. With the exile, they had been scattered. Here Isaiah provides hope that those Jews who had been separated by distance and crisis would regain their community.

Paul appropriates these Old Testament verses intended for Jews and uses them in unexpected ways—ways that are implied in Isaiah. Those who are "far and near" include Gentiles who will be gathered in. This reuse of the text is appropriate because in the wider context of Isaiah, the prophet envisions a future when the ingathering will include *all nations*. "Surely you will summon nations you know not, and nations you do not know will come running to you" (Isa 55:5). This is also the context in Isaiah that Jesus references when he makes his appeal in the temple that it belongs "to all nations."

> And foreigners who bind themselves to the LORD
>     to minister to him,
> to love the name of the LORD,
>     and to be his servants,
> all who keep the Sabbath without desecrating it
>     and who hold fast to my covenant—
> these I will bring to my holy mountain
>     and give them joy in my house of prayer.

> Their burnt offerings and sacrifices
>    will be accepted on my altar;
> *for my house will be called*
>    *a house of prayer for all nations."*
> (Isa 56:6–7, italics added; see Mk 11:17)

Moreover, when Paul refers in Ephesians 2:14 to peace, Isaiah 52:7 and 57:18–19 may well be in mind as a part of this anticipated new era. The hallmark of this renewed Israel is "peace." Indeed, Isaiah himself envisioned a new community of ingathering that brought all nations in alignment with the worship of the one true God. Peace is not something shared among Jews, but something shared between Jews and Gentiles.

Thus in Ephesians 2:13, Paul is reminding Gentiles that they are a part of this new re-creation of Israel. They are *not foreigners* any longer, nor are they without hope. The new creation has begun and Jewish exclusivity has ended.

**2:14** *For he himself is our peace.* Paul no doubt has in mind here the Hebrew *shalom* used with enormous frequency in the Old Testament and in Hebrew culture. (See "Galatians 1:3 Through Old Testament Eyes: Shalom.") While God is the source of peace (Lev 26:6; Isa 2:4; Hag 2:9), the prophets also looked forward to a figure who would bring peace (Isa 53:5), proclaim peace (Zec 9:9–10), be Israel's peace (Mic 5:4–5), and indeed be called the Prince of Peace (Isa 9:6–7).

The use of peace as a greeting in New Testament Greek likely points to this Hebrew use as well (Jn 20:21, 26). However, as a greeting or as a hope, *shalom* did not mean simply the cessation of hostility; it was an active pursuit that brought blessing and life to those who gave and received it. In Ephesians 2:14–15a, Paul now employs three phrases to explain what Christ accomplished.

*Who has made the two groups one.* This is the miracle of the new creation Paul now sees emerging in Christ. The hostility that stood between Jew and Gentile now must end *because* through the grace of God, both communities will live together sharing equal blessing. Neither the Jew nor the Gentile has an advantage since both are recipients of God's grace.

At this point a modern reader has to pause and take this in. This pronouncement was an idea that upended everything Paul had been taught about social order. The Jewish race was *separate* (this is the Hebrew origin of the word for Pharisee). Paul is not imagining that a Gentile church now has replaced the Jewish community of Israel as God's people. Nor is he thinking that Jewish Christians and Gentile Christians would live side by side, living separate lives. He understands that *a new creation* has emerged in Christ and *both categories* are absorbed by it. Therefore, the entire messianic community of Christ lives in direct connection to Abraham because Gentiles and Jews can both be called his children (Ro 4:16; Gal 3:7–9; 26).

## Going Deeper: He Is Our Peace (Eph 2:14)

To appreciate the force of Ephesians 2:11–22, we have to enter Paul's world and recall the sharp divisions he grew up with. If you were a conservative Jew, you would have limited contact with Gentiles. This meant rarely sharing an evening, never sharing a meal, and not letting your children marry someone who was "from the other side." While Gentiles rarely thought about Jews, the Jewish community thought about Gentiles all of the time and worked to promote separation as a cultural value.[19]

We would be naive if we thought that these divisions do not exist today. We may not see this as a Jew/Gentile problem, but Paul's point here carries broadly into our own setting powerfully. Whenever Christians render judgments on others along racial, social, or national lines, they have missed the vision of Ephesians 2:14. Whenever Christians create closed circles that isolate or remove Christians of another tribe, they have missed the vision of Ephesians 2:14.

Diversity is the test of our success in this matter. When some say that we have "peace" but then live in Christian monocultures, they are demonstrating little of the insight and courage this verse requires. As a matter of fact, the cultural majority rarely knows if a community is doing well on this score. It is always those who live on the margin, those *outside* who will be the best barometer. Those on the margin confide in one another and share things that few at the center will ever hear.

Some of us have lived and worked in chiefly white, privileged, somewhat exclusive spaces. And for the most part, members of those communities will say we have little issue with things like race. Our community is "peaceful," they say. A moment's private conversation with a resident "from the margin" of these communities will provide an utterly different perspective.

*Destroyed the barrier.* This is a complex phrase in Greek helpfully eased in the NIV. Paul illustrates this unity now by describing the destruction of the "dividing wall of hostility" (Eph 2:14). He writes (woodenly translated) about "the wall of fencing off," which is nowhere else found in Greek. But as a composite we can make sense of it: Paul is describing a divider, a wall, that existed in the Jerusalem temple, and it relates directly to Gentiles.

Each successive courtyard in the temple held increasing restrictions for entry (first, the court of the Gentiles, then women, then Israelite men, and finally priests). Interpreters generally suggest that Paul is describing the four-foot wall that was built around the entire temple to keep Gentiles away from the inner sanctuaries. Gentiles could see the temple, but they dared never enter it. Portions of this wall were discovered in 1831 and 1937, and we even have a copy of the chiseled warning that was written on the wall: *"No foreigner is to pass the wall and barrier around the precinct. Anyone caught will have himself to thank for his ensuing death."*[20] The prototype for this wall may have been the order given in Exodus 19:21–24 for Moses to build a boundary around Mount Sinai to protect the people so that God does not "break out against them."

Another view is that Paul's word here for "barrier" (Gk, *phragmos*) refers to a divider between homes, creating a boundary. And it was used in the Old Testament (Isa 5:2 LXX) and the New Testament (Mk 12:1) to refer to the hedge that God planted around his vineyard. The rabbis expanded this into a metaphor saying that the law itself *was a hedge/fence* keeping Israelites from sinning. This notion is also in the Jewish oral law (Mishnah) in this same era (*m. Abot* 1.1), where a fence is built *around the law.* Thus, the law taught that if the Sabbath began at sunset, observing Sabbath one hour before sunset protected someone from violations. That is your fence. Similarly in the *Letter of Aristeas* we find the metaphor used to separate Jews from Gentiles: "Now our Lawgiver being a wise man . . . fenced us round with impregnable ramparts and walls of iron, that we might not mingle at all with any of the other nations, but remain pure in body and soul" (*Let. Aris.* 139).

Paul is asserting that all such walls are now destroyed. The barriers built by anyone to protect themselves from outsiders should disappear in this new creation that has emerged.

**2:15** *Setting aside in his flesh the law.* This is Paul's third description of what Christ has done. In his flesh, Christ absorbed the hostility inherent in these divisions. But more, in his coming, crucifixion, and resurrection, he inaugurated an era in which the traditional markers of God's people—markers seen in Torah-obedience—now have undergone complete change.

Those who are committed to the law and those who do not know the law now find their righteousness in Christ, and because of this, the tokens of division may disappear. Paul is alluding to the new covenant (2 Co 3:1–6) anticipated in the Old Testament prophets (Jer 31:32–33) that a new and different means of access to God was now being built (Ro 3:19–31). In Galatians 3:13 Paul wrote, "Christ redeemed us from the curse of the law by becoming a curse for us" (Col 2:14 similarly).

*One new humanity.* This is an echo of Ephesians 2:14, and it repeats the second major purpose in God's plan. God was creating *one new person* (Gk, *anthrōpos*) and thereby building this peace (2:14a). As in 2:14, we cannot let this colossal idea slip by too easily. What Paul is describing is nothing short of phenomenal—both for his context and for ours.

## Ephesians 2:14–18 Through Old Testament Eyes: Jews and Gentiles in Christ

The remarkable vision that Paul is presenting in Ephesians profoundly challenges how Jews and Gentiles reflected on their relationship together. Separation from and judgment of non-Jews is repeated throughout the Old Testament. Israel was to drive out other nations from the land God gave them (Dt 7:1; Jos 3:10; 24:11). More to the point, Israel was to reject the evil practices and idolatry of Gentiles (Lev 18:3, 30; Dt 6:14–15; Jer 7:5–7; 35:15). Marriage to Gentiles was particularly condemned because it could so easily lead to serving other Gods (Ex 34:15–16; Dt 7:3–4; Jos 23:12–13; Jdg 3:6; 14:3; 1 Ki 11:1–12).

The imperative to be separate took on additional force in the Hellenistic period when Israel had to live within an expanding Roman culture. Some Jews resisted fiercely; some made compromises hoping to benefit; others became completely Hellenized and lost many of their Jewish cultural distinctives.

These tensions led to sustained divisions, which were common, and they erupted in churches like Ephesus or Galatia where these two communities tried living together. Paul, however, abandoned the Old Testament notion of separation. Paul does not imagine these two groups living in separate, parallel communities. Rather, in Christ, something new is emerging that dissolves the old battlelines. N. T. Wright comments:

The peculiar thing about what Paul says in this passage (Eph 2:11–22) is that what must have looked to his readers to be the vastly greater and wider river has joined a far smaller one—but it's the smaller one that gives its name to the river that now continues with the two streams merged into one. The great, wide river is the worldwide company of Gentiles, the non-Jewish nations stretching across the world. . . . The smaller river is the single family of Abraham, Isaac and Jacob, described here as the "community of Israel." Somehow, in the strange mapping system that the one God has chosen to operate, Gentiles and Jews have become one in the confluence that is Jesus the Messiah. And as the river continues on its way, it bears only the name of Israel but also the hope that flows from the covenants of promise made with the Israelites' patriarchs.[21]

This does not mean that particular ethnic groups cannot celebrate their unique cultural identities (Messianic Jews or Orthodox Christians, for instance). But it does mean that no one group holds a place of spiritual privilege over any other.

Now Paul has elevated his thinking to a new level. It is not that two divergent peoples can learn to live in one body; but here we have the actual language of new creation. Jesus is *re-creating* what had formerly been created in Genesis. In Christ and through the work of the Spirit, newly created people can form newly created communities that before were impossible.

**2:16** *Reconcile both of them to God.* The goal is now given even more precision. The aim of this community-transforming work is *joint reconciliation* to God (2:15–16). It is a work built on the realization that everyone has equal access to the Father and shares one Spirit (2:18)—meaning, the basis of every relationship to God from this point forward is the promise of God received by faith. Once this is seen, then the possibility of a cessation of hostilities is possible. Only those who see themselves as recipients of gifts can then in humility begin to distribute similar generosity to others.

**2:17** *He came and preached peace to you who were far away and peace to those who were near.* This is the scope of the gospel's invitation to join this new community. Those who are near (Jews) and those who are far (Gentiles) now hold this invitation (see comments on 2:13). While the concept of God being near to Israel and those in need is common (Dt 4:7; Ps 34:18; 46:1; 145:18;

148:14; La 3:57), Paul is again specifically employing language from Isaiah 57:19. (See "Ephesians 2:13 Through Old Testament Eyes: Paul's Use of Isaiah 57:19.")

The NIV "preached" barely describes the weight of the language in this verse (Gk, *euangelizō*). The verb means "to announce good news" and provides the origin of our English word *evangelism*. It represents an announcement of something consequential, generally by a government authority (see "Galatians 1:6-12 Through Old Testament Eyes: The Gospel"). Any Roman citizen reading this line would think immediately of how the same language had been used since the rule of Augustus (27 BC–AD 14). "Peace" was part and parcel of Rome's propaganda preached (Gk, *euangelizō*) regularly, indicating that now a ruler had appeared who would solve the Roman world's political, economic, and military problems. Augustus and his supporters preached "the Peace of Rome." Peace was stamped on coins and carved into building lintels. When the angels announced to the shepherds, "On earth, peace" (Lk 2:14), they were mimicking this same political promise of Augustus. The New Testament abounds with these hidden innuendoes that every careful Roman Christian understood. The gospels repeatedly use this language of announcement (Gk, *euangelizō*) to underscore what was happening. An epoch-making word was now on the street. This is precisely what Paul is signaling here in a code that thoughtful Ephesians would catch. (See also "Galatians 1:3 Through Old Testament Eyes: Shalom.")

**2:18** *Access to the Father by one Spirit.* See "Galatians 4:1-7 Through Old Testament Eyes: God as Father." Regarding the Spirit, see comments at Galatians 3:2-3 and "Galatians 3:2-5 Through Old Testament Eyes: The Holy Spirit."

Note the raw elements of trinitarian thought present already in Paul's thinking (*through Christ, to the Father, by the Spirit*). The NIV "we both" represents a strong term (Gk, *amphoteroi*) meaning, awkwardly, "both the one and the other" (Mt 9:17; Ac 23:8). Paul uses it three times in these verses (Eph 2:14, 16, 18) to say *both parties*—that is, Jew and Gentile—both (again) now have access to the Father. This once more strikes a blow to those who would claim exclusive religious privileges. Christ has opened the door, and the Spirit has ushered each of us into a profound life of access to the Father. The NIV "access" also represents another strong Greek word (*prosagōgē*), which can refer, for instance, to the right of free approach to a king ("to be led before").[22] But it could also be used in reference to access in the temple—which had strict limitations. The holy places were restricted to priests and the high priest, and even for him access was limited to the Day of Atonement (Lev 16). The notion of *this access* is used frequently in Hebrews to describe how believers can now have access to the throne of God located in his temple (Heb 4:16; 7:25; 10:22;

12:22). Paul will use it again in Ephesians 3:12 (see also Ro 5:2; 1 Pe 3:18 both as verb and noun).

**2:19** *No longer foreigners and strangers, but fellow citizens.* On how Jews viewed outsiders see "Through Old Testament Eyes: In-Group and Out-Group" below.

Here Paul describes the latter two (NIV: foreigners and strangers). There were "foreigners" (Gk, *xenoi*) who were from afar (Gk, *xenizo*, "to surprise"), someone suspicious. They were not trusted. Second, there were "strangers" or "resident aliens" (Gk, *paroikos*), outsiders who lived *inside Israel* and were tolerated (Ps 119:19; Isa 16:4) because as Israel was reminded, they too had once been foreigners (*paroikos*) living in Egypt (Ex 22:21; 23:9). The moral question in the Old Testament was always the equal protections of these foreigners and strangers in the land.

Then there were "strangers" (Gk, *xenoi*) who were from afar (Gk, *xenizo*, "to surprise"), someone suspicious. They were not trusted.

Together Paul is loosely referring to those who have no belonging at the center. They were the out-group, some of whom lived close in and were tolerated while others were openly disliked. Neither had a real place and little or no welcome within the Jewish community. In Ephesians 2:13 and 2:17, these are the people "far away," those who have no residential standing, strangers, living in the least desired category. They are Gentiles.

## Ephesians 2:19 Through Old Testament Eyes: In-Group and Out-Group

Every culture works with concentric circles defining a person's relationship to the center of tribal, civic, or social life. Anthropologists call this "in-group" and "out-group" sorting. There are those on the inside, and there are those who receive reminders that they are outside. Roman and Greek cities as well as Second Temple Jewish towns were no different (as are ethnically cohesive communities today). Generally, we see three positions: there were those who belonged at the center, resident foreigners who lived near those at the center (but who never fully belonged), and strangers who were suspect.

Jews could classify Gentiles as resident foreigners who lived in Israel and were only subject to local legal laws and enjoyed the protection of the courts (Lev 25). Grace was often extended to these people because Israel too had once been foreigners living in Egypt. Strangers, on the other hand, were dangerous and approached with fear, lack of hospitality, and opposition (Ge 19:1–10).[23] Strangers spent the "night on the street" (Ge 19:2) and could experience abuse (Ge 19:5). Permanent residents (like traveling Jews) were greeted with culturally mandated hospitality.

The outline of these three classifications can be seen in the Old Testament law describing slavery in Leviticus 25:42–46 (emphasis added):

> Because *the Israelites* are my servants, whom I brought out of Egypt, they must not be sold as slaves. Do not rule over them ruthlessly, but fear your God. Your male and female slaves are to come from *the nations around you*; from them you may buy slaves. You may also buy some of the *temporary residents living among* you and members of their clans born in your country, and they will become your property. You can bequeath them to your children as inherited property and can make them slaves for life, but you must not rule over your *fellow Israelites* ruthlessly.

We can see here that Israelites viewed themselves as living with two out-groups: resident aliens who lived nearby and nations who lived further afield. Both could be enslaved, while Israelites were protected. This is typical tribal behavior throughout the ancient (and modern) world. Paul, on the other hand, is picking up these two out-group categories and challenging their status. They now can belong to the family of God.

Therefore, Paul here is redefining the relationship of Gentiles to the theological center of Israel's story. Throughout the Old Testament, identifying the true in-group and separating from all out-groups is a constant theme. And it is this firm boundary that Paul is challenging. These foreigners will now *in Christ* be called "fellow citizens" (Gk, *sumpolitēs*; Lat, *concivis*), a term potent to any Roman reader. These were citizens of a city and enjoyed all civic privileges; now Gentiles are offered the same in Israel. They are citizens joining with the "holy people" (Eph 2:19; NIV: "God's people"), which, as it is used in 1:18, could mean nothing less than Israel itself. But to strengthen this striking image, their position is not simply citizenship, though this is important, they are now also family members of God's house (2:19: NIV: "members of his household"). This was the common way many early Christians explained their fledgling communities (Heb 3:1–6). They were households, which led to the common familial in-group language of "brother and sister" for believers in the church (1 Co 7:15). The duty of believers was to identify those within the household and be gracious to them (Gal 6:10; 1 Ti 5:8). Thus, the Gentiles are both citizens and family, which gives them a remarkable and intimate place.

**2:20** *Built on the foundation of the apostles and prophets, with Christ Jesus himself as the chief cornerstone.* What is this city to which both Jews in Christ and Gentiles in Christ belong? What is this family in which strangers can call each other brother and sister? This is not a social experiment. It is an effort constructed with Jesus Christ as its cornerstone (Ps 118:22; Mk 12:10; Ac 4:11; 1 Pe 2:7).[24] It is the Father's work achieved through Christ's work and indwelt by the Spirit.

### Ephesians 2:20 Through Old Testament Eyes: Psalm 118:22

Only here does Paul refer to the "chief cornerstone" (Gk, *akrogōniaios*; *gōnia* is a corner, *akron* refers the tip or top). It is a construction term used widely in Greek for a prominent stone. In the Old Testament, Psalm 118 refers to something very similar and it found regular use in the New Testament. In Psalm 118:22 we read, "The stone the builders rejected has become the cornerstone." The language of the LXX (the Old Testament Paul used) is precise: "The stone (Gk, *lithos*) which the builders rejected has become the head (Gk, *kephlē*) of the corner (Gk, *gōnia*)" (in the LXX this is Ps 117:22). In the New Testament this citation of Psalm 118:22 appears in Matthew 21:42, Mark 12:10, Luke 20:17, Acts 4:11, and 1 Peter 2:7.

In the ancient world, stone-builders would receive a stone hewn from a quarry and then determine its usefulness: was it compromised in any manner (cracked or weak)? If the stone needed to be cut or shaped, this was even more important. Psalm 118 imagines a stone-builder rejecting a stone—but only later learning that this stone had been rediscovered and had become the most valuable rock of all, winning a supreme place in the architecture of the building. Perhaps it was final crowning stone set in place. In the psalm, this stone represents the salvation of God the psalmist seeks, something rejected by those around him.

The New Testament cites this psalm because it explains the rejection of Jesus. *He is the rejected stone.* But now he has become the stone of honor, the crowning (Gk, *kephalē*) stone perhaps of a temple (note in Eph 2:21 Paul is building a temple metaphor). Elsewhere Paul even goes further: Jesus was not just the rejected rock; he was a rock on Israel's path that made it stumble. In Romans 9:33 Paul cites Isaiah 8:14, which turns this rock-as-Christ into an obstacle leading to judgment (also 1 Pe 2:8).

Moreover, the image of a stone (Gk, *lithos*) with the heritage of Israel or God was common. Isaiah 51:1–2 says, "Look to the rock from which you were cut and to the quarry from which you were hewn; look to Abraham, your father, and to Sarah, who gave you birth." Psalm 18:31 says, "For who is God besides the Lord? And who is the Rock except our God?" This link between God and rock is frequent in the Old Testament (over one hundred times).

Remarkably this language of stone-symbolizing-God was used widely in Second Temple Judaism for the messiah. The Old Testament texts that are echoed in Jewish writing (Ex 17:6; Nu 20:8; Ps 118:22; Isa 28:16; Da 2:34, 44–45; Zec 4:10) are also used by the New Testament. This becomes clear when we see how the LXX edits the Hebrew Bible to make these messianic connections explicit (Isa 28:16 LXX). Rabbinic commentaries on the stone of Genesis 28:18 refer directly to this stone as messiah.[25]

When Paul refers to "apostles and prophets" (Eph 2:20), he is not referring to Old Testament prophets. In Greek, when one definite article ("the") precedes two nouns (apostles and prophets), the concepts function as one. But in addition, Paul would likely refer to prophets first if he were thinking about the Old Testament. Paul's use in 3:5 and 4:11 also refers to Christian prophets. The foundation of the church is the apostolic witness to Christ and the prophetic teaching that has been preserved in the church by those who were so authorized. But prophets also mediated the voice of the Spirit. The church is thus grounded in right instruction and lives with Spirit-inspired experiences in which the resurrected Jesus can continue to speak. (See comments on "Paul, an apostle" at Gal 1:1.)

## Ephesians 2:19–22 Through Old Testament Eyes: The Temple

The precursor to Solomon's temple was the tabernacle, the portable structure the Israelites would carry with them and set up when stopping during their forty years of wandering (Ex 25–26 and 35–36). Its purpose was to be the place where God would dwell with his people on earth (Ex 25:8). Yet neither the tabernacle nor the temple could contain God (1 Ki 8:27; 2 Ch 2:6). While God fills the whole cosmos (Ps 139:7–12), God is said to sit on his throne and reign in heaven (Ps 103:19; 113:5). The temple was a mere footstool (1 Ch 28:2; Ps 132:7; Isa 66:1). The temple was thus where heaven met earth, where God could live in the midst of his people.

When it came time to construct the temple, this sanctuary of the Lord was built on the highest outcropping of Jerusalem's mountain (called Mount Zion). Its land was first purchased by David (2 Sa 24:24), and it was Solomon who built this structure that survived for centuries (1 Ki 6–7). In the sixth century BC, Babylonian armies destroyed it along with Jerusalem and carried off its treasures (2 Ki 25:9–17). Israel's grief is palpable in many of the Psalms (e.g., 137) and the book of Lamentations.

Israel's returning exiles rebuilt Jerusalem's walls first, but we are not certain how extensive the structures were at the temple site. It wasn't until the first century BC that Herod the Great built the magnificent building known in New Testament times (and still partially visible today). It began in about 20 BC and continued for decades employing thousands of workers. Once when Jesus' visited Jerusalem with his disciples, they were stunned by the size and splendor of the building (Mk 13:1). The temple and its administration was so large that we might think of Jerusalem as a city wrapped around and serving the temple. For this reason, Jews in places like Qumran compared Jerusalem with the camp of Israel in the Old Testament with the tabernacle set up at the center.

If the holy land was sacred in ancient Judaism, Jerusalem was its sacred city. And within this city there were literally ascending levels (stairs) of holiness: the temple, its various courtyards, and its holy places culminating with the most holy space accessed only by the high priest. To refer to the temple's timeless sanctity was something done only with great care.

The New Testament does just this very thing. If the temple is the dwelling place of God and Jesus in his incarnation is likewise this dwelling place, comparisons between Jesus and the temple are inevitable. In John 1:14 we read, "The Word became flesh and made his dwelling among us," which could be rendered "tabernacled among us" (TLV) as God did with Israel in the desert. Jesus also compares himself to the temple where God dwells. One of the most remarkable sayings attributed to him is Mark 14:58, "I will destroy this temple made with human hands and in three days will build another, not made with hands" (also Jn 2:19). Few sayings in Jerusalem were as explosive.

But Paul takes this comparison in a different direction. He argues that since the Spirit of God has now taken up residence in Christ's followers, *they too have become the temple.* This imagery is clear on the Day of Pentecost of Acts 2 when the Spirit with all of the accompanying imagery from the temple rests on Jesus' followers. But this idea is explicit in Paul's letters. "Don't you know that you yourselves are God's temple and that God's Spirit dwells in your midst?" (1 Co 3:16; see 6:19; 2 Co 6:16-17). 1 Peter 2:5 says the same, "You also, like living stones, are being built into a spiritual house to be a holy priesthood, offering spiritual sacrifices acceptable to God through Jesus Christ." In Peter, the imagery is complete.

Ephesians 2:19-22 is making comparable claims. Most of its language points to the temple, but the terms have been changed. Above all, Paul knows that this messianic household is being built with Jews and Gentiles whose affections for each other will be tenuous. Christ must be the cornerstone because, as this large final stone holds together two walls at one corner, so too Christ alone can keep together any church where divisions might live just below the surface.

**2:21-22** *A holy temple.* See "Ephesians 2:19-22 Through Old Testament Eyes: The Temple."

The notion that Gentiles and Jews now form one household leads Paul to a flurry of metaphors expanding on this image. Christ is the cornerstone; the apostles and prophets have built the foundation, and the entire edifice—the church—stone-by-stone now rises to become a holy temple in the Lord. In the New Testament (and Judaism at this time) the Greek term for temple (*hieron*) referred to the sanctuary's larger complex of buildings. But the Greek *naos* was the inner temple where God dwelled. To any Jew, the temple was (and is) a sacred place, but *the naos* held an unparalleled place. The holy temple stood *only* in Jerusalem. It was the dwelling place of the Lord. But just as Paul has shifted the meaning of God's people (2:19), he now shifts the meaning of God's dwelling (2:22). God's people are his handiwork (2:10), and they too are under construction because *they are the dwelling place of God* (2:22) now being built.

The temple of the Lord, therefore, is no longer in Jerusalem. It exists where God's people exist, filled with the Spirit and centered on Jesus. To a Jewish audience with long affection for Jerusalem, no more surprising words could be written.

## Going Deeper: The Temple (Eph 2:19–22)

Over the years, I have led countless people through Israel. Usually it is students, though sometimes I take adult church groups. It simply has become one of the features of my career. When groups come to Jerusalem for the first time, you can feel a tangible excitement as people anticipate that here in this holy city God will be present in ways he is not at their churches. (The same thing happens at the Jordan River, but that is another story.) And when they come to the temple area and we are fortunate enough to climb up onto the site of Israel's ancient temple platform, many are nervous with anticipation. In some manner they have stopped thinking like Christians and now they are thinking like Jews, for whom this site still is held in deep reverence and viewed as the locus of God's presence. I respect the site of the temple for its historical importance but do not see it as holy geography deserving reverence.

Some Christians, particularly in America, have even made Jerusalem and its flourishing a political cause calling on churches to send money and political support to Israel. "This is God's city," I've heard. I've seen believers praying with fervor as they press their hands into the cracks of the retaining walls of Herod's ancient temple. The locals cynically call this Jerusalem Fever.

Jesus changed the spiritual geography of the holy land. And this explains the worldwide mission of the church. No longer would God be located in a city or temple in Israel; no longer would God be represented by one ethnicity with its cultural markers. Instead, the New Testament is announcing something grand and sweeping. The world is God's interest (Ro 4:13) and all peoples belong to him. The community of Christ is a multiplicity of races where each is celebrated and each can be known as "members of God's household" and indeed, as "God's temple." When we let these ideas sink in, suddenly we recognize how shattering this was for those who defended the old structures prevalent in the biblical world. In this sense, Paul preached a revolutionary gospel, and on the foundation of this idea, the worldwide church was born. Pentecostal believers in Kenya, Arab believers in Syria, and Messianic Jewish believers in Tel Aviv share the same identity and privileges within the grace of God.

# EPHESIANS 3

**3:1** *I, Paul, the prisoner of Christ.* Paul wants to resume the prayer for the Ephesians that stemmed from the previous chapters, but he interrupts himself. When he thinks of himself as a prisoner, it is an imprisonment for a cause. He is imprisoned for the sake of the Gentiles because from the beginning he understood that he had been given a commission by Jesus to the Gentiles and he was convinced that Gentile inclusion into the family of God—including them in the family of the patriarch Abraham—was a vital part of the gospel. But this reflection about his imprisonment leads to an impulsive digression (3:2–13) where Paul gives insight into his relationship to this game-changing idea of Gentile inclusion.

## What the Structure Means: Paul's Prayer and Teaching (Eph 1 and 3)

We have seen that much of the structure of Ephesians is organized around liturgies of prayer. It is easy to miss this as we read the essay. Prayers intermingle with digressions that fill out what Paul is affirming.

**Paul's opening prayer and blessing of God (1:3–10)**
*Paul digresses about Christ and the Spirit (1:11–14)*
**Paul's first prayer giving thanks for the Ephesians (1:15–23)**
*Paul describes the Ephesians' distress and hope (2:1–10)*
*Paul describes the Ephesians' unity with God's plan (2:11–22)*
*Paul describes his own role in God's plan (3:1–13)*
**Paul's second prayer interceding for the Ephesians (3:14–19)**
**Paul's closing prayer and blessing of God (3:20–21)**

After these three chapters, Ephesians takes a decidedly different tone. From 4:1 to the end of chapter 6, Paul provides moral and spiritual guidance on a whole host of matters from marriage to spiritual warfare. The liturgical structures are gone, and the essay opens an almost new style of writing. This has led some to wonder if Paul is using liturgical material in 1:3–3:21 that may have been used in his churches. Its beautiful and almost lyrical style has suggested this to many.

**3:2–6** *The administration of God's grace that was given to me.* In 1 Corinthians 4:1 Paul gives a rare insight into his own identity: "This, then, is how you ought to regard us: as servants of Christ and as those entrusted with the mysteries God has revealed." Here in Ephesians, he refers to the administration (*oikonomia*) of God's grace given to him, showing that Paul thinks of himself as a steward (*oikonomos*) or custodian of the mystery (*mustēria*) of God that have been given in Christ. The steward (*oikonomos*) was the most trusted slave in a Roman household, who held enormous responsibility for its management. In Ephesians 3:2 Paul picks up on this same idea, using the noun describing the duties of such a steward: "You have heard about my responsibilities/ stewardship *(oikonmia)* of God's grace" (author's translation). As a steward, he is duty-bound to fulfill his role, managing the mysteries of God and the grace that was intended for the Gentiles.

**3:4–5** *The mystery of Christ.* See comments on "the mystery of his will" at Eph 1:7–10. In the Roman world, *mystery* had a religious sense (recall the many mystery cults flourishing at this time) and so the word might resonate with Paul's readers. But it was also a secular term referring to any undisclosed secret. Paul is actually using the religious sense because he is holding a divine revelation for which he is a steward. This is also paralleled by 1 Corinthians 4:1.

*Not made known.* Paul is a steward of divine secrets that only now have been provided to Paul, the holy apostles, and prophets (3:5). He refers to his previous writing in 3:3, likely pointing to the previous two chapters where he outlined the substance of this mystery. He knows it is dramatic and controversial; it was not known to previous generations,[1] and some would call it novel. But he is not alone in this revelation: there are multiple witnesses (so vital in Judaism), and the Spirit of God has revealed it to many (Christian apostles and prophets).

*Apostles and prophets.* Therefore—and this is the key point—Paul is not alone in holding and promoting this remarkable mystery. His understanding springs from a community of believers (led by Christ's apostles and prophets bringing fresh words from the risen Lord) who also affirm that this Spirit-led revelation is true and reliable. While Paul says this revelation was unknown in the past, this idea has caused controversy. The Old Testament and Second Temple Judaism both described the inclusion of the Gentiles (Ps 22:27; 86:9; 96:3; Isa 2:2–4; 11:10; 52:10; 56:6–7; Jer 3:17; 16:19; Am 9:12; 1 Enoch 10:21; 2 Baruch 72–73; Philo *Moses* 2.43–44).[2]

The solution here is not in the degree of knowledge now held (but previously held back); something now is substantially different. The well-known promise of Gentile inclusion has now been revealed to be something unexpected. In Jesus Christ, Gentiles would not simply be absorbed into Israel, they would become *in Christ* full equals with the people of God.

When did this revelation happen? Each of Paul's three accounts of his conversion in Acts indicates that his unlikely call to the Gentiles was central to this experience. It was revealed to Ananias in Damascus (Ac 9:15). It was also revealed in Paul's vision at the temple (Ac 22:21). He sees this as integral to his commission by Christ (Gal 1:11–16). There is no doubt that this secret, this mystery, was absolutely foundational to Paul's life. But what sort of revelation was it? In Ephesians 3:4 he refers to having an "insight" (into what? The scriptures?) that changed everything.

What is this mystery? Paul believes that when his fellow Jews read their scriptures it is as if a veil has been drawn over their minds (2 Co 3:14–15). But he says whenever anyone turns to the Lord (Christ), "the veil is taken away" (2 Co 3:16). For Paul the revelation included grace, to be sure—but it applied that grace to Gentiles in a way utterly unexpected. Paul was dumbfounded by it. The catalyst for this thought may have been the promises to Abraham (see "Ephesians 3:6 Through Old Testament Eyes: The Three Promises to Abraham") or the fulfillment of prophetic promises that had been misread (see "Ephesians 3:6 Through Old Testament Eyes: The Prophetic Ingathering"). Perhaps it was both. But once Paul had seen it, there was no going back.

## Ephesians 3:6 Through Old Testament Eyes: The Three Promises to Abraham

In Genesis, Abraham meets God and learns of three great promises that will attach to his covenant. Abraham will be a father of many children (15:5), he will receive the land of Canaan (15:18–21), and through him the nations of the world will be blessed (18:18). All three are represented in 26:4, "I will make your descendants as numerous as the stars in the sky and will give them all these lands, and through your offspring all nations on earth will be blessed."

While the first two promises received intense interest in Israel's history, leading to the development of national Israel, the third promise—consistently reinforced in the Old Testament[3]—received less attention, particularly in the Second Temple period. *How would Abraham's tribe bless the nations of the world?* This raised the complex question of Judaism's treatment of and attitudes toward the Gentiles.

Paul understands these three promises, and in his conversion, he suddenly saw that in Christ the third of these promises was being realized. The inclusion of Gentiles would bless the nations of the world and redefine everything about God's saving purposes. Gentiles could be folded into the family of Abraham (Ro 4:9–25). In Galatians 3:8, Paul cites the Genesis promise to the nations and sees its fulfilled as Gentiles embrace Christ.

## Ephesians 3:6 Through Old Testament Eyes: The Prophetic Ingathering

During and after Israel's exile to Babylon, the Old Testament prophets provided hope to Israel by predicting a return to the land. Jeremiah is typical. In a letter to the exiles in Babylon, he wrote expressing God's hope for them (29:10–14):

> This is what the LORD says: "When seventy years are completed for Babylon, I will come to you and fulfill my good promise to bring you back to this place. For I know the plans I have for you," declares the LORD, "plans to prosper you and not to harm you, plans to give you hope and a future. Then you will call on me and come and pray to me, and I will listen to you. You will seek me and find me when you seek me with all your heart. I will be found by you," declares the LORD, "and will bring you back from captivity. I will gather you from all the nations and places where I have banished you," declares the LORD, "and will bring you back to the place from which I carried you into exile."

Other prophets such as Ezekiel promised the same. Note that as a part of this promise, there would be an "ingathering." The dispersed Jews would return.

This ingathering was well-known in Paul's Jewish world, and some believed that it took place in the return from exile. However, many features of the return were not fulfilled. In fact, Israel continued to live under a series of occupying powers, which seemed to invalidate it. For some, it was so bad that it appeared that Israel still lived in exile. We might say that the exile in Babylon was external—foreign—but now, the exile of occupation, first Greek then Roman, was internal.

Here, however, Paul does something extraordinary. He knows the Old Testament promises of ingathering, and he cites them and alludes to them in Ephesians 2. But here in 3:2–6 he makes explicit what he understands. The "mystery" given to him by revelation is that the ingathering is not about Jews rebuilding a nation; it is about the ingathering of Gentiles into God's people. Paul takes these promises and applies them to the church: "This mystery is that through the gospel the Gentiles are heirs together with Israel, members together of one body, and sharers together in the promise in Christ Jesus" (Eph 3:6). We could also view this as Paul's application of the blessing of the nations that reaches back as far as Abraham in Genesis (Ge 12:3; 18:18; 22:18). In Christ, the character of the people of God has become completely inclusive, which is why he can say that the great barrier between Jew and Gentile has been removed in Christ (Gal 3:28; Eph 2:19). Gentiles are now fellow citizens. Of what? Israel. (See sidebar, "Ephesians 3:6 Through Old Testament Eyes: The Three Promises to Abraham.")

Therefore, the great ingathering prophesied in the Old Testament and interpreted through the New Testament is now happening in the worldwide church, which is bringing to faith *every tribe and nation* (not one tribe, not one nation).

**3:6** *Through the gospel the Gentiles are heirs together with Israel.* See "Galatians 1:6–12 Through Old Testament Eyes: The Gospel" and "Ephesians 3:6 Through Old Testament Eyes: The Prophetic Ingathering."

Here at last Paul provides in concise form the mystery that he has been stewarding all along. "This mystery is that through the gospel the Gentiles are heirs together with Israel, members together of one body, and sharers together in the promise in Christ Jesus." The essence of these ideas has already been seen in Ephesians 2 when Paul writes about those who were away who are now near (2:13, 17) and how this movement results in their new citizenship in Israel and their membership in God's household (2:19–20). The end result is a new humanity (2:15) consisting of Jews and Gentiles who together in Christ find unity.

Therefore, Paul's gospel is not simply about grace or Christ's life-giving death on the cross. It is also about the re-creation of human possibilities, a new order of life, a redefining of what it means to be the people of God forged by the work of the Spirit. This worldview and mystery would upend everything Paul knew about his own religious history and the ongoing role of Israel in God's plan. God had surprised everyone. Christ was an agent of reconciliation in ways few expected.

## Going Deeper:
## Ethnicity and the Nations Today (Eph 3:6)

When we reconstruct the worldview of Paul's Jewish culture, no division was greater than that between the Jew and the Gentile. It is easy for us to underestimate how dramatic this was and how explosive it was for Paul to imagine the body of Christ as a community in which ethnicity and nationality could disappear. Let's be clear. There were Christians in the early church who did not want to close that gap. They wanted to privilege one culture over another. This is clear in the aftermath of Peter's conversion of Cornelius in Acts 10. We immediately find the apostle standing in Jerusalem before Christian leaders who are ready to criticize him (Ac 11:2–3).

If Paul had the courage to imagine something like this *for his time*, I cannot help but wonder what this imagining would like *in our time*. We are well aware how racially fueled discrimination appears throughout the world. Bitter conflicts and explicit crimes take place from Myanmar to India to Congo and Sudan. We see it in Europe with immigrants and old residential communities who have come from Turkey and Algeria. America has a long legacy of this.

But perhaps if Paul was with us today, he would ask if followers of Christ were any different from all of this. He might wonder if the church had actually become a place where things were different. He might wonder if the great vision of a community where dividing walls had broken down (Eph 2:14) had been realized in the centuries after his life had passed.

For as Paul says in Ephesians 3:10, breaking down such barriers is nothing less than the announcement to the spiritual forces opposed to God that their defeat is sure. As N. T. Wright said, "It is when the Christian community comes together across barriers which divide us from one another that the principalities and powers know that Jesus Christ is Lord. And that as long as we are divided whether black and white, male and female, rich and poor or whatever, the principalities and powers smile and say, 'We are still in charge here!'"[4]

**3:7-8** *I became a servant of this gospel by the gift of God's grace.* Regarding the pairing of God's gift and Paul's response in service to the gospel, see "Galatians 3:2-6 Through Old Testament Eyes: Grace and Benefaction."

*Grace given me through the working of his power.* Paul continues his digression for another seven verses before reclaiming his prayer in 3:14. Paul now says he is not just a servant or steward of mysteries, but he is one who serves (Gk, *diakonos*; NIV: "servant") the gospel, thanks to the gift of God's grace working powerfully within him. No doubt Paul is thinking here about his conversion (Ac 9) and how he did not encounter a new idea or a new community or a new way of living on the highway to Damascus. *He experienced Christ in his resurrected power.* (On Paul's own account of his experience, see comments on Gal 1:11-17. On Paul's understanding of grace as gift, see "Going Deeper: Paul and the Gift [Gal 2:19-21].")

*The least of all the Lord's people.* Paul is not simply being self-critical. He is being self-effacing. He recognizes the work he has been privileged to complete (preaching to the Gentiles, offering them boundless grace), but he also recalls that grace became for him what it is because of his previous life before his conversion. He never forgot that he persecuted the church, and in every account of this conversion, Paul refers to it (Ac 9:5; 22:4-8; 26:11-15). He says, "I was so obsessed with persecuting them [the church] that I even hunted them down in foreign cities" (Ac 26:11; see Gal 1:13, 23).

But there is more here. Paul views himself as "least" because he understands that he could bring nothing to the table that deserved the generosity he received. Paul reached with an empty hand because, given his history with Christ's church, judgment should have been God's answer, not grace. For Paul, understanding grace increases when we see our own meritless situation.

**3:9-10** *To make plain.* Paul then sees two purposes for his ministry: to preach the grace of God to Gentiles (3:8) and to make plain the *working out* of this great mystery and revelation (3:9). The NIV "administration" is the Greek *oikonomia*, which Paul is now using for the third time (1:7-10; 3:2-6). This is a householder's plan for his estate, and metaphorically it is the working out or the putting into effect the wishes of the household. Household stewards do this (this is how Paul views himself, 3:2). Therefore, Paul's second purpose is the application or unfolding or implementation of this mystery of inclusion that heretofore had not been known.

*Kept hidden in God.* The secrecy of this mystery has sometimes proven difficult for interpreters. Paul here uses a framework of "formerly hidden but now disclosed" scheme to show the limitations of knowledge in Old Testament faith.[5] He says this in 3:5, and he practices it in his use of Isaiah 57:19 in Ephesians 2:17. Isaiah's understanding of those "far off" referred to displaced Jews returning to Judea to rejoin Jews who were "near." Paul's reinterpretation of this promise to refer to Gentiles is part and parcel of the mystery Paul is holding. This view of revelation is also paralleled in Daniel 2 where Nebuchadnezzar's dream is inaccessible to the wise of Babylon. However, Daniel can explain it because "the God of heaven reveals mysteries" (2:18–19 LXX). (See comments on "the mystery of his will" at Ephesians 1:7–10.)

*The rulers and authorities in the heavenly realms.* The twofold mission of Paul was *so that* through the work of the church the multifaceted (Gk, *polupoikilos*, "many-colored") wisdom of God would be shown, not merely to the world but to a heavenly audience. This is unexpected. This likely connects with Paul's view (6:12), shared widely among Romans, that malevolent powers brought harm to human life, and this could be seen directly in the angry suspicions and deep divisions based on race, ethnicity, and nationality in human society. (See comment on "the elemental spiritual forces" at Gal 4:3.) The wisdom of God—to which these powers have no access—could not see this coming. *Christ's work to unite believers into a loving unified community (the church) upends the destructive efforts of these powers.* The mystery of Paul's revelation is not simply good news to those who will benefit by it; but it is an announcement of victory for all creation (3:9)—the very creation God is reclaiming in Christ—that the powers have been defeated. (See comments on "the mystery of his will" at Eph 1:7–10 and "the Spirit of wisdom and revelation" at Eph 1:17.)

## Ephesians 3:10 Through Old Testament Eyes: Paul and Apocalyptic

The Old Testament viewed history as a succession of ages with a beginning (creation) and an ending (judgment). Apocalyptic is a view of history focusing on when this world will end and *another* will emerge in the imminent future. In most cases the view is dramatic and severe, with God bringing judgment on the nations (e.g., Isa 13–23; Eze 25–32) and rescue to his people (e.g., Isa 40–66; Eze 36–37, 40–48). But in all cases, the view is *linear*, with a timeline that moves human history from the past to the present to a new age hallmarked by God's righteousness and restoration of creation. Such views were widespread in the Old Testament prophets and early Judaism.

For some scholars, this apocalyptic worldview has entirely shaped Paul's thinking and contributed to his teaching in Ephesians. Rather than emphasizing merely how the work of Christ brought about personal salvation for believers, Paul is thinking about how Christ has ushered in a new era in which the realities of the future in that linear schema now have erupted in the present. Being "in Christ" is not simply a marker of salvation. It is life ushered into a new reality never before seen in history. We are thus now living in connection with God just as it is promised for the end of time.

Paul says at his conversion he experienced a *revelation* (Gal 1:12; Gk, *apokalupsis*) of what was happening in light of Christ's interruption of the pattern of history. The fullness of time (Gal 4:4) had come and so, rather than two stages (first this world, then the world to come), Christ had inaugurated an interim period in which things of the future (the Spirit) were at work.[6] This is consistent with Jesus' own ministry, which preached that the kingdom was at hand due to his arrival (Mk 1:14–15), but it was not fully realized, as the King himself was rejected by many of his own people (Jn 1:10–11).

In Ephesians, the church was not only a community celebrating its redemption and looking to the future return of Christ, but it was a community living beneath an open heaven in which the powers of all creation were being affected and formed. Mysteries were being revealed *now* (Eph 1:9; 3:3–6) and God's will—which would be imposed on history in the future—was now being enacted on earth (1:11). Christ's followers thus experience immediate power through the Spirit (1:19; 2:18), the same power that can control all powers in all creation (1:20; 3:10). In a word, the future had cast its shadow on the present.

This interim reality means that we continue to be tethered to the earth (as citizens of this world), but also we live in a space that is accessing divine power (as citizens of heaven). Embracing Christ, therefore, is not just about addressing the law and sin; it is about joining Christ, living with Christ, being "in Christ" from now until he returns. Christian life is living in two spheres: remaining in one while also moving substantially into another.

**3:11** *His eternal purpose.* This new creation of a new community was God's plan from the very beginning. It had always been an ancient plan (established from the beginning) and is an expression of God's will today (1:11). Now suddenly we can see with greater clarity the purpose of Christ in the purposes of God. It was not only for revelation or forgiveness of sins.

It was for the restoration of God's creation. This plan, therefore, is a cosmic plan whose scope reaches far beyond the limited interest of Paul's Jewish community. *This was a redemption for the world that invited all peoples to join.*

**3:12** *Freedom and confidence.* A literal translation of 3:12 refers to Jesus thus: "in whom we have boldness and access with confidence through faith in him." Consonant with Paul's surprising mystery, the benefits *for all* now come clear: Access to God is not restricted to the few who claim privilege. Access to God is the bold claim of *anyone* who approaches him while bound to Christ. We need to recall that Paul's world was filled with fear of countless divine powers. The malevolent heavenly authorities that try to harm are now disarmed because Christ's followers are sheltered by God's presence, whose powerful Spirit is undefeatable.

**3:13** *My sufferings.* Paul's own suffering sometimes led to the criticism that this victory he announced could not be believed *because* of Paul's own story. This may have been a charge at Corinth (2 Co 4:16–18). Our mortality, Paul argued there, was no sign of any such thing because despite appearances, God's miraculous, mysterious work was taking root in his inner life. Therefore, Paul's present imprisonment was not a sign of defeat. He was a soldier unfolding the great assault on history's dark order of things, and this worked to the Ephesians' benefit. They should celebrate and not grieve.

**3:14–19** *For this reason I kneel before the Father.* Paul now resumes the thought he began in 3:1 completing his prayer on behalf of the Ephesians. Prayer was commonly practiced in a standing posture in Judaism (1 Sa 1:9; 1 Ki 8:22; Mk 11:25). Kneeling was also well-known (1 Ki 8:54; 19:18; 2 Ch 6:13; Ps 95:6; Da 6:10; Lk 22:41; Ac 21:5) and usually pointed to the depth or pathos of a person's feelings (1 Ch 29:20; Ezr 9:5; Ac 21:5).[7]

The Israelites considered God to be their father (Dt 1:31; 32:6; Ps 103:13; Isa 63:16; 64:8; Mal 2:10; and see "Galatians 4:1–7 Through Old Testament Eyes: God as Father"). When Paul prays to the Father (Gk, *patēr*; Eph 3:14), he opens a wordplay on family (*patria*) in 3:15. The headship of fathers in families and tribes was universal. This is expressed in naming another. The idea of "naming" in antiquity meant exerting authority over another (thus Adam names the animals in Genesis; see Ps 147:4). God is sovereign not simply over Israel—a provincial idea—but he is sovereign over the whole of creation ("*every* family"), including those things beyond the earth in heavenly realms. There is no domain where God is not sovereign (Ex 19:5–6; Dt 10:14; Ps 89:11; 110:6; Isa 6:3).

Thus, Paul is continuing his notion that his God is not limited to one tribe—as was true with most ethnic religions in antiquity. Every family—and here we need to think broadly, because the term *patria* meant a clan or a tribe—now can find its true father in the one God of Israel. Here we have the description of what Paul meant in 1:10. The purpose of God's plan in Christ was to unite "all things in heaven and on earth under Christ." This is a remarkable global concept, a transcultural concept that includes every Gentile, and as we have seen in chapters two and three, this is connected to the mystery of Paul's revelation. Every community of believers despite their national or ethnic place is accorded the same privileges with God.

**3:16** *I pray that out of his glorious riches he may strengthen you with power through his Spirit in your inner being.* This is Paul's first appeal to God—that the Ephesians would be strengthened in power by God's Spirit and this would be drawn from the "glorious riches" of God himself. Glory (Gk, *doxa*) is the radiance or renown that comes from God's presence and is seen in the shekinah glory of Yahweh in the temple. When Paul refers to their "inner being" (Gk, *esō anthrōpos,* "inner person"), he is thinking about the interior life of a person compared with the exterior bodily existence. Paul uses the phrase in two other places (Ro 7:22–23; 2 Co 4:16). In 2 Corinthians he can say that while his outer life is wasting away, still, something miraculous is happening within. This means that while suffering or hardship may be difficult, still, the inner self, the locus of the Spirit's work, will be strengthened. This also means that if the Ephesians are concerned about Paul's imprisonment, they need not be.

**3:17** *So that Christ may dwell in your hearts.* The parallel idea to the interior work of the Spirit is Christ's indwelling (3:17). "In your hearts" mirrors "your inner being" (3:16). This Spirit is the power of Christ himself now at work. The Ephesians have been sealed by the Spirit (1:13) and united with Christ in his resurrection (2:5–6). Conceptually these ideas are moving in the same direction. This is the new humanity Paul has been alluding to all along. This what it means to put on Christ (Gal 3:27). This is the renewal of our minds (Ro 12:2) and the transformation that begins to bring creation back into its place as its creator had planned.[8] Recall what Paul wrote in Galatians 6:15: "Neither circumcision nor uncircumcision means anything; what counts is the new creation." Paul completes the thought with two participles: this transformation happens as we are rooted and grounded in love—a horticultural and a construction metaphor. Being grounded (Gk, *themeliō*) comes from the Greek term for a foundation stone or the root of a mountain (Gk, *themelios*).[9] It is not that we are just grounded but that this transformation has an immovable stone foundation: love.

## Going Deeper: The Love of God (Eph 3:17–19)

Recently I tried adding up the number of college students I have had in class. It was larger than I imagined. Thousands over a long career. There are a lot of memories that accompany this history and many themes that seemed to repeat themselves. One stood out.

These students came from Christian families and grew up in Christian churches. Many were enthusiastically evangelical; some were questioning this heritage; others had walked away from it altogether. But each year I was surprised at how many times students did not have a grasp of God's love *for them*. I am confident that their families talked about it and their churches offered sermons on it. But *in their lived experience* it was not a reality. When a new president came to Wheaton College in 2010, he wisely recognized this at the college (he was a graduate as well), and he decided to focus his inaugural year on the grace of God—a related theme that was equally foreign to students.

If asked, students would tell you that the love and grace of God were central to the gospel. However, for them these had become stale doctrines and clichés. They lived with astonishing degrees of spiritual anxiety fueled by performance-driven lives. In a word, the love of God was not a living reality for them. Had they not experienced unmerited love? Did they not know what grace was (other than a doctrine)? Was personal righteousness promoted so aggressively that it dwarfed any idea of God's affection for them? Sometimes when I said, "You know, God really likes you," I got their attention because it was new language they had not heard.

Ephesians 3:17–19, climaxing perhaps with verse 18, is the one portion of Scripture they so desperately needed. I often showed it to them. The irony was that they knew these verses—some had memorized them—and still they had little effect. A performance-centered legalism had drained many of them of any capacity to believe that love this wide and this deep even existed. And it made me wonder, Was this also true of their parents, their pastors, and, well, all of us?

**3:18–19** *To grasp how wide and long and high and deep is the love of Christ.* God's love is expressed in similar terms in Psalm 103:11—"For as high as the heavens are above the earth, so great is his love for those who fear him" (see also Ps 36:5; 57:10). The imagery may also refer to the newly built temple that dominated Jerusalem in this day. Its grandeur and size would have evoked this very language that we see here for Jesus. And this may be Paul's intent, since the New Testament bears ample evidence of thinking about Jesus in terms of the temple.

It is vital to remember what the mystery religions were offering in Paul's world. They provided secret knowledge and esoteric ceremonies reserved for only those who were selected. Their ecstatic experiences were an end in themselves, linking the worshipper to divine realities. They claimed to have "fullness," a technical term used widely. But knowledge was at the heart of their promise. Paul's language of height and depth would echo many of their promises. Here, however, Paul replaces knowledge with power (Eph 3:18) and love (3:18).

In these sentences (3:18–19) Paul's plea for the Ephesians almost runs away with itself. It is a continuation of petitions that began at 3:16, which we might phrase like this:

> I pray . . .
>> that you would be able to grasp
>>> together with the saints
>>> how wide and long, how high and deep . . .
>> that you would know
>>> the love of Christ that exceeds all comprehension
>> that you would be filled with all the fullness of God.

This remarkable prayer concludes with beautiful language and elevated hopes, which explain its frequent use even today in liturgies. Paul is outlining the ultimate gift of sonship/daughtership (Gal 3:26; 4:7) that belongs to the children of God. This is the culmination of being set apart (Eph 1:4), sealed (1:13), saved (2:5), raised (2:6), called near (2:13), made citizens and family members (2:19), built into a temple (2:22), named heirs (3:6), strengthened by the Spirit (3:16), and having Christ indwell us (3:17)—this is summarized in this singular recognition that we are able to know something otherwise unknowable, that we are invited into a knowledge of God experienced as his indescribable love.

The fullness of God now comes to us not through esoteric religious pursuits but purely through the outpouring of God's love expressed to us in Christ. In a world of fear and uncertainty, this is now the heart of Paul's gospel: that Christ came into the world not to change God's mind, but to show God's mind. And at the very center of God's mind is love. Simply: God is for us, never against us, and he is eager to fold all of his creation into this overwhelming love.

**3:20–21** *Now to him.* This short doxology ends the theological portion of Ephesians. It celebrates God's activity on behalf of his world, now revealed in the gospel of Jesus Christ.

*His power that is at work within us.* Power is the defining mark of this gospel. In Romans 1:16, Paul says the distinguishing feature of the gospel is power—and he is not ashamed of this. In Paul's day (and ours), power evokes thoughts of extreme fanaticism, but for Paul, this is what he experienced when Christ confronted him and transformed him. Power is frequently used by Paul (forty-nine times) to convey what it means to belong to Christ. It is not a remote transaction gaining salvation; it is not a set of theological convictions; it is an encounter, and this experience of power is the confirming feature of Paul's own faith.

*To him [the Father] be glory in the church and in Christ Jesus.* See "Galatians 4:1–7 Through Old Testament Eyes: God as Father." This is the only doxology in Paul's writing that mentions both Christ and the church. Paul sees the church as a sphere where the glory of God is acknowledged.[10] This is not surprising because, here in Ephesians, Paul is explicating the *communal miracle* of the gospel in this world: a new community has formed, called the church. This unity of the church in Christ is a witness, even to the principalities and powers, of the truth and power of God's work in Christ (3:10). It stands as a marker in history, proclaiming not merely the gospel itself but another way to live *where two become one*—where all who have faith are Abraham's children, where everyone on the margin is now invited "in." But glory also belongs to Christ through whom all of this became a reality. Glory is an attribute that belongs to God (Ex 15:11; Ps 57:5, 11), and now (remarkably for a Jewish writer) Paul is willing to apply it to the church and Jesus. (Regarding "glory," see also comments at Eph 1:4–6, 17, and Gal 1:4–5.)

This is also Paul's only use of "generation" (Gk, *genea*) in a doxology, "Glory . . . throughout all generations" (Eph 3:21). This is another signal about time. This event Paul is describing is not one more event among many in the course of human events paraded through time. This is a singular event that will cast its shadow from this point into the future. But it is also a signal about space. This event will not only last "for ever and ever" and be recognized not only in the world but in *all of creation*, including the heavenly realms (1:20; 3:10). It is as if creation has shifted on its moorings and the old categories of religion and religious identity should be no more.

# EPHESIANS 4

**4:1** *Then, I urge you to live a life worthy of the calling you received.* Paul typically followed a major theological section of his letters with a practical exhortation to live into the good things he has just described. Romans 12:1–15:13 is a perfect example of this. In fact, in the Greek, Paul begins Ephesians 4:1 with the same language as Romans 12:1 ("Therefore, I urge you"). While the NIV uses "then," Paul includes *therefore* (Gk, *oun*) in both of these, indicating that what is to follow is anchored in what has just been said. What follows flows from the new realities now at work in the world.

The Greek "I" here is emphatic, underscoring Paul's assumed authority over his churches. But the term *urge* is more richly represented by "encourage" or "exhort" (Gk, *parakaleō*) or, in older translations, "beseech."[1] It conveys a sense of warning as well, often followed by a direct request.

In his first three chapters, Paul offered a dramatic vision for what God has done in the world through Jesus Christ. God was creating something new, re-claiming his creation and charting a way for it to find unity amid its wretched history of disunity and conflict. This story is not simply about *personal salvation*; it is about how saved people will come together and form communities of unity and holiness, thereby offering the world a way out of its dismal state of affairs. In this sense the church in its goodness is not simply an aspiration or a hoped-for reality, but it is inherent in the very definition of what it means for the church to be what it is: a gathering shaped by the Spirit, governed by the Lord Jesus Christ, and finding its life through the Father.[2]

Above all, Paul would never have seen these instructions as a rulebook or some reference list to which we should look to check behavior. This would inspire the very legalism that he had confronted throughout his career. Instead, he urges his readers to conform to the life to which they now belong. (If you are married, now live *as married*! If you have joined the military, embrace honor, courage, and commitment!) Satisfying the rules will never gain entry to this new community, but living by them is what will make the community what it is.

Many see that the two themes that unite chapters 4–6 are unity and purity (or holiness). In 4:1–16, Paul outlines how the church might find unity amid its diversity; but in his longest section, 4:17–5:21, he outlines how the Ephesians can promote holiness despite the cultural pressures surrounding them.

"Live a life" (4:1 NIV) is literally "walking around" (Gk, *peripateō*, Mk 2:9; Jn 5:8) and emphasizes ongoing conduct (such as 1 Pe 5:8, the devil "roams around"). "Walking" is a common metaphor in Hebrew regarding how one is to conduct oneself in God's presence and live faithfully in his ways (Ge 5:22, 24; 6:9; 17:1; 1 Ki 8:25; 2 Ch 6:16; Ps 1:1; Isa 2:3; Mal 2:6). In Hebrew the term for this is *halak* ("to go or walk") and so Judaism's rules of living/walking are called *halakah*. Thus, Paul writes in Colossians 1:10, "That you may live a life (Gk, *peripateō*, "walk") [in a manner] worthy of the Lord."

*As a prisoner for the Lord.* This is literally "a prisoner *in the Lord*" and is similar to 3:1 ("the prisoner of Christ Jesus"). While he is of course a prisoner of Rome, he reframes and transforms his situation into one with a higher reality. Paul is not asking for sympathy. He is showing that being a prisoner is a part of his ministry for Christ, and because of the depth of his commitment to Christ, he now deserves to be heard.

**4:2** *Bearing with one another in love.* Paul opens his encouragement underscoring the need for charity. Three attributes are listed: humility, gentleness, and patience (as in Col 3:12).[3] These were well-known to Paul's audience, but they might have been surprised to see humility (or lowliness) listed as a virtue.

In the Old Testament, humility is a positive character trait associated with obedience (Zep 2:3) and wisdom (Pr 11:2), perhaps because it reflects a rightly ordered relationship of submission to God (Pr 22:4). In Greek and Roman writing, however, humility carried the notion of lacking self-respect or promoting shame. It was the disposition of a cringing slave. In fact, it never appears in any Greek or Roman virtue list as a sought-after quality of life.

Paul, however, uses it frequently (Eph 4:2; Php 2:3; Col 2:18, 23; 3:12; see also Ac 20:19; 1 Pe 5:5) and saw it reflected in Jesus, for whom humility in the cross lived at the center of Christian faith (Mt 11:29; Php 2:5–8).

The same surprise applies to gentleness (or meekness). Proverbs extols gentle speech as a wise approach to resolving tension and conflict (Pr 15:1; 16:14; 25:15; see also Ecc 10:4). Here Paul affirms this disposition that rejects bravado and self-promotion even though those were attitudes that Romans admired. Patience (Gk, *makrothumia*) literally describes a long (Gk, *makro*) anger (Gk, *thumos;* related to words for burning) and evolved to mean someone who did not react quickly, who used self-restraint. Together these three virtues describe how Christians literally "lift up" (or bear—as one carries a litter on shoulders) one another in love.

**4:3** *Keep the unity of the Spirit through the bond of peace.* Regarding the Spirit, see comments at Galatians 3:2–3 and "Galatians 3:2–5 Through Old Testament Eyes: The Holy Spirit."

Paul understandably opens the subject of the church's life with concerns about unity, given his promise that the new community formed by Christ would weaken the divisions so common among us (2:11–22). Within its first generation, the early church began to see fractures in this unity. Virtually each of Paul's letters bears witness to this and in them Paul gives instructions for patience and charity to keep the church unified (Ro 14:13; 1 Co 1:10–17; Php 2:1–11).[4] When Jesus prayed for the church, unity was foremost on his mind (Jn 17:11, 21). Therefore, it is no surprise that here, as Paul imagines the new creation of the church, he urges that peace should reign and unity result. (See "Galatians 1:3 Through Old Testament Eyes: Shalom.")

## Going Deeper: Christian Love, Unity, and War (Eph 4:1–6)

I once had a colleague whose office was near mine. On his door he kept a poster that stood out proudly for years. In the background, two people hug, and in the foreground were these words in bold: "Modest Proposal for Peace. Let the Christians of the world agree that they will not kill each other." When non-Christians in the world look at the strife between Christians in the West, they wonder if the church is living up to its promise of unity and peace.

I spend a lot of time in the Middle East. Despite the fact that the Christian faith was born in the Middle East and local Christians there are grateful for the contributions of the Western churches to their communities, still, they are perplexed at what they see. When I talk to them about violence in places like Syria, Iraq, or Palestine, it takes no time for them to describe European wars and racial violence in the "Christian West." I may talk about the problem of Islamic violence, but they will talk about how often shootings take place on American streets. I try to explain that American isn't "Christian" any more than Syria is "Muslim." But then they ask why American Christians sometimes demand to carry guns to church. They find it incomprehensible to imagine believers listening to a sermon on love, unity, and grace, all the while fully armed and ready to shoot.

All of it is embarrassing. And it makes me think about how Jesus' call to simple "neighbor love" stands apart from what we've become acclimated to seeing.

For some, Ephesians 4:3 has meant uniformity of spiritual or theological belief, and this has led to constraints placed on some and strict definitions of orthodoxy for others. This is not Paul's intent here. He is urging simply that Jesus' followers patiently love one another and not divide the church—which only diminishes its witness to the Spirit who is the architect of this new creation of humanity.

**4:4-6** *One body and one Spirit.* Paul's metaphor for the church (Eph 1:23; 2:11, 16; 3:6; 4:4, 12-16, 25; 5:23-33) saw it as an organic, living body with various constituent parts, all serving and working for the benefit of the whole. In 1 Corinthians 12:4-26 Paul lays out this understanding carefully and keeps in balance the individuality of each person and the imperative to serve the whole (also Ro 12:4-8). The Spirit animates the body by gifting each part with particular skills (1 Co 12:1, 4). This one body then requires a degree of unity and commitment to basic Christian identity so that the church is strengthened (Eph 4:12). This strengthening comes through the active promotion of peace, which, in Paul's mind, is the bond or link or chain (Gk, *sundesmos*) that keeps the church together (2:14).

The repeated use of "one" (six times) in 4:4-6 may well have originated from Israel's famous *Shema* (Dt 6:4-5) that Paul is now adapting for Christian use. This presents a jarring staccato list (without the use of "there is," which is absent in Greek) that presses home the same point. Each term is worthy of reflection. "One hope" (Eph 4:4) expresses the unifying aspiration of our united life together that Paul is expressing for the church. This is the great calling and plan of God in Christ.

Behind each of the terms in 4:5 ("one Lord, one faith, one baptism") we must imagine a teacher who might want to deviate from these and part with Paul's instruction. This also implies that by the time this letter circulated, Christians were nearing a consensus about important fundamental teachings. Paul is alerting the Ephesians to discern between right teaching and deviant teaching. Together these words form a triad that likely should be read together (one Lord in whom we believe and into whom we are baptized). Baptism was the chief marker that identified a person with this confession and which provided entry into the body. Because of its social importance, Paul will not allow any to prohibit someone based on ethnicity, social class, or gender (Gal 3:27–28). He repeats this in 1 Corinthians 12:13, "For we were all baptized by one Spirit so as to form one body—whether Jews or Gentiles, slave or free—and we were all given the one Spirit to drink."

For Christians this confession might have presented a problem. Even though it echoes the Jewish *Shema* ("Hear, O Israel: the LORD is our God, the LORD is one" [Dt 6:4–5]), Christians affirmed not only the one Jewish God but his son, Jesus Christ, who now had claim to the title "Lord" as well. Paul lays this out delicately in 1 Corinthians 8:4–6: "For us there is but one God, the Father, from whom all things came and for whom we live; and there is but one Lord, Jesus Christ, through whom all things came and through whom we live." Paul never saw the affirmation of Jesus' lordship as compromising his monotheism.

*One God and Father of all.* The emphasis here (Eph 4:6) is not on the oneness of God (which has been established) but on the breadth of his father-hood. This has been a repeated theme in Ephesians, where Paul imagines the church as a newly built household where Jews and Gentiles together are in-vited in (2:19) to become joint heirs (3:6). (See also "Galatians 4:1–7 Through Old Testament Eyes: God as Father.")

**4:7** *Grace has been given.* As Paul imagines the church, he now reflects on the diversity of gifts distributed by Christ to his followers much as he does in 1 Corinthians 12. Here he thinks of this as gifts of grace. We are each given gifts (*charis*, gifts or grace) from the measure of the gift (*dōrea*, gift) coming from Christ. This slightly repetitive phrase underscores that not only has Christ called us together, but he has also provided gifts to diversify the abilities of those within the community. In secular Greek, grace (Gk, *charis*) is what delights us (its verbal form meant "to show pleasure"), and so it was closely related to "gift" (see "Galatians 3:2–6 Through Old Testament Eyes: Grace and Benefaction") and the verb, "to give freely or generously." Therefore, Christ's generous giving was not merely seen in redemption or in the new community of the redeemed but in the way he made provision for each member of the church to make a Spirit-given contribution.

**4:8** *He ascended on high.* This Old Testament citation presents various challenges and echoes the main themes found in Psalm 68. God as victor moved from Mount Sinai and ascended Mount Zion (Jerusalem) in victory, receiving bounty from his enemy captives. Paul changes the ending of the Psalm in order to apply it to Christ, who likewise ascended but, in this instance, distributed gifts to his people. This requires us to explain who are Christ's captives. Patristic writers imagined many things: perhaps his captives are sin, darkness, and death. Or they are those who have been *made* captive by Satan. Most likely this is a general statement simply to support Christ's victory. (See below "Ephesians 4:8 Through Old Testament Eyes: Psalm 68:18.")

## Ephesians 4:8 Through Old Testament Eyes: Psalm 68:18

Ephesians 4:8 is one of the few places in his letter where Paul cites the Old Testament directly. Paul uses an introductory phrase that can be rendered "therefore it says" (also at 5:14; Jas 4:6) but does not tell us where it is written. The citation is from Psalm 68:18 in many respects but also deviates from it considerably. Psalm 68:18 (NIV, italics added) offers:

> When *you* ascended on high,
>    *you* took many captives;
>    *you* received gifts *from people.*

In contrast, Paul has written in Ephesians 4:8:

> When *he* ascended on high,
>    *he* took many captives
>    and gave gifts *to his people.*

The psalm describes the mighty victories of God and pictures him moving from Mount Sinai (68:17) to his temple on Mount Zion (Jerusalem, 68:18). He is leading captives and in his holy city receives tribute from them. This is the language of triumph-following-conquest that was commonly understood in antiquity.

To extend this story to Christ, Paul changes the direct address (you) to the third person (he) and now uses it to describe Christ ascending and then distributing gifts to his people. In the first case (the Psalm), gifts come *from people* (captives); in Ephesians, gifts come *to people* (the church).

Paul's reinterpretation presents a difficulty. In later Jewish thought, rabbis used the verse to describe Moses ascending to heaven and there receiving the gift of Torah from God for giving to his people. This illustrates Jewish interpretative freedom and parallels what Paul may be doing. This later Jewish tradition (AD 400) switches the words "receiving gifts" to "giving gifts." For Paul, Christ (not Moses) ascended on high and gave gifts of grace (not law) to his people. Paul then stands in harmony with the Jewish reuse of the Psalm (but not the Psalm itself). Jesus therefore ascended to heaven to give us the gift of the Spirit and this triumphs over anything given by Moses.

The problem is that we have no evidence of this exegetical reuse in Paul's day.[5] Some scholars even think that the Jewish reinterpretation much later may have come from a reaction to what they considered to be Christian misuse of the psalm in preaching. The comparison between Jesus and Moses is well-evidenced in the New Testament (Jn 1:17; 9:28) and in subsequent Christian-Jewish relations.

It is not unusual for Paul to take an Old Testament text and shape it for his own purposes. He is actually using the Old Testament as a springboard for a new idea that may parallel the Old Testament. His use of Habakkuk 2:4 in Galatians 3:11 and Romans 1:17 provides an excellent example. In Ephesians 4:8, Paul begins with an idea parallel to the psalm (God/Christ ascends), describes gifts received, and shifts the ending to his message: gifts are now distributed to the church.

The apparent contradiction between Ephesians 4:8 and Psalm 68:18 may be less than we think.[6] In antiquity the conquering king received tribute from his captives and frequently in turn distributed these received gifts to his people, thus generating greater honor and support from his city. Paul sees Christ in the same manner. Victory and exaltation lead to the blessing of Christ's followers and, in this case, the giving of gifts.

Paul continues his use of these ideas from Psalm 68 in Ephesians 4:9 and this complicates this reuse of the Psalm even further.

The general picture of Jesus' ascent followed by his giving of gifts accords with what we read during Pentecost—first ascension, then the giving of gifts (Ac 1:9; 2:1–4). Moreover Psalm 68 was associated with Pentecost in Jewish use. But there is another feature of the psalm that likely drew Paul's attention. Psalm 68 declares God's mighty victories, and in Ephesians, Paul reminds us that Jesus' triumphal victory defeated the powers that rule this world, thus freeing us from our enemies. The citation (Ps 68:18) is the climax of the psalm celebrating God's victory and this celebration likewise belongs to Jesus.[7]

**4:9** *What does "he ascended" mean?* Paul asks this question to give a deeper interpretation of the movements of Christ. Jesus' *ascent* was preceded by his *descent.* Is this descent his incarnation, when he entered the world? John writes, "No one has ever gone into heaven [ascended] except the one who came from heaven [descended]—the Son of Man" (Jn 3:13). This was the widely held view of Calvin and the Reformers. In this case, the words about descent could be translated, "the area below—that is, the earth," which points to the incarnation as his descent.

Another view is that this refers to Christ's descent into Hades after the cross. Note how Paul refers to the "lower parts of the earth" (KJV, ASV, NASB; see also 1 Pe 3:19; 4:6). This view was common among early patristic writers. In this case, theologians such as Chrysostom could imagine Paul describing the cosmic sweep of Christ's rule: from the bottommost parts of creation (Hades) to the highest expanse of heaven (4:10).[8]

Scribes copying ancient manuscripts recognized this dilemma and tried to resolve it by inserting the word "first" (Gk, *prōton*) after the word "descent" ("he [Christ] descended *first* to the lower, earthly regions"). While we can ignore the scribal addition to the text, still, the view that the addition tries to support has found agreement with most interpreters today. Christ's descent is his incarnation. This is in keeping with Paul's understanding of Christ's movement in his incarnation, particularly in Philippians 2:5–11 (also Heb 2:5–10). Paul views the incarnation as the onset of the sweep of an arc, beginning with Christ in heaven, continuing with his descent into the world, and ending in his exaltation in resurrection/ascension and return to heaven.

**4:10** *Higher than all the heavens.* Confidence in the ability of God to exhibit mastery over the grave is not unknown in the Old Testament (Ps 30:1–4). But in this case, Paul understands that the resurrection is not simply about Jesus' personal fate. This resurrection/ascent of Jesus was not simply his private rescue by God or his resumption of a place held before. These activities alter the "whole universe" (Gk, *hina plērōsē ta panta,* Eph 4:10; NIV: "so that he might fill all things"). This is why all rulers and authorities in heavenly realms are alert to what has just happened (3:10). And if they see this as an assault on their power, then a cosmic struggle has begun. Paul explains, "For our struggle is not against flesh and blood, but against the rulers, against the authorities, against the powers of this dark world and against the spiritual forces of evil in the heavenly realms" (6:12).

**4:11** *Christ himself gave the apostles. . . .* In his ascent, what has Christ distributed to the church? Paul now creates a list of five roles that have been given to serve the church. This list is similar to what we find in Romans 12:3–8 and 1 Corinthians 12:4–11, 28–29. The differences in the lists suggest that no list is exhaustive. Altogether, Paul refers to Spirit-inspired abilities that might be taken up by any Christian and Spirit-created roles serving the church's leadership, which is what we find here. The impression is that these abilities appear widely in the church while these roles are exclusive and fulfilled by particular persons. Note that people holding these roles do not possess an "office"; instead, this is a charismatic gift, a function appointed by the Spirit to build up the church. Note also that there is no reference to bishops, elders, or deacons. Paul's youngest churches have not replaced the Spirit's inspiration with formal ecclesiastical structures such as we see hinted at in Philippians 1:1 or in 1 Timothy 3.

Paul has referred to apostles and prophets twice before (Eph 2:20; 3:5, where he refers to "holy" apostles; see comments on 2:20.) An "apostle" is someone commissioned with a task (Gk, *apostellō*, "to send out or away"; "to commission"). This could apply, for example, to anyone who was sent out by Christ, or it could apply to representatives of churches sent to or by Paul (2 Co 8:23). Finally, there was a smaller group sent and authorized by Christ to serve as eyewitnesses, represent his teaching, and continue his ministry. Ultimately, they were an authoritative circle to which appeals could be made (Gal 2:1–2). Jesus' twelve apostles are the best-known (Mt 10:1–4) and were often called the Twelve (Lk 8:1). Paul understood himself to have this apostolic calling (1 Co 9:1; Gal 1:1; Eph 1:1), but he distinguished this from the Twelve (Gal 1:17, 19). It is likely that these apostles were looked to for teaching roles in the church.

"Prophets" here does not refer to the Old Testament. These are roles in the church whose gifting included an immediate word from the Lord for circumstances pressing on the present (Ac 11:27; 13:1). In some cases, they are named (Judas, Silas, and Agabus, Ac 15:32; 21:10). These are often listed together ("apostles and prophets") and in each case, apostles are given first place (1 Co 12:28; Eph 2:20; 3:5; 4:11; Rev 18:20). It is important to recall that in Paul's churches women were not seen as inferior (Gal 3:28). Junia is a woman referred to as an apostle (Ro 16:7),[9] and women served as prophets in Corinth (1 Co 11:5).

"Evangelists" were likely preachers, whose name (Gk, *euanggelistēs*) comes from the same word as "gospel" (Gk, *euanggelion*) meaning "herald of good news" (see "Galatians 1:6–12 Through Old Testament Eyes: The Gospel"). The noun occurs two other times (Ac 21:8, Philip; 2 Ti 4:5, Timothy) and likely describes public speakers or preachers who could address pagan audiences and make the gospel known.

"Pastors" are shepherds (Gk, *poimēn* from the verb "to tend"), which we imagine to be caregivers of local churches. And finally, "teachers" were persons who could expound the scriptures. When we recall that the New Testament was not in circulation yet and Old Testament texts were rare, the church had to rely on the received traditions heard from authorized sources (apostles) or newly revealed words from God (prophets). Teachers had limited resources and may have had only fragmentary tools with which to work.

**4:12** *To equip his people for works of service.* The aim of this equipping is not the spiritual prowess of church members nor their personal spiritual enhancement. This is what happened in Corinth and led to remarkable divisions fed by spiritual elitism. Rather, Paul says, the aim of this gifting is for building up the body of Christ. Gifts are given for the whole and the benefit is corporate, never private (cf. 1 Co 12). And Paul lists these benefits with three clauses that enumerate in Ephesians 4:13 what the church can attain.

**4:13** *Unity in the faith.* Paul's first hope is that these gifts, when working together, will achieve the unity that he has been describing since 4:1. Paul hopes that every one of us attains this goal. The NIV "reach" (Gk, *katantaō*) means to come to a meeting or consensus, to meet a goal,[10] or perhaps to attain something. We could translate it as, "that you attain the goal of unity found in faith and knowledge of the Son of God." Paul understands that unity must be based on a critical consensus about the nature of our beliefs and the vitality of our experiences with Christ. In this sense faith and knowledge have a reciprocal relationship (both believing and knowing), and when the church pursues this in harmony, unity results.

*Become mature.* The NIV "become mature" disguises the Greek "become a complete man," since the noun is undoubtedly generic. And here Paul is setting up a comparison with infants (4:14) who are expressly immature. The measure of this maturity is Christ (4:13c, "the fullness of Christ") who is the model of who we are to be. Elsewhere Paul refers to Adam, the one "man" through whom sin came (Ro 5:12), while Jesus is the "man" who brought grace (Ro 5:15).

While this is the majority view of the verse, it is an exegetical decision that some say misses the mark.[11] Paul has just said (Eph 4:13) that we are to attain the knowledge of the Son of God, aiming for the perfect man. Paul may not be talking about how we become mature but how we attain knowing Christ *who is* the perfect man (Gk, *anēr*; not *anthrōpos*). The sentence is preceded and followed by reference to Jesus (the Son of God, the fullness of Christ). Throughout these verses Jesus is the measure by which we measure our success in belief and conduct.

We have already read about Paul's understanding that in Christ we not only find redemption, but we find ourselves newly created as one new person, *anthrōpos* (Eph 2:15). This person is becoming not just mature but complete (Gk, *telos*), and this acknowledges the imperfection or incompleteness that characterizes our lives. To be human requires an honest appraisal of where we have been and how far we need to go.

*The whole measure of the fullness of Christ.* This is Paul's description of the completeness (*telos*) he has just described. "Fullness" has the sense of completeness, as in "old and full of years" (Ge 25:8; 35:29) or a family full of children (Ps 127:5). Mature grain is described as full (Ge 41:7). Honesty also calls for giving customers fully what they deserve (Dt 25:15 ESV) and giving a full tithe (Mal 3:10 ESV).

"Fullness" (Gk, *plērōma*) had a long history in Paul's world. In Greek, when a jar is "full," it is *plērēs*. When a ship is fully staffed, it is *plērēs*. A person can be satisfied after a song or full (*plērēs*) after a meal. John can describe Jesus as similarly "full" of grace and truth (Jn 1:14), meaning there is little room for anything else. *Plērōma* is the content that fills (water in a jar, the crew in a ship, the substance of a life), thereby making it "full." In the New Testament it means an abundant endowment of God's presence and grace that is unmistakably a divine gift.

**4:14** *No longer be infants.* Most translations begin a new sentence (or a new paragraph) at Ephesians 4:14, but in Greek it is a continuation of the argument in the preceding verses.

Paul now reverses his view of the subject and explains what we should avoid. While infants and children are cherished and thought of positively (Ps 127:3; Pr 4:3; Jer 31:20), this image can also be used negatively (Isa 28:9; 30:9; Jer 4:22), which is what Paul has in mind. This is the opposite of the maturity described in Ephesians 4:13, which Caird so artfully calls "infantile gullibility."[12] We should flee being childish or foolish (Gk, *nēpios*), which is characterized as someone who is tossed around or carried about "by every wind of teaching" (4:14). The image here is of a ship that cannot withstand wind or sea, that runs without sail, rudder, or skilled captain. The "gullible infant" is ungrounded, unable to recognize false teaching for what it is.

Paul then shifts from his nautical metaphor and moves delightfully to scheming gamers. Such children are sabotaged by human trickery (Gk, *kubeia*; NIV: "cunning"), which literally means "dice-playing." Imagine here a gambler or a con artist working the street in Ephesus. These promoters of false teaching are deceitful and shrewd, duplicitous and underhanded, using cunning to draw in new players.

## Going Deeper: Love, Contention, and Hard Conversations (Eph 4:14–16)

In Ephesians 4:15 Paul talks about the importance of using love whenever we are in a setting filled with strong opinions and potential division.

For the past few years (and for more to come), I am regularly in conversations in church settings about sexual orientation, same-sex attraction, and the LGBTQ+ community. Within one family, within one church, within one seminary or college, we can find people who believe that this is a hill to die on. Many have staked out a position and really cannot hear the other side. I am on a faculty that is wrestling with this at its deepest level.

In one such conversation, a professor of pastoral theology asked us to pause. And he reminded us that when we discuss this issue, we are naive if we think that theology is the only thing that fuels our passions. He challenged us to remember three things: a) that there is pain associated with this question; b) that good Christians with good intentions may disagree; and c) that love should characterize all of our activity or else we will sacrifice our unity.

Paul is certainly aware that there are wrongheaded teachings in Ephesus. He has just called their work crafty and cunning and said we who succumb to it are infants in the faith. *And yet.* And yet Paul here is still able to speak into this situation in love. "Speaking the truth in love" is Paul's overriding expectation despite how passionate we feel about our views.

**4:15** *Speaking the truth in love, we will grow.* Now Paul reverses again showing us that this gullibility need not be our fate (4:15). The alternative is not a dogged defense of the truth or an assertion of orthodoxy against all opponents. Truth must be tied to love, *particularly* where there is disagreement. The solidity of our faith is not only in our adherence to what is right; it is in our reflection of Jesus Christ who has filled us with the fullness of all that he is. Curiously when we speak the truth, every feature of who we are grows into him, into Christ, who is the head.

The imagery of growth (Gk, *auxanō;* 2 Co 10:15) was originally agricultural but became a metaphor for personal (Ps 1:3; 52:8; Pr 11:30; Isa 32:17; Jer 17:7–8) and corporate development (Isa 5:1–7; Hos 14:5–7). (See comments on "the fruit of the Spirit" at Galatians 5:22–23.) Usually, this growth leads to an end: fruit or crops—or maturity (Ps 72:16; Isa 11:1; 27:1–6; Eze 17:23). And this is Paul's meaning: that we grow into becoming like Christ, who is our head. It is a mistake to imagine that Paul or anyone in antiquity thought about the head as the source of thought or intelligence (this was the work of the heart). "Head" (Gk, *kephalē*) can refer to the head on a person's shoulders or something that is prominent (such as a column capital, a king, or a mountain peak on the horizon). Paul is thinking about Christ's prominence and high position above the church. (On head, see further comments on Ephesians 5:23.)

**4:16** *The whole body . . . grows and builds itself up.* See comments on Paul's body metaphor at 1:22–23 and 4:4–6.

The complexity of 4:16 even led the great fifth-century expositor John Chrysostom (a native speaker of Greek) to say that Paul "expresses himself with great obscurity, from his desire to utter everything at once."[13] And indeed there is a congestion of images all tumbling together in these phrases. Paul's reference to Christ's headship over the church now inspires him to draw out his metaphor further. He thinks of the church as the body of Christ and how each person working in unity will strengthen and build that body in love. This parallels the architectural metaphor in 2:21–22, where Christ is the cornerstone and the church is a temple being built up in holiness and filled by the Spirit. Throughout both images we see how the church is less a human endeavor striving to imitate Christ and instead is a living organism that finds itself indwelt by Christ in the Spirit (enjoying the fullness of Christ, 4:13), with each member gifted to their own task as they are empowered. (Paul uses the head/body metaphor similarly in 1 Co 12.)

**4:17** *No longer live as the Gentiles do.* With 4:16, Paul has ended his exhortation to the Ephesians to live in unity, seeing their lives as completely caught up in the life of Christ and therefore sharing with each member of the church equal or parallel giftings in the Spirit. The balance of the letter (to 6:9) emphasizes in a variety of ways how the church should conduct itself in the world. Holiness has been a constant theme in Ephesians (sixteen times), and it is what Paul has in mind throughout these final chapters.

Holiness for a Jew did not mean moral or spiritual perfection as much as it meant *separation* (Lev 20:24, 26; 1 Ki 8:53). God's people should attach themselves to God and create distance (separation) from the pagan world that refused to acknowledge him. Paul does not want them to separate from Gentiles (as he made clear in Galatians) so much as he wanted them to separate from their ways. (See comments on "So that I might preach him among the Gentiles" at Gal 1:15–17.) Futility describes this Gentile world, and Paul knows (as we do) that its habits will find their way into the church regularly. Failed thinking has led to intellectual corruption, and this has welcomed the collapse of all moral judgments. This description is similar to Paul's profile of the pagan world in Romans 1:18–32.

*The futility of their thinking.* The sort of living Paul rejects is described as "futile" (Gk, *mataiotēs*). Its root (*mataios*) refers to emptiness, deceitfulness, or pointlessness. In a person it could be a false confidence that masks the absence of depth or substance. When combined with "word" (*logia, mataio-logia*), it means "empty chatter" or "senseless talking" (1 Ti 1:6). Paul uses *mataiotēs* in Romans 1:21 for those who refuse to honor God and remain fixed in their futile thinking (also 1 Co 3:20).

## Ephesians 4:17 Through Old Testament Eyes: Futility and Ecclesiastes

Paul uses a term here common to the Old Testament to represent an array of Hebrew words (Gk, *mataios*). This refers to something that is pointless, deceptive, vain, or worthless because it is ineffectual. The words of a false prophet, for example, are useless ("futile" in Jer 23:16 NLT, TLB). This is the source of the NIV translation "futility" because it is an effort with impossible odds of success. The Psalms describe the futility of relying on human aid when divine help is needed (Ps 60:11) or the futility of humankind's efforts generally (Ps 62:9). Beauty is "futile" (Pr 31:30 LXX), just as is a religion based on false gods.

Its most famous use is in Ecclesiastes LXX where everything is called *mataios* (1:2, using variations of the word thirty-nine times). In this book, the preacher (1:1) describes the futility and deceptiveness of human efforts to achieve wealth, longevity, prestige, beauty, and power—simply, human prospering. Ecclesiastes describes these as empty efforts because eventually all meaning belongs to God and his purposes. The end of these futile pursuits is despair and hopelessness or, as Ecclesiastes says, "chasing after the wind" (e.g., Eccl 1:14, 17).

Here Paul is applying *mataios* to Gentiles whose despairing lives he goes on to describe in Ephesians 4:18. They are "darkened in their understanding and separated from the life of God," and this has given them lives of complete futility.

**4:18–19** *They are darkened in their understanding and separated from the life of God.* Together with 4:17, this verse describes the hopelessness of the pagan world (quite similar to Ro 1). Two clauses portray this life: they are darkened in their thinking, and they are alienated from God (Eph 2:12; Col 1:21). Their ability to think rightly has collapsed altogether and darkness now pervades their lives. (Regarding spiritual blindness and darkness, see comment on "That the eyes of your heart may be enlightened" at Eph 1:18–19.) Intellectual deterioration (Eph 4:18; NIV: "ignorance") is their state, and it means that they are incapable of understanding the truth about God or the world. Simply put, they are lost in a confusion that parades as bravado. They think they know but they do not. This is also Paul's theme in Romans 1:25 on which Karl Barth once famously wrote in 1928:

> The tiny mist between God and man, by which the far distance is obscured, soon becomes a veritable sea of clouds. Some half-conscious resentment at the unknown God very soon becomes fully conscious. The dazzled eye is soon damaged. Principalities and powers, formerly but seldom exalted to the throne, are soon established there, encircled with a halo of everlasting power and divinity.[14]

*The hardening of their hearts.* Many Gentiles had hard hearts against God, such as Sihon the king of Heshbon (Dt 2:30), the Philistines (1 Sa 6:6), and Nebuchadnezzar (Da 5:20). The most famous example of a hard heart is the story of Pharaoh. Exodus describes God hardening Pharaoh's heart (Ex 9:12; 10:1, 20, 27; 11:10; 14:4, 8) and Pharaoh hardening his own heart (Ex 8:15, 32; 9:34). At times the text says Pharaoh's heart was hardened (Ex 7:13, 22; 8:19; 9:7, 35), and so is not clear who did the hardening. In any case, the reason for this hardening was so that God could multiply his miracles and thus make it clear to the Egyptians that God was the source of their freedom (Ex 7:3–5). As Paul goes on to point out, many of the people he is writing to were themselves miraculously rescued from their own hardened hearts (Eph 4:20–24).

This hardening (Gk, *pōroō*) was originally a medical term for the healing of a fractured bone that soon solidified or became firm. The word could even refer to eyes that become dim (or "hard," Job 17:7 LXX). Metaphorically, "a hard heart" referred to the loss of sensitivity or feeling (all five uses in the New Testament refer to the heart) and suggests someone who is obtuse or dull, whose capacity to intuit what is right and good has been lost.[15] This person (Eph 4:19) is beyond all feeling (Gk, *ap* + *algeō*) and so has no sensitivity for divine things. This describes complete spiritual corruption, where sensitive thoughtfulness has been traded for base sensuality (see Ro 1:26–32). In Romans, Paul sees this as leading to idolatry and callous sexuality (also 2 Pe 2:7); here, Paul refers simply to impurity, which carries the same suggestion of sexual corruption. Note how they are active in this process. "They have given themselves over to sensuality" (Eph 4:19).[16] And in this, they pursue (indulge) all impurity greedily, with an appetite that is unrestrained.

To sum, those capacities that make us human can be lost; gifts acquired by a life lived in proximity to God can be extinguished—which is when human thought, feeling, and spiritual sensitivity collapse on themselves. Ethics itself is abandoned and any hint of a moral universe disappears. When the self is elevated and God is unseeable, Paul argues that sensitivity is converted to sensuality and spiritual instincts for sexual appetite.

**4:20-24** *You . . . were taught in him.*[17] If unity is one hallmark of a healthy church (4:1-16), holiness that stands in contrast to pagan life (4:17-19) is its second attribute. Paul's assumption is that the Christians of Ephesus have been taught how to live rightly, how to live as "saints" or holy ones (1:1, 4, 15, 18; 2:19, etc.). They should have been instructed by teachers or elders who explained not simply what to believe but what activities are appropriate for believers and what things are inappropriate. The reference point within this teaching is always the pagan Roman culture surrounding the church and penetrating its life. This provides an important insight into the early Christian worldview. *This world was theologically binary.* That is, every believer readily understood that they lived *in Christ,* yet surrounding them was a world overtly opposed to Christ. There was no mediating position. Teachers, we can imagine, reinforced and clarified theological and moral boundaries. The guidance Paul provides in these verses and those that follow were likely some of what they taught.

## Ephesians 4:20-21 Through Old Testament Eyes: Codes of Conduct vs. Learning Jesus

Paul uses an odd expression in 4:20-21 to introduce the ethical guidelines that are important to him. He says, "You learned the Messiah" (lit.). The NIV paraphrases it to excess, "That, however, is not the way of life you learned when you heard about Christ." The Greek offers, "But you did not thus learn Christ—if you heard him and were taught in him." This Greek term "to learn" (*manthanō*) generally had an object (e.g., you learn mathematics), and while this is a rare form, it does occur in Greek philosophy as "learning God"—implying that it is for becoming acquainted with a living person. This is Paul's sense. *We learn Christ.* Christian ethical maturity is about cultivating an instinct for Christ's wishes *because* he is known personally so well.[18] The notion could very well be that Christ continues to be a teacher into his resurrection life.[19]

The following words assume this same outlook: "You heard him and were taught by him" (4:21, author's translation). The sense here is not that Christian maturity is about learning what Jesus taught and obeying it. Christian ethical maturity assumes that Christ is alive and he is actively providing guidance to us (through the Spirit). This means that Christians in Paul's churches were (what we call) *charismatic* or *mystical.* They understood they were endowed by the Spirit, gifted by the Spirit, and guided by the resurrected Christ.[20]

This is a quite different outlook than we find in the Old Testament. While the law was not used to gain salvation or access to the covenant (these were anchored in grace), still, the law was central to every aspect of ethical life. Knowing "what was written" and pursuing obedience to it was the moral charge from the Torah to the prophets. No doubt the teachings of Jesus became a historical moral foundation that could be compiled (in the gospels) or referenced to (as in James). However, the church understood that Jesus did not simply speak *in the past* but that he was continuing to speak *in the present* and this was rare in the Old Testament and Second Temple Judaism.

*Put off your old self.* The full break after 4:21 in the NIV is misleading. Paul is trying to outline what the Ephesians have heard and have been taught (4:21)—and this is listed (in Greek) in the three infinitives that follow from 4:22–24. Understanding these three major changes that come to us in Christ defeats the futility that Paul has discussed in 4:17–19.[21]

> 4:22    to put off (your old lifestyle; that is your old personhood, *anthrōpos*)
>
> 4:23    to be renewed (in the spirit of your mind)
>
> 4:24    to put on (the new nature—that is, the new personhood, *anthrōpos*)

The guiding image here is clothing. When the priests took off their ordinary clothes and put on their priestly garments, this set them apart (made them holy) for their sacred service (Ex 29:5–9; 40:12–15; Lev 6:11; 16:3–4). When they took off their priestly garments, it signaled a return to ordinary life (Lev 16:23; Eze 44:19). In contrast, Paul suggests that our change of spiritual clothing (and our life as God's holy people) is not to be temporary and superficial but permanent and complete.

The ruined clothing of our old self must be discarded. It represents not only the identity but the lifestyle that the Ephesians once pursued. The problem is the ruin (Gk, *phtheirō*) of their humanity.[22] The hallmark of this loss of humanity is in their deceptive desires, which attempt to offer promise but instead simply bring ruin. This stands in stark contrast with "the truth" (Eph 4:21) that unmasks what this former way of life once held.

Throughout Paul's writing, the problem with life without God is never simply sinful habits or an unsatisfying life. Paul consistently points to a root cause: the full moral and spiritual collapse of humanity. Our affections and desires have gone astray, and this has led to death (Ro 6:12; 13:14). That this former life has lost any of its divine markers is seen in how they suppress truth (Ro 1:18), become futile in their thinking (1:21), exchange wisdom for foolishness (1:22), and elevate creation rather than its creator (1:23). They may still have echoes of truth in their darkened minds, yet they practice a lie and promote those who do likewise (1:32).

*Be made new in the attitude of your minds.* If our spiritual collapse began with the decay of our minds (Gk, *nous,* 4:17), the solution must begin with the renewal of the mind (Gk, *nous,* 4:23). The term "renewal" (NIV: "be made new") includes the Greek word for fresh or new (Gk, *neos*) combined with a prefix for reviving or bearing up (*ana* + *neoō*). The image here is a darkened or broken mind now resurrected, now reenergized, recovered from its collapse, rising awake to see the truth of what is around it—light penetrating darkness, truth defeating deceit, goodness replacing corrupt desire.

*Put on the new self.* This solution is not cosmetic. It is a reengineering of human self-consciousness, a stripping away and a rebuilding. It is dying and rising. It is removing garments and dressing oneself rightly. The NIV suggests that we put on a new self or gain a new identity; this is true but perhaps incomplete.[23] The Greek text makes a different point, and Paul has something far more dramatic in mind. "Put on the new [person] (*anthrōpos*) created to be like God." This points to the entirety of who we are. The transformation required is not possible apart from *putting on Christ* (Ro 13:14; Gal 3:27). Christ has delivered to the world a *new humanity,* and we appropriate this not by imitating him but by bringing him into the center of our lives through the Spirit. *Our new life is thus his life now taking root in us.* For Paul, this is the source of the new creation that takes place once the old has passed away (2 Co 5:17).[24]

Therefore, we note carefully: the solution of the old *anthrōpos* was not in its repair; it was in its replacement, where we become what we have lost by taking on the *anthrōpos* of God's Son. As a result of this effort, this new creation gains righteousness and holiness, two terms that express in the fullest what humanity has lost through sin and what it can gain in Christ. These are described as "of truth" and likely it does not mean that they modify the two terms (true righteousness, true holiness)—both are self-evidently true. But as deceit grounded the sin of the old person (4:17–19), truth as found in Jesus Christ is now what defines and grounds this righteousness and holiness. These are virtues that belong to the gospel.

**4:25–28** Paul now supplies a list of rules for general conduct inside the Christian community. As this Christ-in-you transformation happens, signs of this transformation should eventually become evident. Such lists as we see here (4:25–5:2) were common in the Greek and Roman worlds and used regularly for instruction. Therefore no one in Ephesus would be surprised by such direct moral instruction. Since Paul is writing to a community that is largely Gentile, he cannot assume that their moral compass is oriented in a manner that will reflect values a Jew or a Jewish Christian might already know.

**4:25** *Therefore.* Paul explicitly connects what preceded these verses—or according to some, it is based on what Paul has said so far in this letter. Theological convictions lead to righteous conduct in each of Paul's letters. Paul then provides three admonitions, which come in a regular pattern: a negative description of what is to be avoided; a positive description of what to pursue; and a justification or motivation for this behavior.

*Put off falsehood.* The order against lying was one of the ten commandments (Ex 20:16; Dt 5:20) and is reemphasized many times (Lev 19:11–12; Ps 52:3; 58:3; Jer 9:5; Mic 6:12). Paul's language here in Ephesians 4:25 recalls 4:22, where he talks about "putting off" the clothing of the former person who lived without Christ. "Falsehood" (NIV) isn't as sharp as the Greek implies; *pseudos* means "lying" or "deception" (also 4:22), and this is always contrasted with truth. The positive admonition "speak truthfully each of you—to your neighbor" comes from the Old Testament (Zec 8:16 LXX), whose context may contribute to its meaning (see "Ephesians 4:25 Through Old Testament Eyes: Paul's Use of Zechariah 8:16").

## Ephesians 4:25 Through Old Testament Eyes: Paul's Use of Zechariah 8:16

The Old Testament prophet Zechariah wrote in the postexilic world after many deportees returned to Jerusalem from Babylon. Along with his contemporary Haggai, Zechariah provided reassurance that hope was within sight, that a return (from east and west) would bring Israel back together and a new blessed era would emerge. Zechariah 7–8 describes this hope, and its lofty picture provides a fantastic eschatological image. "Once again men and women of ripe old age will sit in the streets of Jerusalem, each of them with cane in hand because of their age. The city streets will be filled with boys and girls playing there" (8:4–5). This company will be the remnant of Israel (8:6) who will turn Jerusalem into a faithful city (8:3).

The New Testament frequently takes up these eschatological expectations and sees them fulfilled in the coming of Christ. Zechariah could write,

> "Speak the truth to each other, and render true and sound judgment in your courts; do not plot evil against each other, and do not love to swear falsely. I hate all this," declares the LORD. (Zec 8:16–17)

Paul now echoes this in Ephesians 4:25:

> Therefore each of you must put off falsehood and speak truthfully to your neighbor, for we are all members of one body.

The Greek phrase "speak truth—each of you—with his neighbor" (au. trans.) is an almost perfect rendering of Zechariah 8:16 LXX. Paul may be thinking that Zechariah 8 describes a new era of blessing following the exile. This era now has been fulfilled in the present new creation inaugurated by Christ.[25] Jesus has inaugurated what Zechariah promised. To be sure, some scholars question this eschatological use of Zechariah and wonder if Paul is simply reciting a well-known ethical maxim known in Judaism.

The reason for this truth-telling is that Christians belong to "one body" (Eph 1:22–23; 4:4, 12, 16) and so should consider each other "neighbors" regardless of their racial, ethnic, or national ties. This is an echo of Paul's vision for the new community he sees in Christ. Here we have the reminder of redrawn communal boundaries (see "Ephesians 2:19 Through Old Testament Eyes: In-Group and Out-Group"), and in tribal cultures, this was critically important. The church was to be a cohesive community—a tribe-in-Christ, as it were—people whose unity did not track lines of ethnicity, culture, or nationality. The larger society Paul lived in would find deceit acceptable to outsiders who could not be trusted. No doubt Paul would object to this as well, but this is not his thought here. Lying of any sort within the community is unacceptable in the church.

**4:26–27** *In your anger do not sin.* The reference to anger is taken from Psalm 4:4 ESV (Ps 4:5 LXX). This is a pair of imperatives (literally, "Be angry—and do not sin"), which is a helpful clarification because it gives permission to be angry. As a result, we wonder if Paul is also acknowledging the appropriateness of some anger in some contexts. Jacob was angry with Rachel but replied with a pointed though measured response that did not break the relationship (Ge

30:1–2). Moses was angry with Pharoah but walked out instead of lashing out (Ex 11:8). The key is that we manage this anger so that it does not lead to wrongdoing. It is no surprise that this sin is closely connected to lying in Ephesians 4:25. The link was well-established in Jewish writing since anger could often lead to misrepresenting the opponent.[26]

In the proverb that follows, "Do not let the sun go down while you are still angry" (see Dt 24:13, 15), Paul picks up a different term for anger that helps clarify. "Anger" (Gk, *orgizō*) switches to "wrath or fury" (Gk, *parorgismos*). These may be synonyms, but the second term implies a difference in intensity and duration that Paul warns against. It is this sort of anger that can be exploited by Satan. The proverb itself is cited widely in the ancient world, from Greek moralists to the Dead Sea Scrolls. Even in the Old Testament, Micah 2:1 hints at it (see Ps 36:4). Paul shares it here as useful and practical wisdom. Anger, managed well, should be short-lived.

**4:28** *Anyone who has been stealing must steal no longer.* This is Paul's second admonition. This surprising exhortation (echoing the eighth commandment) reminds us of the economic diversity of the early church. Paul is addressing people for whom theft was an option in life. In 1 Corinthians 1:26–28, Paul is candid:

> Think of what you were when you were called. Not many of you were wise by human standards; not many were influential; not many were of noble birth. But God chose the foolish things of the world to shame the wise; God chose the weak things of the world to shame the strong. God chose the lowly things of this world and the despised things . . . to nullify the things that are.

Names were often codes for social class, and throughout the New Testament we see evidence of slaves, the poor, and common laborers within the church's ranks.[27] Paul follows his exhortation with a positive encouragement, since productive work is the opposite of theft. The text literally says, "but toil working by hand for the good." But the basis of this—sharing—is a quantum leap from what these people have been doing. Rather than acquiring things dishonestly, they can now distribute things in the spirit of Christian generosity.

**4:29** *Do not let unwholesome talk come out of your mouths.* This is Paul's third admonition, and it is related to his concern about deceit. The colorful word for "unwholesome" (Gk, *sapros*) means something that is decayed, putrid, or rancid and beyond use (hence, "rotten" gives it the flair it deserves) and metaphorically can refer to something harmful. Possibly Paul has in mind a crude sexual connotation that he will mention in the next chapter (5:4). The reverse of this is speech that is helpful, that "builds up" (NIV: "benefits") and encourages the body of Christ. It provides grace or favor on those who hear.

**4:30** *Do not grieve the Holy Spirit of God.* Israel grieved the Holy Spirit when they rebelled against God (Isa 63:10) by their idolatry (1 Sa 15:23; Ps 78:17; Jer 2:8) and injustice (Isa 1:17–20; 59:12–13).

While this is not a new admonition in Ephesians 4 (it lacks the triple pattern of the others), it reinforces the preceding verse. The word behind "grieve" is the Greek term for pain or sorrow (Gk, *lupē*), suggesting that this crude and harmful speech found in the mouths of Christians affects the Holy Spirit that is dwelling within them. It is impossible to know the mechanics of this harm, and perhaps "grieving" is sufficient. But if one work of the Spirit is the renewal or sanctification of the new person Christ is forming, then at least this speech becomes an impediment to the transformation of our lives.

## Going Deeper:
## Grieving the Holy Spirit with Words (Eph 4:29–32)

In these verses Paul links grieving the Holy Spirit with speech ethics (4:29–30; cf. 5:4); that is, our speech can impede the power and the joy that the Spirit wants to usher into our lives. Rarely do we think of it this way.

I have taught at three Christian colleges and one theological seminary. Each has been inspiring in its own way, and yet, on occasion, there have been surprising examples of misconduct. Although I should not describe these things in detail, rest assured that I can remember every moment.

Early in my career I recall walking daily in a crowded hallway heading to class and listening to dozens of students talk as they do when they think adults are not around. But in time, I noticed their use of language they would never use in class (or with their parents). Discretion denies me the temptation of writing these words here explicitly. But these were the strongest and crudest words known in English to express anger or disdain for someone *and it was all transpiring in a Christian context*. I began taking note of this and saw that it was consistent.

I was young and idealistic, thinking naively that Christian speech might exclude such language. And yes, I did it. I put a "letter to the editor" in the student paper, gently reflecting on holiness and speech. I even provided a few examples. The response was a barrage of argument about "free speech," the first amendment, and how my being judgmental was worse than their being crude. It was a sobering wakeup for one young professor. One staff person came to me to say "thank you" because she had seen this, and it discouraged her deeply.

Later in my career I encountered faculty who clearly had outgrown sophomoric high-school speech. However, they gathered privately each week for coffee and to roast the school's leadership. Hearty laughter always filled the room. These were powerful, senior faculty who bore a charismatic presence and, well, you simply wanted to be around them. Until you didn't. On another occasion, I witnessed angry, troubled faculty criticize their peers and leaders in deeply uncharitable ways in speech, email, and social media. Sometimes falsehoods were circulated. Rumors were spread. And it left me astonished. Age had robbed me of my earlier naivete, and I wondered if righteousness *in speech* even mattered for them.

These short stories illustrate Paul's point. Too often we think that grieving the Holy Spirit might be a blasphemous word and damaging sin. Paul is painting a portrait of people who have lost "all sensitivity" (4:19), whose hearts now are hardened (4:18), who speak angry falsehoods (4:26), and employ crude speech no differently than the Gentile world (4:29). Paul's hope is very simple: that we would be kind and compassionate (4:32). It strikes me that this is a fairly low bar for righteousness.

The Heidelberg Catechism was written in 1563 in Germany to provide a simplified outline of Christian faith and conduct for the Reformed Churches. Today it circulates widely and offers 129 questions and answers that were often memorized. Question 112 refers to Ephesians 4:25 and is instructive for us:

> Q. What is the aim of the ninth commandment?

> A. That I never give false testimony against anyone, twist no one's words, not gossip or slander, nor join in condemning anyone rashly or without a hearing. Rather, in court and everywhere else, I should avoid lying and deceit of every kind; these are the very devices the devil uses, and they would call down on me God's intense wrath. I should love the truth, speak it candidly, and openly acknowledge it. And I should do what I can to guard and advance my neighbor's good name.

*You were sealed for the day of redemption.* This is one of the few times where Paul describes the Spirit as a seal on the believer's life. Earlier Paul has said, "When you believed, you were marked in him with a seal, the promised Holy Spirit" (Eph 1:13, see comments).[28] The day of redemption ("the day of the Lord") is, in Jewish terms, the great summing up of human history (Isa 13:6; Eze 13:5; 30:3; Joel 1:15; 2:31; Am 5:18; Ob 15; Zep 1:7–10, 14–18; Zec 14:1). It is a day of sorting—when the evil will experience God's wrath and his own, those who are sealed, will enter into their redemption.

Here in Ephesians 4:30, Paul has in mind the fixed mark of God's redemption that appears on every believer (cf. 2 Ti 2:19).[29] This "spiritual sealing" is a mark of ownership, meaning that the Spirit's presence signals that God has placed his authoritative mark on us and displaces any other calls of ownership. Here scholars wonder if there is a legal application as well. A seal is binding and owned by the seal-maker. Thus, themes of security and assurance often follow.

This may have been viewed as linked to baptism, and hints to the effect suggest it. Baptism was the event that initiated new converts (Ac 8:36–38; 10:44–48). In 1 Corinthians 12:13 Paul connects baptism with the Spirit, showing that this was the onset of the Christian life. A fruitful set of images may follow Paul's picture of Christians "putting on" new garments in their new identity. This new covering is akin to a visible marker that announces a new life.

## Ephesians 4:30 Through Old Testament Eyes: Sealing

We have discovered thousands of seals from the ancient Middle East, which indicates how frequently they were used. A seal could be clay, stone, gems like agate, wood, or terracotta carved into a small object that could be pressed onto soft clay or wax as a sign of authority or ownership. A rolled scroll might have soft clay or wax attached to it with an official imprint. Papyrus could be rolled and sealed with wax. Small seals (or "button seals") were often pierced with a hole and worn around the neck, providing a person with their "signature." Cylinder seals were also common. These could roll out a text that then served as authorized marking.

In Genesis 41:42, Joseph obtained a seal (a "signet ring") from Pharaoh, meaning that he could "sign" royal edicts. When Jeremiah purchased property in Anathoth in Benjamin (Jer 32:11–14), he received a witnessed, "sealed" document certifying its authenticity. The king's signet ring plays a significant role in the book of Esther as well, indicating who has the authority to act with the king's approval (Est 3:10; 8:2, 8).

**4:31–32** *Get rid of all bitterness, rage and anger, brawling and slander.* At last, this is Paul's fourth admonition (Eph 4:30–31), which provides five terms that are descriptive of the sort of malice that will destroy the church. Behind each of these terms is a graphic picture of what they do. Bitterness is something sharp or pointed (Gk, *pikros*), which suggests the idea of someone who inflicts harm with embittered, pointed words. Rage (Gk, *thumos*) can also mean boiling, which suggests wrathful anger. Anger (Gk, *orgē*) we have seen in Ephesians 4:26, and in the New Testament era it was synonymous with *thumos*. The NIV "brawling" (Gk, *kraugē*) simply means "an outcry," which can describe the shouts of the wicked as they suffer (Mic 3:4) or a believer's plea to God (Ps 22:5). But here it is an angry demand. "Slander" (Gk, *blasphēmia*) is the word for blasphemy, which also had a general sense of abusive speech or mockery.

## Going Deeper: Anger in Our Age (Eph 4:31–32)

It has become commonplace to think of our era as angry. Some blame social media, which permits anonymous speech. Others wonder if angry speech is more easily expressed in media because we are not personally present. Some point to the politics of our day that erupted sometime after 2015. Maybe it is deeply felt anxiety about our place in history (the economy, the environment, jobs, etc.) Either way, one thing is clear: we have become accustomed to anger and accept the angry rant as normal in the modern world.

In Paul's letters he regularly looked for ways Jesus' followers could be set apart from the world in which they live. He is willing to talk about diet, circumcision, temples, idols—and, here in Ephesians, speech. He is not arguing for suppressing anger in 4:26. Anger has its place, and righteous anger is a regular biblical theme. The question is simply knowing when anger has become destructive. Paul understands that the church is engaged in a battle with supernatural powers, and in 4:27, he suggests that anger is an avenue exploited by these powers to undo us.

I admit that we have become acclimated to anger from our politicians and news sources. But now we see it in the church. The anger of the rest of the world has seeped into the church, and we now find Christians angry about everything from masking in a pandemic to vaccinations. We have short fuses.

Why do I know about this and worry about it? As a seminary professor, I lead mentoring groups of young pastors-in-training who serve as interns in area churches. And for years now, they have reported to me things they can barely say to the leaders at their churches. It discourages them deeply, and they wonder why they would want to choose a profession where this sort of aggressive behavior goes on. The details of their reports haunt me to this day. Paul might imagine that there is no finer moment for a Christian to be set apart, to eliminate falsehood and biting anger that has but one result: the grieving of the Holy Spirit (4:30).

Note that this list centers on speech, and if we look into verses beginning with 4:25, we have here "angry verbiage."[30] These things describe evil (NIV: "malice"), destructive speech (Col 3:8; 1 Pe 2:1) and are to be removed from the church at once. Paul then reverses his command (Eph 4:32).[31] Kindness, compassion, and forgiveness are the hallmarks of this new community in Christ and above all, they are anchored in Christ's own demeanor and behavior. This is not a list simply of Roman virtues (although a Roman might agree with it). Paul's ethics are theologically grounded, and his followers found their inspiration and model in Jesus (4:32).

# EPHESIANS 5

**5:1–2.** *Follow God's example* is literally "become imitators of God." Most scholars consider 5:1 to be a continuation of the exhortations that began in 4:25.[1] Kindness, compassion, and forgiveness concluded chapter four (4:32) as hallmarks of Christian character—and the pursuit of these virtues allows us to imitate God (5:1), whose character embodies these very things. Kindness alone may even be "one of the purist forms of the imitation of God."[2]

In the Old Testament we don't see the language of imitation directly, but we find many analogous ideas, such as "following Yahweh" (Dt 13:4; Jos 14:8–14), "serving him" (Dt 6:13; Jos 24:14), or "walking in his ways" (Isa 2:3; Hos 14:9).[3] A direct example, however, is God's exhortation to "Be holy, because I am holy" (Lev 11:44–45 and 19:2). Peter quotes this directly (1 Pe 1:15–16), and Jesus offers a variation in the Sermon on the Mount: "Be perfect, therefore, as your heavenly Father is perfect" (Mt 5:48).

Imitation (Gk, *mimētēs*) is one of the oldest forms of moral instruction in which a student is told to "mimic" the behavior of a teacher (Heb 6:12; 13:7). Paul uses this regularly (1 Th 2:14; 2 Th 3:7, 9) and has already done so in Ephesians 4:32 ("forgiving each other, just as in Christ God forgave you").

The kindness of 4:32 now becomes "walk in the way of love," which gives sharper definition to this kindness (also in Ro 14:15). "To walk" is a Hebrew idiom that usually means (in a moral context) "to live." *Live in love* or *live as love directs.* (See comments on "live a life" at Eph 4:1 and on "walk by the Spirit" at Gal 5:16–18). Each of us knows that one can be kind without being loving. Paul seeks a deeper and most profound understanding of divine kindness that likely is linked to mercy.

Paul imagines a dearly loved child who finds guidance not in the abstract but in watching the conduct of their model, possibly a parent. We are such children, and Christ is our model, who both loved us and "gave himself up for us" at the cross (5:2). This sacrifice was an offering not unlike those at the temple, where fragrant sacrifices filled Jerusalem with their smoke. (See "Ephesians 5:1–2 Through Old Testament Eyes: A Fragrant Offering.")

## Ephesians 5:1–2 Through Old Testament Eyes: A Fragrant Offering

The Old Testament distinguished between two types of sacrifices. The language was specific, just as Paul is using two terms in 5:2, offering and sacrifice. The first refers to offerings from the tree and field (Heb, *minha*, non-blood offerings), and the second refers to sacrifices of animals, part of which were burned on an altar (Heb, *ōlah*, blood sacrifices). By the Second Temple era after the exile, the language was less carefully employed so that Paul can almost merge the two (Php 4:18). In Ephesians 5:2, Jesus is seen as an altar sacrifice, exactly along the lines of a temple altar sacrifice.

Throughout the Old Testament, such sacrifices are described as a "pleasing aroma" to the Lord many times (Ge 8:21; Ex 29:18, 25, 41; Lev 1:9, 13, 17, etc.). Sacrifices were burned at the temple altar, and the flames were pictured as bringing them to heaven. We need only imagine the tremendous amount of smoke that lifted from the altar daily and settled on the entire city. *Jerusalem smelled of sacrifice* and this could be the fragrance of roasted meat or spices. Because it was an offering and gift to God, the Old Testament depicts this as pleasing to him (Lev 2:9, 12). Paul can thus complete the analogy with Christ, whose death on the cross likewise bore the properties pleasing to God.

The language of fragrance, gift, and offering was so common that they could become metaphors. The gifts Paul received from Epaphroditus in Rome (Php 4:18) bring with them a fragrance "pleasing to God." Even the knowledge of Christ, spreading throughout the world, bears a fragrance of Christ. Paul can write, "But thanks be to God, who . . . uses us to spread the aroma of the knowledge of him everywhere. For we are to God the pleasing aroma of Christ among those who are being saved and those who are perishing" (2 Co 2:14–15).

**5:3** *There must not be even a hint of sexual immorality.* It is difficult for us to imagine the extent of public sexuality present in Roman society. A mere visit to a Mediterranean museum and its statuary hall illustrates easily the

Greek and Roman love for the human form. Jews in this period had never seen anything like this. We also know that Roman society permitted a level of sexual permissiveness for men that was unheard of in Judaism. In addition, connections with fertility (see "Ephesians 5:3–7 Through Old Testament Eyes: Fertility, Sex, and Religion") brought sexual rites into the temples, where cult prostitution was not uncommon. Festivals and parades devoted to the Roman god Dionysus (known as Bacchus by the Greeks) were popular. Their phallic processions (called *phallika* in Greece) were widely celebrated—and repudiated by Roman moralists.[4] The poetry of Ovid rounds out this picture, providing unabashed language for explicit sexual love. It is no wonder that references to sexual immorality appear in many of Paul's letters. In 1 Corinthians, Paul exhorts the church about this very thing because he knows that Roman sexual practices were a moral issue in the church of Corinth.

Sexual modesty was a hallmark of Jews living in these Roman cities. And it is no surprise that here in Ephesians 5:3–7 Paul refers to it. Sexual morality was one among many boundaries that Roman Christians held to. This was how followers of Jesus stood apart from the public sexuality of their day. This is precisely Paul's aim in all of 5:3–14. He is defining what it means to be this new person who is called from darkness to light. He begins with describing the sort of behavior that belongs to those *outside* the church (the darkness) and draws a bright line between them and those who belong to Christ.

For Jews, the Lord ordains human fruitfulness (Ge 1:28) and the exclusive intimacy of husband and wife (Ge 2:23–25). Thus adultery is a cardinal sin (Ex 20:14; Lev 18:20) receiving, along with prostitution, extensive treatment in Proverbs (5:1–23; 6:20–7:27). The story of David and Bathsheba is perhaps the most grievous Old Testament example of sexual immorality—this time sexual abuse—and it shows the far-reaching negative consequences for the family and the nation. So reviled was sexual immorality that it was frequently used as an image for the fundamental sins of idolatry and unfaithfulness to God himself (Ex 34:15; Lev 17:7; Jer 3:6–10; Eze 23:28–30).

Paul refers to sexual immorality, impurity, and greed as practices that do not belong to Christ, and each deserves some explanation. For a Jewish writer, sexual immorality (Gk, *pornē*) was a comprehensive term referring to all inappropriate or illicit sexual conduct among the married or unmarried (adultery is a specialized subset of *pornē*). Here Paul has in mind broader indulgence in the sexualized culture of a typical Roman city (see also 1 Co 6:9; 2 Co 12:19–21; Eph 5:5). Impurity (Gk, *akatharsia*) comes from the ritual world of "cleanness" (*katharos*) and so describes anything that violates holiness. Here it is likely synonymous with immorality or *pornē*. Greed is problematic in this list (literal: "immorality and all impurity—or greed, let none of this be named among you!"). Some wonder if greed may have a sexual connotation because this triad of terms appears elsewhere in Jewish writings.[5] This may mean "insatiability" (see 4:19) or perhaps, in a sexual context, lust. Thus Paul is writing: "*immorality, impurity—and an endless desire for it*—don't let this be named among you!"

## Ephesians 5:3–7 Through Old Testament Eyes: Fertility, Sex, and Religion

We think of human flourishing using business metaphors (success, growth, profitability, etc.), but this image was unused in antiquity. For the agrarian cultures of the ancient world, *fertility* was the primary metaphor for flourishing. Of course, it could be literal: the growth of crops and flocks— even children within a household or clan. Prosperity meant animals born, yields increasing, women "with child." The stories of Abraham (Ge 17:15– 21) and Hannah (1 Sa 1–2) illustrate this. The arrival of God's blessing is seen in pregnancies. Thus ceremonies and prayers for flourishing using fertility symbols were enacted as an appeal to a god.

The Phoenicians worshipped the fertility goddess Astarte.[6] Canaanite religion worshipped the goddess Asherah and the god Baal, both fertility gods. But Asherah's images were widespread, and many references in the Old Testament indicate their importance (1 Ki 15:13; 2 Ki 21:7; 2 Ch 15:16). Jeroboam and Rehoboam both promoted Asherah worship (1 Ki 14:15, 23). Jezebel and Ahab promoted her as well (1 Ki 18:19) and supported this with a religious entourage of four hundred prophets. Israel's leaders continually tried to eliminate Asherah worship (Ex 34:13– 14; Dt 7:5, etc.), and yet, even in the prophetic period, allegiance to her remained (Isa 27:9; Jer 17:1–2, Mic 5:14). Deuteronomy's admonition is stark: "Break down their altars, smash their sacred stones and burn their Asherah poles in the fire; cut down the idols of their gods and wipe out their names from those places" (Dt 12:3).

One mystery is the presence of objects that translations expand and refer to as "Asherah poles," but we are unclear what these are. They were likely fertility symbols (possibly poles, trees, or symbols of trees) often positioned next to Canaanite altars: "They also set up for themselves high places, sacred stones and Asherah poles on every high hill and under every spreading tree. There were even male shrine prostitutes in the land; the people engaged in all the detestable practices of the nations the LORD had driven out before the Israelites" (1 Ki 14:23–24). The fertility rites (performed by Asherah and her consort) expanded widely, leading to cult prostitution throughout the land. The Canaanites even had phallic symbols standing erect in their temples, representing fertility. An intact large phallus was recently excavated at Hazor.

In the Old Testament, God abhors this immoral conduct. Not only does it deny his role in bringing flourishing to Israel, it was also a pagan attempt to manipulate flourishing through a ritual performance. Imagine the landscape of Israel dotted with countless Asherah (poles) promising fertility. The common prophetic demand was to cut these down.

The union of religion, sex, and fertility continued in the ancient world beyond the Old Testament era. It evolved as it entered Persian, Greek, and Roman eras, but the theme was constant: fertility—and prayers and rites enacting it—could be central to worship

**5:4** *Obscenity, foolish talk or coarse joking, which are out of place, but rather thanksgiving.* It is hard to imagine that Paul would take exception to laughter, but this was not uncommon in Jewish moral writings. The Qumran Community, for example, held strict rules for those who spoke foolishly or who laughed aloud.[7] Epictetus of Hierapolis in Phyrgia wrote the same thing in his manual, *The Enchiridion.* "Do not laugh much, nor at many things, nor boisterously" (*Ench.* 33:4). The NIV's "obscenity" stems from a Greek word related to shame (Gk, *aischunō,* see 1 Co 11:4–5) and so in context refers to shameful speech. "Foolish talk" simply combines the terms for foolish (Gk, *mōros*) with word (*logos*). "Coarse joking" appears only here in the New Testament, but Greek literature described speech that was bitingly clever or facetious and hence, tricky or dishonest, sarcastic perhaps. These three should be read together as "shameful, foolish, or vulgar language." But the three might also belong to the first set of three (5:3) and should be understood in the explicit context of Roman sexualized culture. This would be speech that mirrors the inappropriate social behaviors in more base Roman society.

Thanksgiving in the Old Testament is the joyful acknowledgment of God's love and his good gifts for his people (Ezr 3:11; Ps 69:30; 100:4–5) that is often expressed in song (Ne 12:8; 24, 27; Ps 95:2; Isa 51:3). In contrast to Roman society, Paul is hoping to cultivate a mindset and speech habit that is centered on this sort of thanksgiving (1 Co 14:16; 2 Co 4:15; 9:11–12; Php 4:6; Col 2:7; 1 Th 3:9; 5:18) that recognizes and celebrates the grace of God.

**5:5** *For of this you can be sure: No immoral, impure or greedy person—such a person is an idolater—has any inheritance in the kingdom of Christ.* Paul repeats what he said in 5:3 but underscores its importance and expands it. His emphasis is overwhelmingly firm: "knowing this, know that . . ." Or perhaps the RSV paraphrase works well: "Be sure of this, . . ."

Paul is describing people who indulge in this misconduct with idolaters, and while this may seem odd, it fits this setting. In the Old Testament, idolatry was one of the key features of pagan life that repudiated the one true God, Yahweh. The prohibition against idol worship was so strong, it was the topic of Moses' second of ten commandments (Ex 20:4–6). This is because these statues made by hand were viewed as gods (or representing gods) and were a rival to God—in the same manner as Pharaoh was viewed as a divine figure and God's Egyptian rival. This, in Paul's mind, is sheer religious futility (Eph 4:17) as well as an extreme offense to God himself. Therefore, Paul has a strong Hebrew foundation to draw on when he thinks about the pervasive idolatry he encountered daily in the Roman world.

The apostle is drawing a sharp boundary between those who belong to Christ and those who see few problems with participating in the social habits and religion of the Roman world. Idolatry was everywhere in Roman society: temples, public monuments, family altars and figurines, statues, and busts of Roman gods. The consequences of blurring these lines between darkness and light are severe. And Paul even finds it embarrassing to have to mention these things (5:12). Note how in Acts 15:20 anything linked to idols (such as meat sacrificed in pagan temples) is singled out as offensive to Jews who undoubtedly entered the homes of Roman Christians.[8]

Inheritance is one of the key terms of the Old Testament (appearing over two hundred times) to describe the good things God has promised for his people. (See comments on Eph 1:13–14.) It is considerably more complex than how we view it today. Above all, in the Old Testament it refers to land and in Paul's argument, likely the land promises of Abraham. It originally referred to any "portion" (or "lot") connected to land (Ge 31:14; Lev 27:16; Nu 16:14). But it could expand broadly as a metaphor such as what is received in a will controlling an estate. In Deuteronomy 9:29, the Lord is Israel's inheritance (see Ex 34:9; Dt 32:9; 2 Sa 20:19; Isa 19:25; Da 12:13). Paul is using the land-inheritance motif in a figurative sense as he does in 1 Corinthians 6:9–11 and Galatians 5:19–21. Simply, those who participate in the things listed in Ephesians 5:3–5 cannot expect to join in Christ's kingdom any more than a person who participated in Canaanite religion could view themselves as fully a part of Israel's future.

**5:6–7** *Let no one deceive you with empty words, for because of such things God's wrath comes on those who are disobedient.* What is the position of those Paul has in mind in 5:6? In many of his letters, Paul is aware that there are those who will either disagree with him on theological grounds or desire to compromise the force of his ethical teaching. In a moral context (5:3–7) we can expect that these "empty words" that were so deceptive had to do with compromising the moral boundaries Paul is defending (see Ro 1:32). We can imagine Christians here in Ephesus who see few problems with holding a Christian identity and taking part in these things Paul has just listed. They might continue to hold idols or frequent temple festivals—or worse, lead lives that exhibited little moral restraint.

For some interpreters, Paul must be referring to people who have not embraced the gospel. But this seems unlikely. Christian identity is not simply an intellectual embrace of the truth about Jesus. It is also about transformation and the Spirit. It is about conduct and conviction, *and these twin affirmations cannot be used to deny the centrality of grace.* The gift given in grace is a gift that assumes reciprocity and response to the giver. In Paul's exhortation in Galatians 5:13–15, Paul clearly has in mind Galatian believers who *indulge the flesh* and do not conform to the guidance of the Spirit. Paul's list of behaviors that are opposed to the Spirit in Galatians 5:19–21 echoes some of Paul's themes here, and in the same manner, he says they jeopardize their inheritance in God's kingdom (Gal 5:21).

*Do not be partners with them.* With stakes this high, Paul urges that believers make a discerning judgment and *separate* from such deceptive influencers. This is no different from the consistent Old Testament command that the people of God *separate* themselves from those who indulged in Canaanite life (Lev 18:3, 30; Dt 6:14–15; Jer 7:5–7; 35:15). Paul only uses the term *fellow partner* (Gk, *summetochos*) twice in his writings: here in Ephesians 5:7 and in 3:6. A *metochos* is a colleague or accomplice, someone you live or work closely with. A *summetochos* is someone you participate with fully (it is emphatic): a joint-investor or collaborator. Our deep partners in life should be those who share prominently in the gospel of Christ (3:7) and reflect Christ's righteousness to the world.

**5:8** *Now you are light in the Lord.* The contrast between the "before and after" of Christian belief could not be more dramatic. As he did in 4:17–19, Paul uses the imagery of light and darkness to represent the stark transition evident to the believers he is addressing. (Regarding spiritual blindness and darkness, see comment on "That the eyes of your heart may be enlightened" at Eph 1:18–19.) Note that Paul does not say that formerly the Ephesians were "in darkness." They *were darkness.* Nor does he say that they are now "in the light." They *are now light* itself since they are in the Lord. What had changed was not their environment but their lives.[9] And as light they have the ability to change the environments in which they live.

The difference between light and dark is primal. When the world was dark, chaotic, and unformed, God's first act was to create light and bring order by separating light and dark (Ge 1:2–5, 16; Job 26:10). Evil is associated with darkness, where it may seek to hide (Job 34:22; Ps 11:2; 74:20). It represents not just ignorance but deliberately walking away from God's wisdom and knowledge (Job 24:13; Ps 82:5; Ecc 2:13–14). God's word is a light that guides the path of how we should live (Ps 119:105). The righteous walk by light while the wicked are in the dark (Pr 4:18; 13:9).

*Live as children of light.* The Jewish idiom here is hidden in the NIV. "Walk as children of the light." This phrase was common in Judaism (especially in Qumran and the Old Testament apocrypha),[10] and Paul uses "walking" frequently (thirty-two times) to express our conduct. In Galatians 5:16, Paul says to "walk by the Spirit," with a similar formula (see also comments on "live a life" at Eph 4:1). In 1 Thessalonians 2:12, we are to walk "worthy of God." Above all, light and darkness are mutually exclusive. "Either light rules or darkness does."[11] There is no grey in this black and white universe, no middle ground, no neutrality. "Light and darkness can be mixed as little as Spirit and flesh, light and death, fertility and sterility."[12]

**5:9** *The fruit of the light consists of all goodness, righteousness and truth.* When Paul thinks about the results or outcomes of a life of light or darkness, he employs the metaphor of fruit (see "Ephesians 5:3–7 Through Old Testament Eyes: Fertility, Sex, and Religion"). In Romans 6:21, "What benefit [lit.: "fruit"] did you reap at that time from the things you are now ashamed of? Those things result in death" (cf. Gal 5:22). Here in Ephesians 5:9, Paul lists the fruit of a life lived as children of light: goodness, righteousness, and truth. Goodness evokes images of kindness, generosity, and someone who brings well-being to their world. Righteousness suggests a standard of what is right, shaped, no doubt, by God's word. And truth grounds all of these activities in what we know with clarity about God and his son, Jesus Christ. It rejects hypocrisy, duplicity, and dishonesty and will not compromise in what it knows. This sort of life cannot be achieved through a book of rules. This is—as Paul says in Galatians 5—simply and purely a work of the Spirit. This requires a renewed mind (Eph 4:23) or what Paul can call having the mind of Christ (1 Co 2:16).

**5:10** *Find out what pleases the Lord.* We are not simply to "find out" (NIV) what pleases the Lord, but we are to investigate and discern—put things to the test (Gk, *dokimazō*), which is the fullest meaning of the verb (similarly the Gk, *dokimos*, which is a test or something reliable). This suggests an active moral life that is weighing constantly what things are good and righteous and true *so that* our lives might bring about the fruit pleasing to God.

**5:11** *Fruitless deeds of darkness.* The flip side of this discernment is avoiding those matters of falsehood and evil that are discovered. These things are displeasing to the Lord. But not only are we to shun them, we are to *expose* them (Gk, *elegchō*). The verb Paul uses here has many dramatic nuances. It means to test something by holding it up, to bring it into the light (thus the parallel with *dokimazō* above).[13] This leads to the related idea of conviction when the lie is exposed and the truth prevails (perhaps in court). In John 16:7-8, this is a work of the Spirit, and so, among those filled with the Spirit, this active and courageous role calls for us to name and rebuke the darkness when we see it.

**5:12-13** *But everything exposed by the light becomes visible.* Paul's line of thought moves here from exposure or conviction of the darkness to its illumination. If the first effort is to expose what is truly of the darkness (and what is shameful, 5:12), the second effort is to make these things crystal clear by comparison with the light of God's revelation. Being in the light is not simply about personal clarity. It is about living in the light that comes from the Spirit. In this sense, Paul might imagine that the criticism of the darkness is not by way of natural law or utilitarian ethics but by revelation. It is in divine light that we see reality for what it is. The confusion of right and wrong vanish; the vanity of human intelligence is unmasked, and the concoction of religion is judged *only* in the light God shines on them.[14]

**5:14** *Wake up sleeper, rise from the dead!* Paul's citation here is one of the great mysteries of Ephesians. Most scholars agree that it is a verse from a hymn well-known among the early Christians (Paul refers to such hymns in 5:19), and this is why Paul can cite it without context or clarification. It may have been influenced by the Old Testament at some point (possibly Isa 26:19; 60:1) but likely this has been forgotten, and its common use gave it a life of its own.[15]

Some believe that this may have been a baptismal hymn applying resurrection to the notion of new life found in Christ as we find it in Romans 6:1-4. Baptisms used this imagery of movement from death to life, from darkness to light. Thus, the verse serves Paul's purposes here quite well. As darkness and light describe the transformation of discipleship, so now sleep and wakefulness do the same. And in this awakening, "Christ will shine on you" (Eph 5:14). This new life then brings together light, life, and their source: Christ known in the community through the Spirit.

**5:15** *Be careful, then, how you live—not as unwise but as wise.* Just as disciples are to be discerning about light and darkness, so too they must be discerning about how they "walk" (NIV: "live"). They are to be self-aware in a manner that they were not before their transformation. They are to be wise, not in a manner common to the world—not by education—but by revelation, with a wisdom that comes from God. Paul has already prayed "that the God of our Lord Jesus Christ, the glorious Father, may give you the Spirit of wisdom and revelation, so that you may know him better" (Eph 1:17; see comments there). This wisdom is part of his gift of grace "lavished on us. With all wisdom and understanding" (1:7–8; see comments on "the mystery of his will" at Eph 1:7–10).

**5:16** *The days are evil.* This godly wisdom is needed so badly because of the condition of the world. It is rife with evil. The NIV paraphrase, "making the most of every opportunity," represents a very few Greek words (lit.: "buying [or redeeming] the time." This word (Gk, *exagorazō*) comes from the term for the market (*agora*) because it originally meant buying something "out" and was used for manumission of slaves whose money could buy them freedom. Thus Christ "bought" us through the price of his death (1 Co 6:20; 7:23). Paul reminds us that we should look at the present time as something that likewise can be "bought up" or taken back away from the evil; that is, the disciple's work is not simply preparation for a redemptive future and a private enlightenment but a focused effort to change the present wisely.

**5:17** *Do not be foolish, but understand what the Lord's will is.* This, as in the book of Proverbs, is the reverse of wisdom. The foolish are lazy and naive, while the wise are deliberate and thoughtful (Pr 14:15; 22:3). Ultimately a fool simply won't take advice or fear God (Pr 1:29–30). As Derek Kidner says, "The root of his trouble is spiritual, not mental. He likes his folly, going back to it like 'a dog that returns to his vomit' (Pr 26:11)."[16] Paul's comment echoes Ephesians 5:10, contrasting fools with disciples who will deliberately seek the Lord's will (Pr 14:16; 15:33) and pursue it to please him (Pr 14:35; 15:20; 23:24).

**5:18** *Do not get drunk on wine.* Verses such as this probably win more attention in Ephesians than they deserve. The contrast Paul is making is between being drunk with wine and being filled with the Holy Spirit—a parallel already found in Acts 2:13–15 on the Day of Pentecost. Wine was a widely used beverage both in the Old Testament (see "Ephesians 5:18 Through Old Testament Eyes: Wine") and in the Roman world. Jews used it commonly as well. In fact, it would be hard to find a Mediterranean culture that did not drink wine. However, the abuse of wine was also well known among Jews as well as Romans (Pr 20:1; 23:29–35; Isa 5:11, 22). Paul's concern is not with the consumption of wine but with its misuse. Drunkenness is a concern in many of Paul's letters (Ro 13:13; 1 Co 5:11; 6:10; 11:21; Gal 5:21; 1 Th 5:7; 1 Ti 3:3; Tit 1:7).

# Ephesians 5:18 Through Old Testament Eyes: Wine

The Mediterranean climate was ideal for the cultivation of grapes, and it was a staple of any diet. Grapes were pressed to give up their juices, the liquid was filtered, and fermentation came quickly. Sometimes spices were mixed with the wine (Ps 75:8). But generally, the wine harvest was a time of joy and thanksgiving (Isa 16:10; Jer 48:33). Drunkenness, however, was viewed negatively (Ge 9:21; 1 Sa 1:13–17; Pr 23:21; Isa 19:14; Jer 48:26; Eze 23:33; Joel 1:5–6). Still, wine is a joy-bringing gift. Ecclesiastes 9:7 tells us, "Go, eat your food with gladness, and drink your wine with a joyful heart, for God has already approved what you do."

The Roman world was no different. All classes of society drank wine regularly, and they preferred a sweet white wine. "It was also a key component of one of the central social institutions of the elite, the dinner and drinking party."[17] Since Rome was an agrarian society, those who owned vineyards enjoyed special prestige. Farms in Italy, Spain, and Gaul were prized for the prestige of their harvests.

Wine was preserved with difficulty because fermentation, if unchecked, ruined the beverage and made vinegar. Wine stored in jars was often given an olive oil "cap" that floated on the top and sealed the wine from the air. This was then fixed with pitch. The jars were then kept in a cellar (1 Ch 27:27) or placed in the ground to keep cool. It was left to the Greeks and Romans to turn viticulture into a science.[18]

Diluting wine with water was commonplace. Greeks even experimented mixing it with marble dust, salt, pitch, resin, ash, or seawater to "enliven a wine's smoothness" (Pliny, *Nat. Hist.,*14.24). But on occasions when "large quantities of wine were drunk, it was invariably heavily diluted with water. It was considered a mark of uncivilized peoples, untouched by classical culture, that they drank wine (neat) with supposed disastrous effects on their mental and physical health."[19] Pliny talks about how wine has "commissioned thousands of crimes" (*Nat. Hist.* 14.28).

Hot water was used in winter (perhaps with spices and honey) to make a cold-weather beverage. In Paul's day, Jews imitated this Roman practice of diluting wine. In 2 Maccabees 15:39 we read, "It is harmful to drink wine alone, or, again, to drink water alone, while wine mixed with water is sweet and delicious and enhances one's enjoyment."[20] At the Jewish Passover, we know that a kettle for hot water was on the table (m. *Pesah*

7.13), and so we suspect that, at Jesus' final supper, this wine too had been mixed with water.

Paul says the chief problem is where such overuse leads: to debauchery. This rarely used English word translates *asōtōs*, used only twice in the Greek Old Testament (Pr 7:11; 28:7) and rarely in the New Testament (Eph 5:18; Tit 1:6; 1 Pe 4:4). In Luke 15:13, it describes the character of the prodigal's life in the far country. The word refers to someone who is reckless, undisciplined, or intemperate—whose behavior may lead to sensual indulgence. It suggests a morally disordered life. This difficulty requires little imagination. Alcohol misuse and moral problems are often twins.

**5:19-20** *Speaking to one another with psalms, hymns, and songs from the Spirit.* Paul is here imagining a new rhythm of life that is directed entirely by the Holy Spirit (5:19–20; cf. Col 3:16). He uses three terms: psalms (Gk, *psalmoi*), hymns (*humnoi*), and songs (*ōdai*). The last is modified: songs in the Spirit. And this activity sets the tone for how the Ephesians should "speak" to one another. It is impossible to say if Paul is limiting this activity to the Old Testament Psalms. Paul has in mind a community that is shaped by Spirit-inspired worship—by music, song, and psalms—and this sets the tone for how the Ephesian community would live together.

Note how the verse continues, Paul began with a participle (speaking) and now this is mirrored with another participle (singing). The NIV uses the second participle as an imperative, *sing (and make) music from our heart* which it may be. But simply Paul says, *singing music or melodies.* The community uses music inspired by the Spirit to grace its life together.

Some interpreters warn that these instructions should not be taken legalistically, as if singing hymns will awaken spiritual renewal. Instead, they say, these gestures emerge as a result of a life *already* immersed in the Spirit. Others disagree and wonder if here Paul is describing the beginning of *spiritual disciplines*, that pursuing these exercises will bring with them the awakening sought by us. Many who are skilled at spiritual disciplines take this view seriously and recognize that disciplined efforts can draw us nearer to God in ways we can barely imagine without them.

## Ephesians 5:19 Through Old Testament Eyes: The Psalms and Worship

The Psalms were the hymnbook of the Old Testament. But it is not entirely clear how they were used or when. We can be tempted to imagine large congregations of Israelites singing the Psalms in Hebrew much as we sing in congregations today. But this is not at all clear.

In the Old Testament, the psalms (Heb, *t*ᵉ*hillim*) refer to songs of praise. Over fifty times the psalms are introduced in the LXX with the Gk *psalmoi*, which points to a stringed instrument such as a harp (Gk, *psallō*, "to pluck;" *psalmos*, a tune played with strings, hence our "Psalms"). We know that musical instruments accompanied the Psalms since fifty-seven of them refer to musical accompaniment. There is also a subset of hymns called the "Songs of Ascent," for pilgrims climbing to Jerusalem (Ps 120–34).

It was likely David who brought definition to Israel's public worship. In 1 Chronicles 25:1–31, we see the how David assigned tasks to divisions of leaders and among these were musicians and singers. A choir of Levites hosted 288 singers (25:7)! When Solomon brought the ark to its new temple, again we see the array of musicians in service (2 Ch 5:12–14).

Worship in antiquity was more performative than it was participatory. The temple provided the presentation of music with teams of singers with many instruments. We can imagine it centered on the temple, sacrifice, formal prayers, and performed singing of Psalms known by the gathered audience. In the Second Temple era, fifteen steps leading from the court of the women to the court of Israel were used for the Levitical choirs to sing (*m. Middot* 2:5). We also think that in this period the Court of the Women held a chamber ("The Chamber of Music") for storing instruments. The much later Talmud describes this chamber in full.[21]

However, the full range of human experience referred to in the Psalms suggests that they also took on a private, devotional use that was highly personal. Some are liturgical, such as Psalm 117's call to worship. Some recited Israel's sacred history (8; 105; 136, etc.). Others provided for lament (44) and thanksgiving (18; 20; 21). But use within organized worship was likely limited to approved choirs.

Paul refers to "psalms and hymns" (Eph 5:19), and this pair of terms (which are likely synonyms) appears in the Second Temple period. The LXX refers to the beauty of the Psalms (2 Sa 23:1), and Josephus says David wrote "psalms and hymns" (*Ant* 7.305). When Judas Maccabaeus rededicated the temple, his followers used "psalms and hymns" (*Ant.* 12.323) to thank God. This suggests the wide corporate use of the Psalms that anticipated Paul's time. And it likely means that these two terms (psalms and hymns) were synonyms.

**5:21** *Submit to one another out of reverence for Christ.* Grammatically the list of participles in Ephesians 5:19–20 suggests that the participle in 5:21 (*submitting* to one another) is to be linked to the previous verses. This is the view of most scholars. This anchors the exhortation in Paul's only active imperative in 5:18 and views each activity as led by the Spirit:

> Be filled with the Spirit (18)
> - speaking to one another with psalms . . . (19)
> - singing . . .
> - making music . . .
> - giving thanks . . . (20)
> - submitting to one another . . . (21)
>     women to their own husbands as to the Lord (22)

This arrangement might be the case. But it is also problematic since submission is a theme foreign to 5:15–20. Ephesians 5:21 thus might be a bridge to what follows. The connection with the earlier verses, therefore, is only in form but not in substance.[22]

Another view sees 5:21 as heading up a new section because 5:22 has no verb and must rely on 5:21.[23] In this case, the participle of 5:21 ("submitting") functions as an imperative verb ("submit!"), a use not uncommon in Greek.[24] This is not a minor issue since Ephesians 5:21 makes *mutual submission* the central exhortation of Paul for the entire following section. Too often readers have begun with 5:22 and concluded that Paul's interest is in a wife's submission. Paul sees submission *to one another* as a mandate for both men and women, as the following verses will show. A literal translation would read:

> Submit yourselves to one another out of reverence for Christ, wives to your husband as to the Lord.

Or:

> Because you fear Christ, subordinate yourselves to one another, e.g., wives to your husbands as to the Lord.[25]

Note that the participle ("submitting") is to be read as in the Greek middle voice (where the subject acts upon itself), indicating the agency of the person ("submit yourself").[26] Paul sees this as a voluntary decision related to our discipleship. It is not subjection, where one forces submission on another. Each person takes up this call freely; it is never imposed.

This highly debated section (5:21–33) reflects something that was common in Roman society. These were called "household codes." They were as old as Aristotle[27] and Plutarch.[28] Josephus provides a similar list[29] as does Philo.[30] In each of these, rules outlined the roles of husband and wife, parent and child, and master and slave. Aristotle's ideal family consisted of master/slave, husband/wife, father/child—with the father playing all three roles (master/husband/father).[31] Paul knows that his Roman readers would expect such a "household code" in any moral exhortation and so he regularly supplies one (Col 3:18–4:1; 1 Ti 2:8–15; 5:1–10; Tit 2:1–10; cf. 1 Pe 2:18—3:7).

## Ephesians 5:21 Through Old Testament Eyes: Marriage

Paul's moral guidance on marriage, seen here in chapter five, is framed in conversation with Roman expectations at the time. These were the social forces—powerful forces—that were at work in his diaspora churches. But this does not mean that Paul wasn't indebted to the Old Testament's presentation of these same ideas.

In the Old Testament, marriage was assumed to be the norm in society and referred to as a covenant or contract (Heb, *berith*; Jer 31:32). Husbands were generally older than their wives (Joseph was 30; Isaac was 40; Ge 41:45–46; 25:20), but there is no minimum age for young women. Romantic attraction often played a part, and the wise parent no doubt looked for this (Ge 24:67; 29:20; 34:3–4; Jdg 14:1–3; 1 Sa 18:20; SS) because marriages were generally arranged by parents (Ge 21:21; 24:33–38; 27:46–28:2). Esau is an exception when he chooses his wife alone (Ge 28:6–9). The aim of marriage was producing children, particularly a male heir who would serve the patrilinear culture for inheritance.

The Old Testament provides ample evidence of bridal gifts or "bride prices" (Ge 34:12; Ex 22:16; Pr 18:16), the ceremonies and their expected garments (SS 3:11; Ps 45:13–14), feasts (Ge 29:22), and even the wedding canopy (Heb, *huppa*; NIV: "chamber") that was built (Ps 19:5–6) and where the young couple was blessed (Ru 4:11). There is also good evidence that monogamy was the ideal (Ps 128:3; Pr 12:4; 18:22; Isa 50:1; Jer 2:2), but polygamy was never illegal (see Jacob with Leah and Rachel). This was as true in the Old Testament as it was in Second Temple Judaism (*m. Sanh.* 2:4). Esau had five wives, Solomon, many more.

Restrictions also existed against marrying relatives (except cousins; see Isaac with cousin Rebekah, Ge 24:15, and Jacob with Rachel, Ge 28:2), and laws prohibited marriage to tribal "outsiders"—namely, non-Israelites (Ex 34:15–16; Dt 7:3–4), though there are exceptions (see Moses' marriage to Zipporah, a Midianite, Ex 2:21). In the post-exilic period, this prohibition was strictly enforced (Mal 2:11–12).

Everything we say about Old Testament marriage must be framed within the strict patriarchy that was common in the ancient Near East. The Hebrew wife was restricted but respected and this can be seen in the husband using the title Lord (Heb, *ba'al;* Ge 18:12; 1 Pe 3:6–8); but she was not classified as a concubine, she was not owned, she was protected (particularly by her family of origin), and she was free. In many narratives, such as Abraham and Sarah, the wife exhibits the behavior of an equal with her husband.

The covenant language of marriage spilled over to the treaty language between God and Israel (both use Heb, *berit*). This is explicitly seen in Ezekiel 16:60 and 37:26 as well as Jeremiah 11:10 compared with 11:15. This link explains the affectionate language God uses for Israel (Hos) and the jealousy God has for Israel in terms of marriage jealousy (Dt 5:9). Therefore, we can view the treaty covenant affections of God as a window into how Israelites in the Old Testament experienced their own marriages. They demonstrated love, fidelity, exclusivity, and blessing. If the Song of Solomon is any indication, here too we see that, despite its patriarchy, still, Israel enjoyed marital relationships of respect, love, and mutuality.

However, while humility is a virtue in light of Pr 11:2; 22:4, we do not see anything like the language Paul is using in Ephesians 5 for full reciprocity expressed as mutual submission.[32]

What we miss when we read these sections is how different Paul's guidance is. Roman codes focused entirely on rank and power. Their society was honor driven, and those with position and authority gained honor and prestige through these roles. Their assumption was that those who were subordinate had less ability to reason and understand moral order and so it built a firm hierarchy: husbands, wives, children, and slaves. There was little interest in mutuality and the primacy of the husband/father was central in the cast of family roles.[33] All of this sounds very foreign to us who live with individual autonomy and an interest in the rights of the person. But these modern ideas of personhood did not exist in antiquity.

The Christian innovation was to promote humility by putting others first. This would sound revolutionary to any Roman reading these verses since Paul's code inverts traditional values drastically. Romans would be comfortable with the notion of submission in certain circumstances (slaves/masters, subjects/kings), but humility is never promoted in Roman virtue lists as an aspiration. To imagine submission or humility as universal virtues in the church would be shocking. This call to mutual submission "demands readiness to renounce one's own will for the sake of others, i.e., *agapē*, and to give precedence to others."[34]

*Out of reverence for Christ.* Paul's reference to reverence for Christ in 5:21 actually translates as "fear" of Christ (Gk, *phobos*) and most modern translations soften it. This is the only occurrence of the phrase in the New Testament. It may well evoke the Old Testament idea of the "fear of God" or the "fear of the Lord," which Jews knew well (Ex 9:30; Lev 19:14; Dt 31:12; 1 Ch 16:25; Ps 19:9; Pr 1:7; etc.). In the Old Testament fear is a term linked to the covenant of Israel and is natural to those who love and obey God (Dt 6:2, 4; 10:12; Ps 103:17–18). The New Testament continues this tradition (2 Co 5:11; Php 2:12).[35] Paul's word choice strengthens this command to mutually submit because it is a holy command, directed to us by a holy God for whom *phobos* was an appropriate response.

Reverence for Christ or fear of Christ, however, gives us a clue to Paul's understanding. Jesus had set this pattern of mutual submission in motion through *his understanding* of rank and power. "Whoever wants to become great among you must be your servant, and whoever wants to be first must be slave of all. For even the Son of Man did not come to be served, but to serve, and to give his life as a ransom for many" (Mk 10:43–45). And of course, the cross was the ultimate display of this descent-in-humility: "Whoever wants to be my disciple must deny themselves and take up their cross and follow me" (Mk 8:34). Status was something to be sacrificed and powerlessness something to be cherished. In Philippians 2:5–11 Paul lays out this reasoning fully.

## Ephesians 5:21 Through Old Testament Eyes: Old Testament Descent

The Old Testament presents an idea that we often miss when we consider Ephesians 5:21 in its context. If Paul is talking about the model of what Christ relinquished, the power he surrendered, and his descent to the cross, we can find a corollary in the Old Testament.

Israel is reminded many times that as a nation, its own prowess or power were not the reasons God had chosen them and given them the protection and privileges that came with their departure from Egypt. Deuteronomy 7:7–8 records, "The LORD did not set his affection on you and choose you because you were more numerous than other peoples, for you were the fewest of all peoples. But it was because the LORD loved you and kept the oath he swore to your ancestors that he brought you out with a mighty hand and redeemed you from the land of slavery, from the power of Pharaoh king of Egypt." Therefore, Israel cannot boast in its own worth. Instead, their worth is assigned by God's love and faithfulness.

This idea of God "reaching below" to bless can be illustrated in a variety of ways. It is not Abraham's inherent worth or successes that provide what he desires; it is God's generosity. His covenant is not earned; it is given as a gift. When the tribal assignments are given, Reuben, the firstborn, is given land on the margin in the eastern deserts while Benjamin, the youngest, is blessed with the premium gift of land near Bethel. The lesser becomes the greater. When Samuel is examining the parade of Jesse's sons in Bethlehem, seeking the one who will become the next king, at last he finds the youngest, who is absent, keeping sheep (1 Sa 16:11). We can imagine Jesse's sons presenting themselves with stature, retelling their stories of greatness. The instruction the Lord gives to Samuel is instructive: "Do not consider his appearance or his height, for I have rejected him. The LORD does not look at the things people look at. People look at the outward appearance, but the LORD looks at the heart" (1 Sa 16:7).

Here we find a motif "The last will be first, and the first will be last" (Mt 20:16). And we can imagine that this notion of grace finding those "below" could be a framework in which early Christians like Paul could understand the cross and its call on the lives of Jesus' followers. It was "Jesus-in-descent" that became a role model for the church, and likewise Paul can use it here in Ephesians. Paul will tell husbands to love their wives *as Christ loved the church*, which is a path directly to the cross.

Paul's interest in his codes is less about upending the social order itself but instead, subverting it. His audience had been living with hierarchical household codes their entire lives. Instead, Paul examines how each pair (husband/wife; master/slave; etc.) relate to each other and applies his own insight into how, *living in Christ*, these relationships should change.

**5:22 *Wives, submit yourselves to your own husbands.*** As we have seen, the verbal action in this verse comes from 5:21, "submit to one another . . . wives

. . . to your own husbands as you do to the Lord." Interpreters who view the command of 5:21 as absolute see it as the controlling command of the entire section that follows. This means that in a setting of voluntary submission, Paul is supplying a reminder to wives that mirrors the command in 5:21. As both are submitting, so too the wife should submit. It is also important to see that Paul is speaking to *wives* here. He does not refer to women or females (Greek has other words for this). He sees this as a gesture that is limited to one relationship—not an organizing of gender-submission for all settings. Paul's Greek makes this explicit: this regards a wife's "own" husband only.

## Going Deeper: Gender, Marriage, and New Creation (Eph 5:21–33)

The controversial topic of Paul and gender should always be framed within the larger theological idea of new creation. Paul understands that salvation includes transformation. Therefore, we are to have renewed minds (Eph 4:23) and clothe ourselves with a "new self" that reflects the true righteousness and holiness of God (4:24). At the very least, it means that followers of Christ *do not* reflect the conventions of ordinary patriarchal culture but in some manner either overturn it or sanctify it.

Among those who wish to embrace a husband's headship as a creation-mandated role requiring his wife's submission (a complementarian view), at least we can expect that the husband must rethink his role through the prism of Christ's demeanor. Headship is not about authority; it is about love and sacrifice.

More and more Christian leaders are inclined to view these roles differently (an egalitarian view). They will see the command of 5:21 (and Gal 3:28) as determinative and see that Paul is subtly and substantially reversing patriarchy, particularly as it was known in Roman culture. In this view, Ephesians 5 provides a sharp exhortation to husbands to relinquish traditional roles in light of their faith—roles they assumed they deserved by virtue of their birth.

I have spoken on these subjects countless times to college students who would come to me privately. These were conservative evangelical students worried less about Paul's teaching and more about how an egalitarian view would upend the way society works. "Someone has to be in charge," is the unfortunate refrain I have heard frequently. In evangelical culture, many of these young men and women had been socialized to promote male leadership, both within marriage and society in general.

But here is what surprised me. It was not merely young women who looked for freedom from patriarchy; it was young men. Privately, young men would admit to me that the "burden" (their word) was too much to bear. They assumed that biblical headship meant providing a financially secure future, guiding their family's decision-making, being the spiritual leader, and bringing wisdom to parenting as "the father." Young men didn't want the assignment and confessed that they avoided thoughts of marriage because of this load.

I have had many conversations with "pre-engaged" couples in my office. And I often made a suggestion. "Imagine if you are in this project called marriage equally, not only as equal persons but in equal roles. Your leadership will be determined by your gifts, not your gender. Each of you will have your shoulder to the plow—and if this marriage works, you both will deserve the credit. And if it fails, you both will deserve the blame. But you will be in it together, fully, for life. If one of you falters, the other will pick them up—financially, spiritually, personally."

It was one of my personal joys to see the relief and happiness wash over these young adults. "Are you sure this is Christian?" they would ask. Indeed. This is Paul's vision for a new creation marriage that you are invited to build together.

**5:23** *For the husband is the head of the wife as Christ is the head of the church.* There is endless discussion about the meaning of the term "head" (Gk, *kephalē*) in 5:23. But we should avoid the common modern notion that *kephalē* always means authority over another. The term refers to something that is prominent or sticks out (a point, the top of a wall, a mountain on the horizon, the prow of a ship, the crown of a column) and generally means "prominence."[36] There are over twenty metaphorical uses of *kephalē*, and we must be cautious when interpreting Paul here. For example, *kephalē* can also mean "source" (the headwaters of a river), and many interpreters think Paul may have in mind Genesis 2:18–24 where Adam is the source of Eve's life. I regularly remind students that Paul never said the husband is the head of the wife. Paul said: the husband is the *kephalē* of the wife. "Head" wasn't in his vocabulary.

Paul's chief interest is in "how people in paired hierarchal relationships" (not those in peer relationships) should treat one another.[37] Because in Paul's mind, the household—which was viewed everywhere in the Roman world as the foundation of society—should reflect the person of Christ, *who is known for his self-giving love.* The bulk of Paul's interest is directed to the prominent member of this traditional hierarchy: the husband (5:25–33). Paul is gesturing to Roman convention, where husbands are legally prominent, but he is about to upend the husband's role. The Roman husband would recognize his role as *kephalē* but then learn that Paul has redefined it. It is as if the *kephalē* (or capital or crown) of a marble column suddenly learned that the column was turning upside down and the *kephalē* was suddenly at the bottom. This is why Paul nowhere teaches that the husband should demand this subordination from his wife. This would violate his command in 5:21 for the husband's own submission, and it would violate the husband's calling to love her sacrificially.[38]

## Going Deeper: Calling and Abuse (Eph 5:21–25)

Over the years, I have met many young women who decided to attend seminary. They were gifted, inspiring, and passionate, and they had been exhibiting leadership skills since they were young. They are a delight to have in class.

But when they trust you, suddenly a different, darker story emerges. An astounding number of them came from conservative evangelical churches where they were told that women had limits on their roles: they could not be deacons, elders, pastors—and in some cases, young girls were forbidden to read Scripture in church or lead in prayer. One talked to her pastor about coming to seminary and was told, "You can. But our church will not support you nor pray for you." Scriptures like Ephesians 5:22 were often cited. These women were not "submitting."

These women had overcome enormous obstacles to arrive at seminary. And the wounds they were carrying were profound. Some were angry. Some doubted themselves deeply. Many found that therapy helped them overcome abusive church experiences. But it was these very wounds *from the church* that made them compassionate healers and wise counselors. Many developed prophetic voices. Most were viewed as wise friends that younger students turned to for help. Academically they were often at the top of the class because they had determination.

My own confidence in the future of the church is imagining these women in leadership: imagining them in families and congregations that celebrate their gifts and shelter them from the criticism that seems to so often follow them in church life.[39]

**5:24** *Now as the church submits to Christ.* The church elevates Christ and worships him. But this is where Paul's analogy has its limits. The husband does not have the glorified role of Christ in a marriage. Instead, through his sacrificial love for his wife (5:25), a wife finds the inspiration to embrace the command of 5:21 for mutual submission. All of this must be framed in Paul's teaching that we are new persons in Christ, filled with the Spirit, and therefore live differently than the conventions of common society. This was a world where subjects were expected to sacrifice their interests or lives for those who were their leaders. Paul will say the reverse: his is a world where the head sacrifices himself for those in the family (or church).

**5:25** *Husbands, love your wives, just as Christ loved the church and gave himself up for her.* Paul's exhortation—still governed by the imperative of 5:21—now continues the Christ-centered metaphor for the husband. The imperative is in the present tense, suggesting continuous activity (lit. trans., "keep loving your wife"). This is a strong, ongoing requirement. Paul imagines a marital relationship of mutual submission in which the husband is reminded to love his wife. But this love is modeled on Christ, whose sacrificial love characterized his headship. *Nothing in the Roman world parallels this.* And in fact, many would rightly see that Paul is undercutting traditional roles through this exhortation. Both husbands and wives are called to submit; but here, husbands are called to die.

This subverting of custom parallels what Paul had done for slavery. In Philemon, the slave Onesimus is still a slave when he returns to Philemon, but the master now must reckon with a Spirit-led evolution: Philemon must love Onesimus as a brother (16). Paul's strategy is to erode conventional social values by reframing them in light of Christ.

Therefore, what Paul imagines here is a marriage in which the wife is not subordinated to her husband's authority or whims, but she voluntarily subordinates to her husband's love as he subordinates to her love. It is a selfless life from beginning to end.[40]

## Ephesians 5:25–33 Through Old Testament Eyes: God's Sacred Marriage

It was not unusual for the gods of antiquity to be accompanied by a consort or even a wife. The great pantheons in ancient religion could stem from these unions. The Old Testament stands out in that Yahweh has no such "partner." However, the motif of marriage is employed in a way unique in antiquity. Yahweh views Israel as his bride (Isa 54:4–5; 62:4–5; Eze 16:7–8; Hos 2:16). The language of love and care for Israel is found particularly in the prophets, who use this marriage motif to explain why God will not abandon "his bride." "For your Maker is your husband—the Lord Almighty is his name" (Isa 54:5).

This concept was likely the inspiration for Paul's depiction of the church as the bride of Christ (2 Co 11:2; Eph 5:25–26; cf. Rev 19:7). As Yahweh was to Israel, so now Christ is to the church. Paul's language in Ephesians 5:26 describing how Christ made the church holy through cleansing and washing may also be a direct echo of Ezekiel 16:9–10, where the prophet describes Yahweh's (futile) care for Israel, "I bathed you with water and washed the blood from you and put ointments on you. I clothed you with an embroidered dress and put sandals of fine leather on you. I dressed you in fine linen and covered you with costly garments."

**5:26–27** *To make her holy . . . and to present her.* Paul continues to describe the sacrificial service of Christ (5:26–27) using two purpose clauses: Christ gave himself up

- in order to make her (the church) holy
    by cleansing her, washing (her) with water in the word

- in order to present the church to himself
    in splendor and radiance
        not having stain, wrinkle, or blemish
        but holy and without blame.

This washing may be an allusion to baptism, and "the word" likely refers to the truth of the gospel (see 6:17). But the aim of this effort is restoration: so that the community of Christ may reclaim the goodness and righteousness it had lost through sin. This is so that creation, once tarnished by darkness, now can be reclaimed. Since Paul's subject here is marriage, to what extent is he inferring that the husband serves his wife in order for her to reflect a splendor similar to what Christ has given to the church? And since this love and submission is mutual (5:21), Paul's ideal opens the possibility that every husband and wife *in Christ* should aim to restore their partner to the person they were always meant to be. They are meant to encourage their respective spiritual and personal growth, to bring them to a place of goodness and flourishing that once may have been lost.

**5:28–31** *In this same way, husbands ought to love their wives as their own bodies.* Paul now applies the principle directly and Paul's Greek makes this unmistakable: "In the very same manner" (Gk, *houtōs*), husbands should love. Ephesians 5:26–27 was thus not a digression about the life-giving work of Christ. It was also contributing directly to the husband's mandate to love as Christ loves. In other words, Paul has redefined *kephalē* (head) in terms of Christ as *kephalē*, which is why the old order of the Roman household must change. *Kephalē* now suggests descent and sacrifice.

Two ideas converge here. Christ loves the church, his body (Ro 7:4; 1 Co 12:27; Eph 5:30); and second, the husband loves the very "body" that was created in his marriage. His wife is not a "body" for him; rather, when husband and wife join their lives (5:28; Ge 2:24) they become "one flesh," and this creates a redeemed body *together*, as we have in the church (see "Ephesians 5:31 Through Old Testament Eyes: Genesis 2:24"). The mistake is to fail to see that marriage is a union in which the man and woman share together in this one flesh, and therefore loving this new creation of two-made-one is akin to loving ourselves (5:28).

## Ephesians 5:31 Through Old Testament Eyes: Genesis 2:24

Genesis 2:24 climaxes the story of Adam and Eve following her creation from Adam's side. Adam exclaims, "Bone of my bone and flesh of my flesh" (2:23). The union of husband and wife was widely discussed in Jewish literature, and Genesis 2:24 is used by Jesus in Matthew 19:5–6 to underscore that they become "one flesh." For the Old Testament and Judaism, marriage was not simply a social contract: it was a unique union of two lives.

As Paul develops his understanding of the husband/wife relationship, he also reflects on Christ and the church. There is a symmetry here, and for both, the language of "one flesh" or "one body" are at work. In Ephesians 5:31, Paul cites Genesis 2:24 as the basis of this symmetry. "That is why a man leaves his father and mother and is united to his wife, and they become one flesh (Gk, *sarx*)." *Sarx* is used both for the husband's care for his wife and its parallel in Christ's care for the church (Eph 5:29).

In Ephesians 5:31, Paul copies the Greek Old Testament (LXX) almost perfectly, with very few changes. He omits "his" after "father" and "mother," probably to shorten the quote. But he also changes the beginning of it. Paul replaces the LXX *heneken toutou* ("for this reason") with *anti toutou*, which is synonymous. The words are close and he is reinforcing a point. Paul is making a comparison. *Similarly, a man will leave . . .* This strengthens his purpose: to show a symmetry between the church and marriage. Both the church and marriage illustrate the mysterious (5:32) union that God has created.

Paul turns these two ideas over and over again in 5:29–32. Indeed, we share in one body in marriage, and indeed, we belong to the body of Christ, the church. As Christ has loved the church in self-giving, so too husbands and wives share this same rhythm of loving sacrifice. In 5:29 Paul says in Greek, "For no one ever hates his own *flesh*" (NRSVue; Gk, *sarx; emphasis added*), and this echoes directly his quotation of Genesis 2:24 in Ephesians 5:31. Marriage creates *one flesh*. And thus marital union and the union of Christ with the church share properties that Paul finds intriguing (5:32).

**5:32** *This is a profound mystery.* Paul uses the term "mystery" six times in Ephesians (1:9; 3:3–6, 9; 5:32; 6:19; see comments on "the mystery of his will" at 1:7–10), and each time it suggests a secret meaning hidden from the world but now being revealed in the messianic age. Here Paul senses that in Genesis 2:24 something is being revealed that exceeds conventional wisdom. These sacred words of marriage share profound meaning for the church *just as* Christ's role in the church offers profound meanings for marriage. There is reciprocity, and for Paul, it is profound.

**5:33** *Each one of you also must love.* Paul continues to address husbands when he departs from his analogy with Christ and speaks in simple, direct terms. Husbands must love their wives and wives must respect their husbands. Paul's command for husbands to love their wives *as they love themselves* may well be an Old Testament echo from Leviticus 19:18 ("love your neighbor as yourself"), a text well-known among Christians. The respect expressed by wives translates once again *phobos* or "fear" (see 5:21; but here as a verb, *phobeō*). This shows the elasticity of the word. Wives are not to fear their husbands—here the English translation of *phobos* fails us. Outside of covenant language with God, *phobos* means an attitude of respect that does not subvert her husband's role. Some want to see *phobos* as more and include ideas of honor, deference, and reverential respect. But this edges toward the problem of authority-based headship, which Paul has overturned throughout these verses.

# EPHESIANS 6

**6:1–3** *Children, obey your parents in the Lord, for this is right.* This is a continuation of the household code that began in 5:21 and is the second part of the triad (husbands/wives, parents/children, masters/slaves). The expectation in most of these ancient codes is for children to exhibit full respect and duty to their parents because they were the source of the child's life. This was the basis of obligation and obedience. From Aristotle to the Roman writers, the expectation was inflexible. A Jewish contemporary of Paul named Philo could describe parents as benefactors and rulers and masters—while their children were recipients of benefits and subjects and servants. Parents, Philo said, are of a superior class, while children are inferior. These truths were "derived from reason" and are "undeniable."[1]

In the Jewish mind, infants and children are cherished and thought of positively (Ps 127:3; Pr 4:3; 17:6; Jer 31:20), but sons are often admonished to listen to the instructions of parents (Pr 1:8; 6:20) because it leads to reverence for and knowledge of God (Pr 2:1–5) as well as long life and prosperity (Pr 3:1–2; 4:10). Fathers were expected to discipline children (Pr 3:12; 19:18; 29:17).

Paul qualifies the obedience children are to give by saying that it is "in the Lord" (Eph 6:1),[2] which recalls Ephesians 5:21 where submission is qualified by being "in Christ." In other words, this duty of obedience and respect springs from discipleship and how a child understands his or her life in Christ.

Paul then grounds this in the Old Testament reciting of the fifth commandment (see sidebar "Ephesians 6:2 Through Old Testament Eyes: Exodus 20:12"). This command—as Paul reminds his readers—provides a promise of blessing. The command is for honor, however, which is a more complex and interesting thought than subordination or obedience. Honor suggests a relationship that is elevated when people live together.

## Ephesians 6:2 Through Old Testament Eyes: Exodus 20:12

Paul finds a basis for children's obedience in his citation of the fifth commandment from Exodus 20:12 (LXX). The quote is quite close; in the Old Testament (LXX) we read:

> Honor your father and mother, so that it will go well for you and so that you will be long-lived on the *good* land *which the Lord your God gave to you.* (Ex 20:12, emphasis added)

> Honor your father and mother . . . so that it may go well with you and so that you may enjoy long life on the earth. (Eph 6:2–3)

Paul follows Exodus 20:12 carefully but abbreviates it after he inserts his own comment ("which is the first command with a promise," Eph 6:2). The blessing in Exodus is directly related to the Promised Land of Israel. Paul removes this reference to Israel and instead makes the location of this blessing universal. Both citations use the word for the land (Gk, gēs), but gēs can also refer to the earth, which is Paul's intent here. Leaving out the application of the promise to Israel fits with Paul's zeal to view all lands of the entire world as places of God's blessing. Christians in Ephesus can be blessed *where they are* and are not required to come to Israel. We see this throughout Paul (see Ro 4:13). The land of Israel slips to the background and all lands, including Gentile lands, move to the foreground. Paul is upending the sacred geography of the Old Testament in order to promote a new reality that is centered in the gospel.

**6:4** *Fathers, do not exasperate your children.* We know that in the Roman world, the father's authority was seen as absolute. His common title, the *paterfamilias* ("the family father"), reinforced this and some household codes could even compare him to a king. Just as in the first teaching (husbands/wives), the focus returns to the father who is told not to provoke their children to anger. The term "exasperate" (Gk, *parorgizō*) comes from the word group for anger (Gk, *orgē*) and puts constraints on a father's behavior. Paul is calling for honoring behavior that reflects in some manner the behavior expected by the child. Once again, Paul is subverting a cultural freedom and viewing it in Christ as having a new dimension.

*Bring them up in the training and instruction of the Lord.* Upper class Roman households would either assign the education of children to a slave or have a teacher that was hired. Jews had a long tradition of seeing the home as the locus of education, where fathers were responsible primarily for religious education (Dt 6:6–7; 32:7; Pr 13:1, 24; 15:5). In the Second Temple period, synagogue schools for boys supplemented family instruction. In this tradition, Paul calls for fathers to oversee their education so that boys will know how to live (Gk, *paideia*) and how to think (Gk, *nouthesia*). The words are close, but the first is often used for directing or discipling children so that they cultivate proper habits (thus its use for vocations).[3] The latter is narrower and often refers to disciplines of the mind such as philosophy or reasoning skills. Together they provide a complete picture of childhood formation.

**6:5–9** *Slaves, obey your earthly masters with respect and fear, and with sincerity of heart, just as you would obey Christ.* Paul walks a fine line when he now picks up the last part of the household triad: masters/slaves. The Roman world had an unimaginable number of slaves, and some believe that Rome's slave population was 30 percent of the total. In some cities, the slaves may have been equal to citizens in number.[4] They were fully integrated into society and could be found at a variety of levels (from estate managers to educators to field laborers). There were many writings from the period on how to manage slaves, though for many of these writers, they were little more than "living tools" (Aristotle). (See sidebar "Ephesians 6:5 Through Old Testament Eyes: Slavery.") Slavery in antiquity should not be romanticized nor should it be compared with modern race-based slave narratives.[5]

## Ephesians 6:5 Through Old Testament Eyes: Slavery

It is certainly disconcerting to hear Paul tell slaves to be obedient to their masters. Moreover, he says, they are to obey with respect and fear. Living in the twenty-first century, we find this extremely difficult to comprehend. Passages such as Ephesians 6:5 were misused in American history to justify the right of enslavers to own people. We should not forget this history.

But in the Old Testament world, the idea of slavery was common and accepted, and this was true throughout both the Old and New Testament periods. Slavery was owning another person and having the power to control everything they did (mainly as laborers). Slavery was such a common idea that Israel referred to itself as a slave owned by God (Ex 32:13; Ps 31:16). But Israelites also owned slaves. They are listed as property (Ge 12:16) and could be bought and sold. Sarah owned an Egyptian slave, Hagar, and Abraham owned many others (Ge 17:23;

21:12). The Israelites were slaves in Egypt, and this tempered their view of slavery but did not end it. Deuteronomy 20:10–14 typically gives directions for conquering cities: if the city surrenders, all are put into slavery; if it resists, all the males are killed and women and children, like cattle, become Israel's slave property.

But we must carefully distinguish what we may call "chattel slavery" from other forms of servitude. The former treats the enslaved as property, and these usually came through conquest; the latter has entered slavery for a limited time (usually through debt, Pr 22:7), and these people can be from within the ranks of Israel. Thus in Exodus 21:1–6, we find directions for an Israelite father that sells his family into slavery (no doubt due to debt). They must be freed in six years.

The Old Testament presents many case studies of how slavery disputes are resolved. What if a man has sex with a slave woman—is the child born to her an Israelite or a slave (Lev 19:20–21)? If an Israelite beats a slave to death, this is a crime, but not if the slave recovers from a beating in a few days *because* the slave is property (Ex 21:20–21). Leviticus 25 indicates that Israelite debt slaves could not be sold as chattel slaves, and rules said Israelite debt slaves could not be abused or overworked. Foreign chattel slaves were not so protected. However, the protections for Israelite slaves were often ignored, and this inspired criticism from the prophets (Jer 34).

Intertestamental Judaism right through to the Roman period diverges little from the common and severe practice of slave-keeping. It is simply everywhere, with occasional refinements protecting those slaves who "belong" to the society that writes the rules. Even Jesus tells stories using slaves as characters (Lk 14:15–24). In Luke 12:47–48 Jesus describes the duties of a slave that any Roman would like: "The servant [slave] who knows the master's will and does not get ready or does not do what the master wants will be beaten with many blows. But the one who does not know and does things deserving punishment will be beaten with few blows."[6]

The prominence of this enormous cultural assumption helps us understand the difficulty for Paul or any New Testament writer to swim against the tide. Paul no doubt is clear that, in Christ, a rearrangement of the slave/master relationship is at hand (Gal 3:28; Phm). And yet, in passages such as 1 Corinthians 7:20–24, he sustains the traditional roles. The early church even adopts the name "slave" for its own membership

(Ro 6:16–17; see Ro 1:1, 2 Co 4:5; NIV: "servant") and recognizes slaves in its communities (1 Co 7:21), while encouraging them to gain their freedom. A trajectory is therefore in place that should have led to a critique of slavery on theological grounds, and this did happen.

Some scholars have suggested a "story of ascent," arguing that "the rise of Christianity gradually caused the decline of the institution of slavery."[7] But this took centuries. We might point to the erosion of slavery gradually, but this argument is weakly attested. Within two generations of Paul, the apocryphal writing *The Didache* presents an egalitarian view of slaves and masters while keeping slavery in place, but also exhorts masters in a manner rarely found among the Romans (*Didache* 4:10–11).

Rome was also alert to religious or political movements that would challenge social structures, leading to slave uprisings. We know that many slaves were drawn to the church, and there they found men and women for whom slavery was not seen as a class marker (Gal 3:28). Slaves were integrated in ways that were uncommon in Roman society. Thus, the church too had to be alert in how it was viewed on this matter. Was Christianity a religion that freed slaves? Such a view would put churches at grave risk.

We should imagine that throughout this social triad Paul is referring to Christians because these are instructions for the church. These are Christian slaves who may or may not be living in Christian households. Paul's most explicit instructions are, in 1 Corinthians 7:20–24, summarized well in 7:21, "Were you a slave when you were called? Don't let it trouble you—although if you can gain your freedom, do so."[8] Paul is willing to leave the social institution in place while viewing the gospel as eroding the institution itself. Here in Ephesians 6:9 and in Philemon, Paul assumes a relationship between master and slave, and he assumes that Christ will transform this into more of a family bond (Phm 16).

But since Paul is giving directions to slaves *and masters*, we can assume that he is imagining something remarkable transpiring in a slave-holding household that now names Christ as Lord. Slaves should interpret their station in life in light of Christ's call and conduct themselves with integrity and honesty (Eph 6:5–7), viewing their work as service. However, the ability to do this is viewed in a context where masters are likewise aiming to "do good" (6:8) and not be threatening *because* both slave and free live under the One Master, Christ. Remarkably, Paul can say that there is no partiality in God's eyes between slave and free. He writes in Colossians 4:1, "Masters, provide your slaves with what is right and fair, because you know that you also have a Master in heaven."

Paul's aim then is the erosion of an institution for which Roman society had rules. But here (as with marriage) there is another inversion. Christ would have us deny violence, brutality, insensitivity, dehumanizing behavior and, moreover, begin viewing slaves as persons worthy of good and right treatment. When a master-in-Christ is living with a slave-in-Christ, Paul expects a Spirit-led change to begin its work reimagining what Rome had built.

Of course, this leaves unanswered what a slave is to do when he is brutalized by an unbelieving master. If we use 1 Corinthians 7:20–24 as a guide, Paul calls slaves to remain with integrity *but to take every opportunity to acquire freedom.*

**6:10–12** *Finally, be strong in the Lord and in his mighty power.* Paul writes (lit.), "And for now what's left." Here Paul begins to bring this letter to a close.[9] The phrase draws together what has just been said and, based on this, looks forward to what comes next. Paul understands that what he has just written is needed to strengthen the church for the battles it will encounter. Similar to Jesus' teachings in Mark 13 or John 17, Paul is looking to the far horizon and sees deeper levels of conflict than most believers imagine.

Among many scholars, it is common to view these struggles in Ephesians 6:10–17 with rulers and authorities as secular. The twentieth century had seen two world wars, a war in Korea and southeast Asia, multiple civil wars, systemic issues of race and gender, and societal upheaval. The church, we were told, was struggling with economic and political structural evils. Other uses of "rulers and authorities" in the New Testament suggest this. In Luke 20:20, the words "rulers" and "authorities" appear when the high priest wants to turn Jesus over to Rome. Jesus even warns his followers that they will be turned over to such secular powers (Lk 12:11), while Paul sees these powers as something Christians should subject themselves to (Ro 13:1–3; cf. Tit 3:1).

If the motive for this interpretation is a rejection of a worldview that recognizes personal powers of evil, then it is mistaken. Paul's uses of the phrase elsewhere in Ephesians make this clear. In Ephesians 1:20–21, the exaltation of Christ "above all rule and authority" says his place is in heaven at God's right hand and thus is consequential for heavenly realities. In 3:10, the wisdom of God is being made known to the "rulers and authorities *in the heavenly realms,*" and in 6:12, we learn that the struggle is "not against flesh and blood" but "against the spiritual forces of evil *in the heavenly realms*" (emphasis added). This places the domain of the struggle clearly in the spiritual setting. In 4:27, Paul has already introduced the devil as operating against the work of the church, and this parallels 6:11, where the devil is mentioned again as scheming to defeat the church. Paul refers to Satan or the devil almost twenty times in his letters, showing his worldview clearly: *earthly struggles may well be more than they appear to the naked eye.* (See comment on "the elemental spiritual forces" at Gal 4:3.)

## Going Deeper: Rulers and Authorities (Eph 6:10–12)

The church has often made two mistakes when discussing "rulers and authorities" (or in older translations, "principalities and powers"). The first is to think that every Christian effort of struggle for the kingdom of God is won through prayer and the many spiritual disciplines. Their opponent is Satan and his forces. They see spiritual warfare "vertically" and privately and rarely look critically at the powers of this world. The second mistake is to reduce this warfare to "horizontal" realities such as government abuses, economic corruption, or systemic social evils (such as racism). They see evil as manifest in *this world* and find their Christian calling confronting these powers.

What they often fail to realize is that both realities may be at work in the same instant, in the same event.

This is perhaps one of the many helpful insights given from the African American church. Their theological leaders (Howard Thurman, Willie Jennings, James Cone, Esau McCaulley, and Matt Vega, among others) see that evil does not simply afflict us privately and spiritually, but it afflicts us in the necessary structures of this world. For example, a call for justice against racism is an engagement with evil and darkness that can be exploited by Satan, since he is the origin of all that kills and corrupts. Such public work is spiritual warfare, and it must be joined to the traditional tools of prayer, preaching, and prophetic truth-telling. Dr. Martin Luther King symbolizes this well.

Too often we have viewed horizontal "spiritual warfare" as liberal and vertical "spiritual warfare" as conservative and evangelical. It is the same with the kingdom of God. The mission of the church is to ready our souls for our entry into that heavenly kingdom—and to advance that kingdom *in this world* through our prayerful prophetic efforts.

Throughout his letter, Paul has drawn a picture of Christ upending not simply social structures but as affecting the heavenly realities of creation. The arrival of Christ was not a local revival within Judaism; it was a cosmic rearrangement of time and history, planned from the beginning of creation (Eph 1:3–10).

Judaism was necessarily swept up in these changes and blessed by them since the kingdom of God had now changed its borders: both Jew and Gentile now held equal places. However, such a seismic shift *inevitably* brings a response from those who want to protect the status quo, both in heaven and on earth. Christians will be personally assaulted by these dark forces, and many will be arrested. Paul is saying that believers must anticipate the *strategies* of the devil and lean into the Spirit for empowerment. "They are standing on ground that God's anointed king, Jesus, has already won for them (1:20–23; 4:8), but they must stand against the devil's cleverly planned counterinsurgency tactics."[10]

## Going Deeper: The Plans of the Adversary (Eph 6:10–17)

Jerome (c. 342–420) was one of the church's most important scholars, who is best known for bringing to the Roman world the first complete translation of the Bible into Latin (the Vulgate). His theological writings were equally valued. Writing on themes similar to Ephesians 6, Jerome captures the plan of evil in our lives effectively:

> Just as wise leaders of armies are accustomed to assault especially those places of a city which are least protected so that, when they have broken in through those places, the protected areas may be easily captured, so also the devil seeks to break in and reach the very citadel of our heart and soul through those places which he sees lying open and perhaps not shut up firmly.[11]

*The powers of this dark world.* Knowing your enemy is the first necessary task of any military operation. Paul uses four terms for this opposition: the rulers, the authorities, the powers of this dark world, and the spiritual forces of evil. The widespread view of antiquity was that spiritual forces had genuine impact on or could determine the fate of common life. Pagan Romans might look to the stars or planets affecting them—or even the pantheon of gods. Jews believed in spiritual forces (Satan in particular) contesting with God for the fates of his people (Job). Paul points to these ideas in Ephesians 1:3, describing a plan executed in heaven that is now unfolding in the world. When Paul refers in 2:2 to the "ruler of the kingdom of the air" who inspires disobedience, he has this very thing in mind. Spiritual forces are in contention (see comment on "the elemental spiritual forces" at Gal 4:3).

"Rulers and authorities" simply refer to the powers that contend in a particular domain, which here, is spiritual. The NIV "powers" represents the Greek *kosmokratōr*, which is actually a world (cosmos) ruler—but it is a rare word, appearing here for the first time in Greek. In later literature it was used for planets that, some thought, could control the world. Some Jewish literature refers to these planets as metaphors for demons who bring vices to the world (T. Sol. 8.2–4). However, we are told clearly that their domain is darkness. All of this can be summed up in Paul's final term, "spiritual forces" or literally, "spirits of evil in the heavens" (Eph 6:12). This means that the opposition against Christians is not simply the devil but an array of spiritual powers intent on destroying the work that Christ has done.

**6:13–17** *Put on the full armor of God.* The language here is military, and it is striking that all of the equipment Paul lists is defensive, save for his last entries. He is describing the posture of a sentry or infantry soldier holding the line against threatening foes. Here the apostle imagines spiritual warfare to its fullest extent. He describes a "day of evil"—not a generalized temptation by the devil, but a full-on conflict where the successful defensive posture is standing firm: "So that you will resist—and after having done all things—you still will be standing" (6:13, au. trans). In 6:16 Paul imagines an infantry line absorbing a hail of fire-tipped arrows, and thanks to the right armor and training, the line never fails.

The equipment list offers a dramatic picture of a Roman legionnaire preparing for battle. The belt, the breastplate, sandals, shield, helmet, and sword would be immediately recognized by any reader in that world. Together they represent the virtues, shaped by the Spirit, that equip the believer for battle with the powers described in 6:10–12. Truth, righteousness, readiness with the gospel, faith, salvation—these are the attributes of the vital Christian whose preparations will assure success against attack. But the reverse is also true. Failure to know the truth, failure to live a life of righteousness, failure to hold dear the faith—these will make us vulnerable as would battle dress that was missing critical parts. No one faces arrows without a shield (6:16).

**6:15** *With your feet fitted with readiness that comes from the gospel of peace.* In Isaiah 52:7 we read:

> How beautiful on the mountains
>> are the feet of those who bring good news,
> who proclaim peace,
>> who bring good tidings,
>> who proclaim salvation,
> who say to Zion,
>> "Your God reigns."

It was common for a herald to bring news of victory in battle (1 Sa 31:9; Na 1:15). The context in Isaiah is one of redemption and restoration of God's people. When the cry "Your God reigns" is heard, however, it would not just suggest God's rule over Israel but over all the nations (Ps 22:27–28; 47:7–8; 99:1–2; 113:4; Isa 14:26–27; Zec 14:9).

As Paul has said, in Christ the divisions between Jews and Gentiles (the nations) are ended with God's reign over both: "For he himself is our peace . . . to create in himself one new humanity out of the two, thus making peace. . . . He came and preached peace to you who were far away and peace to those who were near" (Eph 2:14–17). In Christ we find not just personal peace with God but also peace between groups who were once hostile to each other. This is the message Christ preached, that Paul preached, and that we are to preach (see also "Galatians 1:6–12 Through Old Testament Eyes: The Gospel").

**6:16–17** *Take up the shield of faith . . . and the sword of the Spirit.* The shield and sword were the soldier's chief battle tools. The legionnaire's shield was long and curved, standing from knee to shoulder. It could be covered with leather or metal and at the outside center was a metal boss (a small dome) that protected the soldier's hand inside but also was an attack tool. The heavy metal boss could be pushed against the enemy in hand-to-hand combat while the sword in his opposite hand did its work. The sword (Gk, *machaira*, called a *gladius* in Latin) was very short (twenty inches; fifty centimeters) and appears in other settings as a knife or dagger. The Roman soldier did not want a long sword in close combat where fighting often turned to chaos. His weighted shield and *gladius* worked in harmony, protecting him and permitting him to use his short sword for stabbing.

## Ephesians 6:1–17 Through Old Testament Eyes: Isaiah's Messiah Warrior

The Old Testament commonly refers to God as a warrior (Ps 35:1–3; Isa 42:13; Hab 3:8–9) and describes his people going to battle relying on his strength (Ps 18:1–2, 32, 39; 28:7; 59:11, 16–17; 68:35). However, the references to battle preparation in Isaiah 11:4–5 and 59:17 may have shaped Paul's imagery in Ephesians 6. Isaiah describes the Messiah: "He put on righteousness as his breastplate, and the helmet of salvation on his head; he put on the garments of vengeance and wrapped himself in zeal as in a cloak" (Isa 59:17).

Isaiah 11:4–5 adds, "He will strike the earth with the rod of his mouth; with the breath of his lips he will slay the wicked. Righteousness will be his belt and faithfulness the sash around his waist." However, the LXX adjusts a few words in the verses: "He will strike the earth with the word (*logos*) of his mouth and with his spirit (*pneuma*)." In the LXX, righteousness and truth (not faithfulness) accompany him. These are the words Paul picks up in Ephesians 6.

These parallels are striking. In Ephesians 6, Paul is thinking about the promised equipping of the Messiah and how, with the preparation of the Spirit, Jesus' followers will have the same ability.

*The word of God.* The "word [Gk, *rhēma*] of God" can be seen in two ways. First, it may be strategic uses of Scripture for when we are under attack. In this sense, Jesus models such use in his temptations. Following each test in the wilderness, he cites from Deuteronomy as he resists Satan. Jesus also promised this: "Whenever you are arrested and brought to trial, do not worry beforehand about what to say. Just say whatever is given you at the time, for it is not you speaking, but the Holy Spirit" (Mk 13:11; cf. Jn 14:26). This is the kind of help Moses was promised when he was commissioned to speak to the Israelites and to Pharoah (Ex 4:10–12). Isaiah and Jeremiah were given similar aid from the Lord (Isa 50:4; 51:16; Jer 1:9; 5:14). Now the Spirit gives help not just to leaders and prophets but to all his people (see comments at Gal 3:2–3 on "Did you receive the Spirit?").

Second, the word of God may also refer to the truth of the gospel that Paul has been describing, a broader term encompassing the full message about Christ. Paul uses *rhema* or "word" in this manner in Romans 10:8, 17–18 as well as Ephesians 5:26 (the only other place he uses *rhēma*). This is also Paul's prayer for himself in 6:19–20. Therefore, the prepared Christian is one who has a robust understanding of the faith and who can absorb criticism as well as speak confidently about Christ in difficult circumstances.

**6:18–20** *And pray in the Spirit on all occasions.* These words are a continuation of Paul's exhortation for the spiritual soldier about to enter into battle. The sentence actually begins in 6:14 ("stand firm") and continues through 6:20 (using many participles). Attentiveness (6:18; NIV: "be alert") is a frequent New Testament discipline (1 Co 16:13; Col 4:2; 1 Th 5:6; 1 Pe 5:8; Rev 3:2) that matches the soldier's readiness. It is the same request Jesus gave to the disciples in Gethsemane (Mk 14:34; see 13:35). Prepared disciples listen, watch, and discern the events happening around them, remembering that the devil is also watching for opportunities.

The exhortation to pray (Eph 6:18) repeats itself for reinforcement ("praying at all times and places in the Spirit, in every prayer and request," au.

trans.). This is followed immediately by another participle that may describe this type of prayer. It is prayer that keeps alert and perseveres in all things. It is prayer that is sustained in strength and is participating in the Spirit. But its subject becomes clear at the close of 6:18. Paul asks for us to be alert in regular prayers for "the saints" (NIV: "the Lord's people"), which leads him to ask for prayer for himself as well (6:19).

What does Paul ask? He is not thinking about courage in the face of death, as he does in 2 Timothy. He is in prison, but he is active, writing, and speaking, enjoying free custody, and able to see visitors such as Tychicus (Eph 6:21). Paul wants to be fearless when he communicates and particularly when he explains the "mystery of the gospel" (6:19). We have seen this the word "mystery" now five times (1:9; 3:3–6, 9; 5:32; 6:19), and clearly it is important to Ephesians (see comments on "the mystery of his will" at 1:7–10).

We have seen, particularly in Ephesians 3, that Paul is bearing a message that has remained as yet undisclosed to Judaism and the world. For Judaism, it includes the dissolution of the old boundaries maintained between Jew and Gentile (Eph 2–3). For the world, it includes the world-encompassing significance of Christ for all nations. Jesus is not simply the Messiah, he is a turning point in history, a divine marker God has brought into the world by which all persons will be judged.

**6:21–24** *Tychicus . . . will tell you everything.* We know that various emissaries and friends accompanied Paul during his Roman imprisonment. When he arrived in Italy, still under guard, Christians met him at the port of Puteoli giving him hospitality and an escort to Rome (Ac 28:13–14). In Rome, even more Christians joined him (Ac 28:15). During his free custody, churches sent emissaries. For instance, the Philippians sent a man named Epaphroditus to him (Php 2:25). But Paul had many others working with him, and a brief note in Acts 20:4 names several of them. The Letter of Romans (while not a prison letter) shows Paul using a scribe (Tertius, Ro 16:22), a woman named Phoebe serving as a courier (Ro 16:1), and other colleagues whom Paul calls fellow workers (Timothy, Lucius, Jason, and Sosipater, Ro 16:21).

Tychicus is one of these. He was originally from the Roman province of Asia (western Turkey today) and accompanied Paul on his final voyage to Jerusalem, likely as a bearer of his church's financial gift for Judea (Ac 20:4; cf. 24:17; 1 Co 16:1). He must have been Paul's messenger on other occasions (Tit 3:12) and some wonder if he later became a leader in Ephesus, possibly his home church (2 Ti 4:12).[12] Paul calls him a beloved brother and a faithful servant in the Lord. In Colossians 4:7, Paul commends Tychicus similarly but adds that he is also a "faithful minister and fellow servant [slave] in the Lord."

A courier, however, is not simply a letter carrier. Tychicus, as a trusted disciple of Paul, would bring the church up to date on Paul's circumstances, read Paul's letter aloud to the Ephesians, and then be ready to answer questions about Paul's meaning. This was an oral culture, for the most part, and emissaries like Tychicus played a crucial role.

*Peace to the brothers and sisters, and grace to all who love our Lord.* What is absent in Ephesians are the personal greetings we generally find at the end of Paul's letters. This fact, along with the impersonal third-person language (NIV: "peace to the brothers and sisters"), suggests that Ephesians was meant to be used in a number of churches, making it an encyclical. However, the use of family language such as "brothers" was common to Paul. He uses it ten times in Galatians, but here in Ephesians, it only occurs twice at the end (6:21, 23).

Paul began Ephesians with grace and peace (1:2), and he bookends his whole message with this same sentiment. Peace was a common greeting, particularly among Jews (see "Galatians 1:3 Through Old Testament Eyes: Shalom"), but here in Ephesians it is connected to the work of Christ (2:14–18; also Ro 5:1). Since peace now reigns with God, so too it should reign within the church (Eph 4:1–6).

The reference to grace (6:24) is uniquely Christian and Paul uses it regularly, generally in the phrase "the grace of our Lord Jesus Christ" (1 Co 16:23; 2 Co 13:14; Gal 6:18; see "Galatians 3:2–6 Through Old Testament Eyes: Grace and Benefaction").[13] Grace here is extended to all who love our Lord Jesus Christ. But the last word describing this love has proven difficult (Gk, *aphtharsia*). Is it "undying love" (NIV, NRSVue), sincere love (NKJV), or incorruptible love (ESV)? Elsewhere in the New Testament (Ro 2:7; 1 Co 15:42, 50, 53; 2 Ti 1:10) it seems to mean something that is not subject to decay and so could infer something not susceptible to death or dissolution. This is the legacy of the word, where it is often translated as immortality.[14] It is unending. So here Paul blesses those whose love for Jesus is uncompromised and unwavering, something that time itself will not erode.

# ACKNOWLEDGMENTS

***After many years as a professor of New Testament*** with both undergraduate and graduate students, I have seen how foreign our biblical texts are to us. We are removed in culture, theological framework, and range of metaphors. A well-read Christian two thousand years ago knew a wide number of images and stories from the Old Testament. They could echo an Old Testament story with tremendous subtlety and their readers would understand it at once. In fact, this early Christian's culture shared many values with the Old Testament world, and this made the meaning of the biblical texts that much easier. But today we are separated from the Bible by time, distance, language, culture, and religious history. Our minds are congested with modern images and metaphors completely foreign to the Bible, and they often interfere with our ability to read and understand it.

When Andy Le Peau originally conceived this series, I knew at once that it was sorely needed. His own volume on Mark (2017) modeled the skills of an expert interpreter drawing the reader back into a world that is substantially lost to us. These books will be the sort of tools students and pastors will return to in order to rethink the New Testament's words through the lens of the Old Testament.

I need to express my appreciation to Andy and how he imagined this series. I am also grateful to be asked to join the series to work on Galatians and Ephesians. For someone who generally works in the Gospels, this was new and exciting territory allowing me to work deeply in two of my favorite Pauline letters. Andy has also been an excellent editor. He is skilled at wordcraft, and his long years in publishing and editing have given him a wide array of experiences that few editors can match. He kept this ship off the rocks on many occasions and pointed me to new lines of inquiry that I had completely missed. This is a better book thanks to Andy's work.

Andy assigns all of our manuscripts to an anonymous peer reviewer who is also a New Testament scholar. I am grateful for his/her careful reading of the text and numerous excellent suggestions. From Greek syntax minutiae to current bibliography, this scholar provided many helpful redirections. This is also a better book thanks to their scholarly review.

I am also grateful to Kregel Academic publishers. This is my first book with them, and throughout they have proven to be enormously helpful, professional, and creative. The finished volumes are beautifully designed and produced, which means they care for what we are building together right to the final step. In particular I need to thank a remarkable editorial team at Kregel who brought expertise and precision to their close reading of the text. Thanks to: Kristina Vandiver, Russ Meek, Amie Vaughan, Thom Blair, and Shawn Vander Lugt. Kevin McKissick contributed to marketing and inspiration as the book went forward.

A quick word about the book's dedication. Each of us are formed and influenced by friends, teachers, and mentors who help us become who we are. These four professors (Drs. Ken Bailey, Ralph Martin, Howard Marshall, and James Dunn) each contributed personally to who I am and how I view the New Testament. When I work on a book, I often hear their voices echoing in my mind (from a letter, a classroom, a phone call, a meeting, a conference, a publication) and hope that I am honoring their investment in me. They have left us now and are in the presence of our Lord Jesus. And I am sure they have already heard those good words, "Well done, good and faithful servant" (Mt 25:21).

# LIST OF FIGURES

# LIST OF WHAT THE STRUCTURE MEANS

# LIST OF THROUGH OLD TESTAMENT EYES

## EPHESIANS

# LIST OF GOING DEEPER

**GALATIANS**

## EPHESIANS

# ABBREVIATIONS

| | |
|---|---|
| *1QS* | *Serekh ha-Yahad* or "Community Rule," from Qumran Cave 1 |
| ACCS | Ancient Christian Commentary on Scripture |
| *Ag. Apian* | *Against Apian,* Josephus |
| *Antiquities* | *The Antiquities of the Jews,* Josephus |
| au. trans. | Author's Translation |
| BDAG | The Greek-English Lexicon of the New Testament (2nd ed) |
| *CBQ* | *Catholic Biblical Quarterly* |
| *Ench.* | *The Enchiridion,* Epictetus of Hierapolis |
| ESV | English Standard Version |
| *Gen. Rab.* | Genesis Rabbah |
| Gk | Greek |
| Heb | Hebrew or book of Hebrews |
| *Histories* | *Histories,* Tacitus |
| JBL | *Journal of Biblical Literature* |
| Jubilees | Jubilees |
| Lat | Latin |
| *Let. Aris.* | *Letter of Aristeas* |
| LXX | Septuagint |

| | |
|---|---|
| *m. Abot* | Mishnah, Tractate Abot |
| *m. Middot* | Mishnah, Tractate Middot |
| *m. Pesah* | Mishnah, Tractate Pesahim |
| *m. Sabb.* | Mishnah, Šabbat |
| *m. Sanh.* | Mishnah, Sanhedrin |
| NASB | New American Standard Bible |
| NET | New English Translation |
| NIV | New International Version |
| NLT | New Living Translation |
| NRSVue | New Revised Standard Version Updated Edition |
| P. Oxy. | Oxyrhynchus Papyri |
| *Pro Rabirio* | Cicero, *Pro Rabirio Postumo* |
| RSV | Revised Standard Version |
| *Spec. Laws* | Philo, *On the Special Laws* |
| T. Sol. | Testament of Solomon |
| TOTC | Tyndale Old Testament Commentaries |
| *TDNT* | *Theological Dictionary of the New Testament* |
| TLV | Tree of Life Version |
| *Wars* | *Jewish Wars*, Josephus |

# SELECT BIBLIOGRAPHY

## GALATIANS

Bruce, F. F. *Commentary on Galatians*. New International Greek Testament Commentary. Grand Rapids: Eerdmans, 1982.

Burton, Ernest De Witt. *The Epistle to the Galatians*. Edinburgh: T&T Clark, 1921.

deSilva, David. *The Letter to the Galatians*. The New International Commentary on the New Testament. Grand Rapids: Eerdmans, 2018.

Dunn, James D. G. *The Epistle to the Galatians*. Black's New Testament Commentary. Peabody: Hendrickson, 1993.

Fung, Ronald Y. K. *The Epistle to the Galatians*. The New International Commentary on the New Testament. Grand Rapids: Eerdmans, 1988.

Keener, Craig. *Galatians: New Cambridge Bible Commentary*. Cambridge: Cambridge University Press, 2018.

Keener, Craig. *Galatians: A Commentary*. Grand Rapids: Baker Academic, 2019.

Lightfoot, J. B. *The Epistle of Paul to the Galatians*. 1865. Repr., Grand Rapids: Zondervan, 1957.

Longenecker, Richard N. *Galatians*. Word Biblical Commentary. Dallas: Word, 1990.

Martyn, J. Louis. *Galatians*. Anchor Bible Commentary 33A. New York: Doubleday, 1997.

McKnight, Scot. *Galatians*. The NIV Application Commentary. Grand Rapids: Zondervan Academic, 1995.

Moo, Douglas J. *Galatians*. Baker Exegetical Commentary on the New Testament. Grand Rapids: Eerdmans, 2013.

Witherington, Ben III. *Grace in Galatia: A Commentary on Paul's Letter to the Galatians.* Grand Rapids: Eerdmans, 1998.

Wright, N. T. *Galatians: Commentaries for Christian Formation.* Grand Rapids: Eerdmans, 2021.


## EPHESIANS

Abbott, T. K. *Ephesians.* International Critical Commentary. Edinburgh: T&T Clark, 1902.

Arnold, Clinton E. *Ephesians, Power and Magic: The Concept of Power in Ephesians in Light of Its Historical Setting.* SNTS Monograph Series 63. Cambridge: Cambridge University Press, 1992.

Barth, Markus. *The Broken Wall: A Study of the Epistle to the Ephesians.* Valley Forge, PA: Judson, 1959.

Barth, Markus. *Ephesians.* Anchor Bible Commentary 34a, 34b. New York: Doubleday, 1974.

Bock, Darrell. *Ephesians.* Tyndale New Testament Commentaries. Downers Grove, IL: IVP Academic, 2019.

Bruce, F. F. *The Epistles to the Colossians, Philemon, and to the Ephesians.* The New International Commentary on the New Testament. Grand Rapids: Eerdmans, 1984.

Caird, G. B. *Paul's Letters from Prison.* Oxford: Oxford University Press, 1976.

Cohick, Lynn. *The Letter to the Ephesians.* New International Commentary on the New Testament. Grand Rapids: Eerdmans, 2020.

deSilva, David A. *Ephesians.* New Cambridge Bible Commentary. Cambridge: Cambridge University Press, 2022.

Lincoln, Andrew T. *Ephesians.* Word Biblical Commentary. Dallas: Word, 1990.

Snodgrass, Klyne. *Ephesians.* The NIV Application Commentary. Grand Rapids: Zondervan Academic, 1996.

Stott, John. *The Message of Ephesians.* Downers Grove, IL: IVP Academic, 1979.

Thielman, Frank. *Ephesians.* Baker Exegetical Commentary on the New Testament. Grand Rapids: Baker Academic, 2010.

Witherington, Ben III. *The Letters to Philemon, the Colossians, and the Ephesians: A Socio-Rhetorical Commentary on the Captivity Epistle.* Grand Rapids: Eerdmans, 2007.

Wright, N. T. *Paul for Everyone: The Prison Letters.* Louisville: Westminster John Knox Press, 2004.

# ENDNOTES

## INTRODUCTION TO GALATIANS

1. I always encourage students to purchase one of two atlases: (1) Adrian Curtis, *The Oxford Bible Atlas*, 4th edition (Oxford University Press, 2007) or (2) Paul Lawrence, *The IVP Atlas of Bible History* (Downers Grove, IL: IVP Academic, 2006). IVP published a concise, shorter edition of the Lawrence atlas in 2012.
2. Throughout the late nineteenth century and into the mid-twentieth century, critical scholars only accepted Galatians, 1–2 Corinthians, and Romans as the "four authentic" Pauline letters.
3. For more on the Septuagint, see Gregory R. Lanier and William A. Ross, *The Septuagint: What It Is and Why It Matters* (Wheaton, IL: Crossway, 2021).

## GALATIANS 1

1. J. B. Lightfoot, *The Epistle of St. Paul to the Galatians*, 10th ed. (1896; repr., Grand Rapids: Zondervan, 1957), 71.
2. Esau McCaulley, "Galatians, Letter to the," Scott McKnight, ed., *Dictionary of Paul and His Letters* (Downers Grove, IL: IVP Academic, 2023), 349.
3. Clinton E. Arnold, "I Am Astonished That You Are So Quickly Turning Away! (Gal 1:6): Paul and Anatolian Folk Belief," *New Testament Studies* 51, no. 3 (2005): 434. For a popular fictional reconstruction of a world where fear and sacrifice intermingled, see C. S. Lewis, *Till We Have Faces: A Myth Retold* (Harcourt Brace, 1956).
4. Kenneth L. Schenck, "Gospel: Good News," Joel B. Green, et al., eds., *Dictionary of Jesus and the Gospels*, 2nd ed. (IVP Academic, 2013), 343.

## GALATIANS 2

1. James D. G. Dunn, *The Epistle to the Galatians*, Black's New Testament Commentary (London: A&C Black, 1993), 91.
2. See further, Matthew Thiessen, *Contesting Conversion: Genealogy, Circumcision, and Identity in Ancient Judaism and Christianity* (Oxford: Oxford University Press, 2018).
3. Keener, *Galatians*, 126.
4. David A. deSilva, *The Letter to the Galatians* (Grand Rapids: Eerdmans, 2018), 184.
5. deSilva, *Galatians*, 184.
6. Keener, *Galatians*, 129.
7. This should not be confused with Psidian Antioch located in Lower Central Anatolia.

8   Although some scholars do not accept this. See Keener, *Galatians*, 139n521 and Dunn, *Galatians*, 116n1.
9   Burton, *Galatians*, 102–03.
10  Keener, 146.
11  Dunn, *Galatians,* 130.
12  Dunn, *Galatians*, 130.
13  For a thorough and helpful treatment, see Keener, *Galatians*, 177–83.
14  Gary M. Burge, *Whose Land? Whose Promise? What Christians Are Not Being Told about Israel and the Palestinians* (Cleveland: Pilgrim Press, 2003, 2013); *Jesus and the Land: The New Testament to Holy Land Theology* (Grand Rapids: Baker Academic, 2010).
15  See Dunn, *Galatians*, 142.
16  Note that Paul uses the perfect tense for this death rather than the aorist. His crucifixion is not something limited to the past (a completed event) but an event with ongoing implications (hence the perfect tense). See similarly Galatians 3:1 and Romans 6:5.
17  Keener, *Galatians*,193; similarly deSilva, *Galatians*, 247–50.
18  John Barclay, *Paul and the Gift* (Grand Rapids: Eerdmans, 2015). For readers who would rather not work through this weighty tome (625 pages), Barclay offers a condensed version (258 pages) that still offers his essential insights. See *Paul and the Power of Grace* (Grand Rapids: Eerdmans, 2020).
19  Barclay, *Paul and the Gift*, 189–193.
20  Barclay, *Paul and the Gift*, 400, as cited by Keener, *Galatians*, 202.
21  Keener, *Galatians*, 202.

## GALATIANS 3

1   Chrysostom on Galatians 3:1, cited in Ben Witherington III, *Grace in Galatia: A Commentary on St. Paul's Letter to the Galatians* (Grand Rapids: Eerdmans, 1998), 201–04; see also Keener, *Galatians*, 207; deSilva, *Galatians*, 267. There has been a long tradition in the church of seeing this problem as the practice of magic or sorcery, something that was well-known in the Roman world.
2   David deSilva, "Excursus: A Contextual Understanding of Grace," *Galatians*, 254–262. This sidebar chiefly relies on deSilva's excellent essay.
3   deSilva, "Excursus," 254.
4   David deSilva refers to one of the cultural icons of the ancient world called the Three Graces. These are goddesses dancing together, and they are intended to exemplify the relationships created by grace. He cites Seneca: "There is one for bestowing a benefit, another for receiving it, and a third for returning it" (*On Benefits*, 1:3.3–5). This understanding of benefit distribution as a dance is as old as Aristotle, and for many, it built a network of benefaction that gave society its solidity.
5   Keener, *Galatians*, 217, with many references.
6   The Greek verb *paschó* literally refers to suffering, but there is a more figurative use that most lexicons will apply here. It can mean "endure" or "experience," *which may* be suffering. *Theological Dictionary of the New Testament*, 5:905.
7   The Greek text actually says "sons of Abraham," and this language may have value if we are talking about inheritance and blessing, something that in a patriarchal society followed sons. Nevertheless, the NIV is right to make this inclusive to show contemporary readers that this includes both men and women (which would be Paul's intention as seen just a few verses later in Gal 3:28).
8   The cave of Machpelah is one of the great sites in Hebron today. Located at the center of the Old City, the site was covered with a remarkable building by Herod the Great, which still stands. Beneath its floors is an inaccessible labyrinth of cave tunnels with many tombs. Abraham, Sarah, Isaac, Rebecca, Leah, and Jacob (Ge 49:28–33) are all buried here and today represented by cenotaphs (monument tomb markers).

9   Keener, *Galatians*, 231–32.

10  Barclay, *Paul and the Gift*, 405–06.

11  The technical term for this is *covenantal nomism* (from Gk, *nomos*, "law"), a term made popular by Richard Longenecker, *Paul, Apostle of Liberty* (Grand Rapids: Baker, 1964) and is used widely by Pauline scholars. In this view, Jews understood obedience to the law not as a means of gaining covenant righteousness but as a response to covenant righteousness given freely.

12  This is the important concession of Longenecker in *Paul, Apostle of Liberty*, that in a religious life shaped by law, it would not be unusual to see many who would view obedience to law as a prerequisite for remaining in the covenant.

13  Scot McKnight, *Galatians*, The NIV Application Commentary (Grand Rapids: Zondervan Academic, 1995), 153.

14  McKnight, *Galatians*, 153.

15  Much turns on the reference in Habakkuk 1:6 to the Chaldeans who defeated the Egyptians at the Euphrates River in 605 BC (the battle of Carchemish). Others point to 1:9 and suggest that "Chaldeans" (Heb, *kasdim*) refers to *kittim*, which would refer to Greeks or perhaps Alexander much later. The earlier date is usually preferred.

16  Keener, *Galatians*, 249–250.

17  Barclay, *Paul and the Gift*, 406.

18  See Moisés Silva, "Galatians," in G. K. Beale and D. A. Carson, eds., *Commentary on the New Testament Use of the Old Testament* (Grand Rapids: Baker Academic, 2007), 801–04.

19  Chris Bruno, Jared Compton, and Kevin McFadden, *Biblical Theology According to the Apostles: How the Earliest Christians Told the Story of Israel* (Downers Grove, IL: IVP Academic: 2020), 98.

20  See deSilva, *Galatians*, 309–310, and Michael Wilcox, "The Promise of the 'Seed' in the New Testament and the Targumim," *Journal of the Study of the New Testament* 5 (1979), 2–20. Keener, *Galatians*, 266–67, provides multiple examples from Jewish writings. For instance, in the Mishnah, rabbis could argue based on the plural/singular of seed in this same way (*m. Sabb.* 9.2). In another example, women could be exempt from certain duties because the biblical text said "sons" even though it is a generic masculine in Hebrew.

21  The importance of one line over another is indicated in Genesis by following the line of one son in favor of the other(s). Thus Cain's line is mentioned in Genesis 4 and then dropped before following Seth's line in Genesis 5 through to Noah. The descendants of Noah's three sons are noted in Genesis 10, but only that of Shem's line is followed thereafter through to Abraham. The same pattern is found for Ishmael and Isaac, as well as Esau and Jacob. In this way Genesis conveys the priority of Isaac's line over Ishmael's.

22  Keener, *Galatians*, 278n634, for copious references.

23  The term here is *parabasis*, "transgressions," and is an unusual word used rarely by Paul (Ro 2:23; 4:15; 5:14; Gal 3:19; 1 Ti 2:14). It means "to let something slip" or "to overstep." In the LXX it is used regularly for violations of the law (LXX Ex 32:8; Dt 9:12).

24  J. B. Lightfoot, *The Epistle to the Galatians* (1895; 1957 reprint), 146, says the number of interpretations must exceed two hundred and fifty!

25  *ho de mesitēs henos ouk estin.*

26  Dunn represents a quite different view: Israel commonly understood that angels directed the affairs of other nations, but Israel was different since God directed Israel personally. But Paul is saying that the understanding that Israel needed angelic mediators compromised the exclusivity of Israel's unique claims. Thus in 4:9–10 Paul can worry that submission to the law *is submission to angelic intermediaries*. Those who belong to Christ do nothing of the sort. Dunn, *Galatians*, 192.

27    Keener, *Galatians*, 286. Cited from Mark J. Edwards, *Galatians, Ephesians, and Philippians* ACCS (Downers Grove, IL: IVP Academic, 1999).

28    M. Robert Mulholland Jr. and Ruth Haley Barton, *Invitation to a Journey: A Road Map for Spiritual Formation,* rev. ed. (Downers Grove, IL: IVP Formatio, 1993, 2016), 6.

29    See *huios* in *TDNT* 8:351–5, 359–60, for numerous references.

30    Dunn, *Galatians,* 202.

31    The language Paul uses here for clothing oneself appears in the LXX with some frequency. See Lightfoot, *Galatians,* 149–50 for references.

32    One Greek prayer available at the time of Paul thanked the gods that he was born a human being and not one of the brutes; that he was born a man and not a woman; and that he was born a Greek and not a barbarian.

33    Richard Hayes, *Echoes of Scripture in the Letters of Paul* (New Haven, CT: Yale University Press, 1989), 29–32, where we see obvious links to male and female.

34    Troy W. Martin, "The Covenant of Circumcision: Genesis 17:9–14 and the Situational Antitheses of Galatians 3:28," *JBL* 122.1 (2003), 116–19.

35    Martin, "Covenant," 121.

36    Greeks were fully capable of the same thing: there were Greeks and there were barbarians, which included everyone else.

37    Paul prefers the formal name Prisca (Ro 16:3), just as he uses the formal name Silvanus. Luke prefers the informal names Priscilla and Silas (Ac 18:2). Prisca was a well-known name in Rome and meant "ancient." See Keener, *Acts*, 3:2711. The NIV translates all references to her as "Priscilla."

38    "Inheritance" in Leland Ryken, et al., eds., *Dictionary of Biblical Imagery* (Downers Grove, IL: IVP Academic, 1998), 420.

## GALATIANS 4

1    Paul's use of "observing (*paratēreō*) special days" was commonly used by Jews to refer to *observing* the Sabbath. Josephus, *Antiquities*. 3:91, "We must keep (*paratēreō*) the seventh day."

2    Keener, *Galatians*, 365–369, excursus on Pathos.

3    Keener, *Galatians*, 383, with many references. In a Jewish commentary near Paul's time (*Sifre Deuteronomy* 313.1.4), a rabbi explains Abraham's faithfulness, saying that the patriarch was willing even to sacrifice the pupil of his eye if needed.

4    Note how Paul seems to present himself in letter more strongly than he does in person—2 Co 10:10 shows his critics saying that he is unimpressive in person but firm on paper.

5    This is the only occurrence of this word in biblical Greek, but it had a long legacy within classic Greek writers. In Paul's day, Philo used allegory regularly to interpret the Old Testament. Allegory simply assigns symbolic meaning to most elements of a story.

6    4:25 NIV, "corresponds"; Gk, *sustoixeō*, meaning "to stand in a column or alignment," which suggests Paul is thinking about a linear display of linkages in history.

7    See Dunn, *Galatians*, 253–54; Keener, *Galatians*, 417–420.

8    deSilva, *Galatians*, 400.

9    The NIV translates Jer 15:17 as "revelers" and Pr 26:19 as "joking." The LXX uses *paizō* for these, implying a play that has a darker side.

## GALATIANS 5

1    Greek employs three "voices" to express action: active (when the subject acts); middle (when the subject acts upon him/herself); and passive (when the subject is acted upon). "I see you" would express the active voice and often had a direct object (you). "I see myself" would express this middle voice. "I am seen" expresses the passive voice

but often adds in a clause who acted upon the subject ("I am seen by you"). This is a simple explanation. However, the middle voice can also have a variety of other uses as well. In Galatians, Paul wants to be clear: this decision for circumcision is about a person's choice—they are bringing this on themselves.

2    Another dimension of Paul's argument might arise from the eight-day rule. Genesis 17 says circumcision was to take place when a male baby was eight days old (17:12). However, Abraham was ninety-nine years old (17:24) and Ishmael was thirteen (17:25). These two were clearly exceptions since the covenant was new. When Isaac is born, he is circumcised on the eighth day (Ge 21:4). But what about those who neglected this rule?

The Book of Jubilees is a Jewish writing from this era that reports private revelations given by God to Moses while he was on Mount Sinai. In some sense, it serves as a commentary on the law. In Jubilees 15 we have a remarkable description of circumcision and the eight-day rule:

> This law [circumcision] is for all the eternal generations and there is no circumcising of days and there is no passing a single day beyond eight days because it is an eternal ordinance ordained and written in the heavenly tablets. And anyone who is born whose own flesh is not circumcised on the eighth day is not from the sons of the covenant which the LORD made for Abraham since (he is) from the children of destruction. And there is therefore no sign upon him so that he might belong to the LORD because (he is destined) to be destroyed and annihilated from the earth. . . . (James H. Charlesworth, *The Old Testament Pseudepigrapha* [Doubleday, 1985], 2:87.)

If this view was well-known, Paul may be arguing not only that Gentiles should decline circumcision but that Gentiles *cannot* follow the law by being circumcised. Is this Paul's point in Romans 2:25–27?

3    These metaphors come from J. D. G. Dunn, *Galatians*, 268–69. Scot McKnight compares this choice to the difference between a typewriter and a computer. The first is laborious, requiring our full effort; the computer is supplying us with successes we could not have imagined ourselves (*Galatians*, 242–250).

4    The church has always been divided on the permanence of our salvation. Theologians emphasizing God's sovereignty (often in the Calvinist tradition) will speak of the perseverance of our faith and the security of our salvation. Theologians who emphasize human agency (often in the Arminian or Anabaptist tradition) will speak about the possibility of apostasy. Both themes are in the New Testament. We are sustained by God's grace, and it is only a persistent, aggressive, conscious rejection of God that can move us away from that grace. It might be fair to say that a believer who is worried about apostasy has not committed it.

5    *hēmeis gar*, which invites a very strong contrast for what has just been said.

6    See J. D. G. Dunn, *The Theology of Paul the Apostle* (Grand Rapids: Eerdmans, 1998), 399.

7    Burton E. DeWitt, *The Epistle to the Galatians* (Edinburgh: T&T Clark, 1921), 280.

8    Günther Bornkamm, *Paul* (New York: Harper and Row, 1971), 219, cited in F. F. Bruce, *The Epistle to the Galatians: A Commentary on the Greek Text* (Grand Rapids: Eerdmans, 1982), 233.

9    See W. Günther, "Love," in *The New International Dictionary of New Testament Theology*, ed. C. Brown (Grand Rapids: Zondervan, 1976), 2:538–532; similarly, Patrick Mitchell, "Love," in McKnight, *Dictionary of Paul and His Letters*, 665.

10    On Greek voices, see comments on 5:2.

11    Paul's idea of sin is similar to that expressed by Jesus: "What comes out of a person is what defiles them. For it is from within, out of a person's heart, that evil thoughts come—sexual immorality, theft, murder, adultery, greed, malice, deceit, lewdness, envy, slander, arrogance and folly. All these evils come from inside and defile a person" (Mk 7:20–23).

12    Dunn, *Galatians*, 289, cites a tradition how Rabbi Akiba cited Leviticus 19:18 as "the greatest general principle of the Torah" (*Gen. Rab.* 19:7; *Sipra* on Lev 19:18).
13    For an excellent summary of each Greek term, see Bruce, *Galatians*, 247–50; R. Y. G. Fung, *The Epistle to the Galatians* (Grand Rapids: Eerdmans, 1988), 253–60; or Keener, *Galatians*, 510–15, with copious references to Roman and Jewish parallels. Such vice lists were common throughout antiquity and are attested from the Old Testament (Jer 7:9; Eze 16:6–8) to the Dead Sea Scrolls (1QS 4:2–14). The New Testament offers more as well (Ro 1:29–30; 1 Co 6:9–10). Even Christians after the New Testament era wrote these (Didache 1:1–6:3; Epistle of Barnabus 18:1–21:9). Roman and Greek writers wrote similar lists that circulated widely.
14    Wright, *Galatians*, 336.
15    Dunn, *Galatians*, 303.
16    Virtue lists were also common among Greek, Roman, and Jewish writers. Paul's Galatian audience would have recßognized these immediately.
17    See "Fruit, Fruitfulness" in *Dictionary of Biblical Imagery*, 310–11.
18    Martin Hengel, *Crucifixion: In the Ancient World and the Folly of the Message of the Cross* (Philadelphia: Fortress, 1977).
19    Fung, *Galatians*, 278; Bruce, *Galatians*, 257–58.

## GALATIANS 6

1    *Theological Dictionary of the New Testament*, 4:15–16.
2    Many scholars have doubted that Paul is thinking about the ethical teaching of Jesus and doubted if Paul had known it (given the absence of references to it in his letters). But this does not mean Paul was unaware of the love command that is represented widely in the New Testament.
3    Richard B. Hayes, "Christology and Ethics in Galatians: The Law of Christ," *CBQ* 49 (1987) 268–90.
4    This is a Greek idiom: "For if someone thinks (himself) to be something—he is nothing."
5    Ernest De Witt Burton, *Galatians*, 330.
6    The Greek term "share" (*koinōneō*) leads the sentence, giving it special emphasis. It is also a present imperative, which gives it continuous force: continue to share regularly.
7    Dunn, *Galatians*, 336; Keener, *Galatians*, 564.
8    The offense of circumcision was so strong in Roman society that it could not appear in Roman athletic contests. Some Jews tried to reverse the signs of circumcision to integrate into the Roman world (1 Maccabees 1:14–15; Josephus, *Antiquities* 12.241; cited by Keener, *Galatians*, 564n54).
9    Lightfoot, *Galatians*, 222.
10    Bruce, *Galatians*, 271, who cites Cicero, *Pro Rabirio*, 16.
11    Wright, *Galatians*, 378.
12    Keener, *Galatians*, 578–579.
13    This includes Lightfoot, Fung, Hayes, Barclay, Dunn, Longenecker, Witherington, Beale, Köstenberger, deSilva, Fee, Schreiner, Moo, Keener, McKnight, and Wright. See Keener, *Galatians*, 579n180.
14    McKnight suggests a chiasm here: A. Whoever follows this rule; B. Peace; B.' Mercy; A.' Israel of God. This would make the followers of the rule of Christ align naturally with Israel. McKnight, *Galatians*, 303.
15    Dunn, *Galatians*, 344.
16    Wright, *Galatians*, 377.
17    In the Greek Old Testament it is usually translated as *génoito*, "let it be so."

## INTRODUCTION TO EPHESIANS

1  Scholars have debated if this was the imprisonment these letters refer to. Some point to Paul's Ephesian experiences (Ac 19). The majority of scholars point to Rome.

2  These manuscripts represent some of our earliest and most important, such as Papyrus 46 and Codex Sinaiticus. However this shows the complexity of the problem. P46 does not have these words in its text, but "To the Ephesians" remains in its title. In addition, the P46 copyist may not have been too skilled. In the first few verses, he skips an entire line from the text in front of him. Some modern translations move the reference to Ephesus to a footnote or leave it in the text and footnote the problem (NIV).

3  In addition, while the letter addresses general problems Christians might encounter in the region (see "The World of Ephesus and Its Neighbors" and "The Message of Ephesians"), he is not answering questions or issues raised by a particular congregation, which prompted the writing of other letters from Paul.

4  On this see E. Randolph Richards, *Paul and First-Century Letter Writing: Secretaries, Composition and Collection* (Downers Grove, IL: IVP Academic, 2004).

5  For a list, see Thomas K. Abbott, *Epistles to the Ephesians and to the Colossians* (Edinburgh: T&T Clark, 1897), xxiii.

6  David deSilva, *Ephesians* (Cambridge: Cambridge University Press, 2022), 31; Frank Thielman, *Ephesians* (Grand Rapids: Baker Academic, 2010), 11.

7  George B. Caird, *Paul's Letters from Prison* (Oxford: University Press, 1976), 29.

8  Markus Barth, *Ephesians*, 2 vols (Doubleday, 1974), 2:27.

9  See Ephesians 2:17; 5:31; 6:2–3.

10  See Ephesians 1:20–23; 2:13–17; 4:8–11, 25–27; 5:31–32; 6:3–4.

11  M. Barth, *Ephesians*, 29.

12  Andrew Lincoln, *Ephesians* (Grand Rapids: Zondervan, 1990), 47.

13  Today the port is silted up and can only be imagined.

14  P. Bohstrom, "Archaeologists Unveil Blazing Mosaics From Apostle Paul-era Ephesus," *Haaretz*, August 11, 2016, https://www.haaretz.com/archaeology/2016-08-11/ty-article/1-900-year-old-mosaics-restored-in-ephesus/0000017f-df38-d3ff-a7ff-ffb8adb70000.

15  Visitors to Ephesus today will see the famous Library of Celsus, but this was built about sixty years after Paul. Ephesus is today a UNESCO World Heritage Site.

16  Christine Sourvinou-Inwood, "Artemis," in S. Hornblower and A. Spawforth, eds., *The Oxford Classical Dictionary*, 3rd Edition (Oxford: Oxford University Press, 1996), 182–84.

17  Pliny, *Natural History*, 36.96, as cited in Clinton E. Arnold, "Ephesus," Gerald F. Hawthorne, Ralph P. Martin, and Daniel Reid, eds., *Dictionary of Paul and His Letters* (Downers Grove, IL: IVP, 1993), 250.

18  Craig Keener, *Acts: An Exegetical Commentary* (Grand Rapids: Baker Academic, 2014), 3:2897. More of the temple can be seen in the British Museum, London, in "the Ephesus Room" than at the site itself. Another impressive collection is in the Ephesus Museum in Vienna, Austria, located in the *Kunst Historische Museum Wein*). Austrian archaeologists began excavating the site in 1895, and as was typical in the era, they shipped countless discoveries back to Vienna until 1906. For an overview of this collection, see https://www.khm.at/en/.

19  Steven J. Friesen, *Imperial Cults and the Apocalypse of John: Reading Revelation in the Ruins* (Oxford: Oxford University Press, 2001), 95, cited in deSilva, *Ephesians*, 21. See further, Christoph Heilig, *The Apostle and the Empire: Paul's Implicit and Explicit Criticism of Rome* (Grand Rapids: Eerdmans, 2022).

20  Keener, *Acts*, 3:2827–2830.

21  John Stott, *The Message of Ephesians* (Downers Grove, IL: IVP Academic, 1979), 10.

22  Thielman, *Ephesians*, 21–22; Friesen, *Imperial Cults*, 125.

23  Clinton Arnold, *Ephesians: Power and Magic. The Concept of Power in Ephesians in Light of Its Historical Setting* (Cambridge: Cambridge University Press, 1992).
24  Stott, *Ephesians*, v.

## EPHESIANS 1

1   M. Barth, *Ephesians*, 105.
2   Frequently this verb is used to mean chosen, select, and elect—and this loads its intention with an entire history of interpretation and theology that may not be on Paul's mind. See the full critique of theological misuse of election in Ephesians in M. Barth, *Ephesians*, 105–109.
3   M. Barth, *Ephesians*, 1:80.
4   M. Barth, *Ephesians*, 123–25; Lincoln, *Ephesians*, 30–31; deSilva, *Ephesians*, 168–70.
5   Lincoln, *Ephesians*, 33.
6   Darryl Bock, *Ephesians* (Downers Grove, IL: IVP Academic, 2019), 42.
7   This is a Greek difficulty. The correct translation is, "Which is" (neuter), referring to the Spirit in the previous line (Spirit is neuter in Greek). Many Greek manuscripts insert "he," which is used by the NIV. This is right and may be the original. Grammatically, the masculine pronoun was likely attracted to the following noun (*arrabōn*), as in Mark 15:16 and Galatians 3:16. This is not uncommon in Koine. However, the Father and the Son have been praised as persons, and so now the Spirit is likewise praised not as an ambiguous power but as another feature of God's own presence. See M. Barth, *Ephesians*, 96, or Abbott, *Ephesians and Colossians*, 23, for technical details.
8   "Inheritance," *Dictionary of Biblical Imagery*, 420–421.
9   Thielman, *Ephesians*, 84–86.
10  deSilva, *Ephesians*, 79; M. Barth, *Ephesians*, 97.
11  Stott, *Ephesians*, 32; Caird, *Paul's Letters from Prison*, 42–43.
12  J. Weima, *Neglected Endings: The Significance of the Pauline Letter Closings* (Sheffield: JSOT Press, 1994), 34–39.
13  Bock, *Ephesians*, 49–50.
14  This is a perfect participle showing activity completed.
15  Some interpreters here see *hagioi* referring to angels (as it does in the LXX), but this is widely rejected.
16  There is a complex array of genitives in 1:19–20 that underscores the nature of this power. But it is beyond the scope of this commentary to untangle them. Thielman remarks, "We probably do more justice to Paul's intentions . . . if we resist the temptation to parse the logic of the phrase and meaning of its terms precisely," *Ephesians*, 101.
17  Gk, *eis*, followed by the accusative rather than the dative.
18  The LXX (Septuagint) numbering of the Psalms is different than what we have in our English translations. See further Karen Jobes and Moisés Silva, *Invitation to the Septuagint*, 2nd ed. (Grand Rapids: Baker Academic, 2015).
19  For a full survey, see M. Barth, *Ephesians*, 1:170–176.
20  Compare, deSilva, *Ephesians*, 96.
21  Abbot, *Colossians and Ephesians*, 34, citing J. B. Lightfoot, *Unpublished Notes*, 1895.
22  M. Barth, *Ephesians*, 1:201.

## EPHESIANS 2

1   Stott, *Ephesians*, 47; Klyne Snodgrass, *Ephesians* (Grand Rapids: Zondervan Academic, 1996), 93–94.
2   Snodgrass, *Ephesians*, 94, citing Leslie Mitton, *Ephesians* (London: Oliphants, 1976), 155.
3   Caird, *Ephesians*, 50.

4   Some translations will pick up the verb in 2:5 and introduce it in 2:1 just for the sake of clarity (RSV). This is not done in the NIV, NASB, NRSVue, and the ESV, leaving 2:1 "hanging" until 2:5.

5   Some wish to make this difference, transgressions representing deliberate decisions to break law and sin being the propensity to be in a condition.

6   The NIV "those who are disobedient" is actually another Hebrew expression from Paul, "those who are the sons of disobedience." This is one more illustration of how Paul is bilingual, writing in eloquent Greek but sometimes thinking in Hebrew idioms.

7   deSilva, *Ephesians*, 115.

8   Caird, *Ephesians*, 52, writes "'By nature' does not mean that evil is inherent in human nature as God created it, but simply that it is the natural proclivity of fallen men as in fact they are. Neither here nor in Ro 9:22 is there any justification for the idea of Augustine and Calvin that some men are reprobate by God's eternal decree. On the contrary, the point of the argument is that those who by their natural state were exposed to retribution have now by grace been redeemed."

9   R.V.G. Tasker, "Wrath," Douglas, J.D., and Hillyer, N., and Wood, D.R.W., eds., *The New Bible Dictionary*, 3rd ed. (London: IVP, 1996), 1250.

10  The verb's prefix (*sun* contracted in *su*) means "making alive *together*."

11  The Greek text refers to "the ages," but Paul uses this commonly to describe simply the future. Attempts to interpret this as a specific period of eschatological time are misdirected.

12  Snodgrass, *Ephesians*, 111, complains, "What pernicious and devious force has so subverted the meaning of the word 'faith?' Paul's understanding of 'faith' includes attachment, union, and solidarity with Christ, whereas in much of the church—including the evangelical church—faith means assent, decision, or the teaching one affirms."

13  Caird, *Ephesians*, 53; similarly, Thielman, *Ephesians*, 143.

14  Paul almost always uses the future tense, seeing salvation as something acquired in the end of our lives or of history.

15  See deSilva's helpful explanations, *Ephesians*, 124–25.

16  F. F. Bruce, *Ephesians*, 52; cited in Stott, *Ephesians*, 59.

17  From the Latin, *gentilis*, meaning "family" or "tribe"; in Greek: *ethnos*. It is a term used by Jews almost exclusively to describe non-Jews.

18  Good evidence suggests that Paul's use of "handmade" (2:11; NIV: "done in the body by human hands") had consistent negative connotations in biblical literature. In the LXX it is used for idols: "handmade" idols (Lev 26:1; 2 Ki 19:18; Ps 115:4; Da 5:4). In the New Testament it is used critically to describe the "handmade" temple (Mk 14:58; Ac 7:48). See Thielman, *Ephesians*, 160. The term is used to contrast things made by God. Thus in Ephesians 2:11 Paul is denigrating circumcision as "handmade" and so, possibly, of lesser value than the new creation that God is making.

19  See further, L. Feldman, *Jew and Gentile in the Ancient World: Attitudes and Interactions from Alexander to Justinian* (Princeton: Princeton University Press, 1996).

20  Josephus describes this wall in *Antiquities* 15.417 (15.11.5) and *Wars* 5.227 (5.5.6).

21  N. T. Wright, *Paul for Everyone: The Prison Letters* (Louisville: Westminster John Knox Press, 2004), 25–26.

22  Caird, *Ephesians*, 60.

23  M. Barth, *Ephesians*, 1:269.

24  Paul here is likely referring to the cornerstone above two walls (not the keystone to a stone arch) locking them together and securing the strength of the building.

25  See J. Jeremias, "*lithos*," *TDNT* 4:268–280.

## EPHESIANS 3

1 The text actually refers to "the sons of men" (NIV: "people"). This is a Hebrew expression that is rarely used in the New Testament and is very regional idiomatic Greek.

2 See further, Joachim Jeremias, *Jesus' Promise to the Nations*, trans. S. Hooke (Philadelphia: Fortress Press, 1982).

3 See Ge 12:3, 5; 22:18; 49:10; Dt 32:21; Ps 2:8; 22:27–31; 65:5; 72:1–20; 86:9; 102:15, 18–22; 145:10–12; Isa 2:2–5; 9:1–7; 11:1–10; 35:1–20; 40:4–11; 42:1–12; 45:6, 8, 22–24; 49:1, 5–6, 18–23; 55:5; 60:1–14; 66:7–23; Jer 3:17; 4:2; 16:19–21; Da 2:35, 44–45; 7:13–14; Hos 2:23; Joel 2:28–32; Am 9:11–12; Mic 4:3–4; Hag 2:7; Zec 2:10–11; 6:15; 8:1–23; 9:1, 9–17; 14:8–21; Mal 1:11.

4 N. T. Wright, in a question-and-answer session after a joint lecture with Paul Barnett, "Fresh Perspectives on Paul," MacQuarie University (Sydney, Australia), March 16, 2006 (Vancouver: Regent Bookstore/Regent Audio).

5 deSilva, *Ephesians*, 169.

6 Dunn, *The Theology of Paul the Apostle*, 461–471.

7 Thielman, *Ephesians*, 227.

8 Note the trinitarian language that again Paul is using: he prays to the Father for the strengthening of the Spirit, which means Christ dwelling in us.

9 Today this word, *Themelios*, is cleverly used as the title of a student-oriented journal about Christian theology. See https://www.thegospelcoalition.org/themelios/.

10 Lincoln, *Ephesians*, 217.

## EPHESIANS 4

1 M. Barth, *Ephesians*, 2:426. Of course, this is the term (often translated Paraclete) John uses four times in his gospel and once in his letters to describe the Holy Spirit (Jn 14:16, 26; 15:26; 16:7; 1 Jn 2:1).

2 Caird, *Ephesians*, 71.

3 Although the grammar could suggest two features: "with all humility and gentleness—and with patience."

4 In 1 Corinthians 1:10–17 Paul describes this sort of dissension at work ("I appeal to you . . . that all of you agree . . . and that there be no divisions"). Philippians 1:27–2:11 shows the same ("If there is any encouragement in Christ . . . complete my joy by being of the same mind" [RSV]). In Romans 14 Paul gives guidelines for showing needed charity ("Let us stop passing judgment on one another" [v. 13]).

5 For full evidence, see M. Barth, "The Interpretation of Ps 68," *Ephesians*, 2:473–477; Thielman, "Ephesians," in Beale, and Carson, eds, *Commentary on the New Testament Use of the Old Testament*, 819–825.

6 Abbott, *Ephesians*, 111–113.

7 Timothy Gombis, "Cosmic Lordship and Divine Gift-Giving: Psalm 68 in Ephesians 4:8," *Novum Testamentum* (2005), 47:367–80.

8 Chrysostom, *Homily* 11 on Ephesians 4:9, cited in deSilva, *Ephesians*, 206n589.

9 This interpretation of Junia is frequently contested. See further Yii-Jan Lin, "Junia: An Apostle before Paul," JBL 139(2020), 191–209.

10 This is a common Pauline construction (Ro 10:2), also occurring in Acts (26:7).

11 M. Barth, *Ephesians*, 2:484–497 and deSilva, *Ephesians*, 201–215. Barth notes that every reference to "man" (*anēr*) in Ephesians refers to Christ. And deSilva says Paul does not use the abstract word for maturity (*teleiotēs*) but rather uses *telos*.

12 Caird, *Ephesians*, 77.

13 deSilva, *Ephesians*, 217, referring to Homily 11 on Ephesians 4:16 (*Ephesians*, 105).

14 K. Barth, *The Epistle to the Romans*, 6th ed., trans. E. C. Hoskyns (Oxford: Oxford University Press, 1933), 52.

15 BDAG 732.

16 The verse employs the reflexive pronoun, ἑαυτοῦ, with the verb. They gave *themselves* over . . .

17 The Greek text of 4:20–24 is notoriously complex. It is often used to explain how Paul's words can "run away with him," so that sentences are broken and clauses are interrupted. Every translator and interpreter is forced to make choices throughout. A comparison of the NIV with, for example, the NRSVue or the ESV makes this clear.

18 Thielman, *Ephesians*, 300–301.

19 M. Barth, *Ephesians*, 2:530.

20 See M. Barth, *Ephesians,* 2:530–31.

21 Here the Greek is using indirect discourse with a series of infinitive verbs: "you were taught: to put off . . . to be renewed . . . to put on."

22 This verb can take on the meaning of destruction or corruption.

23 See alternatives given in M. Barth, *Ephesians*, 2:537–540, where collective and individualistic interpretations are compared.

24 deSilva, *Ephesians*, 230; Caird, *Ephesians,* 81.

25 See Thielman, *Ephesians,* 312, citing Peter T. O'Brien, *The Letter to the Ephesians* (Grand Rapids: Eerdmans, 1999), 338: "What is predicated of the eschatological future of God's people in terms of new Jerusalem language in the Old Testament is picked up by Paul in relation to the "new person," God's new community in Christ upon whom the ends of the ages have come."

26 Jewish apocryphal writings often make this connection. In particular, see *Testament of Dan* 4:7–5:2, which connects anger with lying and provides a clear echo of Zechariah 8:16 exactly as Paul has done in Ephesians 4.

27 R. Bauckham, *Jesus and the Eyewitnesses: The Gospels as Eyewitness Testimony* (Grand Rapids: Eerdmans, 2008).

28 In John 6:27 Jesus himself was sealed by the Spirit. A seal is designed for ownership (see sidebar, "Ephesians 4:30 Through Old Testament Eyes: Sealing"), generally for a letter. Paul views the Spirit in just this manner: Christ "set his seal of ownership on us, and put his Spirit in our hearts as a deposit, guaranteeing what is to come" (2 Co 1:22).

29 In Galatians 6:17 Paul uses this term literally to refer to the lasting marks on his body gained through following Christ.

30 Thielman, *Ephesians*, 318.

31 This reversal is signaled by the Gk, *dev, de*, "beginning," 4:32.

## EPHESIANS 5

1 The same imperative is used and is grounded in the behavior of Christ *who loved us.*

2 Wright, *The Prison Letters*, 54.

3 See M. Barth, *Ephesians*, 2:556n8 for many Old Testament examples.

4 Greek and Roman fertility was centered on the male role (phallus). They had no idea of female ovulation because they could not see it and instead imagined fertility resulting when a man "planted his seed" in a woman's "fertile field." Thus fertility and flourishing—if ritually enacted—would center on phallic rites.

5 M. Barth, *Ephesians*, 527fn158 for many references.

6 A 3,400-year-old figurine of Astarte was recently found (2016) in Israel. See Robin Ngo, "Canaanite Worship? 3,400-Year-Old Figurine Found at Tel Rehov," *Bible History* (Biblical Archaeology Society), Feb 26, 2016, at: https://www.biblicalarchaeology. org/daily/ancient-cultures/ancient-israel/canaanite-worship-figurine-tel-rehov/.

7 See Qumran *1QS* 7:9, 16. Cited in deSilva, *Ephesians*, 251.

8 Keener, *Acts*, 3:2270–71.

9 Edmund K. Simpson, "Commentary on the Epistle to the Ephesians," in Edmund K. Simpson and F. F. and Bruce, *Commentary on the Epistles to the Ephesians and the Colossians* (London: Marshall, Morgan and Scott, 1957), 145, cited by Stott, *Ephesians*, 152.

10   "Choose for yourselves, light or darkness, the law of the Lord or the works of Beliar," *Testament of Levi* 19:1; see *Testament of Benjamin* 5:3. The Gospel of John makes extensive use of the light/darkness motif (1;4, 5, 7–9, etc.).

11   M. Barth, *Ephesians*, 2:601.

12   M. Barth, *Ephesians*, 2:601.

13   BDAG 249

14   K. Barth, *Romans*, 48–52.

15   See further, Jonathan M. Lunde and John A. Dunne, "Paul's Creative and Contextual Use of Isaiah in Ephesians 5:14." *JETS* 55 (2012): 87–110.

16   Derek Kidner, *Proverbs* TOTC (Downers Grove, IL: IVP Academic, 1964, 2008), 37.

17   John R. Paterson, "Wine," in Hornblower and Spawforth, *The Oxford Classical Dictionary*, 1623.

18   Among the Romans, wine production was an enormous industry and technological advances influenced European methods for centuries. Manuals were written (Cato's *De agri cultura*. Pliny has entire section of his *Natural History* devoted to it: sec 14) discussing everything from terracing to harvest timing to hygiene. Even far-off colonies required imports from Italy. One of our sources for this shipping trade is through shipwrecks that held hundreds of jars (amphorae) of wine in their holds.

19   Paterson, "Wine," 1623, citing the Roman historian *Ammianus Marcellinus* (AD 330–395), 15.12.

20   Cited in Edwin M. Yamauchi and Marvin R. Wilson, *Dictionary of Daily Life in Biblical and Post Biblical Antiquity* (Peabody: Hendrickson Academic, 2017), 50.

21   *m. Middot* 2:6, "And there were chambers under the Court of Israel, which opened into the Court of the Women, where the Levites played upon harps and lyres and the cymbals and all instruments of music." Some archaeologists think we may have found remnants of the entrance to this chamber near the likely location of the ancient temple.

22   Abbott, *Ephesians*, 164.

23   See further, P. Gurry, "The Text of Eph 5.22 and the Start of the Ephesian Household Code." *New Testament Studies,* 67.4 (2021), 560–81. A wide consensus of scholars finds no verb in 5:22. Gurry argues for a variant in later Greek manuscripts that inserts a verb in 5:22, arguing that this is not a scribal clarification but originating with Paul (see 1 Co 14:34, which has this verb).

24   Gurry, *New Testament Studies*, 560–81; also see M. Barth, *Ephesians*, 2:608; 2:453–457; Friedrich Blass and Albert Debrunner, *A Greek Grammar of the New Testament* (Chicago: University of Chicago Press, 1961), 245 (§468).

25   This is the suggested translation of M. Barth, *Ephesians*, 2:607–608.

26   This is an interpretative decision. In the participle, this middle and passive both have the same form, and the reader must decide. Reading this as a middle voice is the majority view.

27   Aristotle, *Politics* 1.3, 6–7, 12–13.

28   Plutarch, "Advice on Marriage," 11; and "Advice to Bride and Groom."

29   Josephus, *Contra Apion* 2:199, 206, 215–17.

30   Philo, *Decalogue*, 165–67; *Special Laws*, 225–227.

31   See deSilva, *Ephesians* 275–77.

32   See Edwin Yamauchi, "Marriage," in Yamauchi and Wilson, *Dictionary of Daily Life*, 1065–1093; Ronald Pierce, "From Old Testament Law to New Testament Gospel," in Ronald Pierce and Rebecca M. Groothuis, eds., *Discovering Biblical Equality: Complementarity without Hierarchy* (Downers Grove, IL: IVP Academic, 2004), 96–109; David Instone-Brewer, *Divorce and Remarriage in the Bible: The Social and Literary Context* (Grand Rapids: Eerdmans, 2002), 1–58; Craig Keener, "Marriage," in Craig Evans and Stanley Porter, *Dictionary of New Testament Background,*" (Downers Grove, IL: IVP, 2000), 680–693.

33  However, a major movement to empower women was growing in the first century. See M. Barth, *Ephesians*, "Comment II: The Position of Women and Marriage at Paul's Time," 2:655–662; also Lynn Cohick, *Women in the World of the Earliest Christians: Illuminating Ancient Ways of Life* (Grand Rapids: Baker Academic, 2009); Cynthia Westfall, *Paul and Gender: Reclaiming the Apostl's Vision for Men and Women in Christ* (Grand Rapids: Baker Academic, 2016).

34  Gerhard Delling, "ὑποτάσσω," TDNT 8:45; cited in Lincoln, *Ephesians*, 365.

35  Snodgrass, *Ephesians*, 293.

36  Whether *kephale* implies authority of a husband over his wife is hotly debated today and perhaps represents one of the critical ideas in the egalitarian/complementarian discussion.

37  deSilva, *Ephesians*, 278, who refers (278n789) to Ben Witherington, *The Letters to Philemon, the Colossians, and the Ephesians: A Socio-Rhetorical Commentary on the Captivity Epistles* (Grand Rapids: Eerdmans, 2007), 324.

38  deSilva, *Ephesians*, 281.

39  See further Westfall, *Paul and Gender*. See chapter 7 ("Calling") where she outlines how vocation and call are interpreted differently among men and women. Men's calling is celebrated; women's is viewed skeptically.

40  deSilva, *Ephesians*, 284, citing Lincoln, *Ephesians*, 373.

## EPHESIANS 6

1  Philo, *Spec. Laws* 2:226–227 (Loeb); cited in part by deSilva, *Ephesians*, 294.

2  This phrase is absent in some Greek manuscripts, but the NIV rightly retains it, agreeing with most interpreters.

3  See J. Louw and E. Nida, *The Greek-English Lexicon of the New Testament Based on Semantic Domains,* (United Bible Society, 1988) Domain: 333.226.

4  Keener, "Slaves and Slavery," *Acts*, 2:1907.

5  Roman slavery should not be compared directly with the American slave experience. One could enter slavery in Roman antiquity a number of ways: conquest, debt relief, ancestry-slavery, etc. One could even find ways to be free. It was not based on race and so slaves and their masters could look exactly alike. However, Roman society was carefully stratified, and so slaves were nevertheless given few if any of the privileges of free citizens.

6  See the excellent article by Jonathan DeFelice, "Slavery," in Yamauchi and Wilson, *Dictionary of Daily Life*, 1515–1539, and its extensive bibliography. See further Keener, "Slaves and Slavery," in *Acts*, 2:1906–1942; Keith Bradley and Paul Cartledge, eds., *The Cambridge World History of Slavery: Volume 1, The Ancient Mediterranean World* (Cambridge: Cambridge University Press, 2011).

7  Jennifer A. Glancy, *Slavery in Early Christianity* (Minneapolis: Fortress Press, 2006), as cited in Yamauchi and Wilson, *Dictionary of Daily Life*, 1533.

8  Scholars will commonly note that this is a notoriously difficult text to translate.

9  A textual variation (or variant) appears at 6:10. The majority of interpreters view Paul's first words, *to loipon* as meaning "finally;" but a very close variant is *tou loipou*, which may be an abbreviation of *tou loipou chronou*; this uses a genitive, which means, "from now on or henceforth" and means believers are to leave the past behind and look forward. The latter reading is in most new Greek texts and defended by Thielman, *Ephesians*, 417, 430, and many others. M. Barth, 2:760, rejects the idea, and Lincoln, *Ephesians*, 441, believes the two terms are synonymous. (See 2 Co 13:11; Php 4:8; 1 Th 4:1, 2; 2 Th 3:1.)

10  Thielman, *Ephesians*, 419.

11  Thielman, *Ephesians*, 419, citing Ronald E. Heine, *Commentaries of Origen and Jerome on St. Paul's Epistle to the Ephesians* (Oxford: Oxford University Press, 2002), 254, who supplies a new translation.

12  That Tychicus was an Ephesian has a long tradition and appears in a Greek variant naming him as an Ephesian. But we are generally not confident in this reading.

13  Paul's formula here in Ephesians is different than the usual Pauline usage and sometimes is used to suggest whether this stylistic difference suggests another author or a scribe. However, with Thielman, *Ephesians,* 445, we can note that most of Paul's closing benedictions have minor variations, and this one in Ephesians may be just one example.

14  BDAG, second edition, 125.

# SCRIPTURE INDEX

*All Scripture references are indexed except for those in Galatians and Ephesians.*